Libre
The Document Foundation

Getting Started with LibreOffice 4.0

Copyright

Contributors

Jean Hollis Weber
Martin Fox
Andrew Pitonyak
John A Smith
Jeremy Cartwright
Dan Lewis
Hazel Russman
Laurent Balland-Poirier
Ron Faile Jr.
David Michel
Peter Schofield

Cover art:
Drew Jensen
Jean Hollis Weber
Christoph Noack
Klaus-Jürgen Weghorn

Acknowledgements

This book is adapted and updated from *Getting Started with OpenOffice.org 3.3*. The contributors to that book are listed on page 13.

Feedback

Please direct any comments or suggestions about this document to:
documentation@global.libreoffice.org

Publisher

Friends of OpenDocument, Inc.
544/60 Beck Drive North
Condon, QLD 4815, Australia
http://friendsofopendocument.com/

ISBN 978-1-921320-31-6

Publication date and software version

Published 28 February 2013. Based on LibreOffice 4.0.

Contents

Preface

Who is this book for?

Anyone who wants to get up to speed quickly with LibreOffice will find this Getting Started Guide valuable. You may be new to office software, or you may be familiar with another office suite.

What's in this book?

This book introduces the main components of LibreOffice:

- Writer (word processing)
- Calc (spreadsheets)
- Impress (presentations)
- Draw (vector graphics)
- Base (database
- Math (equation editor)

It also covers some of the features common to all components, including setup and customization, styles and templates, macro recording, and printing. For more detail, see the user guides for the individual components.

Where to get more help

This book, the other LibreOffice user guides, the built-in Help system, and user support systems assume that you are familiar with your computer and basic functions such as starting a program, opening and saving files.

Help system

LibreOffice comes with an extensive Help system. This is your first line of support for using LibreOffice.

To display the full Help system, press *F1* or select **LibreOffice Help** from the Help menu. In addition, you can choose whether to activate Tips, Extended tips, and the Help Agent (using **Tools > Options > LibreOffice > General**).

If Tips are enabled, place the mouse pointer over any of the icons to see a small box ("tooltip") with a brief explanation of the icon's function. For a more detailed explanation, select **Help > What's This?** and hold the pointer over the icon.

Free online support

The LibreOffice community not only develops software, but provides free, volunteer-based support. See Table 1 and this web page: http://www.libreoffice.org/get-help/

Users can get comprehensive online support from the community through mailing lists. Other websites run by users also offer free tips and tutorials. This forum provides community support for LibreOffice: http://en.libreofficeforum.org/

This site provides support for LibreOffice, among other programs:

http://user.services.openoffice.org/en/forum/

Paid support and training

Alternatively, you can pay for support services. Service contracts can be purchased from a vendor or consulting firm specializing in LibreOffice.

Table 1: Free support for LibreOffice users

Free LibreOffice support	
FAQs	Answers to frequently asked questions http://www.libreoffice.org/get-help/faq/ http://wiki.documentfoundation.org/Faq
Documentation	User guides, how-tos, and other documentation. http://www.libreoffice.org/get-help/documentation/ https://wiki.documentfoundation.org/Documentation/Publications
Mailing lists	Free community support is provided by a network of experienced users http://www.libreoffice.org/get-help/mailing-lists/
International support	The LibreOffice website in your language. http://www.libreoffice.org/international-sites/ International mailing lists http://wiki.documentfoundation.org/Local_Mailing_Lists
Accessibility options	Information about available accessibility options. http://www.libreoffice.org/get-help/accessibility/

What you see may be different

Illustrations

LibreOffice runs on Windows, Linux, and Mac OS X operating systems, each of which has several versions and can be customized by users (fonts, colors, themes, window managers). The illustrations in this guide were taken from a variety of computers and operating systems. Therefore, some illustrations will not look exactly like what you see on your computer display.

Also, some of the dialogs may be differ because of the settings selected in LibreOffice. You can either use dialogs from your computer system (default) or dialogs provided by LibreOffice. To change to using LibreOffice dialogs:

1) On Linux and Windows operating systems, go to **Tools > Options >LibreOffice > General** on the main menu bar to open the dialog for general options.
2) On a Mac operating system, go to **LibreOffice > Preferences > General** on the main menu bar to open the dialog for general options.
3) Select *Use LibreOffice dialogs* in *Open/Save dialogs* and, in Linux and Mac OS X operating systems only, *Print dialogs* to display the LibreOffice dialogs on your computer display.
4) Click **OK** to save your settings and close the dialog.

Icons

The icons used to illustrate some of the many tools available in LibreOffice may differ from the ones used in this guide. The icons in this guide have been taken from a LibreOffice installation that has been set to display the Galaxy set of icons.

If you wish, you can change your LibreOffice software package to display Galaxy icons as follows:

1) On Linux and Windows operating systems, go to **Tools > Options >LibreOffice > View** on the main menu bar to open the dialog for view options.
2) On a Mac operating system, go to **LibreOffice > Preferences > View** on the main menu bar to open the dialog for view options.
3) In *User interface > Icon size and style* select *Galaxy* from the options available in the drop-down list.
4) Click **OK** to save your settings and close the dialog.

Note	Some Linux operating systems, for example Ubuntu, include LibreOffice as part of the installation and may not include the Galaxy set of icons. You should be able to download the Galaxy icon set from the software repository for your Linux operating system.

Using LibreOffice on a Mac

Some keystrokes and menu items are different on a Mac from those used in Windows and Linux. The table below gives some common substitutions for the instructions in this chapter. For a more detailed list, see the application Help.

Windows or Linux	*Mac equivalent*	*Effect*
Tools > Options menu selection	**LibreOffice > Preferences**	Access setup options
Right-click	*Control+click* and/or *right-click* depending on computer setup	Open a context menu
Ctrl (Control)	*⌘ (Command)*	Used with other keys
F5	*Shift+⌘+F5*	Open the Navigator
F11	*⌘+T*	Open the Styles and Formatting window

What are all these things called?

The terms used in LibreOffice for most parts of the *user interface* (the parts of the program you see and use, in contrast to the behind-the-scenes code that actually makes it work) are the same as for most other programs.

A *dialog* is a special type of window. Its purpose is to inform you of something, or request input from you, or both. It provides controls for you to use to specify how to carry out an action. The technical names for common controls are shown in Figure 1. In most cases we do not use the technical terms in this book, but it is useful to know them because the Help and other sources of information often use them.

1) Tabbed page (not strictly speaking a control).
2) Radio buttons (only one can be selected at a time).
3) Checkbox (more than one can be selected at a time).
4) Spin box (click the up and down arrows to change the number shown in the text box next to it, or type in the text box).
5) Thumbnail or preview.
6) Drop-down list from which to select an item.
7) Push buttons.

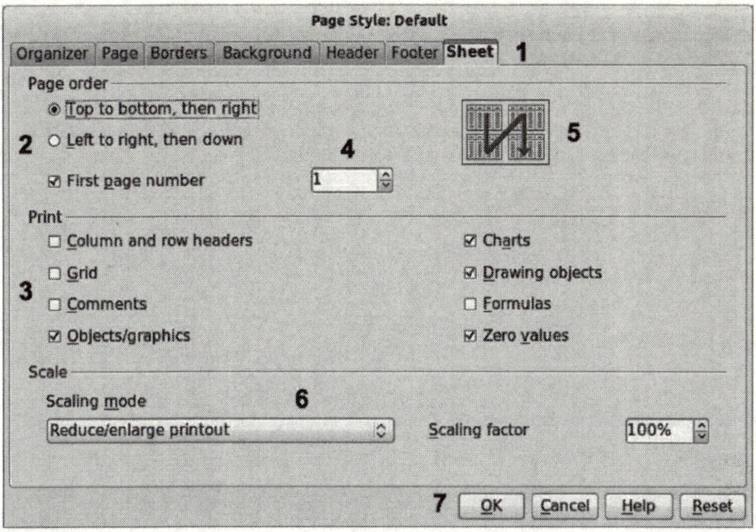

Figure 1: Dialog showing common controls

In most cases, you can interact only with the dialog (not the document itself) as long as the dialog remains open. When you close the dialog after use (usually, clicking **OK** or another button saves your changes and closes the dialog), then you can again work with your document.

Some dialogs can be left open as you work, so you can switch back and forth between the dialog and your document. An example of this type is the Find & Replace dialog.

Who wrote this book?

This book was written by volunteers from the LibreOffice community. Profits from sales of the printed edition will be used to benefit the community.

Acknowledgements

This book is adapted from *Getting Started with OpenOffice.org 3.3*. The contributors to that book are:

Jean Hollis Weber
Thomas Astleitner
Chris Bonde
JiHui Choi
Laurent Duperval
Peter Hillier-Brook
Rachel Kartch
Michael Kotsarinis
Dan Lewis
Andrew Pitonyak
Hazel Russman
Joe Sellman
Alex Thurgood
Linda Worthington
Michele Zarri
Richard Barnes
Nicole Cairns
Richard Detwiler
Spencer E. Harpe
Richard Holt
Stefan A. Keel
Peter Kupfer
Alan Madden
Carol Roberts
Gary Schnabl
Janet Swisher
Barbara M. Tobias
Magnus Adielsson
Agnes Belzunce
Daniel Carrera
Alexander Noël Dunne
Regina Henschel
John Kane
Jared Kobos
Ian Laurenson
Michel Pinquier
Iain Roberts
Robert Scott
Jim Taylor
Claire Wood

Frequently asked questions

How is LibreOffice licensed?

LibreOffice is distributed under the Open Source Initiative (OSI) approved Lesser General Public License (LGPL). The LGPL license is available from the LibreOffice website: http://www.libreoffice.org/download/license/

May I distribute LibreOffice to anyone?

Yes.

How many computers may I install it on?

As many as you like.

May I sell it?

Yes.

May I use LibreOffice in my business?

Yes.

Is LibreOffice available in my language?

LibreOffice has been translated (localized) into over 40 languages, so your language probably is supported. Additionally, there are over 70 *spelling*, *hyphenation*, and *thesaurus* dictionaries available for languages, and dialects that do not have a localized program interface. The dictionaries are available from the LibreOffice website at: www.libreoffice.org.

How can you make it for free?

LibreOffice is developed and maintained by volunteers and has the backing of several organizations.

I am writing a software application. May I use programming code from LibreOffice in my program?

You may, within the parameters set in the LGPL. Read the license: http://www.libreoffice.org/download/license/

Why do I need Java to run LibreOffice? Is it written in Java?

LibreOffice is not written in Java; it is written in the C++ language. Java is one of several languages that can be used to extend the software. The Java JDK/JRE is only required for some features. The most notable one is the HSQLDB relational database engine.

Note: Java is available at no cost. If you do not want to use Java, you can still use nearly all of the features of LibreOffice.

How can I contribute to LibreOffice?

You can help with the development and user support of LibreOffice in many ways, and you do not need to be a programmer. To start, check out this webpage: http://www.documentfoundation.org/contribution/

May I distribute the PDF of this book, or print and sell copies?

Yes, as long as you meet the requirements of one of the licenses in the copyright statement at the beginning of this book. You do not have to request special permission. In addition, we request that you share with the project some of the profits you make from sales of books, in consideration of all the work we have put into producing them.

New features in LibreOffice 4

LibreOffice 4.0 offers a large number of new characteristics, which are listed on this page: https://www.libreoffice.org/download/4-0-new-features-and-fixes. Here are some highlights:

- Integration with several content and document management systems – including Alfresco, IBM FileNet P8, Microsoft Sharepoint 2010, Nuxeo, OpenText, SAP NetWeaver Cloud Service and others – through the CMIS standard.
- Better interoperability with DOCX and RTF documents, thanks to several new features and improvements like the possibility of importing annotations and attaching comments to text ranges.
- Possibility to import Microsoft Publisher documents, and further improvement of Visio import filters with the addition of 2013 version (just announced).
- Additional UI incremental improvements, including Unity integration and support of Firefox Themes (Personas) to give LibreOffice a personalized look.
- Different header and footer on the first page of a Writer document, without the need of a separate page style.
- Several performance improvements to Calc, plus new features such as export of charts as images (JPG and PNG) and new spreadsheet functions as defined in ODF OpenFormula.
- First release of Impress Remote Control App for Android, supported only on some Linux distributions. (The second release, coming soon, will be supported on all platforms: Windows, MacOS X, and all Linux distros and binaries.)
- Significant performance improvements when loading and saving many types of documents, with particular improvements for large ODS and XLSX spreadsheets and RTF files.
- Introduction of the widget layout technique for dialogs, which makes it easier to translate, resize and hide UI elements, reduces code complexity, and lays a foundation for a much improved user interface.
- Improved code contribution thanks to Gerrit: a web based code review system, facilitating the task for projects using Git version control system (although this is not specific of LibreOffice 4.0, it has entered the production stage just before the 4.0 branch).

Chapter 1
Introducing LibreOffice

What is LibreOffice?

LibreOffice is a freely available, fully-featured office productivity suite. Its native file format is Open Document Format (ODF), an open standard format that is being adopted by governments worldwide as a required file format for publishing and accepting documents. LibreOffice can also open and save documents in many other formats, including those used by several versions of Microsoft Office.

LibreOffice includes the following components.

Writer (word processor)

Writer is a feature-rich tool for creating letters, books, reports, newsletters, brochures, and other documents. You can insert graphics and objects from other components into Writer documents. Writer can export files to HTML, XHTML, XML, Adobe Portable Document Format (PDF), and several versions of Microsoft Word files. It also connects to your email client.

Calc (spreadsheet)

Calc has all of the advanced analysis, charting, and decision making features expected from a high-end spreadsheet. It includes over 300 functions for financial, statistical, and mathematical operations, among others. The Scenario Manager provides "what if" analysis. Calc generates 2D and 3D charts, which can be integrated into other LibreOffice documents. You can also open and work with Microsoft Excel workbooks and save them in Excel format. Calc can also export spreadsheets in several formats, including for example Comma Separated Value (CSV), Adobe PDF and HTML formats.

Impress (presentations)

Impress provides all the common multimedia presentation tools, such as special effects, animation, and drawing tools. It is integrated with the advanced graphics capabilities of LibreOffice Draw and Math components. Slideshows can be further enhanced using Fontwork special effects text, as well as sound and video clips. Impress is compatible with Microsoft PowerPoint file format and can also save your work in numerous graphics formats, including Macromedia Flash (SWF).

Draw (vector graphics)

Draw is a vector drawing tool that can produce everything from simple diagrams or flowcharts to 3D artwork. Its Smart Connectors feature allows you to define your own connection points. You can use Draw to create drawings for use in any of the LibreOffice components, and you can create your own clip art then add it to the Gallery. Draw can import graphics from many common formats and save them in over 20 formats, including PNG, HTML, PDF, and Flash.

Base (database)

Base provides tools for day-to-day database work within a simple interface. It can create and edit forms, reports, queries, tables, views, and relations, so that managing a relational database is much the same as in other popular database applications. Base provides many new features, such as the ability to analyze and edit relationships from a diagram view. Base incorporates HSQLDB as its default relational database engine. It can also use dBASE, Microsoft Access, MySQL, or Oracle, or any ODBC compliant or JDBC compliant database. Base also provides support for a subset of ANSI-92 SQL.

Math (formula editor)

Math is the LibreOffice formula or equation editor. You can use it to create complex equations that include symbols or characters not available in standard font sets. While it is most commonly used to create formulae in other documents, such as Writer and Impress files, Math can also work as a standalone tool. You can save formulae in the standard Mathematical Markup Language (MathML) format for inclusion in web pages and other documents not created by LibreOffice.

Advantages of LibreOffice

Here are some of the advantages of LibreOffice over other office suites:

- **No licensing fees**. LibreOffice is free for anyone to use and distribute at no cost. Many features that are available as extra cost add-ins in other office suites (like PDF export) are free with LibreOffice. There are no hidden charges now or in the future.
- **Open source.** You can distribute, copy, and modify the software as much as you wish, in accordance with either of the LibreOffice Open Source licenses.
- **Cross-platform.** LibreOffice runs on several hardware architectures and under multiple operating systems, such as Microsoft Windows, Mac OS X and Linux.
- **Extensive language support**. The LibreOffice user interface is available in over 40 languages and the LibreOffice project provides spelling, hyphenation, and thesaurus dictionaries in over 70 languages and dialects. LibreOffice also provides support for both Complex Text Layout (CTL) and Right to Left (RTL) layout languages (such as Urdu, Hebrew, and Arabic).
- **Consistent user interface.** All the components have a similar "look and feel," making them easy to use and master.
- **Integration.** The components of LibreOffice are well integrated with one another.
  - All the components share a common spelling checker and other tools, which are used consistently across the suite. For example, the drawing tools available in Writer are also found in Calc, with similar but enhanced versions in Impress and Draw.
  - You do not need to know which application was used to create a particular file. For example, you can open a Draw file from Writer.
- **Granularity.** Usually, if you change an option, it affects all components. However, LibreOffice options can be set at a component level or even at document level.
- **File compatibility.** In addition to its native OpenDocument formats, LibreOffice includes PDF and Flash export capabilities, as well as support for opening and saving files in many common formats including Microsoft Office, HTML, XML, WordPerfect, and Lotus 1-2-3 formats. An extension (included) provides the ability to import and edit some PDF files.
- **No vendor lock-in.** LibreOffice uses OpenDocument, an XML (eXtensible Markup Language) file format developed as an industry standard by OASIS (Organization for the Advancement of Structured Information Standards). These files can easily be unzipped and read by any text editor, and their framework is open and published.
- **You have a voice.** Enhancements, software fixes, and release dates are community-driven. You can join the community and affect the course of the product you use.

You can read more about LibreOffice and The Document Foundation on their websites at http://www.libreoffice.org/ and http://www.documentfoundation.org/.

Minimum requirements

LibreOffice 4.0 requires one of the following operating systems:

- **Microsoft Windows** XP, Vista, Windows 7, or Windows 8
- **GNU/Linux** Kernel version 2.6.18, glibc2 v2.5 or higher, and gtk v2.10.4 or higher
- **Mac OS X** 10.4 (Tiger) or higher

Administrator rights are needed for the installation process.

Some LibreOffice features (wizards and the HSQLDB database engine) require that the Java Runtime Environment (JRE) is installed on your computer. Although LibreOffice will work without Java support, some features will not be available.

For a more detailed listing of requirements, see the LibreOffice website, http://www.libreoffice.org/download/system-requirements/.

How to get the software

The software can be downloaded from http://www.libreoffice.org/. You can also download the software by using a Peer-to-Peer client, such as BitTorrent, at the same address.

Linux users will find LibreOffice included in many of the latest Linux distributions; Ubuntu is just one example.

How to install the software

Information on installing and setting up LibreOffice on the various supported operating systems is given here: http://www.libreoffice.org/get-help/installation/.

Extensions and add-ons

Extensions and add ons are available to enhance LibreOffice. Several extensions are installed with the program and others are available from the official extensions repository, http://extensions.libreoffice.org/. See *Chapter 14 Customizing LibreOffice* for more information on installing extensions and add ons.

Starting LibreOffice

The most common way to launch any component of LibreOffice is by using the system menu, the standard menu from which most applications are started. On Windows, it is called the Start menu. On GNOME, it is called the Applications menu. On KDE it is identified by the KDE logo. On Mac OS X, it is the Applications menu.

When LibreOffice was installed on your computer, a menu entry for LibreOffice and each LibreOffice component was added to your system menu if your computer uses a Windows or Linux operating system. On computers operating Mac OS X, only a menu entry for LibreOffice is added to the Applications menu.

Clicking on the LibreOffice menu entry opens the LibreOffice Start Center (Figure 2) from where you can select the individual components of LibreOffice. You can also select to open an existing file or use a template.

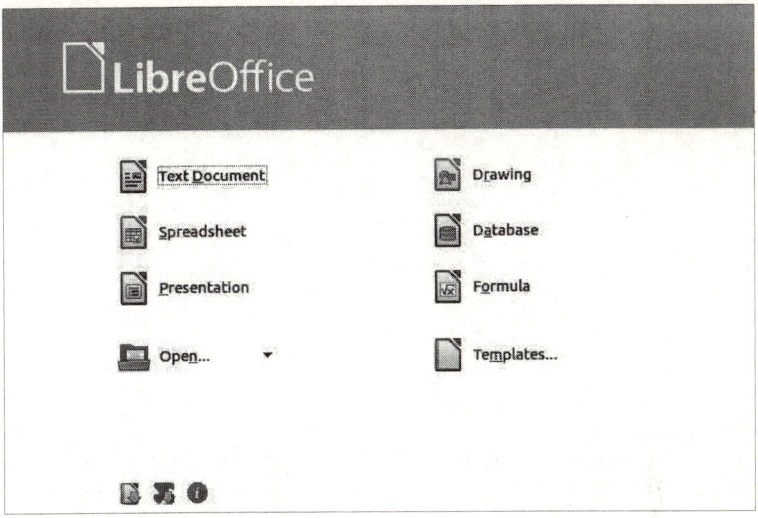

Figure 2: LibreOffice Start Center

Starting from an existing document

You can start LibreOffice by double-clicking the filename that is an ODF document in a file manager such as Windows Explorer. The appropriate component of LibreOffice will start and the document will be loaded.

If Microsoft Office is installed on your computer and you have associated Microsoft Office file types with LibreOffice, when you double-click on the file:

- For a Word file (*.doc or *.docx), it opens in Writer.
- For an Excel file (*.xls or *.xlsx), it opens in Calc.
- For a PowerPoint file (*.ppt or *.pptx), it opens in Impress.

If you did not associate the file types and Microsoft Office is installed on your computer, then when you double-click on a Microsoft Office file, it opens using the appropriate Microsoft Office component.

For more information on opening files, see “Opening existing documents” on page 27.

Quickstarter for Windows

The LibreOffice installation process installs Quickstarter on computers using the Windows operating system. Quickstarter is installed in the Windows system tray and is automatically loaded during system startup. It loads `*.DLL` library files required by LibreOffice, resulting in a shorter startup time for LibreOffice components. If Quickstarter has been disabled, see “Reactivating Quickstarter” on page 22 to enable it.

Using Quickstarter

Right-click the **Quickstarter** icon in the system tray to open a pop-up menu (Figure 3) from which you can open a new document, or open the Templates Manager, or choose an existing document to open. You can also double-click the **Quickstarter** icon to open the Templates Manager.

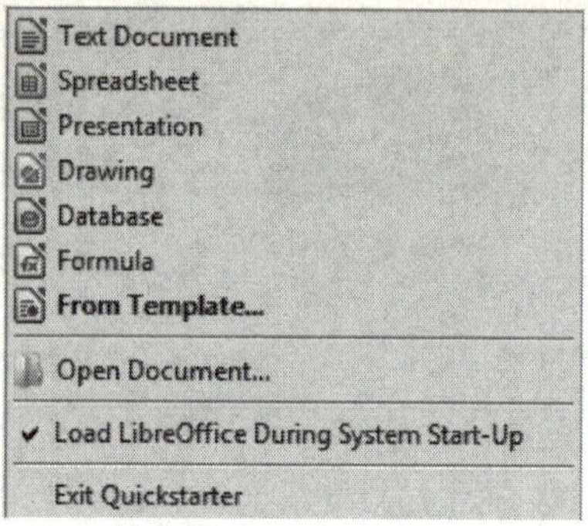

Figure 3: Quickstarter menu in Windows

Disabling Quickstarter

To close Quickstarter, right-click on the icon in the system tray, and then click **Exit Quickstarter** in the pop-up menu. The next time the computer is restarted, Quickstarter will be loaded again.

To prevent LibreOffice from loading Quickstarter during system startup, deselect the **Load LibreOffice during system start-up** item on the pop-up menu. You might want to do this if your computer has insufficient memory, for example.

Reactivating Quickstarter

If Quickstarter has been disabled, you can reactivate it by selecting the **Load LibreOffice during system start-up** check box in **Tools > Options > LibreOffice > Memory**.

Linux and Mac OS X

Computers operating Linux and Mac OS X do not have a Quickstarter module. To launch LibreOffice you have to click on the LibreOffice icon in Applications. This opens the LibreOffice startup screen (Figure 2) from where you can select the various LibreOffice components or select to open an existing file or use a template.

Parts of the main window

The main window is similar for each component of LibreOffice, although some details vary. See the relevant chapters in this guide about Writer, Calc, Draw, and Impress for descriptions of those details.

Common features include the main menu bar, standard toolbar, and formatting toolbar at the top of the window and the status bar at the bottom.

Main menu bar

The *Main menu bar* is located across the top of the LibreOffice window, just below the Title bar. When you select one of the menus listed below, a sub-menu drops down to show commands.

- **File** – contains commands that apply to the entire document such as Open, Save, and Export as PDF.

- **Edit** – contains commands for editing the document such as Undo: xxx (where xxx is the command to undo) and Find & Replace. It also contains commands to cut, copy, and paste selected parts of your document.
- **View** – contains commands for controlling the display of the document such as Zoom and Web Layout.
- **Insert** – contains commands for inserting elements into your document such as Header, Footer, and Picture.
- **Format** – contains commands, such as Styles and Formatting and AutoCorrect, for formatting the layout of your document.
- **Table** – contains all commands to insert and edit a table in a text document.
- **Tools** – contains functions such as Spelling and Grammar, Customize, and Options.
- **Window** – contains commands for the display window.
- **Help** – contains links to the LibreOffice Help file, What's This?, and information about the program.

Toolbars

LibreOffice has two types of toolbars: docked (fixed in place) and floating. Docked toolbars can be moved to different locations or made to float, and floating toolbars can be docked.

In a default LibreOffice installation, the top docked toolbar, just under the Main menu bar, is called the *Standard* toolbar. It is consistent across the LibreOffice applications.

The second toolbar at the top, in a default LibreOffice installation, is the *Formatting* bar. It is context-sensitive; that is, it shows the tools relevant to the current position of the cursor or the object selected. For example, when the cursor is on a graphic, the Formatting bar provides tools for formatting graphics; when the cursor is in text, the tools are for formatting text.

Displaying or hiding toolbars

To display or hide toolbars, go to **View > Toolbars** on the main menu bar, then click on the name of a toolbar from the drop-down list. An active toolbar shows a check-mark beside its name. Toolbars created from tool palettes are not listed in the View menu.

To close a toolbar, click on the X on the right of the toolbar title or go to **View > Toolbars** on the main menu bar and deselect the toolbar.

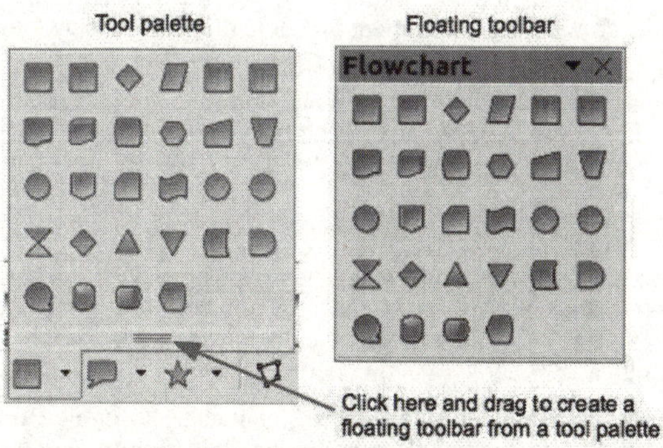

Figure 4: Example of tearing off a tool palette

Sub-menus and tool palettes

Toolbar icons with a small triangle to the right will display *sub-menus*, *tool palettes*, and other ways of selecting things, depending on the icon.

Tool palettes can be made into a floating toolbar and Figure 4 shows an example of a tool palette from the Drawing toolbar made into a floating toolbar. See "Moving toolbars" and "Floating toolbars" below for more information on moving and floating these toolbars created from tool palettes.

Moving toolbars

Docked toolbars can be undocked and moved to a new docked position or left as a floating toolbar.

1) Move the mouse cursor over the toolbar handle, which is the small vertical bar to the left of a docked toolbar and highlighted in Figure 5.
2) Hold down the left mouse button and drag the toolbar to the new location. The toolbar can be docked in a new position at the top, sides or bottom of the main window, or left as a floating toolbar.
3) Release the mouse button.
4) To move a floating toolbar, click on its title bar and drag it to a new floating location or dock the toolbar at the top or bottom of the main window.

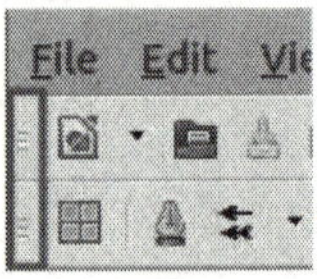

Figure 5: Toolbar handles

Note	You can also dock a floating toolbar by holding down the *Ctrl* key and clicking in the title bar of the toolbar.

Floating toolbars

LibreOffice includes several additional toolbars, whose default setting appear as floating toolbars in response to the current position of the cursor or selection. You can dock these toolbars to the top or bottom of the main window, or reposition them on your computer display (see "Moving toolbars" above).

Some of these additional toolbars are context sensitive and will automatically appear depending on the position of the cursor. For example, when the cursor is in a table, a *Table* toolbar appears, and when the cursor is in a numbered or bullet list, the *Bullets and Numbering* toolbar appears.

Customizing toolbars

You can customize toolbars in several ways, including choosing which icons are visible and locking the position of a docked toolbar. You can also add icons and create new toolbars, as described in *Chapter 14 Customizing LibreOffice*. To access the customization options for a toolbar, right-click between the icons on a toolbar. A context menu opens.

- To show or hide icons defined for the selected toolbar, click **Visible Buttons**. Visible icons on a toolbar are indicated by an outline around the icon (Figure 6) or by a check mark beside the icon, depending on your operating system. Select or deselect icons to hide or show them on the toolbar.

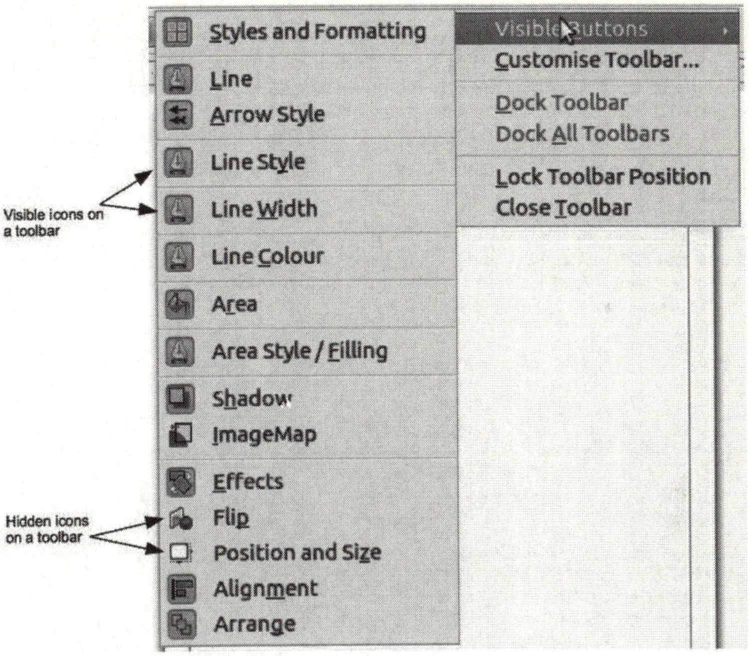

Figure 6: Selection of visible toolbar icons

- Click **Customise Toolbar** to open the Customise dialog, see *Chapter 14 Customizing LibreOffice* for more information.
- Click **Dock Toolbar** to dock the selected toolbar. By default, a toolbar will dock at the top of the workspace. You can reposition the toolbar to a different docked position; see "Moving toolbars" on page 24.
- Click **Dock All Toolbars** to dock all floating toolbars. By default, toolbars will dock at the top of the workspace. You can reposition the toolbars to different docked positions; see "Moving toolbars" on page 24.
- Click **Lock Toolbar Position** to lock a docked toolbar into its docked position.
- Click **Close Toolbar** to close the selected toolbar.

Docking/floating dialogs

When dialogs open, they are floating dialogs, unless they have been docked when LibreOffice was last opened. These floating dialogs can be docked by holding down the *Ctrl* key and double-clicking in a vacant area near the icons at the top of the floating dialog. The dialog will then dock in its last docked position on the workspace. After docking, you can resize the docked dialog and reposition in a new docked position.

To undock a docked dialog and make it floating, hold down the *Ctrl* key and double-click in a vacant area near the icons at the top of the docked dialog. Alternatively, click and hold in a vacant area near the icons at the top of the docked dialog and drag it to a floating position.

Context menus

Context menus are a quick access to many menu functions and are opened by right-clicking on a paragraph, graphic, or other object. When a context menu opens, the functions or options available will be dependent on the object that has been selected. A context menu can be the easiest way to reach a function, especially if you are not sure where a function is located in the menus or toolbars.

Status bar

The status bar is located at the bottom of the workspace. It provides information about the document and convenient ways to quickly change some features. It is similar in Writer, Calc, Impress, and Draw, but each LibreOffice component includes some component-specific items. An example of the Writer status bar is shown in Figure 7.

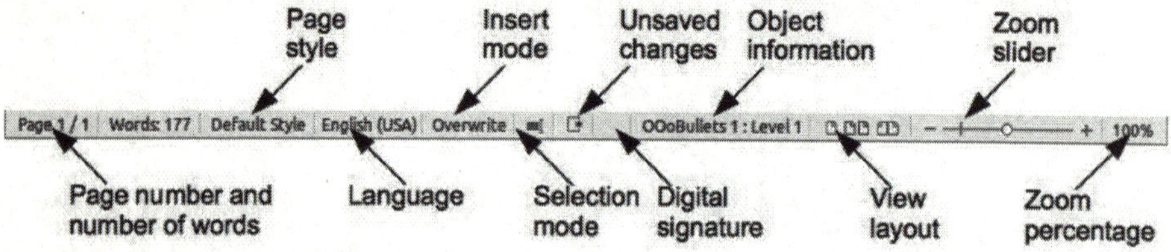

Figure 7: Example status bar from Writer

Page, sheet, or slide number
: Shows the current page, sheet, or slide number and the total number of pages and words, sheets, or slides in the document. Double-click on this field to open the Navigator. Other uses of this field depend on the LibreOffice component.

Page style or slide design
: Shows the current page style or slide design. To edit the current page style or slide design, double-click on this field.

Language
: Shows the current language of the whole document.

Insert mode
: Shows the type of insert mode the program is in. This field is blank if the program is in Insert mode. Press the *Ins* key to change modes.

Unsaved changes
: An icon appears here if changes to the document have not been saved.

Digital signature
: If the document has been digitally signed, an icon shows here. You can double-click the icon to view the certificate.

Object information
: Displays information relevant to the position of the cursor or the selected element of the document. Double-clicking in this area usually opens a relevant dialog.

Zoom slider
: Drag the Zoom slider, or click on the + and – signs to change the view magnification.

Zoom percentage

Indicates the magnification level of the document. Right-click on the percentage figure to open a list of magnification values from which to choose. Double-clicking on this percentage figure opens the **Zoom & View Layout** dialog.

Starting new documents

You can start a new, blank document in LibreOffice in several ways.

When LibreOffice is open but no document is open, the Start Center (Figure 2 on page 21) is shown. Click one of the icons to open a new document of that type, or click the **Templates** icon to start a new document using a template.

You can also start a new document in one of the following ways:

- Use **File > New** on the main menu bar and select the type of document from the context menu.
- Use *Ctrl+N* on the keyboard to start a new text document.
- Use **File > Wizards** on the main menu bar and select the type of document from the context menu.
- If a document is already open in LibreOffice, click the **New** icon on the Standard toolbar and a new document of the same type opens in a new window. For example, if Calc is open, a new spreadsheet is opened. The New icon changes depending on which component of LibreOffice is open.

Note	If all documents are closed without closing LibreOffice, then the Start Center will be displayed.

Opening existing documents

You can also open an existing document in one of the following ways:

- When no document is open, click the **Open** icon on the Start Center and select from a list of available documents.
- Click the small triangle to the right of the Open icon and select from a list of recently opened documents.
- Go to **File > Open** on the main menu bar
- Click the **Open** icon on the Standard toolbar if there is a document already open.
- Press *Control+O* on the keyboard.

In each case above, an Open dialog opens. Navigate to the folder you want and select the file you want, and then click **Open**. If a document is already open in LibreOffice, the second document opens in a new window.

In the Open dialog, you can reduce the list of files by selecting the type of file you are looking for. For example, if you choose **Text documents** as the file type, you will only see documents Writer can open (including... `.odt`, `.doc`, `.txt`); if you choose **Spreadsheets**, you will see `.ods`, `.xls`, and other files that Calc opens.

You can also open an existing document that is in a format that LibreOffice recognizes by double-clicking on the file icon on the desktop or in a file manager such as Windows Explorer. LibreOffice has to be associated with file types that are not ODF files for the appropriate LibreOffice component to open.

Note	On computers operating Microsoft Windows or Mac OS X, you can select to use the LibreOffice Open/Save dialogs or the ones provided by the computer operating system. See “Open and Save As dialogs” on page 31 for more information.

Saving documents

You can save documents as follows:

- Using the **Save** command if you are keeping the document, its current filename and location.
- Using the **Save As** command if you want to create a new document, or change the filename and/or file format, or save the file in a different location on your computer.
- Using password protection if you want to restrict who can open and read the document, or open and edit the document.

Save command

To save a document if you are keeping the document, its current filename and location, do one of the following:

- Use the keyboard shortcut *Ctrl+S*.
- Go to **File > Save** on the main menu bar.
- Click the **Save icon** on the standard toolbar.

Using the Save command will overwrite the last saved version of the file.

Save As command

To save a document if you want to create a new document, or change the filename and/or file format, or save the file in a different location on your computer:

- Use the keyboard shortcut *Ctrl+Shift+S*.
- Go to **File > Save As** on the main menu bar.

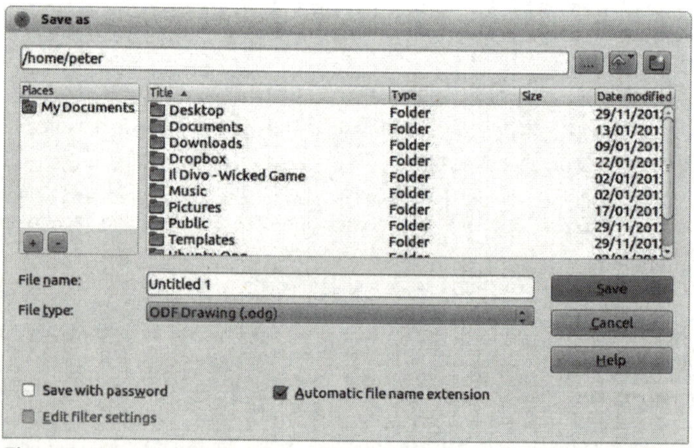

Figure 8: Example of LibreOffice Save As dialog

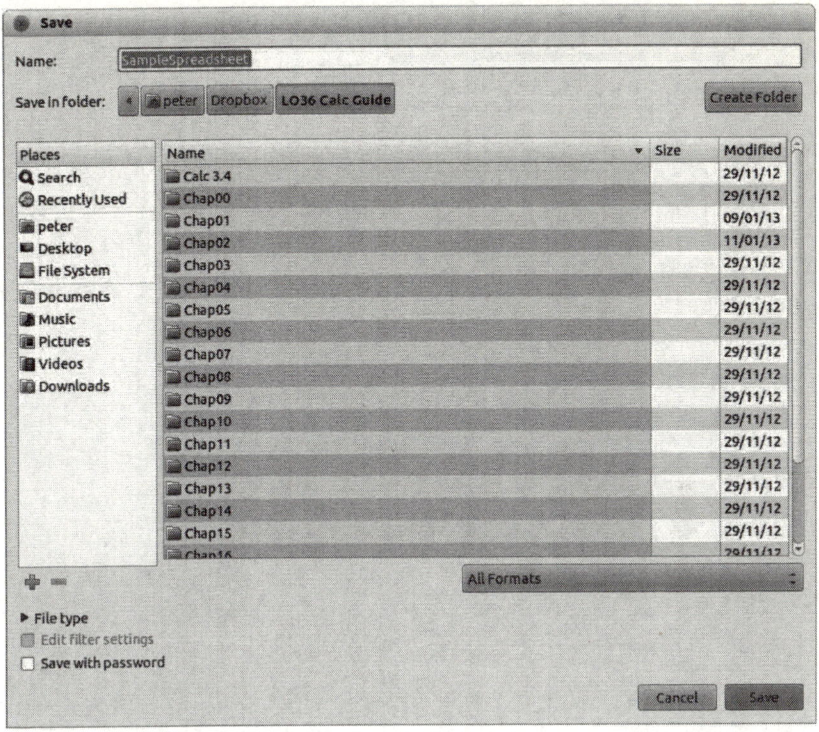

Figure 9: Example of an operating system Save dialog

When the **Save As** dialog (Figure 8) or **Save** dialog (Figure 9) opens, enter the file name, change the file format (if applicable), navigate to a new location (if applicable), and click **Save**.

The dialog that opens when using the Save As command depends on the options that have been set in LibreOffice. See "Open and Save As dialogs" on page 31 for more information.

Password protection

To protect a document and restrict who can open and read the document, or open and edit the document, you have to use password protection.

1) Using the Save As command above, select the **Save with password** option in the Save As dialog or Save dialog.
2) Click **Save** and the **Set Password** dialog opens (Figure 10).
3) In *File encryption password*, enter a password to open the document and then enter the same password as confirmation.
4) To restrict who can edit the document, click the **More Options** button. This button changes to **Fewer Options** when clicked.
5) In *File sharing password*, select **Open file read only** and enter a password to allow editing and then enter the same password as confirmation.
6) Click **OK** and the dialog closes. If the passwords match, the document is saved password protected. If the passwords do not match, you receive an error message.

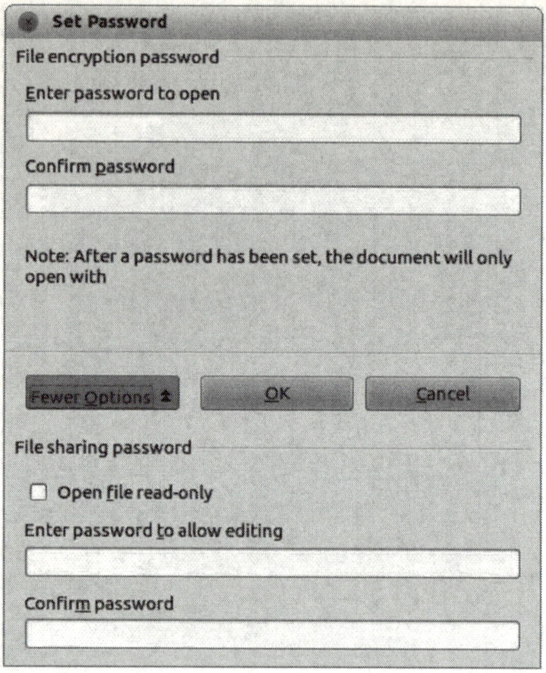

Figure 10: Set Password dialog

Caution	LibreOffice uses a very strong encryption mechanism that makes it almost impossible to recover the contents of a document if you lose or forget the password.

Changing password

When a document is password-protected, you can change the password while the document is open. Go to **File > Properties > General** on the main menu bar and click the **Change Password** button in the Properties dialog. This opens the Set Password dialog where you can enter a new password.

Saving documents automatically

LibreOffice can save files automatically, which is part of the **AutoRecovery** feature included in LibreOffice. Automatic saving, like manual saving, overwrites the last saved state of the file. To set up automatic file saving:

1) Go to **Tools > Options > Load/Save > General** on the main menu bar.
2) Select **Save AutoRecovery information every** and set the time interval.
3) Click **OK**.

Renaming and deleting files

You can rename or delete files within the LibreOffice dialogs, just as you can in a file manager. Select a file and then right click to open a context menu. Select either **Delete** or **Rename**, as appropriate. However, you cannot copy or paste files within the dialogs.

Open and Save As dialogs

You can choose whether to use the LibreOffice Open and Save As dialogs or the ones provided by your operating system.

- To use LibreOffice dialogs for saving or opening files, go to **Tools > Options > LibreOffice > General** and check the option **Use LibreOffice dialog boxes**. An example of a LibreOffice dialog is shown in Figure 8 on page 28.
- To use the operating system dialogs for saving or opening files, go to **Tools > Options > LibreOffice > General** and uncheck the option **Use LibreOffice dialog boxes**. An example of an operating system dialog is shown in Figure 9 on page 29.

The three icons in the top right of the LibreOffice Open and Save As dialogs are as follows:

- **Connect To Server** – a dialog opens allowing you to connect to a network server if the file you want is not located on your computer.
- **Up One Level** – moves up one folder in the folder hierarchy. Click and hold the mouse button on this icon to display a drop down a list of higher level folders. Move the cursor over a higher level folder and release the mouse button to navigate to that folder
- **Create New Folder** – creates a new sub-folder in the folder that is displayed in the dialog.

Use the **File type** field to specify the type of file to be opened or the format of the file to be saved.

The **Read-only** option on the Open dialog opens the file for reading and printing only. Most of the icons and most menu options are disabled on the toolbars. The **Edit File** icon becomes active on the Standard toolbar. Click on this icon to open the file for editing.

Using the Navigator

The LibreOffice Navigator lists objects contained within a document, collected into categories. For example, in Writer it shows Headings, Tables, Text frames, Comments, Graphics, Bookmarks, and other items, as shown in Figure 11. In Calc it shows Sheets, Range Names, Database Ranges, Graphics, Drawing Objects, and other items. In Impress and Draw it shows Slides, Pictures, and other items. An example of the Navigator used in Calc is shown in Figure 11.

To open the Navigator, click the **Navigator** icon on the Standard toolbar, or press the *F5* key, or go to **View > Navigator** on the main menu bar.

You can dock the Navigator to either side of the main LibreOffice window or leave it floating (see "Docking/floating dialogs" on page 25 for more information).

Click the marker (+ or triangle) by any of the categories to display the list of objects in that category.

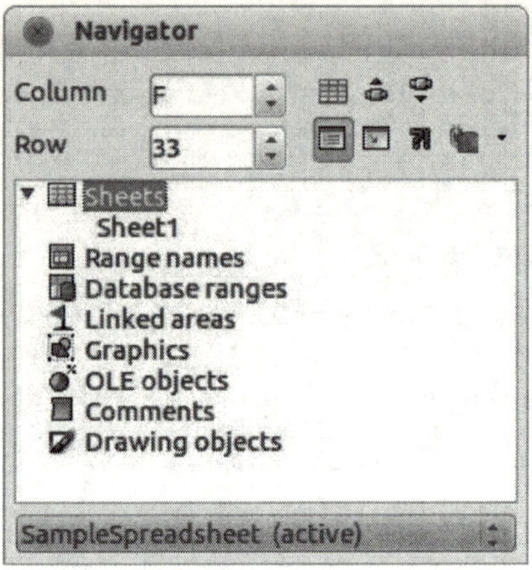

Figure 11: Navigator in Calc

The Navigator provides several convenient ways to move around a document and find items in it:

- When a category is showing the list of objects in it, double-click on an object to jump directly to that object location in the document.
- Objects are much easier to find if you have given them recognisable names when creating them, instead of keeping the LibreOffice default names, for example Sheet1, Table1, Table2, and so on. The default names may not correspond to the actual position of the object in the document.
- Each Navigator in the individual LibreOffice components has a different range of functions and these functions are further explained in the appropriate user guides for each LibreOffice component.

Undoing and redoing changes

To undo the most recent change in a document, use the keyboard shortcut *Ctrl+Z*, or click the **Undo** icon on the Standard toolbar, or go to **Edit > Undo** on the main menu bar. Click the small triangle to the right of the **Undo** icon to get a list of all the changes that can be undone. You can select multiple changes and undo them at the same time.

After changes have been undone, you can redo changes. To redo a change use the keyboard shortcut *Ctrl+Y*, or click the **Redo** icon, or go to **Edit > Redo** on the main menu bar. As with Undo, click on the triangle to the right of the arrow to get a list of the changes that can be reapplied.

To modify the number of changes LibreOffice remembers, go to **Tools > Options > LibreOffice > Memory** on the main menu bar. In the Undo section increase or decrease the **Number of steps**. Be aware that asking LibreOffice to remember more changes consumes more computer memory.

Closing a document

If there is only one document open and you want to close the document, go to **File > Close** on the menu bar or click on the X on the menu bar.

If more than one document is open, go to **File > Close** on the menu bar or click on the X on the title bar of the window. The X may be located on either the right or left end of the title bar. When the last document is open, the X on the menu bar appears.

If the document has not been saved since the last change, a message box is displayed. Choose whether to save or discard your changes.

Caution ⚠	Not saving your document could result in the loss of recently made changes, or worse still, your entire file.

Closing LibreOffice

To close LibreOffice completely, go to **File > Exit** on the Menu bar in Windows and Linux operating systems. In a Mac operating system, go to **LibreOffice > Quit LibreOffice** on the menu bar.

When you close the last document using the X on the title bar of the window, then LibreOffice will close completely. A Mac operating system does not have this function; instead, you need to go to **LibreOffice > Quit LibreOffice** on the menu bar.

You can also use a keyboard shortcut as follows:

- In Windows and Linux – *Ctrl+Q*
- In Mac OS X – *Command* ⌘*+Q*

If any documents have not been saved since the last change, a message box is displayed. Choose whether to save or discard your changes.

LibreOffice
The Document Foundation

Chapter 2
Setting up LibreOffice

Choosing options to suit the way you work

Choosing options for all of LibreOffice

This section covers some of the settings that apply to all the components of LibreOffice. For information on settings not discussed here, see the online help.

Click **Tools > Options**. The list in the left-hand box of the Options – LibreOffice dialog varies depending on which component of LibreOffice is open. The illustrations in this chapter show the list as it appears when a Writer document is open.

Click the marker (+ or triangle) by LibreOffice on the left-hand side. A list of pages drops down. Selecting an item in the list causes the right-hand side of the dialog to display the relevant page.

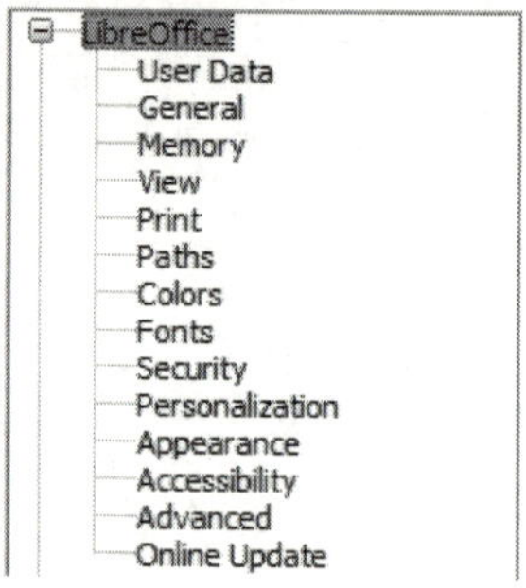

Figure 12: LibreOffice options

Note	The **Revert** button (not shown in the illustration; located in the lower right of the full Options dialog) has the same effect on all pages of the Options dialog. It resets the options to the values that were in place when you opened the dialog.

User Data options

Because LibreOffice uses the name or initials stored in the *LibreOffice – User Data* page for several things, including document properties (created by and last edited by information) and the name of the author of comments and changes, you will want to ensure that the correct information appears here.

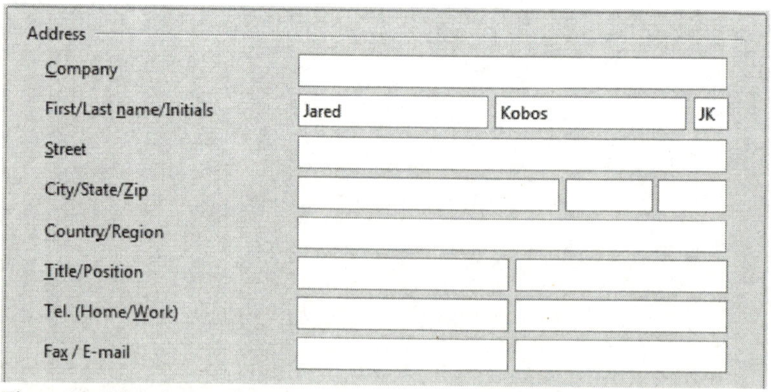

Figure 13: Filling in user data

Fill in the form (shown in Figure 13), or amend or delete any existing incorrect information.

If you are using a version of LibreOffice other than US English, some field labels may be different from those shown in the illustrations.

General options

The options on the *LibreOffice – General* page are described below.

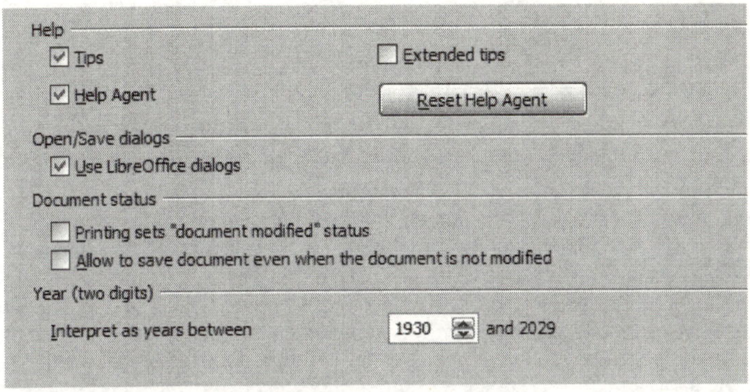

Figure 14: Setting general options for LibreOffice

Help - Tips

When *Tips* is active, one or two words will appear when you hold the mouse pointer over an icon or field, without clicking.

Help - Extended tips

When *Extended tips* is active, a brief description of the function of a particular icon or menu command or a field on a dialog appears when you hold the mouse pointer over that item.

Help Agent

To turn off the *Help Agent* (similar to Microsoft's Office Assistant), deselect this option. To restore the default behavior, click **Reset Help Agent**.

Open/Save dialogs – Use LibreOffice dialogs

To use the standard Open and Save dialogs for your operating system, deselect the **Use LibreOffice dialogs** option. When this option is selected, the Open and Save dialogs supplied with LibreOffice will be used. See Chapter 1, Introducing LibreOffice, for more about the LibreOffice Open and Save dialogs. This book uses the LibreOffice Open and Save dialogs in illustrations.

Print dialogs – Use LibreOffice dialogs

(Mac only) To use the standard Print dialogs for your operating system, deselect the **Use LibreOffice dialogs** option. When this option is selected, the Print dialogs supplied with LibreOffice will be used. This book uses the LibreOffice Print dialogs in illustrations.

Document status – Printing sets "document modified" status

If this option is selected, then the next time you close the document after printing, the print date is recorded in the document properties as a change and you will be prompted to save the document again, even if you did not make any other changes.

Document status – Allow to save document even when the document is not modified
Normally when a document has not been modified, the **File > Save** menu option and the Save icon on the Standard toolbar are disabled and the keyboard shortcut *Ctrl+S* has no effect. Select this option to allow documents to be saved even when they have not been modified.

Year (two digits)
Specifies how two-digit years are interpreted. For example, if the two-digit year is set to 1930, and you enter a date of 1/1/30 or later into your document, the date is interpreted as 1/1/1930 or later. An "earlier" date is interpreted as being in the following century; that is, 1/1/20 is interpreted as 1/1/2020.

Memory options

The options on the *LibreOffice – Memory* page control how LibreOffice uses your computer's memory and how much memory it requires. Before changing them, you may wish to consider the following points:

- More memory can make LibreOffice faster and more convenient (for example, more undo steps require more memory); but the trade-off is less memory available for other applications and you could run out of memory altogether.
- If your documents contain a lot of objects such as images, or the objects are large, LibreOffice's performance may improve if you increase the memory for LibreOffice or the memory per object. If you find that objects seem to disappear from a document that contains a lot of them, increase the number of objects in the cache. (The objects are still in the file even if you cannot see them on screen.)

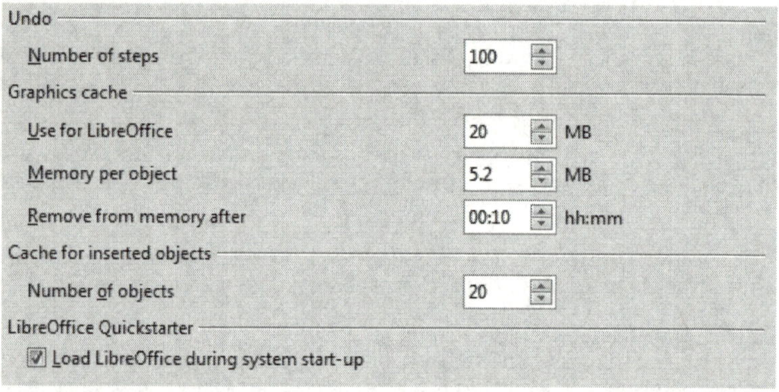

Figure 15: Choosing Memory options for the LibreOffice applications

- To load the Quickstarter (an icon on the desktop or in the system tray) when you start your computer, select the option near the bottom of the dialog. This makes LibreOffice start faster; the trade-off is LibreOffice uses some memory even when not being used. This option (called **Enable systray quickstarter** on Linux) is not available on Mac OS X or on systems where the Quickstarter module has not been installed.

View options

The options on the *LibreOffice – View* page affect the way the document window looks and behaves. Some of these options are described below. Set them to suit your personal preferences.

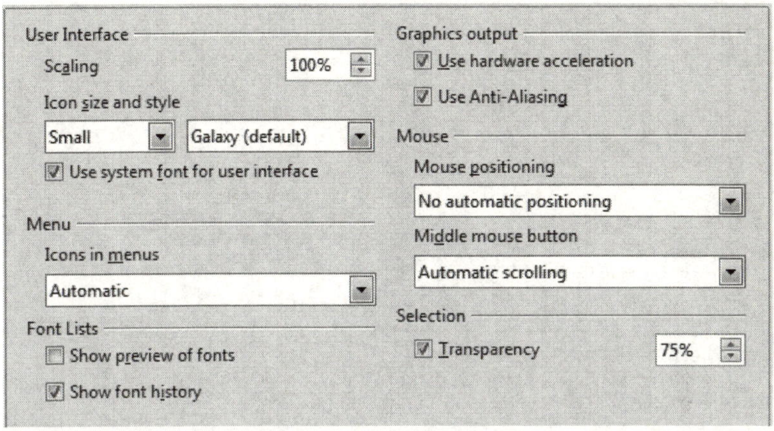

Figure 16: Choosing View options for LibreOffice applications

User Interface – Scaling

If the text in the help files or on the menus of the LibreOffice user interface is too small or too large, you can change it by specifying a scaling factor. Sometimes a change here can have unexpected results, depending on the screen fonts available on your system. However, it does not affect the actual font size of the text in your documents.

User Interface – Icon size and style

The first box specifies the display size of toolbar icons (Automatic, Small, or Large). The Automatic icon size option uses the setting for your operating system. The second box specifies the icon style (theme); here the Automatic option uses an icon set compatible with your operating system and choice of desktop: for example, KDE or Gnome on Linux.

User Interface – Use system font for user interface

If you prefer to use the system font (the default font for your computer and operating system) instead of the font provided by LibreOffice for the user interface, select this option.

User interface – Screen font anti-aliasing

(Not available in Windows; not shown in Figure 16.) Select this option to smooth the screen appearance of text. Enter the smallest font size to apply anti-aliasing.

Menu – icons in menus

Causes icons as well as words to be visible in menus.

Font Lists - Show preview of fonts

Causes the font list to look like Figure 17, Left, with the font names shown as an example of the font; with the option deselected, the font list shows only the font names, not their formatting (Figure 17, Right). The fonts you will see listed are those that are installed on your system.

Fonts which are tuned for use with a specific script, such as Arabic, Hebrew, Malayalam, and so on, now show an additional preview of some sample text in the target script.

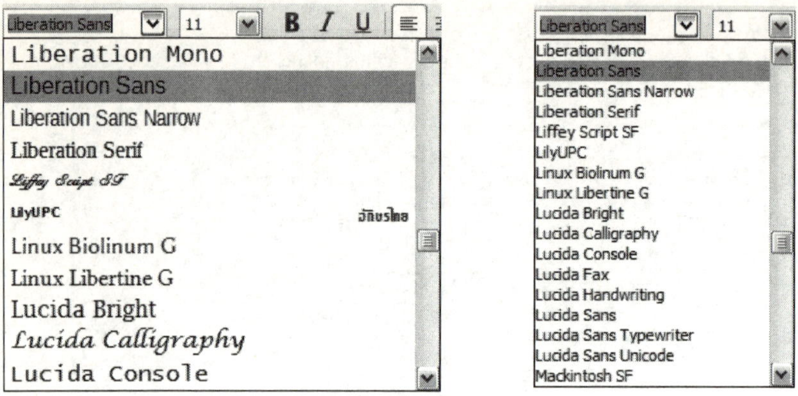

Figure 17. Font list (Left) With preview; (Right) Without preview

Font Lists - Show font history
Causes the last five fonts you have assigned to the current document to be displayed at the top of the font list. Otherwise fonts are shown in alphabetical order.

Graphics output – Use hardware acceleration
Directly accesses hardware features of the graphical display adapter to improve the screen display. Not supported on all operating systems and LibreOffice distributions.

Graphics output – Use anti-aliasing
Enables and disables anti-aliasing, which makes the display of most graphical objects look smoother and with fewer artifacts. Not supported on all operating systems and LibreOffice distributions.

Tip	Press *Shift+Ctrl+R* to restore or refresh the view of the current document after changing the anti-aliasing settings, to see the effect.

Mouse positioning
Specifies if and how the mouse pointer will be positioned in newly opened dialogs.

Middle mouse button
Defines the function of the middle mouse button.

- **Automatic scrolling** – dragging while pressing the middle mouse button shifts the view.
- **Paste clipboard** – pressing the middle mouse button inserts the contents of the "Selection clipboard" at the cursor position.

The "Selection clipboard" is independent of the normal clipboard that you use by **Edit > Copy/Cut/Paste** or their respective keyboard shortcuts. Clipboard and "Selection clipboard" can contain different contents at the same time.

Function	Clipboard	Selection clipboard
Copy content	**Edit > Copy** *Ctrl+C*	Select text, table, or object.
Paste content	**Edit > Paste** *Ctrl+V* pastes at the cursor position.	Clicking the middle mouse button pastes at the mouse pointer position.
Pasting into another document	No effect on the clipboard contents.	The last marked selection is the content of the selection clipboard.

Selection – Transparency

Determines the appearance of selected text or graphics, which appear on a shaded background. To make the shaded background more or less dark, increase or decrease the Transparency setting.

If you prefer selected material to appear in reversed color (typically white text on a black background), deselect this option.

Print options

On the *LibreOffice – Print* page, set the print options to suit your default printer and your most common printing method.

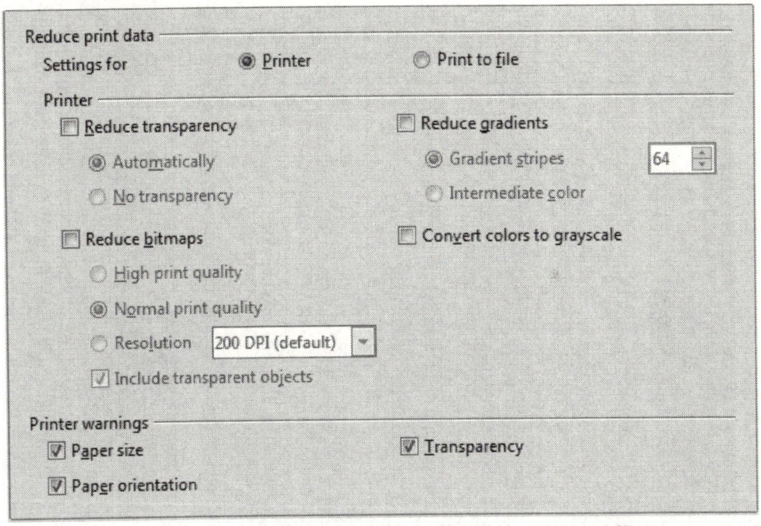

Figure 18: Choosing general printing options to apply to all LibreOffice components

In the *Printer warnings* section near the bottom of the page, you can choose whether to be warned if the paper size or orientation specified in your document does not match the paper size or orientation available for your printer. Having these warnings turned on can be quite helpful, particularly if you work with documents produced by people in other countries where the standard paper size is different from yours.

Tip	If your printouts are incorrectly placed on the page or chopped off at the top, bottom, or sides, or the printer is refusing to print, the most likely cause is page size incompatibility.

Paths options

On the *LibreOffice – Paths* page, you can change the location of files associated with, or used by, LibreOffice to suit your working situation. In a Windows system, for example, you might want to store documents by default somewhere other than My Documents.

To make changes, select an item in the list shown in Figure 19 and click **Edit**. On the Select Path dialog (not shown; may also be titled Edit Paths), add or delete folders as required, and then click **OK** to return to the Options dialog. Note that some items can have at least two paths listed: one to a shared folder (which might be on a network) and one to a user-specific folder (normally on the user's personal computer).

Tip	You can use the entries on the *LibreOffice – Paths* page to compile a list of files, such as those containing AutoText, that you need to back up or copy to another computer.

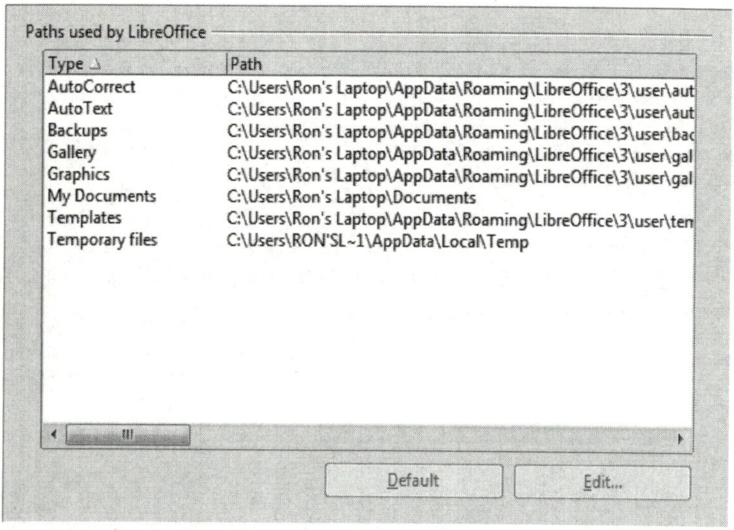

Figure 19: Viewing the paths of files used by LibreOffice

Color options

On the *LibreOffice – Colors* page, you can specify colors to use in LibreOffice documents. You can select a color from a color table, edit an existing color, and define new colors. These colors are stored in your color palette and are then available in all components of LibreOffice.

To modify a color:

1) Select the color to modify from the list or the color table.
2) Enter the new values that define the color. You can choose the RGB (Red, Green, Blue) or the CMYK (Cyan, Magenta, Yellow, Black) system to specify your color. The changed color appears in the lower of the two color preview boxes at the top.
3) Modify the *Name* as required.
4) Click the **Modify** button. The newly defined color is now listed in the Color table.

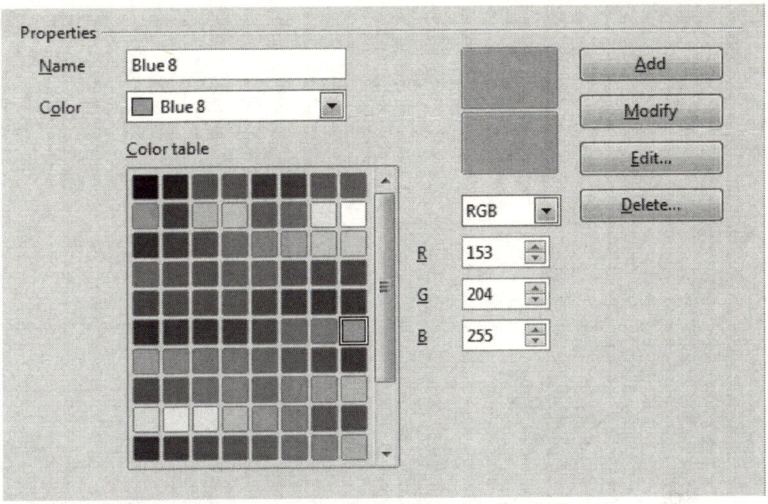

Figure 20: Defining colors to use in color palettes in LibreOffice

Alternatively, click the **Edit** button to open the Color Picker dialog, shown in Figure 21. Here you can select a color from the window on the left, or you can enter values on the right using your choice of RGB, CMYK, or HSB (Hue, Saturation and Brightness) values.

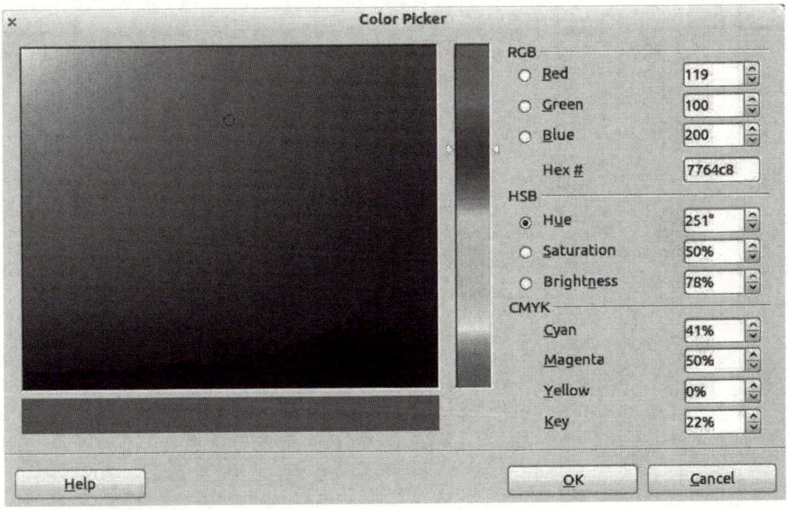

Figure 21: Editing colors

The color window on the left is linked directly with the color input fields on the right; as you choose a color in the window, the numbers change accordingly. The color field at the lower left shows the value of the selected color on the left and the currently set value from the color value fields on the right.

Modify the color components as required and click **OK** to exit the dialog. The newly defined color now appears in the lower of the color preview boxes shown in Figure 20. Type a name for this color in the *Name* box, then click the **Add** button. A small box showing the new color is added to the Color table.

Another way to define or alter colors is through the Colors page of the Area dialog, where you can also save and load palettes, a feature that is not possible here. In Calc, draw a temporary draw object and use the context menu of this object to open the Area dialog. If you load a palette in one component of LibreOffice, it is only active in that component; the other components keep their own palettes.

Font options

You can define replacements for any fonts that might appear in your documents. If you receive from someone else a document containing fonts that you do not have on your system, LibreOffice will substitute fonts for those it does not find. You might prefer to specify a different font from the one that the program chooses.

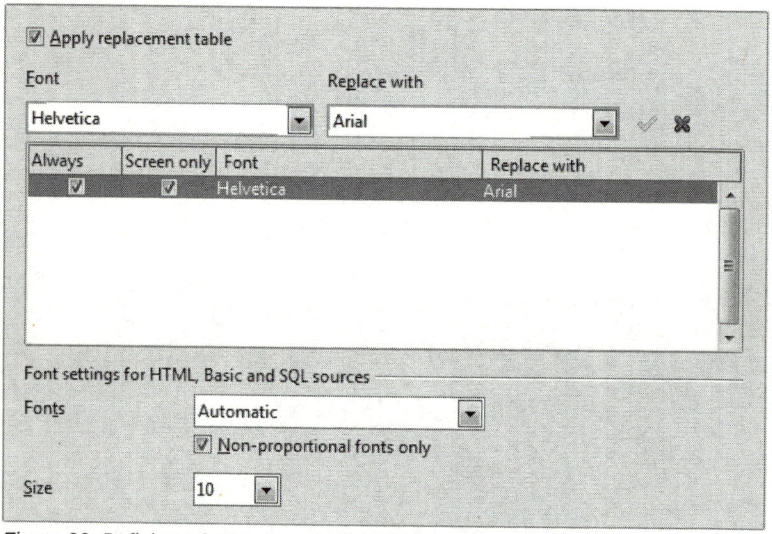

Figure 22: Defining a font to be substituted for another font

On the *LibreOffice – Fonts* page:

1) Select the **Apply Replacement Table** option.
2) Select or type the name of the font to be replaced in the **Font** box. (If you do not have this font on your system, it will not appear in the drop-down list in this box, so you need to type it in.)
3) In the **Replace with** box, select a suitable font from the drop-down list of fonts installed on your computer.
4) The checkmark to the right of the **Replace with** box turns green. Click on this checkmark. A row of information now appears in the larger box below the input boxes. Select **Always** to replace the font, even if the original font is installed on your system. Select **Screen only** to replace the screen font only and never replace the font for printing. The results of combining these selections are given in Table 2.
5) In the bottom section of the page, you can change the typeface and size of the font used to display source code such as HTML and Basic (in macros).

Table 2. Font substitution replacement actions

Always checkbox	***Screen only checkbox***	***Replacement action***
checked	blank	Font replacement on screen and when printing, whether the font is installed or not.
checked	checked	Font replacement only on screen, whether the font is installed or not.
blank	checked	Font replacement only on screen, but only if font is not available.
blank	blank	Font replacement on screen and when printing, but only if font is not available.

Security options

Use the *LibreOffice – Security* page to choose security options for saving documents and for opening documents that contain macros.

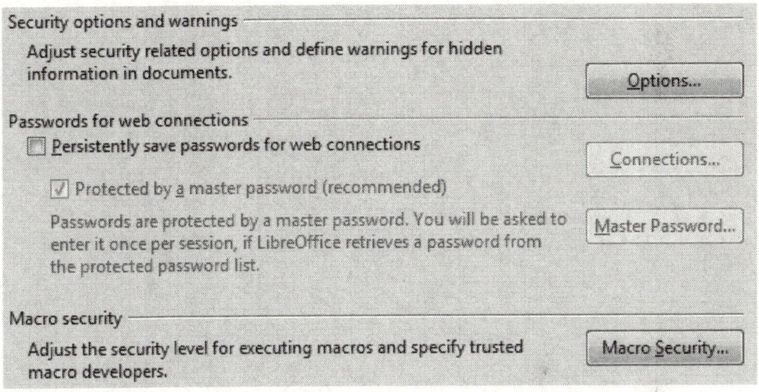

Figure 23: Choosing security options for opening and saving documents

Security options and warnings

If you record changes, save multiple versions, or include hidden information or notes in your documents, and you do not want some of the recipients to see that information, you can set warnings to remind you to remove it, or you can have LibreOffice remove some of it automatically. Note that (unless removed) much of this information is retained in a file whether the file is in LibreOffice's default OpenDocument format, or has been saved to other formats, including PDF.

Click the **Options** button to open a separate dialog with specific choices (Figure 24).

Macro security

Click the **Macro Security** button to open the Macro Security dialog (not shown here), where you can adjust the security level for executing macros and specify trusted sources.

Security options and warnings

The following options are on the Security options and warnings dialog (Figure 24).

Remove personal information on saving

Select this option to always remove user data from the file properties when saving the file. To manually remove personal information from specific documents, deselect this option and then use the **Delete** button under **File > Properties > General**.

Ctrl-click required to follow hyperlinks

The default behavior in LibreOffice is to *Ctrl+click* on a hyperlink to open the linked document. Many people find creation and editing of documents easier when accidental clicks on links do not activate the links. To set LibreOffice to activate hyperlinks using an ordinary click, deselect this option.

The other options on this dialog should be self-explanatory.

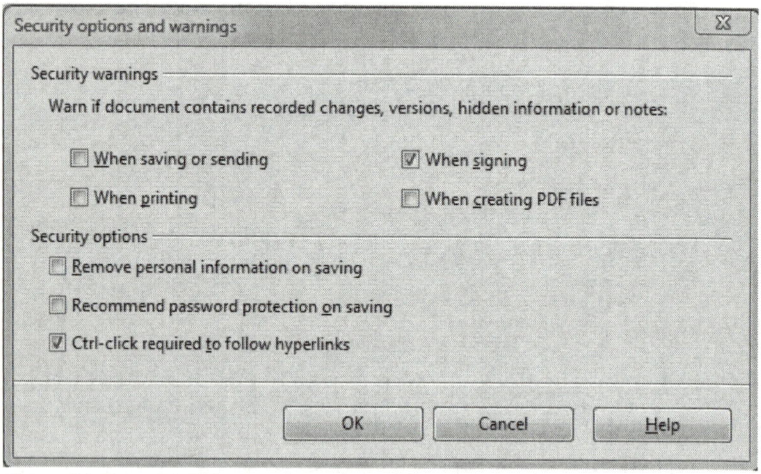

Figure 24: Security options and warnings dialog

Personalization

Personalization allows you to add a theme to your LibreOffice installation. You can choose to not use a Persona, to use a pre-installed Persona if one is available, to select a ready-made persona from the Mozilla Firefox site, or to add your own design. This option defaults to **Pre-installed Persona (if available)** at installation time.

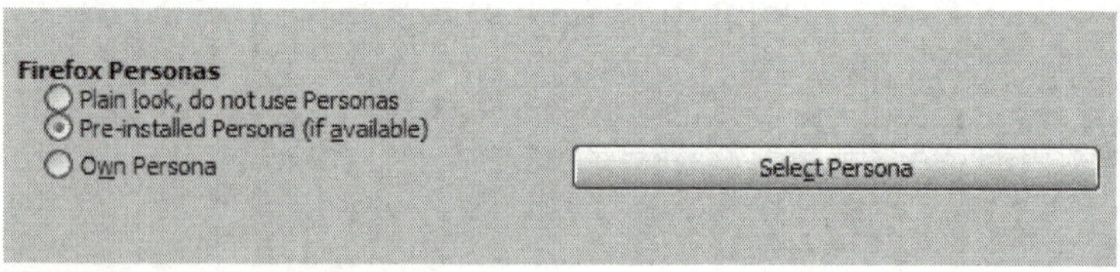

Figure 25: Personalization options

To install a persona, click the **Select Persona** button to open the install dialog, shown in Figure 27. From here you can install your persona by either entering a local URL to the persona, or by clicking the **Visit Firefox Personas** button (an internet connection is required for this choice). Installation instructions are on the dialog.

Full details about Personas are on the website http://www.getpersonas.com

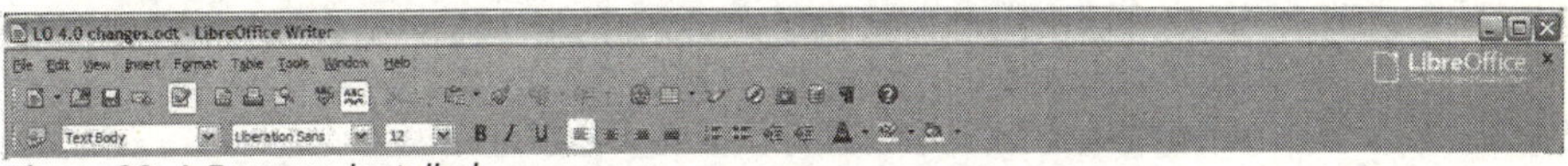

Figure 26: A Persona installed

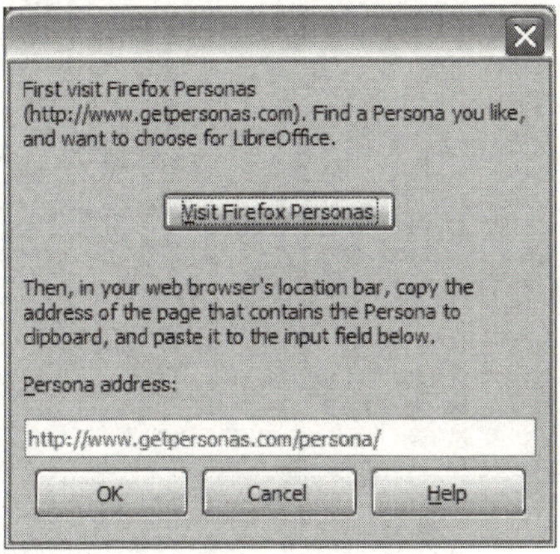

Figure 27: Persona installation dialog

Appearance options

Writing, editing, and (especially) page layout are often easier when you can see the page margins (text boundaries), the boundaries of tables and sections (in Writer documents), page breaks in Calc, grid lines in Draw or Writer, and other features. In addition, you might prefer to use colors that are different from LibreOffice's defaults for such items as comment indicators or field shadings.

On the *LibreOffice – Appearance* page (Figure 28), you can specify which items are visible and the colors used to display various items.

- To show or hide items such as text boundaries, select or deselect the options next to the names of the items.
- To change the default colors for items, click the down-arrow in the *Color Setting* column by the name of the item and select a color from the list box. Note that you can change the list of available colors as described in “Color options” on page 42.
- To save your color changes as a color scheme, click **Save,** type a name in the *Scheme* box, and then click **OK**.

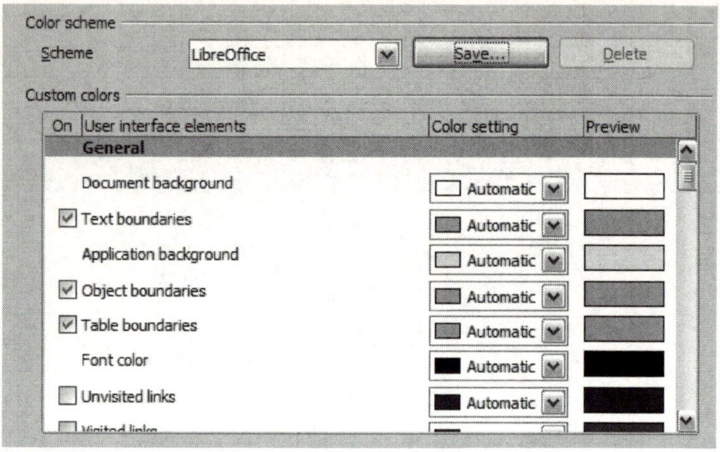

Figure 28: Showing or hiding text, object, and table boundaries

Accessibility options

Accessibility options include whether to allow animated graphics or text, how long help tips remain visible, some options for high contrast display, and a way to change the font for the user interface of the LibreOffice program.

Accessibility support relies on the Java Runtime Environment for communication with assistive technology tools. The *Support assistive technology tools* option is not shown on all LibreOffice installations. See *Assistive Tools in LibreOffice* in the Help for other requirements and information.

Select or deselect the options as required.

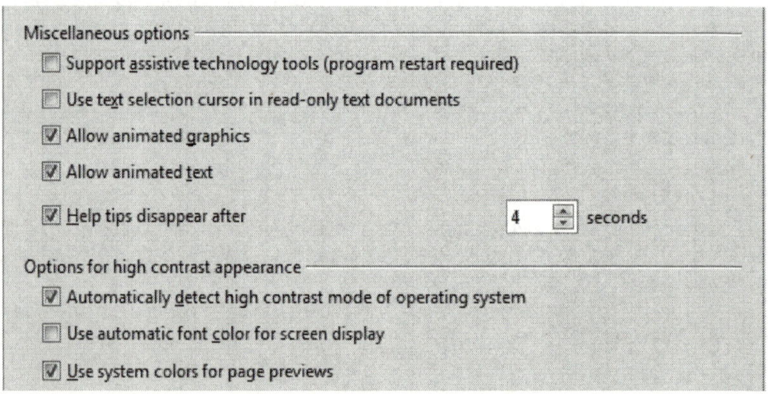

Figure 29: Choosing accessibility options

Advanced

Java options

If you install or update a Java Runtime Environment (JRE) after you install LibreOffice, or if you have more than one JRE installed on your computer, you can use the *LibreOffice – Java options* page to choose the JRE for LibreOffice to use.

If you are a system administrator, programmer, or other person who customizes JRE installations, you can use the Parameters and Class Path pages (reached from the Java page) to specify this information.

If you do not see anything listed in the middle of the page, wait a few minutes while LibreOffice searches for JREs on the hard disk.

If LibreOffice finds one or more JREs, it will display them there. You can then select the **Use a Java runtime environment** option and (if necessary) choose one of the JREs listed.

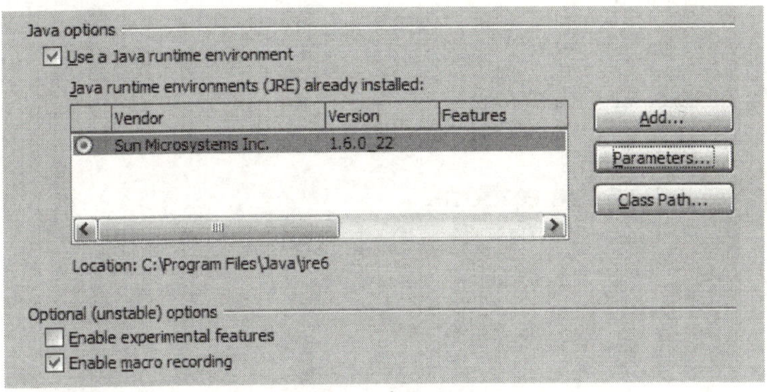

Figure 30: Choosing a Java runtime environment

Optional (unstable) options

Enable experimental features

Selecting this option enables features that are not yet complete or contain known bugs. The list of these features is different version by version.

Enable macro recording

This option enables macro recording with some limitations. Opening a window, switching between windows, and recording in a different window to that in which the recording began, is not supported. Only actions relating to document contents are recordable, so changes in Options or customizing menus are not supported. For more about macro recording, see Chapter 13, Getting Started with Macros.

Online update options

On the *LibreOffice – Online Update* page (Figure 31), you can choose whether and how often to have the program check the LibreOffice website for program updates. If the **Check for updates automatically** option is selected, an icon appears at the right-hand end of the menu bar when an update is available. Click this icon to open a dialog where you can choose to download the update.

If the **Download updates automatically** option is selected, the download starts when you click the icon. To change the download destination, click the **Change** button and select the required folder in the file browser window.

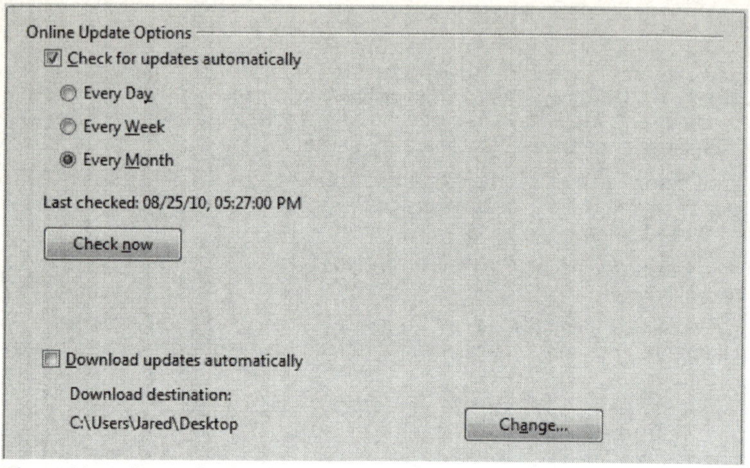

Figure 31: Online update options

Choosing Load/Save options

You can set the Load/Save options for loading and saving documents to suit the way you work.

If the Options dialog is not already open, click **Tools > Options**. Click the expansion symbol (+ or triangle) to the left of **Load/Save**.

General

Most of the choices on the *Load/Save – General* page are familiar to users of other office suites. Some items of interest are described below.

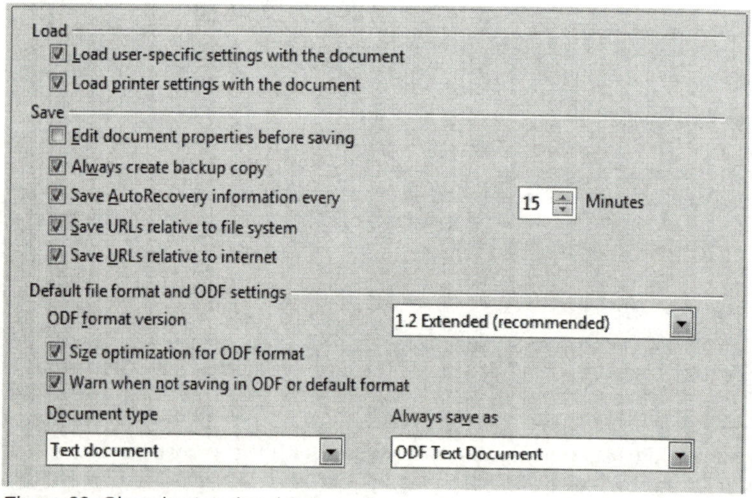

Figure 32. Choosing Load and Save options

Load user-specific settings with the document

A LibreOffice document contains certain settings that are read from the user's system. When you save a document, these settings are saved with it.

Select this option so that when a document loads, it ignores the stored settings in favor of the settings on your computer.

Even if you do not select this option, some settings are taken from your LibreOffice installation:

- Settings available in **File > Print > Options**
- Name of Fax
- Spacing options for paragraphs before text tables
- Information about automatic updating for links, field functions and charts
- Information about working with Asian character formats.

The following settings are **always** loaded with a document, whether or not this option is marked:

- Data source linked to the document and its view.

If you deselect this option, the user's personal settings do not overrule the settings in the document. For example, your choice (in the options for LibreOffice Writer) of how to update links is affected by the **Load user-specific settings** option.

Load printer settings with the document

If enabled, the printer settings will be loaded with the document. This can cause a document to be printed on a distant printer (perhaps in an office setting), if you do not change the printer manually in the Print dialog. If disabled, your standard printer will be used to print this document. The current printer settings will be stored with the document whether or not this option is selected.

Edit document properties before saving

If you select this option, the Document Properties dialog pops up to prompt you to enter relevant information the first time you save a new document (or whenever you use **Save As**).

Always create backup copy

Saves the previous version of a document as a backup copy whenever you save a document. Every time LibreOffice creates a backup copy, the previous backup copy is replaced. The backup copy gets the extension BAK. Authors whose work may be very lengthy should always consider using this option.

Save AutoRecovery information every __ Minutes

Choose whether to enable AutoRecovery and how often to save the information used by the AutoRecovery process.

AutoRecovery in LibreOffice saves the information needed to restore all open documents in case of a crash. If you have this option set, recovering your document after a system crash will be easier.

Save URLs relative to file system / internet

Use this option to select the default for relative addressing of URLs in the file system and on the Internet. Relative addressing is only possible if the source document and the referenced document are both on the same drive.

A relative address always starts from the directory in which the current document is located. In contrast, absolute addressing always starts from a root directory. The following table demonstrates the difference in syntax between relative and absolute referencing:

Examples	File system	Internet
relative	../images/img.jpg	../images/img.jpg
absolute	file:///c|/work/images/img.jpg	http://myserver.com/work/images/img.jpg

If you choose to save relatively, the references to embedded graphics or other objects in your document will be saved relative to the location in the file system. In this case, it does not matter where the referenced directory structure is recorded. The files will be found regardless of location, as long as the reference remains on the same drive or volume. This is important if you want to make the document available to other computers that may have a completely different directory structure, drive or volume names. It is also recommended to save relatively if you want to create a directory structure on an Internet server.

If you prefer absolute saving, all references to other files will also be defined as absolute, based on the respective drive, volume or root directory. The advantage is that the document containing the references can be moved to other directories or folders, and the references remain valid.

Default file format and ODF settings

ODF format version. LibreOffice by default saves documents in OpenDocument Format (ODF) version 1.2 Extended. While this allows for improved functionality, there may be backwards compatibility issues. When a file saved in ODF 1.2 Extended is opened in an editor that uses earlier versions of ODF (1.0/1.1), some of the advanced features may be lost. Two notable examples are cross-references to headings and the formatting of numbered lists. If you plan to share documents with people who use editors that use older versions of ODF, you may wish to save the document using ODF version 1.0/1.1.

Size optimization for ODF format. LibreOffice documents are XML files. When you select this option, LibreOffice writes the XML data without indents and line breaks. If you want to be able to read the XML files in a text editor in a structured form, deselect this option.

Document type. If you routinely share documents with users of Microsoft Office, you might want to change the **Always save as** attribute for documents to one of the Microsoft Office formats. Current versions of Microsoft Word can open ODT files, so this may no longer be needed.

Note	Although LibreOffice can open and save files in the DOCX and XLSX formats produced by Microsoft Office 2007 and 2010, it does not yet save in PPTX format. This capability is planned for a future release.

VBA Properties

On the *VBA Properties* page, you can choose whether to keep any macros in Microsoft Office documents that are opened in LibreOffice.

If you choose **Load Basic code**, you can edit the macros in LibreOffice. The changed code is saved in an ODF document but is not retained if you save into a Microsoft Office format.

If you choose **Save original Basic code**, the macros will not work in LibreOffice but are retained unchanged if you save the file into Microsoft Office format.

If you are importing a Microsoft Word or Excel file containing VBA code, you can select the option **Executable code**. Whereas normally the code is preserved but rendered inactive (if you inspect it with the StarBasic IDE you will notice that it is all commented), with this option the code is ready to be executed.

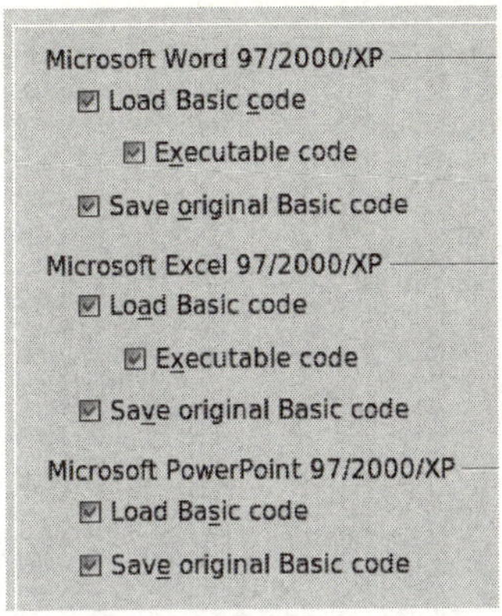

Figure 33: Choosing Load/Save VBA Properties

Save original Basic code takes precedence over **Load Basic code**. If both options are selected and you edit the disabled code in LibreOffice, the original Microsoft Basic code will be saved when saving in a Microsoft Office format.

To remove any possible macro viruses from the Microsoft Office document, deselect **Save original Basic code**. The document will be saved without the Microsoft Basic code.

Microsoft Office

On the *Load/Save – Microsoft Office* page, you can choose what to do when importing and exporting Microsoft Office OLE objects (linked or embedded objects or documents such as spreadsheets or equations).

Select the [L] options to convert Microsoft OLE objects into the corresponding LibreOffice OLE objects when a Microsoft document is loaded into LibreOffice (mnemonic: "L" for "load").

Select the [S] options to convert LibreOffice OLE objects into the corresponding Microsoft OLE objects when a document is saved in a Microsoft format (mnemonic: "S" for "save").

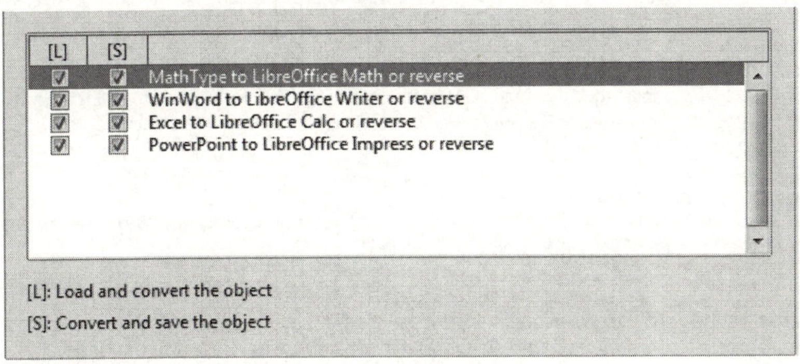

Figure 34: Choosing Load/Save Microsoft Office options

HTML compatibility

Choices made on the *Load/Save – HTML Compatibility* page affect HTML pages imported into LibreOffice and those exported from LibreOffice. See *HTML documents; importing/exporting* in the Help for more information.

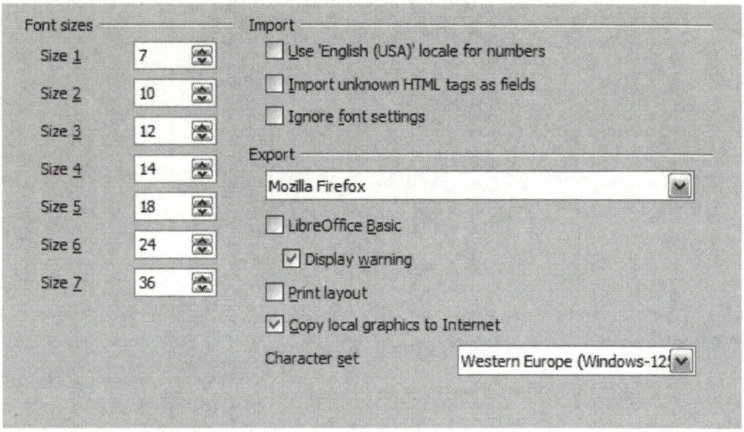

Figure 35. Choosing HTML compatibility options

Font sizes

Use these fields to define the respective font sizes for the HTML <font size=1> to <font size=7> tags, if they are used in the HTML pages. (Many pages no longer use these tags.)

Import - Use 'English (USA)' locale for numbers

When importing numbers from an HTML page, the decimal and thousands separator characters differ according to the locale of the HTML page. The clipboard, however, contains no information about the locale. If this option is **not** selected, numbers will be interpreted according to the **Locale setting** in **Tools > Options > Language Settings > Languages** (see page 55). If this option is selected, numbers will be interpreted as for the English (USA) locale.

Import - Import unknown HTML tags as fields

Select this option if you want tags that are not recognized by LibreOffice to be imported as fields. For an opening tag, an HTML_ON field will be created with the value of the tag name. For a closing tag, an HTML_OFF will be created. These fields will be converted to tags in the HTML export.

Import - Ignore font settings

Select this option to have LibreOffice ignore all font settings when importing. The fonts that were defined in the HTML Page Style will be used.

Export

To optimize the HTML export, select a browser or HTML standard from the **Export** box. If LibreOffice Writer is selected, specific LibreOffice Writer instructions are exported.

Export - LibreOffice Basic

Select this option to include LibreOffice Basic macros (scripts) when exporting to HTML format. You must activate this option *before* you create the LibreOffice Basic macro; otherwise the script will not be inserted. LibreOffice Basic macros must be located in the header of the HTML document. Once you have created the macro in the LibreOffice Basic IDE, it appears in the source text of the HTML document in the header.

If you want the macro to run automatically when the HTML document is opened, choose **Tools > Customize > Events**. See Chapter 13, Getting Started with Macros, for more information.

Export - Display warning
When the **LibreOffice Basic** option (see above) is *not* selected, the **Display warning** option becomes available. If the **Display warning** option is selected, then when exporting to HTML a warning is shown that LibreOffice Basic macros will be lost.

Export - Print layout
Select this option to export the print layout of the current document as well. The HTML filter supports CSS2 (Cascading Style Sheets Level 2) for printing documents. These capabilities are only effective if print layout export is activated.

Export - Copy local graphics to Internet
Select this option to automatically upload the embedded pictures to the Internet server when uploading using FTP.

Export - Character set
Select the appropriate character set for the export.

Choosing language settings

There are several options to customize the language setting in LibreOffice:

- Install the required dictionaries
- Change some locale and language settings
- Choose spelling options

Install the required dictionaries

LibreOffice automatically installs several dictionaries with the program. To add other dictionaries, be sure you are connected to the Internet, and then use **Tools > Language > More Dictionaries Online**. LibreOffice will open your default web browser to a page containing links to additional dictionaries that you can install. Follow the prompts to select and install the ones you want.

Change some locale and language settings

You can change some details of the locale and language settings that LibreOffice uses for all documents, or for specific documents.

In the Options dialog, click **Language Settings > Languages**. The exact list shown depends on the *Enhanced language support* settings (see Figure 37).

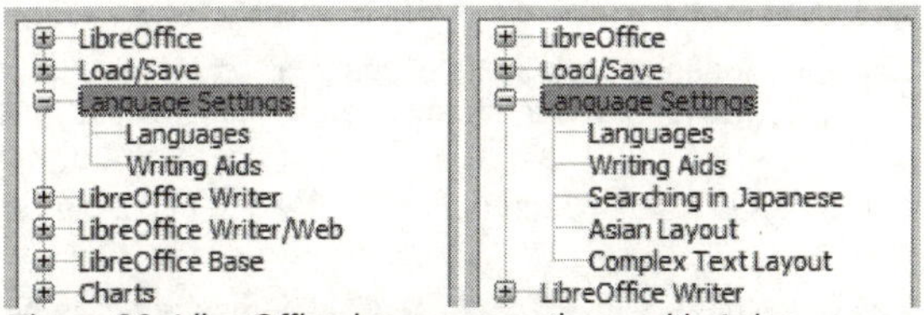

Figure 36: LibreOffice language options, with Asian language options enabled on the right side

On the right-hand side of the *Language Settings – Languages* page, change the *User interface*, *Locale setting*, *Default currency*, and *Default languages for documents* as required. In the example, English (USA) has been chosen for all the appropriate settings.

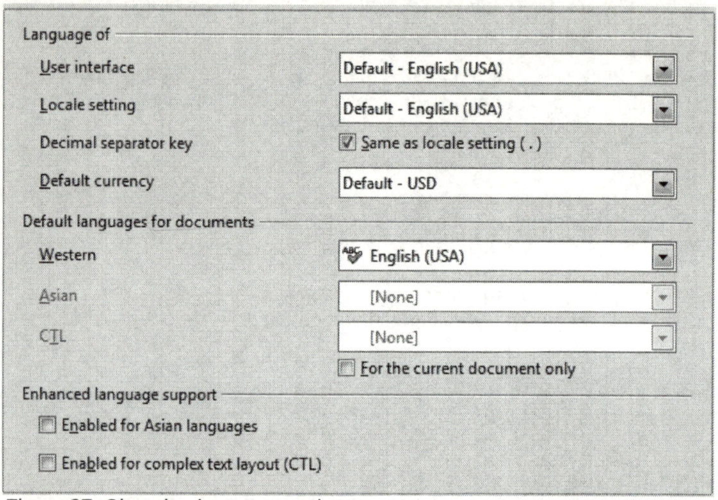

Figure 37: Choosing language options

If you want the language setting to apply to the current document only, instead of being the default for all new documents, select **For the current document only**.

If necessary, select the options to enable support for Asian languages (Chinese, Japanese, Korean) and support for CTL (complex text layout) languages such as Urdu, Thai, Hebrew, and Arabic. If you choose either of these options, the next time you open this dialog, you will see some extra choices under Language Settings, as shown in Figure 36. These choices (*Searching in Japanese*, *Asian Layout*, and *Complex Text Layout*) are not discussed here.

Choose spelling options

To choose the options for checking spelling, click **Language Settings > Writing Aids**. In the *Options* section of the page (Figure 38), choose the settings that are useful for you.

Some considerations:

- If you do not want spelling checked while you type, deselect **Check spelling as you type**. This option can also be deselected using the **AutoSpellcheck** button on the Standard toolbar.
- If you want grammar to be checked as you type, you must have **Check spelling as you type** enabled too.
- If you use a custom dictionary that includes words in all upper case and words with numbers (for example, AS/400), select **Check uppercase words** and **Check words with numbers**.
- **Check special regions** includes headers, footers, frames, and tables when checking spelling.

Here you can also check which user-defined (custom) dictionaries are active by default, and add or remove user-installed dictionaries, by clicking the **New** or **Delete** buttons. Dictionaries installed by the system cannot be deleted.

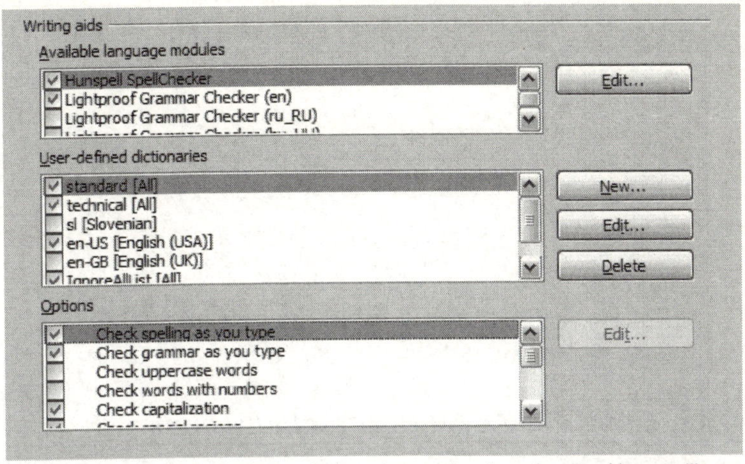

Figure 38: Choosing languages, dictionaries, and options for checking spelling

Choosing Internet options

Use the Internet Options pages to define search engines and save proxy settings for use with LibreOffice.

If you are using a Mozilla browser (such as Firefox) on Windows or Linux, you can enable the Browser Plug-in so you can open LibreOffice files in your browser, print them, save them, and work with them in other ways.

If you are using a Unix- or Linux-based operating system (including Mac OS X), an additional page of E-mail options is available, where you can specify the e-mail program to use when you send the current document as e-mail. Under Windows the operating system's default e-mail program is always used.

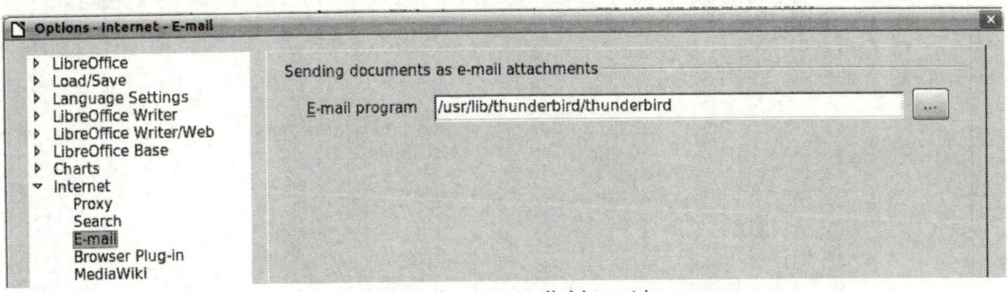

Figure 39: Internet options, showing E-mail page available to Linux users

A MediaWiki publisher is included. To enable it, select MediaWiki in the Internet options, then click the **Add** button to open the dialog shown in Figure 40. Here you can specify the address (URL) and login information for a wiki. You can add several wikis to the list.

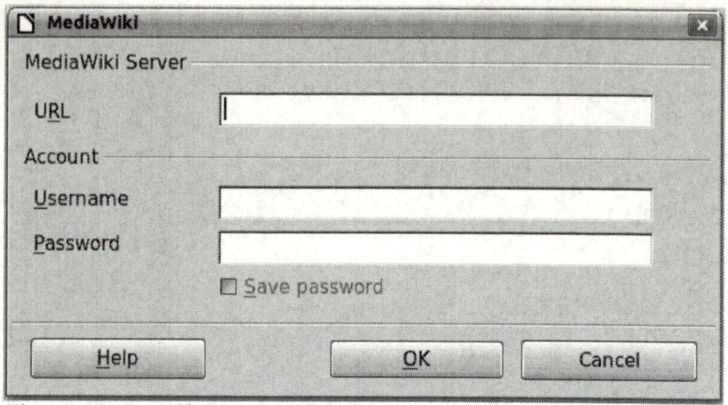

Figure 40: Specifying a MediaWiki server account

Controlling LibreOffice's AutoCorrect functions

Some people find some or all of the items in LibreOffice's AutoCorrect function annoying because they change what you type when you do not want it changed. Many people find some of the AutoCorrect functions quite helpful; if you do, then select the relevant options. But if you find unexplained changes appearing in your document, this is a good place to look to find the cause.

To open the AutoCorrect dialog, click **Tools > AutoCorrect Options**. (You need to have a document open for this menu item to appear.) In Writer, this dialog has five tabs, as shown in Figure 41. In other components of LibreOffice, the dialog has only four tabs. More details are given in the component guides.

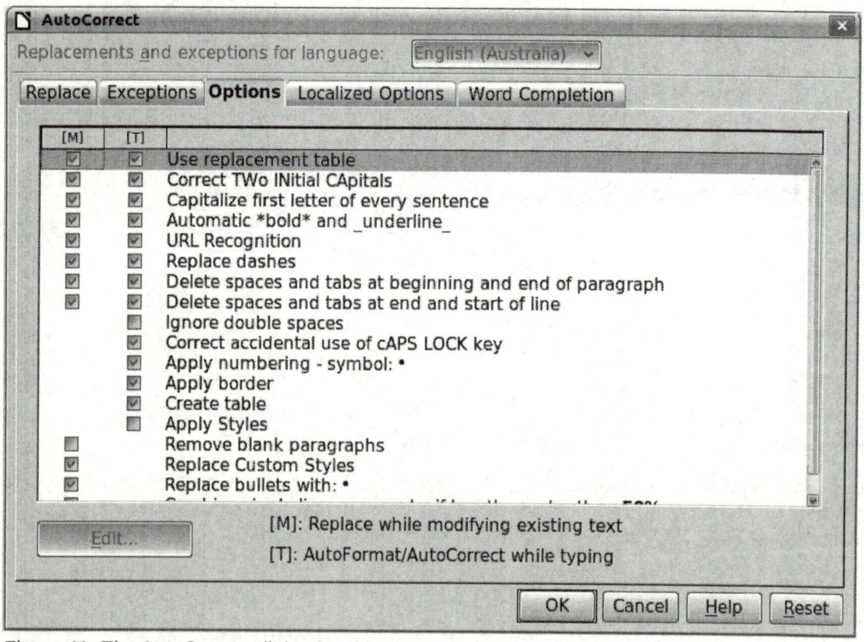

Figure 41: The AutoCorrect dialog in Writer, showing some of the choices on the Options tab

LibreOffice
The Document Foundation

Chapter 3
Using Styles and Templates

What is a template?

A *template* is a document model that you use to create other documents. For example, you can create a template for business reports that has your company's logo on the first page. New documents created from this template will all have your company's logo on the first page.

Templates can contain anything that regular documents can contain, such as text, graphics, a set of styles, and user-specific setup information such as measurement units, language, the default printer, and toolbar and menu customization.

All documents in LibreOffice are based on templates. You can create a specific template for any document type (text, spreadsheet, drawing, presentation). If you do not specify a template when you start a new document, then the document is based on the default template for that type of document. If you have not specified a default template, LibreOffice uses the blank template for that type of document that is installed with LibreOffice. See "Setting a default template" on page 74 for more information.

LibreOffice 4.0 supplies one user-selectable text template, MediaWiki, as an alternative to the default in documents (Writer). Note that German is the default document language in the MediaWiki template. This can be changed on the **Languages** page in **Tools > Options > Language Settings.**

Ten colored backgrounds are supplied for presentations (Impress). No alternative templates are supplied for drawings (Draw) or spreadsheets (Calc).

What are styles?

A *style* is a set of formats that you can apply to selected pages, text, frames, and other elements in your document to quickly change their appearance. When you apply a style, you apply a whole group of formats at the same time.

Many people manually format paragraphs, words, tables, page layouts, and other parts of their documents without paying any attention to styles. They are used to writing documents according to *physical* attributes. For example, you might specify the font family, font size, and any formatting such as bold or italic.

Styles are *logical* attributes. Using styles means that you stop saying "font size 14pt, Times New Roman, bold, centered", and you start saying "Title" because you have defined the "Title" style to have those characteristics. In other words, styles means that you shift the emphasis from what the text (or page, or other element) looks like, to what the text *is*.

Styles help improve consistency in a document. They also make major formatting changes easy. For example, you may decide to change the indentation of all paragraphs, or change the font of all titles. For a long document, this simple task can be prohibitive. Styles make the task easy.

In addition, styles are used by LibreOffice for many processes, even if you are not aware of them. For example, Writer relies on heading styles (or other styles you specify) when it compiles a table of contents. Some common examples of style use are given in "Examples of style use" on page 77.

LibreOffice supports the following types of styles:

- *Page styles* include margins, headers and footers, borders and backgrounds. In Calc, page styles also include the sequence for printing sheets.
- *Paragraph styles* control all aspects of a paragraph's appearance, such as text alignment, tab stops, line spacing, and borders, and can include character formatting.
- *Character styles* affect selected text within a paragraph, such as the font and size of text, or bold and italic formats.

- *Frame styles* are used to format graphic and text frames, including wrapping type, borders, backgrounds, and columns.
- *Numbering styles* apply similar alignment, numbering or bullet characters, and fonts to numbered or bulleted lists.
- *Cell styles* include fonts, alignment, borders, background, number formats (for example, currency, date, number), and cell protection.
- *Graphics styles* in drawings and presentations include line, area, shadowing, transparency, font, connectors, dimensioning, and other attributes.
- *Presentation styles* include attributes for font, indents, spacing, alignment, and tabs.

Different styles are available in the various components of LibreOffice, as listed in Table 3.

LibreOffice comes with many predefined styles. You can use the styles as provided, modify them, or create new styles, as described in this chapter.

Table 3. Styles available in LibreOffice components

Style Type	***Writer***	***Calc***	***Draw***	***Impress***
Page	X	X		
Paragraph	X			
Character	X			
Frame	X			
Numbering	X			
Cell		X		
Presentation			X	X
Graphics	(included in Frame styles)		X	X

Applying styles

LibreOffice provides several ways for you to select styles to apply.

Using the Styles and Formatting window

1) Click the **Styles and Formatting** icon located at the left-hand end of the formatting toolbar, or click **Format > Styles and Formatting**, or press *F11*. The Styles and Formatting window shows the types of styles available for the LibreOffice component you are using. Figure 42 shows the window for Writer, with Page Styles visible.

   You can move this window to a convenient position on the screen or dock it to an edge (hold down the *Ctrl* key and drag it by the title bar to where you want it docked).
2) Click on one of the icons at the top left of the Styles and Formatting window to display a list of styles in a particular category.
3) To apply an existing style, position the insertion point in the paragraph, frame, page or word, and then double-click on the name of the style in one of these lists. To apply a character style to more than one word, select the characters first.

Tip	At the bottom of the Styles and Formatting window is a drop-down list. In Figure 42 the window shows *Automatic*, meaning the list includes only styles applied automatically by LibreOffice. You can choose to show all styles or other groups of styles, for example only custom styles.

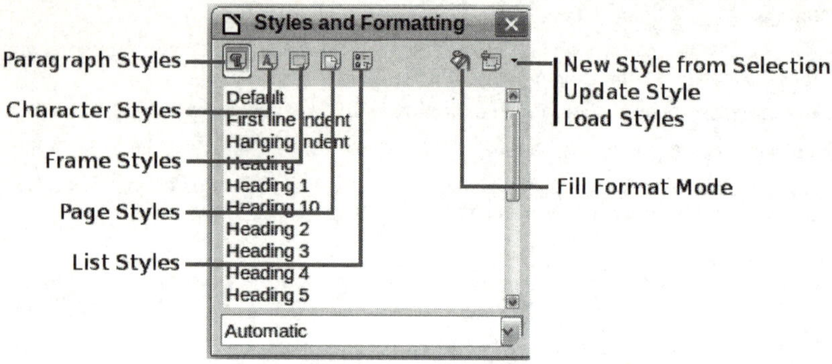

Figure 42: The Styles and Formatting window for Writer, showing paragraph styles

Using Fill Format Mode

Use Fill Format to apply a style to many different areas quickly without having to go back to the Styles and Formatting window and double-click every time. This method is quite useful when you need to format many scattered paragraphs, cells, or other items with the same style.

1) Open the Styles and Formatting window and select the style you want to apply.
2) Click the **Fill Format Mode** icon .
3) To apply a paragraph, page, or frame style, hover the mouse over the paragraph, page, or frame and click. To apply a character style, hold down the mouse button while selecting the characters, Clicking on a word applies the character style for that word. Repeat step 3 until you have made all the changes for that style.
4) To quit Fill Format mode, click the **Fill Format Mode** icon again or press the *Esc* key.

Caution	When this mode is active, a right-click anywhere in the document undoes the last Fill Format action. Be careful not to accidentally right-click and thus undo actions you want to keep.

Using the Apply Style list

After you have used a style at least once in a document, the style name appears on the Apply Style list at the left-hand end of the Formatting toolbar, next to the Styles and Formatting icon.

You can open this list and click once on the style you want, or you can use the up and down arrow keys to move through the list and then press *Enter* to apply the highlighted style.

Tip	Select **More** at the bottom of the Apply Style list to open the Styles and Formatting window.

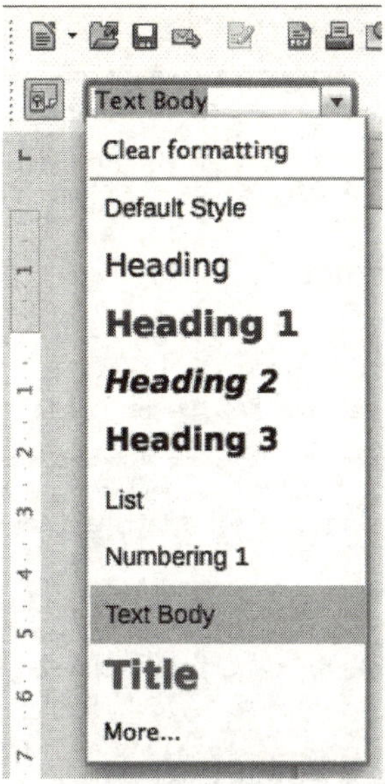

Figure 43: The Apply Style list on the Formatting toolbar

Using keyboard shortcuts

Some keyboard shortcuts for applying styles are predefined. For example, in Writer *Ctrl+0* applies the *Text body* style, *Ctrl+1* applies the *Heading 1* style, and *Ctrl+2* applies the *Heading 2* style. You can modify these shortcuts and create your own; see Chapter 14, Customizing LibreOffice, for instructions.

Caution	Manual formatting (also called *direct formatting*) overrides styles, and you cannot get rid of the manual formatting by applying a style to it. To remove manual formatting, select the text, right-click, and choose **Clear Direct Formatting** from the context menu, or use *Ctrl+M* after selecting the text.

Modifying styles

LibreOffice provides several ways to modify styles (both the predefined styles and any custom styles that you create):

- Changing a style using the Style dialog
- Updating a style from a selection
- Use AutoUpdate (paragraph and frame styles only)
- Load or copy styles from another document or template

Note	Any changes you make to a style are effective only in the current document. To change styles in more than one document, you need to change the template or copy the styles into the other documents as described on page 66.

Changing a style using the Style dialog

To change an existing style using the Style dialog, right-click on the required style in the Styles and Formatting window and select **Modify** from the pop-up menu.

The Style dialog displayed depends on the type of style selected. Each style dialog has several tabs. See the chapters on styles in the user guides for details.

Updating a style from a selection

To update a style from a selection:

1) Open the Styles and Formatting window.
2) In the document, select an item that has the format you want to adopt as a style.

Caution	Make sure that there are unique properties in this paragraph. For example, if there are two different font sizes or font styles, that particular property will remain the same as before.

3) In the Styles and Formatting window, select the style you want to update (single-click, not double-click), then click on the arrow next to the **New Style from Selection** icon and click on **Update Style**.

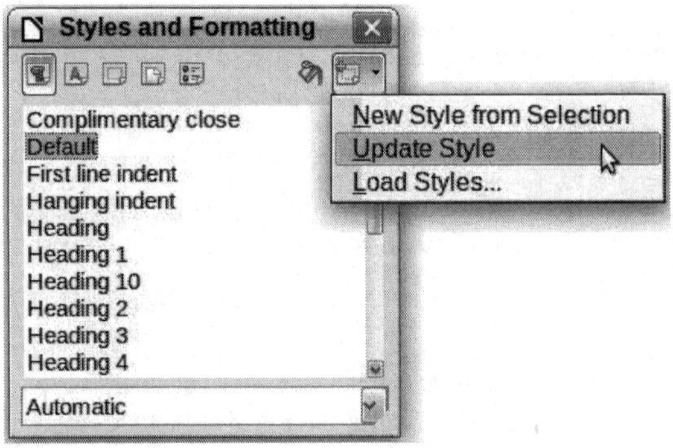

Figure 44: Updating a style from a selection

Using AutoUpdate

AutoUpdate applies to paragraph and frame styles only. If the AutoUpdate option is selected on the Organizer page of the Paragraph Style or Frame Style dialog, applying direct formatting to a paragraph or frame using this style in your document automatically updates the style itself.

Tip	If you are in the habit of manually overriding styles in your document, be sure that AutoUpdate is **not** enabled.

Updating styles from a document or template

You can update styles by copying or loading them from a template or another document. See "Copying styles from a template or document" on page 66.

Creating new (custom) styles

You may want to add some new styles. You can do this in two ways:

- Creating a new style using the Style dialog
- Creating a new style from a selection

Creating a new style using the Style dialog

To create a new style using the Style dialog, right-click in the Styles and Formatting window and select **New** from the pop-up menu.

If you want your new style to be linked with an existing style, first select that style and then right-click and select **New**.

If you link styles, then when you change the base style (for example, by changing the font from Times to Helvetica), all the linked styles will change as well. Sometimes this is exactly what you want; other times you do not want the changes to apply to all the linked styles. It pays to plan ahead.

The dialogs and choices are the same for defining new styles and for modifying existing styles. See the chapters on styles in the user guides for details.

Creating a new style from a selection

You can create a new style by copying an existing manual format. This new style applies only to this document; it will not be saved in the template.

1) Open the Styles and Formatting window and choose the type of style you want to create.
2) In the document, select the item you want to save as a style.
3) In the Styles and Formatting window, click on the **New Style from Selection** icon.
4) In the Create Style dialog, type a name for the new style. The list shows the names of existing custom styles of the selected type. Click **OK** to save the new style.

Figure 45: Naming a new style created from a selection

Dragging and dropping to create a style

You can drag and drop a text selection into the Styles and Formatting window to create a new style.

Writer

Select some text and drag it to the Styles and Formatting window. If Paragraph Styles are active, the paragraph style will be added to the list. If Character Styles are active, the character style will be added to the list.

Calc

Drag a cell selection to the Styles and Formatting window to create cell styles.

Draw/Impress

Select and drag drawing objects to the Styles and Formatting window to create graphics styles.

Copying styles from a template or document

You can copy styles into a document by loading them from a template or from another document:

1) Open the document you want to copy styles into.
2) In the Styles and Formatting window, click on the arrow next to the **New Style from Selection** icon, and then click on **Load Styles** (see Figure 44).
3) Select the categories of styles to be copied. Select **Overwrite** if you want the styles being copied to replace any styles of the same names in the document you are copying them into.
4) On the Load Styles dialog (Figure 46);
   - To copy the styles from a template, find and select the template.
   - To copy the styles from another document, click the **From File** button to open a window from which you can select the required document.

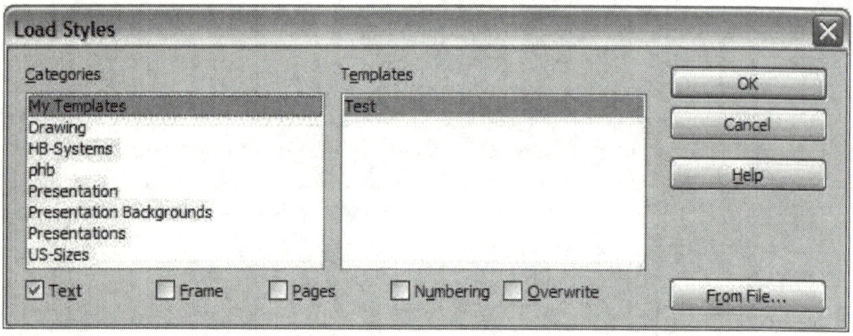

Figure 46. Copying styles from a template into the open document

5) Click **OK** to copy the styles. You will not see any change on screen.

Caution ⚠	If your document has a table of contents, and if you have used custom styles for headings, the heading levels associated with outline levels in **Tools > Outline Numbering** will revert to the defaults of Heading 1, Heading 2, and so on when you load styles. You will need to change these back to your custom heading styles.

Deleting styles

You cannot remove (delete) any of LibreOffice's predefined styles from a document or template, even if they are not in use.

You can remove any user-defined (custom) styles; but before you do, you should make sure the styles are not in use in the current document. If an unwanted style is in use, you will want to replace it with a substitute style.

To delete unwanted styles, right-click on them (one at a time) in the Styles and Formatting window and click **Delete** on the context menu.

If the style is not in use, you receive a confirmation message; click **Yes** to delete the style. If the style is in use, you receive a warning message asking you to confirm deletion.

Caution	Make sure the style is not in use before deletion. Otherwise, all objects with that style will return to the default style and retain their formatting as manual formatting.

Using a template to create a document

To use a template to create a document:

1) From the main menu, choose **File > New > Templates**. The Template Manager dialog opens.
2) From the tabs at the top of the dialog, select the category (type) of template you want to use. Folders containing templates are listed in category page of the dialog. If no folders are visible, there are no templates available.
3) Double-click the folder that contains the template that you want to use. All the templates contained in that folder are listed on the page (as shown in Figure 47).

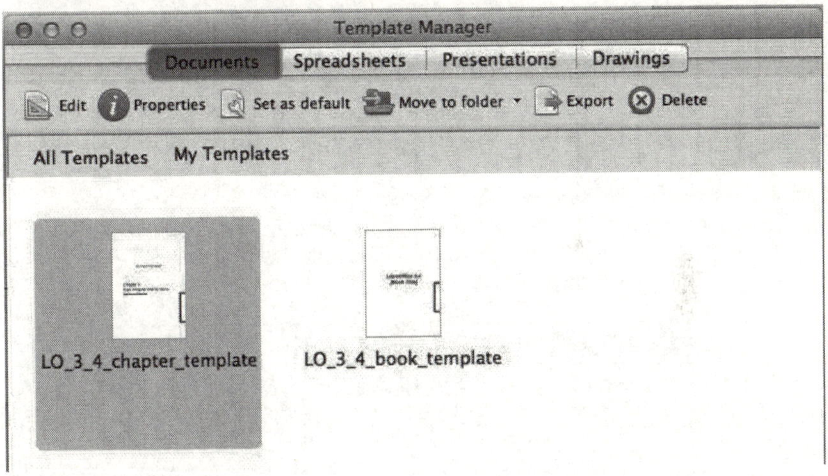

Figure 47: Template Manager dialog

4) Select the template that you want to use. If you wish to view the template's properties, click the **Properties** button above the list of templates. The template's properties appear in a pop-up window. Click **Close** to close this pop-up window.
5) Double-click on the required template. A new document based on the selected template opens in LibreOffice.

Creating a template

Note	In a new installation, only the MediaWiki folder in Documents, and the Presentation Backgrounds folder in Presentations are visible. Other folders become visible only when content is added (My Templates, for example). If this is the case when you come to save your template, follow the instructions in Saving a template to a hidden folder on page 69, to save your template to one of these folders, or to another user folder. In an upgrade, other folders will be visible if you had other than the default installation templates saved.

You can create your own templates in two ways: from a document or using a wizard.

Creating a template from a document

To create a template from a document and save it to My Templates:

1) Open a new or existing document of the type you want to make into a template (text document, spreadsheet, drawing, or presentation).
2) Add the content and styles that you want.
3) From the Menu bar, choose **File > Save As Template**. The Template Manager dialog opens at the **Documents** page.
4) If the My Templates folder is visible, select it. If it is not, from the tabs at the top of the dialog, select a category in which the folder is visible and select it.

Note	It does not matter which tab is selected. The object is to select a My Templates folder. The template will be automatically saved into the My Documents folder in the correct page (tab), according to the meta-data stored in the properties of the file. To learn more about template folders, see "Organizing templates" on page 75.

5) Click **Save**.
6) In the dialog that opens, type a name for the new template and click **Accept**. You can view the My Templates folder on the relevant page to confirm the template is correctly located.
7) Close the Template Manager dialog.

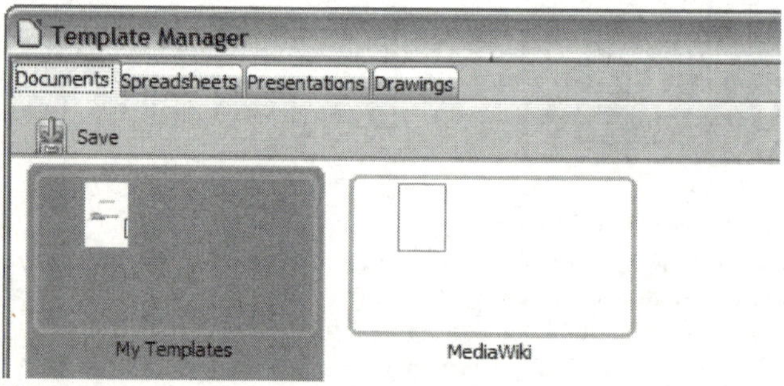

Figure 48: Saving a new template

Any settings that can be added to or modified in a document can be saved within a template. For example, below are some of the settings (although not a full list) that can be included in a Writer document and then saved in the template for later use:

- Printer settings: which printer, single-sided or double-sided printing, paper size, and so on
- Styles to be used, including character, page, frame, numbering and paragraph styles
- Format and settings regarding indexes, tables, bibliographies, table of contents

Templates can also contain predefined text, saving you from having to type it every time you create a new document. For example, a letter template may contain your name, address, and salutation.

You can also save menu and toolbar customizations in templates; see Chapter 14, Customizing LibreOffice, for more information.

Saving a template to a hidden folder

This procedure is for an installation that has yet to have any user installed templates in place. Because empty template folders are hidden in the Template Manager, a work-around is necessary to save the first template into a My Templates folder.

Tip	You can also import a template into a hidden folder by using a similar technique.

It does not matter what document type you are saving as a template, text, spreadsheet, drawing or presentation, follow this procedure. In this example we will save a drawing document which we will title Floor Plan, as a template. Selecting the Drawings tab before starting shows a completely empty category listing (this is our **first** save).

1) Choose **File > Save As Template**. The Template Manager **Save** dialog opens at the **Documents** page. Click once on the MediaWiki folder to select it.
2) Click **Save**, specify the template name in the pop-up dialog (for example, Floor Plan), and click **Accept**. The template is saved into the MediaWiki folder. This appears in the MediaWiki folder in the category of the file type being saved (in our example Drawings).

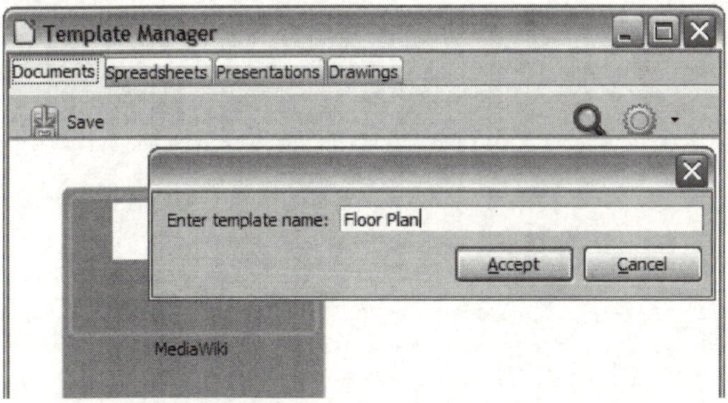

Figure 49: Saving into MediaWiki in Documents

3) Close the Template Manager Save dialog. Open the Template Manager and select the category tab of the template type just saved (**Drawings** in the example). Double-click the **MediaWiki** folder to open it. Select the template you just added. The file handling controls are displayed.

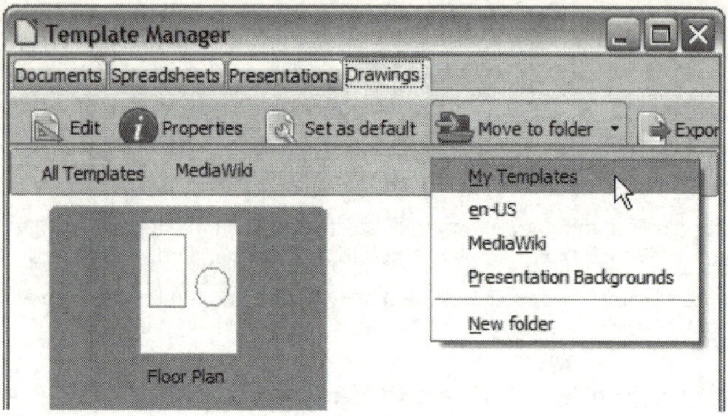

Figure 50: Moving a file to My Templates

4) Click on **Move to folder** to open a menu of destination folders. Select a destination folder for the template. In the example above, **My Templates** is selected. The file is moved.
5) Now click on **All Templates**. The **My Templates** folder is no longer hidden and shows the Floor Plan template file in the folder.

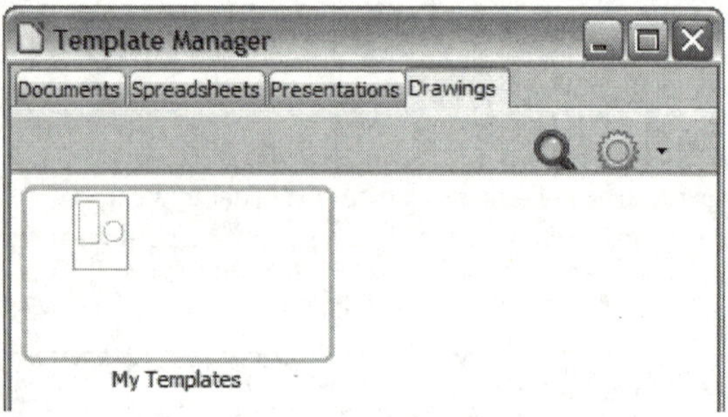

Figure 51: My Templates folder is no longer hidden

Note	The procedure outlined above could also have been carried out using the Presentations Backgrounds folder as the starting folder.

Creating a template using a wizard

You can use wizards to create templates for letters, faxes, agendas, and to create presentations, and Web pages.

For example, the Fax Wizard guides you through the following choices:

- Type of fax (business or personal)
- Document elements like the date, subject line (business fax), salutation, and complementary close
- Options for sender and recipient information (business fax)
- Text to include in the footer (business fax)

To create a template using a wizard:

1) From the main menu, choose **File > Wizards > [type of template required]**.

Figure 52. Creating a template using a wizard

2) Follow the instructions on the pages of the wizard. This process is slightly different for each type of template, but the format is very similar.
3) In the last section of the wizard, you can specify the template name which will show in the Template Manager, and also the name and location for saving the template. The two names can be different but may cause you confusion if you choose two different names. The default location is your user templates directory, but you can choose a different location if you prefer.
4) Selecting the **Path** button to set the file name, and perhaps change the directory, causes the **Save As** dialog to open. Setting the file name and clicking **Save** closes the dialog.
5) Finally, you have the option of creating a new document from your template immediately, or manually changing the template by clicking **Finish**. For future documents, you can re-use the template created by the wizard, just as you would use any other template.

You may have to open the Template Manager and click **Refresh** on the **Action** menu to have any new templates appear in the listings.

Note	In this early release of LibreOffice, clicking **Finish** reopens the Save As dialog in which you set the file name at Step 4. Clicking **Save** now, in the reopened dialog, causes the file to be saved to the hard drive and the template to open. Clicking **Save** in Step 4 only saved the dialog in memory and not to the hard drive.

Editing a template

You can edit a template's styles and content, and then, if you wish, you can reapply the template's styles to documents that were created from that template. (Note that you can only reapply styles. You cannot reapply content.)

To edit a template:

1) From the main menu, choose **File > New > Templates**. The Template Manager dialog opens.

2) Navigate to the template that you want to edit. Click once on it to activate the file handling controls (see Figure 50). Click **Edit**. The template opens in LibreOffice.
3) Edit the template just as you would any other document. To save your changes, choose **File > Save** from the main menu.

Updating a document from a changed template

The next time you open a document that was created from the changed template, the following message appears.

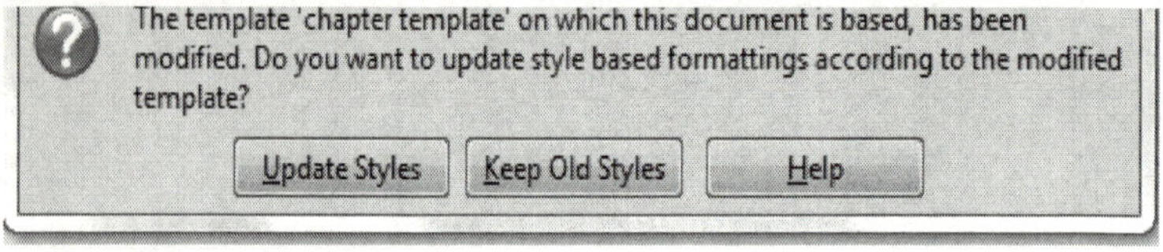

Figure 53. Update styles message

Click **Update Styles** to apply the template's changed styles to the document. Click **Keep Old Styles** if you do not want to apply the template's changed styles to the document (but see the Caution notice below).

Caution

If you choose **Keep Old Styles** in the message box shown in Figure 53, that message will not appear again the next time you open the document after changing the template it is based on. You will not get another chance to update the styles from the template, although you can use the macro given in the Note below to re-enable this feature.

Note

To re-enable updating from a template:

1) Use **Tools > Macros > Organize Macros > LibreOffice Basic**. Select the document from the list, click the expansion symbol (+ or triangle), and select Standard. If Standard has an expansion symbol beside it, click that and select a module.
2) If the **Edit** button is active, click it. If the Edit button is not active, click **New**.
3) In the Basic window, enter the following:

```
Sub FixDocV3
 ' set UpdateFromTemplate
  oDocSettings = ThisComponent.createInstance( _
   "com.sun.star.document.Settings" )
  oDocSettings.UpdateFromTemplate = True
End Sub 'FixDocV3
```

4) Click the **Run BASIC** icon, then close the Basic window.
5) Save the document.

The next time you open this document, you will be prompted to update the styles from the modified template.

Adding templates obtained from other sources

You can download templates for LibreOffice from many sources, including the official template repository at http://templates.libreoffice.org/, and install them on your computer. On other websites you may find collections of templates that have been packaged into extension (OXT) files. These are installed a little differently, as described below.

Installing individual templates

To install individual templates:

1) Download the template and save it anywhere on your computer.
2) Import the template into a template folder by following the instructions in "Importing a template" on page 77.

Tip	(For advanced users) If you know the location of LibreOffice template folders, you can manually copy new templates into them. The location varies with your computer's operating system. To learn where the template folders are stored on your computer, go to **Tools > Options > LibreOffice > Paths**.

Installing collections of templates

The Extension Manager provides an easy way to install collections of templates that have been packaged as extensions. Follow these steps:

1) Download the extension package (.OXT file) and save it anywhere on your computer.
2) In LibreOffice, select **Tools > Extension Manager** from the menu bar. In the Extension Manager dialog (Figure 54), click **Add** to open a file browser window.

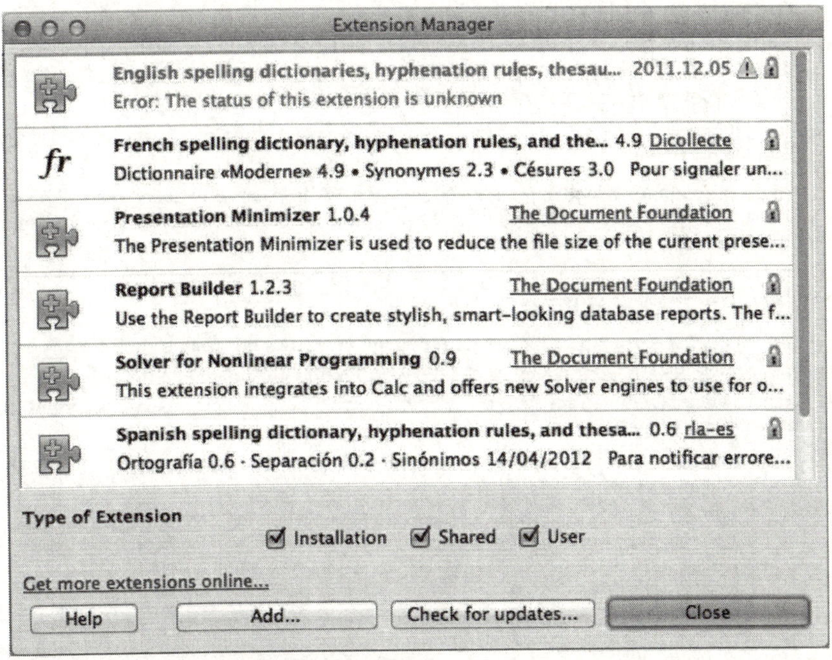

Figure 54: Newly-added package of templates

3) Find and select the package of templates you want to install and click **Open**. The package begins installing. You may be asked to accept a license agreement.

4) When the package installation is complete, the templates are available for use through **File > New > Templates** and the extension is listed in the Extension Manager.

See Chapter 14, Customizing LibreOffice, for more about the Extension Manager.

Setting a default template

If you create a document by choosing **File > New > Text Document** (or **Spreadsheet**, **Presentation**, or **Drawing**) from the main menu, LibreOffice creates the document from the default template for that type of document. You can, however, set a custom template to be the default. You can reset the default later if you choose.

Note for Windows users	You may know that Microsoft Word employs a `normal.dot` or `normal.dotx` file for its default template and how to regenerate it. LibreOffice does not have a similar default template file; the "factory defaults" are embedded within the software.

Setting a custom template as the default

You can set any template to be the default, as long as it is in one of the folders displayed in the Template Manager dialog.

To set a custom template as the default:

1) From the main menu, choose **File > New > Template**.
2) In the Template Management dialog, open the folder containing the template that you want to set as the default, then select the template.
3) Click the **Set as default** icon above the list of templates (see Figure 50).

The next time that you create a document by choosing **File > New,** the document will be created from this template.

Although many important settings can be changed in the **Tools > Options** dialog (see Chapter 2) for the default template, for example default fonts and page size, more advanced settings (such as page margins) can only be changed by replacing the default template with a new one.

Resetting the default template

To re-enable LibreOffice's default template for a document type as the default:

1) In the Template Manager dialog, click the **Action Menu** icon on the right
2) Point to **Reset Default Template** on the drop-down menu, and click **Text Document** (or other template type).

   These choices do not appear unless a custom template has been set as the default, as described in the previous section.

The next time that you create a document by choosing **File > New**, the document will be created from the default template for the document type.

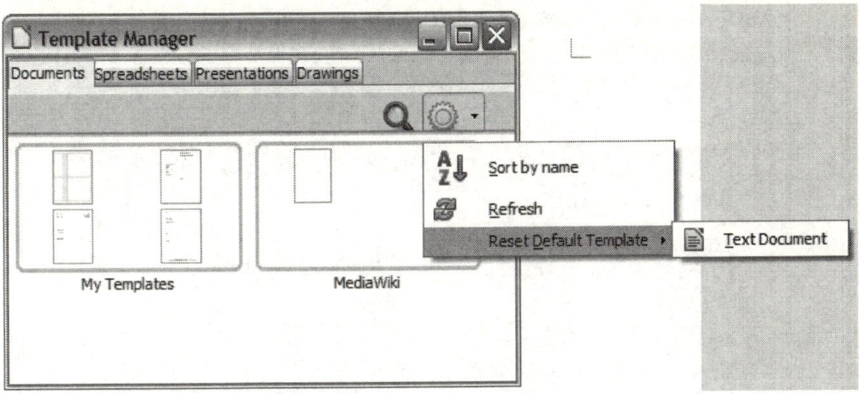

Figure 55: Resetting the default template for text documents

Associating a document with a different template

At times you might want to associate a document with a different template, or perhaps you are working with a document that did not start from a template.

One of the major advantages of using templates is the ease of updating styles in more than one document, as described on page 72. If you update styles by loading a new set of styles from a different template (as described on page 66), the document has no association with the template from which the styles were loaded—so you cannot use this method. What you need to do is associate the document with the different template.

Note	In LibreOffice 3.x, you could use the Template Changer extension to simplify this process. Unfortunately, this extension does not work in LibreOffice 4.0.

For best results, the names of styles should be the same in the existing document and the new template. If they are not, you will need to use **Edit > Find & Replace** to replace old styles with new ones. See Chapter 4, Getting Started with Writer, for more about replacing styles using Find & Replace.

1) Use **File > New > Templates**. In the Template Manager dialog, double-click the template you want to use. A new document opens, containing any text or graphics that were in the template. Delete any unwanted text or graphics from this new document.
2) Open the document you want to change. (It opens in a new window.) Press *Ctrl+A* to select everything in the document. Click in the blank document created in step 1. Press *Ctrl+V* to paste the content from the old document into the new one.
3) Update the table of contents, if there is one. Use **Save As** to save this file with the name of the file from which content was taken. Close the old file without saving.

Organizing templates

LibreOffice can only use templates that are in LibreOffice template folders. You can create new LibreOffice template folders and use them to organize your templates. For example, you might have one template folder for report templates and another for letter templates. You can also import and export templates.

To begin, choose **File > New > Templates** to open the Template Manager dialog.

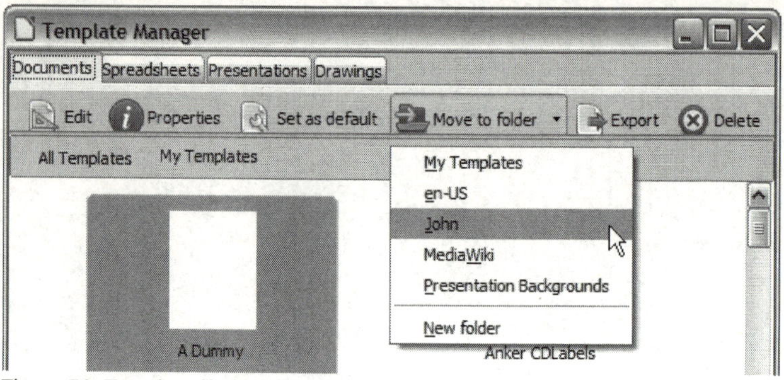

Figure 56: Template file handling icons

Creating a template folder

To create a template folder:

1) In the Template Manager dialog, doube-click any folder, then click any template to activate the row of icons above the list of templates (see Figure 56).
2) Click the **Move to folder** button and choose **New folder** from the drop-down menu.
3) In the pop-up dialog, type a name for the new folder and click **Accept**.

Deleting a template folder

You cannot delete template folders supplied with LibreOffice or installed using the Extension Manager; you can only delete template folders that you have created.

To delete a template folder that you have created:

1) In the Template Manager dialog, select the folder that you want to delete.
2) In the row of icons above the list of folders, click the **Delete** button. A message box appears, asking you to confirm the deletion. Click **Yes.**

Caution	Folders which contain no files are hidden. If the folder is visible, ensure that you want to delete the files that are inside. You may have to put a dummy template into an empty folder in order to delete it (just select **File > Save As Template** for any file you have opened, move it into the folder to be deleted, and then delete the folder; see Figure 56).

Moving a template

To move a template from one template folder to another template folder:

1) In the Template Manager dialog, double-click the folder that contains the template you want to move.
2) Click the template that you want to move and click the **Move to folder** button above the list of templates (see Figure 56).

Deleting a template

You cannot delete templates supplied with LibreOffice or installed using the Extension Manager; you can only delete templates that you have created or imported.

To delete a template:

1) In the Template Manager dialog, double-click the folder that contains the template you want to delete.
2) Click the template that you want to delete.
3) Click the **Delete** button above the list of templates. A message box appears and asks you to confirm the deletion. Click **Yes.**

Importing a template

If the template that you want to use is in a different location, you must import it into a LibreOffice template folder.

To import a template into a template folder:

1) In the Template Manager dialog, select the folder into which you want to import the template.
2) Click the **Import** button above the list of template folders. A standard file browser window opens.
3) Find and select the template that you want to import and click **Open.** The file browser window closes and the template appears in the selected folder.

Exporting a template

To export a template from a template folder to another location:

1) In the Template Manager dialog, double-click the folder that contains the template you want to export.
2) Click the template that you want to export.
3) Click the **Export** button above the list of template folders. The Save As window opens.
4) Find the folder into which you want to export the template and click **Save**.

Examples of style use

The following examples of common use of page and paragraph styles are taken from Writer. There are many other ways to use styles; see the guides for the various components for details.

Defining a different first page for a document

Many documents, such as letters and reports, have a first page that is different from the other pages in the document. For example, the first page of a letterhead typically has a different header, or the first page of a report might have no header or footer, while the other pages do. With LibreOffice, you can define the *page style* for the first page and specify the style for the following pages to be applied automatically.

As an example, we can use the *First Page* and *Default* page styles that come with LibreOffice. Figure 57 shows what we want to happen: the first page is to be followed by the default page, and all the following pages are to be in the *Default* page style. Details are in Chapter 4, Formatting Pages, in the *Writer Guide*.

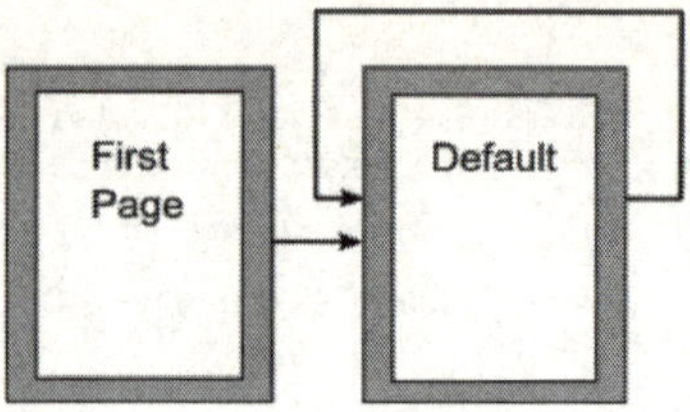

Figure 57: Flow of page styles

Dividing a document into chapters

In a similar way, you can divide a document into chapters. Each chapter might start with the *First Page* style, with the following pages using the *Default* page style, as above. At the end of the chapter, insert a manual page break and specify the next page to have the *First Page* style to start the next chapter, as shown in Figure 58.

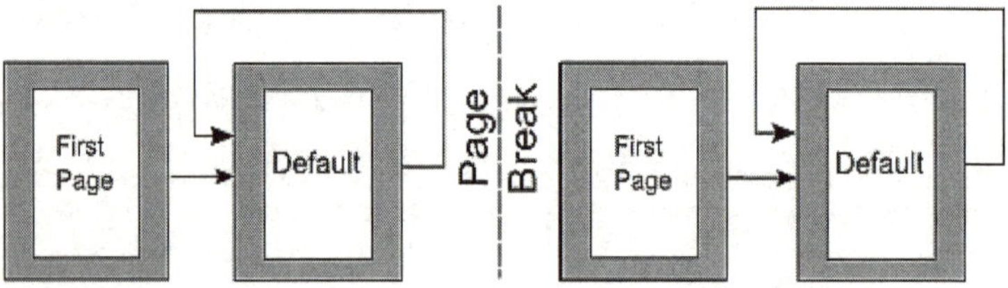

Figure 58: Dividing a document into chapters using page styles

Changing page orientation within a document

A Writer document can contain pages in more than one orientation. A common scenario is to have a landscape page in the middle of a document, whereas the other pages are in a portrait orientation. This can also be done with page breaks and page styles.

Different headers on right and left pages

Page styles can be set up to have the facing left and right pages *mirrored* or only right (first pages of chapters are often defined to be right-page only) or only left. When you insert a header on a page style set up for mirrored pages or right-and-left pages, you can have the contents of the header be the same on all pages or be different on the right and left pages. For example, you can put the page number on the left-hand edge of the left pages and on the right-hand edge of the right pages, put the document title on the right-hand page only, or make other changes.

Controlling page breaks automatically

Writer automatically flows text from one page to the next. If you do not like the default settings, you can change them. For example, you can require a paragraph to start on a new page or column and specify the style of the new page. A typical use is for chapter titles to always start on a new right-hand (odd-numbered) page.

Compiling an automatic table of contents

To compile an automatic table of contents, first apply styles to the headings you want to appear in the contents list, then use **Tools > Outline Numbering** to tell Writer which styles go with which level in the table of contents. See Chapter 4 for more information.

Defining a sequence of styles

You can set up one paragraph style so that when you press *Enter* at the end of that paragraph, the following paragraph automatically has the style you wish applied to it. For example, you could define a *Heading 1* paragraph to be followed by a *Text Body* paragraph. A more complex example would be: *Title* followed by *Author* followed by *Abstract* followed by *Heading 1* followed by *Text Body*. By setting up these sequences, you can avoid manually applying styles in most cases.

LibreOffice
The Document Foundation

Chapter 4
Getting Started with Writer

Word Processing with LibreOffice

What is Writer?

Writer is the word processor component of LibreOffice. In addition to the usual features of a word processor (spelling check, thesaurus, hyphenation, autocorrect, find and replace, automatic generation of tables of contents and indexes, mail merge and others), Writer provides these important features:

- Templates and styles (see Chapter 3)
- Page layout methods, including frames, columns, and tables
- Embedding or linking of graphics, spreadsheets, and other objects
- Built-in drawing tools
- Master documents—to group a collection of documents into a single document
- Change tracking during revisions
- Database integration, including a bibliography database
- Export to PDF, including bookmarks (see Chapter 10)
- And many more

These features are covered in detail in the *Writer Guide*.

The Writer interface

The main Writer workspace is shown in Figure 59. The menus and toolbars are described in Chapter 1, Introducing LibreOffice.

Some other features of the Writer interface are covered in this chapter.

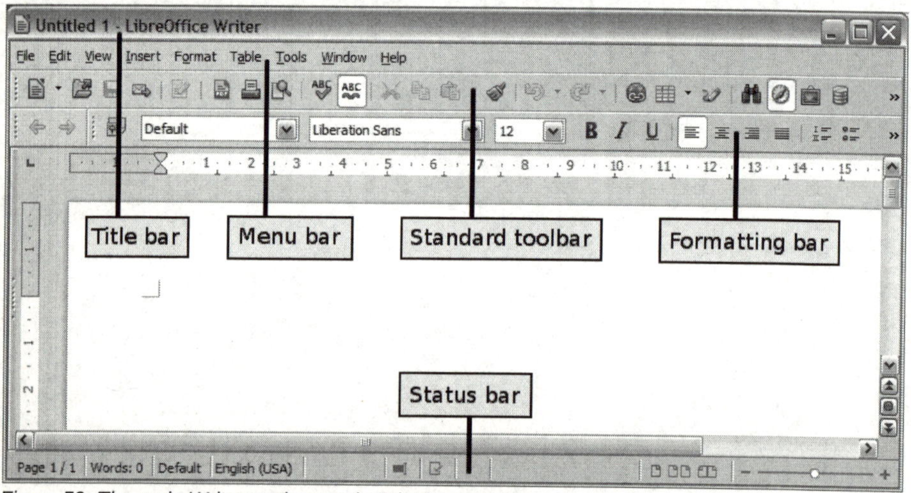

Figure 59: The main Writer workspace in Print Layout view

Status bar

The Writer status bar provides information about the document and convenient ways to quickly change some document features.

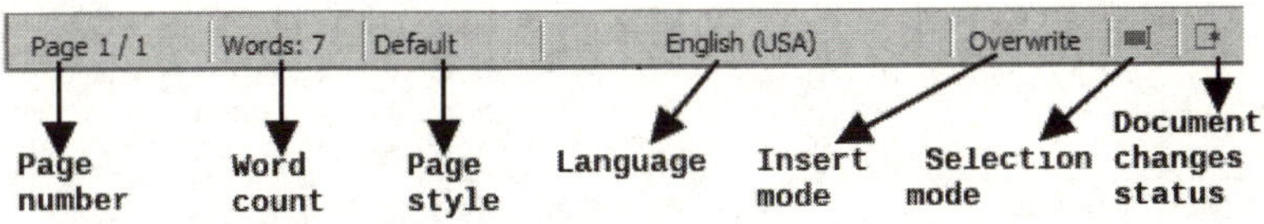

Figure 60: Left end of status bar

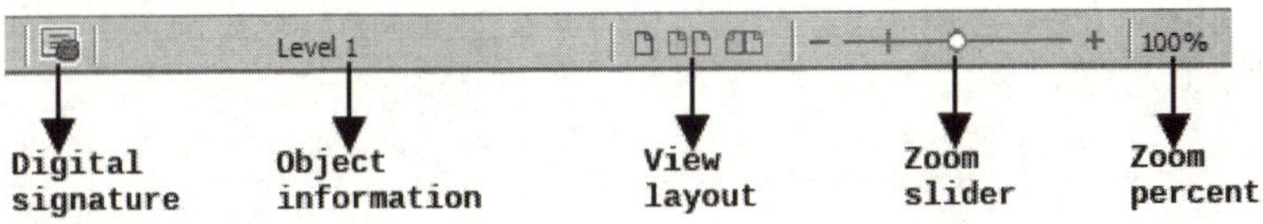

Figure 61: Right end of status bar

Page number

Shows the current page number, the sequence number of the current page (if different), and the total number of pages in the document. For example, if you restarted page numbering at 1 on the third page, its page number is 1 and its sequence number is 3.

If any bookmarks have been defined in the document, a right-click on this field pops up a list of bookmarks; click on the required one.

To jump to a specific page in the document, double-click on this field. The Navigator opens. Click in the Page Number field and type the *sequence* number of the required page and press *Enter*.

Word count

The word count is shown in the status bar, and is kept up to date as you edit. Any text selected in the document will be counted and displayed alongside the total count.

To display extended statistics such as character count, double-click the word count in the status bar, or choose **Tools > Word Count.**

Page style

Shows the style of the current page. To change the page style, right-click on this field. A list of page styles pops up; choose a different style by clicking on it.

To edit the current page style, double-click on this field. The Page Style dialog opens.

Language

Shows the language for the selected text.

Click to open a menu where you can choose another language for the selected text or for the paragraph where the cursor is located. You can also choose **None (Do not check spelling)** to exclude the text from a spelling check or choose **More...** to open the Character dialog.

Insert mode

This area is blank when in Insert mode. Double-click to change to *Overwrite* mode; single-click to return to Insert mode. In Insert mode, any text after the cursor position moves forward to make room for the text you type; in Overwrite mode, text after the cursor position is replaced by the text you type. This feature is disabled when in **Edit > Changes > Record** mode.

Selection mode

Click to choose different selection modes. The icon does not change, but when you hover the mouse pointer over this field, a tooltip indicates which mode is active.

When you click in the field, a context menu displays the available options.

Mode	*Effect*
Standard selection	Click in the text where you want to position the cursor; click in a cell to make it the active cell. Any other selection is deselected.
Extending selection (*F8*)	Clicking in the text extends or crops the current selection.
Adding selection *(Shift+F8)*	A new selection is added to an existing selection. The result is a multiple selection.
Block selection *(Ctrl+Shift+F8)*	A block of text can be selected.

On Windows systems, you can hold down the *Alt* key while dragging to select a block of text. You do not need to enter the block selection mode.

Document changes status

The icon that is displayed here changes from this one if the document has no unsaved changes, to this one if it has been edited and the changes have not been saved.

Digital signature

If the document has been digitally signed, this icon is displayed here; otherwise, it is blank. To view the certificate, double-click the icon.

Section or object information

When the cursor is on a section, heading, or list item, or when an object (such as a picture or table) is selected, information about that item appears in this field. Double-clicking in this area opens a relevant dialog. For details, consult the Help or the *Writer Guide*.

View layout

Click an icon to change between single page, side-by-side, and book layout views. The effect varies with the combination of window width and zoom factor in use. You can edit the document in any view.

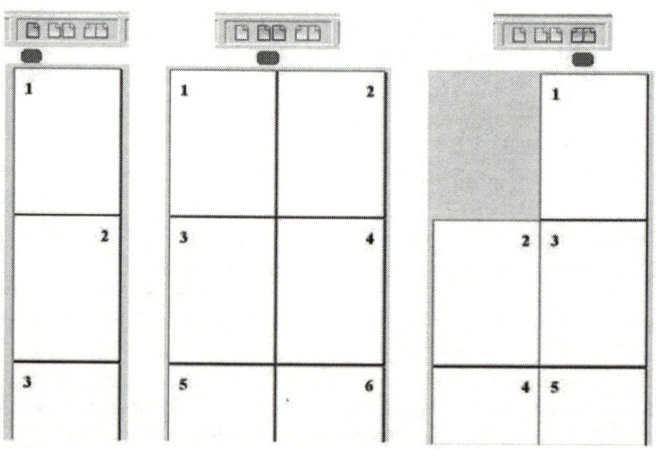

Figure 62: View layouts: single, side-by-side, book.

Zoom

To change the view magnification, drag the Zoom slider, or click on the + and – signs, or right-click on the zoom level percent to pop up a list of magnification values from which to choose. Zoom interacts with the selected view layout to determine how many pages are visible in the document window.

Changing document views

Writer has several ways to view a document: Print Layout, Web Layout, and Full Screen. To access these and other choices, go to the **View** menu and click on the required view. (When in Full Screen view, press the *Esc* key to return to either Print or Web Layout view.)

Print Layout is the default view in Writer. In this view, you can use the Zoom slider and the View Layout icons on the Status bar to change the magnification.

You can also choose **View > Zoom** from the menu bar to display the Zoom & View Layout dialog, where you can set the same options as on the Status bar. In Web Layout view, most of the choices are not available.

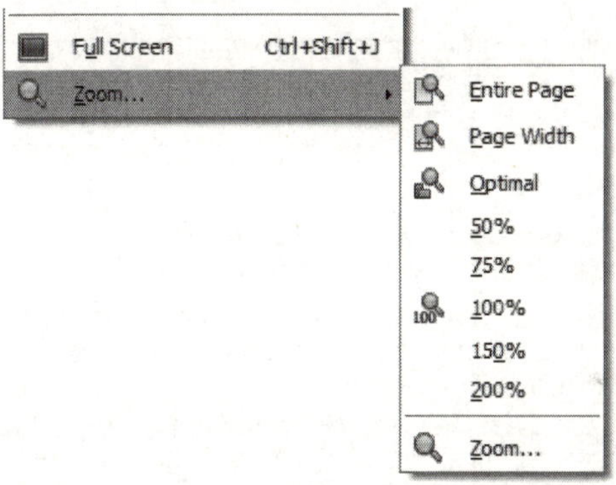

Figure 63: Choosing Zoom and View Layout options.

Moving quickly through a document

In addition to the navigation features of the Status bar (described above), you can use the main Navigator window and the Navigation toolbar as described in Chapter 1, Introducing LibreOffice.

In Writer, you can also display the Navigation toolbar by clicking on the small Navigation icon near the lower right-hand corner of the window below the vertical scroll bar, as shown in Figure 64.

Figure 64: Navigation icons

The Navigation toolbar (Figure 65) shows icons for all the object types shown in the Navigator, plus some extras (for example, the results of a **Find** command).

Figure 65: Navigation toolbar

Click an icon to select that object type. Now all the **Previous** and **Next** icons (in the Navigator itself, in the Navigation Toolbar, and on the scroll bar) will jump to the next object of the selected type. This is particularly helpful for finding items like index entries, which can be difficult to see in the text. The names of the icons (shown in the tooltips) change to match the selected category; for example, **Next Graphic**, **Next Bookmark**, or **Continue search forward**.

For more uses of the Navigator in Writer, see the *Writer Guide*.

Working with documents

Chapter 1, Introducing LibreOffice, includes instructions on starting new documents, opening existing documents, saving documents, and password-protecting documents. Chapter 3, Using Styles and Templates, covers how to create a document from a template.

Saving as a Microsoft Word file

If you need to exchange documents with users of Microsoft Word who are unwilling or unable to receive ODT files, you can save a document as a Microsoft Word file.

1) **Important**—First save your document in the file format used by LibreOffice Writer (ODT). If you do not, any changes you made since the last time you saved will appear only in the Microsoft Word version of the document.
2) Then choose **File > Save As**. On the Save As dialog (Figure 66), in the **File type** (or **Save as type**) drop-down menu, select the type of Word format you need. Files cannot be saved to the Word version 6.0/95 file format. Click **Save.**

From this point on, *all changes you make to the document will occur only in the new document*. You have changed the name and file type of your document. If you want to go back to working with the ODT version of your document, you must open it again.

Tip	To have Writer save documents by default in the Microsoft Word file format, go to **Tools > Options > Load/Save > General**. In the section named *Default file format and ODF settings*, under **Document type**, select **Text document**, then under *Always save as*, select your preferred file format.

Caution	It is recommended that if you use a Microsoft Word format, you use the **DOC** and not the **DOCX** format. Saving in ODF format gives you the option to redo the document if the recipient of your document experiences trouble with the Microsoft format.

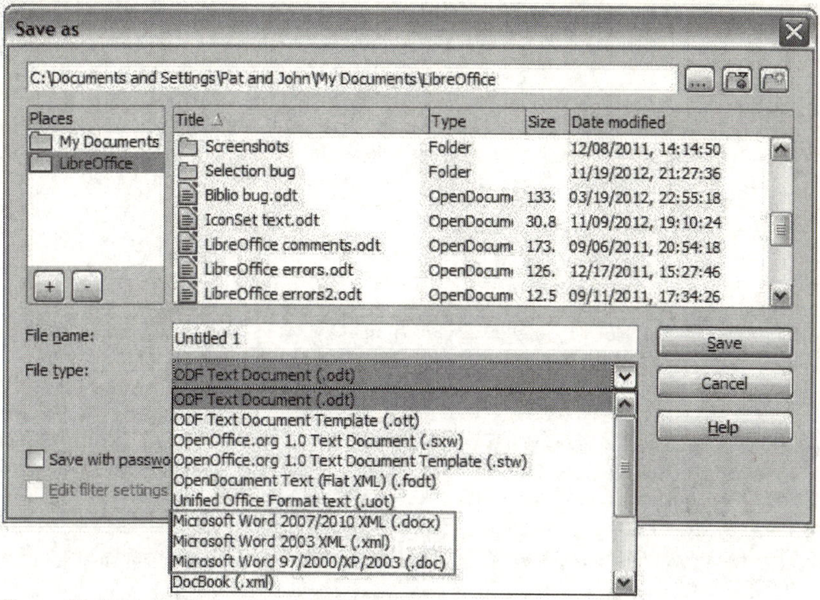

Figure 66. Saving a file in Microsoft Word format

Working with text

Working with text (selecting, copying, pasting, moving) in Writer is similar to working with text in any other program. LibreOffice also has some convenient ways to select items that are not next to each other, select a vertical block of text, and paste unformatted text.

Selecting items that are not consecutive

To select nonconsecutive items (as shown in Figure 67) using the mouse:

1) Select the first piece of text.
2) Hold down the *Ctrl* key and use the mouse to select the next piece of text.
3) Repeat as often as needed.

Now you can work with the selected text (copy it, delete it, change the style, or whatever).

Note	Macintosh users: substitute the *Command* key when instructions in this chapter say to use the *Ctrl* key.

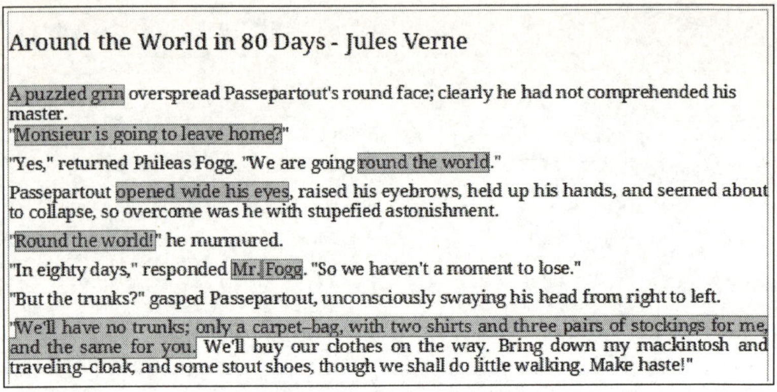

Around the World in 80 Days - Jules Verne

A puzzled grin overspread Passepartout's round face; clearly he had not comprehended his master.
"Monsieur is going to leave home?"

"Yes," returned Phileas Fogg. "We are going round the world."

Passepartout opened wide his eyes, raised his eyebrows, held up his hands, and seemed about to collapse, so overcome was he with stupefied astonishment.

"Round the world!" he murmured.

"In eighty days," responded Mr. Fogg. "So we haven't a moment to lose."

"But the trunks?" gasped Passepartout, unconsciously swaying his head from right to left.

"We'll have no trunks; only a carpet-bag, with two shirts and three pairs of stockings for me, and the same for you. We'll buy our clothes on the way. Bring down my mackintosh and traveling-cloak, and some stout shoes, though we shall do little walking. Make haste!"

Figure 67: Selecting items that are not next to each other

To select nonconsecutive items using the keyboard:

1) Select the first piece of text. (For more information about keyboard selection of text, see the topic "Navigating and selecting with the keyboard" in the Help.)
2) Press *Shift+F8*. This puts Writer in "Adding selection" mode.
3) Use the arrow keys to move to the start of the next piece of text to be selected. Hold down the *Shift* key and select the next piece of text.
4) Repeat as often as required.

Now you can work with the selected text.

Press *Esc* to exit from this mode.

Selecting a vertical block of text

You can select a vertical block or "column" of text that is separated by spaces or tabs (as you might see in text pasted from e-mails, program listings, or other sources), using LibreOffice's block selection mode. To change to block selection mode, use **Edit > Selection Mode > Block Area**, or press *Ctrl+F8*, or click on the **Selection** icon in the status bar and select **Block selection** from the list.

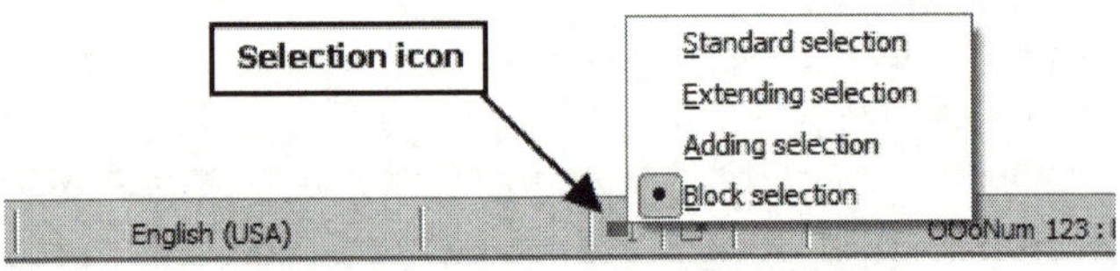

Now highlight the selection, using mouse or keyboard, as shown below.

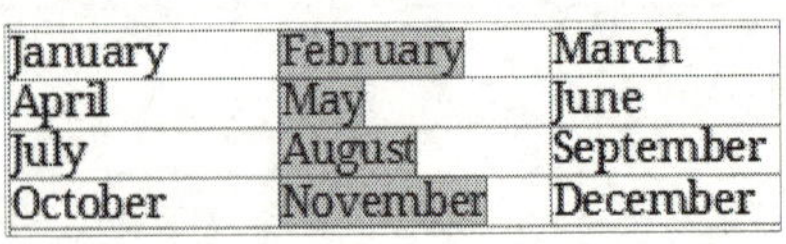

January	February	March
April	May	June
July	August	September
October	November	December

Figure 68: Selecting a vertical block of text

Cutting, copying, and pasting text

Cutting and copying text in Writer is similar to cutting and copying text in other applications. You can use the mouse or the keyboard for these operations. You can copy or move text within a document, or between documents, by dragging or by using menu selections, icons, or keyboard shortcuts. You can also copy text from other sources such as Web pages and paste it into a Writer document.

To *move* (drag and drop) selected text using the mouse, drag it to the new location and release it. To *copy* selected text, hold down the *Ctrl* key while dragging. The text retains the formatting it had before dragging.

To *move* (cut and paste) selected text, use *Ctrl+X* to cut the text, insert the cursor at the paste-in point and use *Ctrl+V* to paste. Alternatively, use the icons on the **Standard** toolbar.

When you paste text, the result depends on the source of the text and how you paste it. If you click on the **Paste** icon, any formatting the text has (such as bold or italics) is retained. Text pasted from Web sites and other sources may also be placed into frames or tables. If you do not like the results, click the **Undo** icon or press *Ctrl+Z*.

To make the pasted text take on the formatting of the surrounding text where it is being pasted:

- Choose **Edit > Paste Special**, or
- Click the triangle to the right of the **Paste** icon, or
- Click the **Paste** icon without releasing the left mouse button.

Then select **Unformatted text** from the resulting menu.

The range of choices on the Paste Special menu varies depending on the origin and formatting of the text (or other object) to be pasted. See Figure 69 for an example with text on the clipboard.

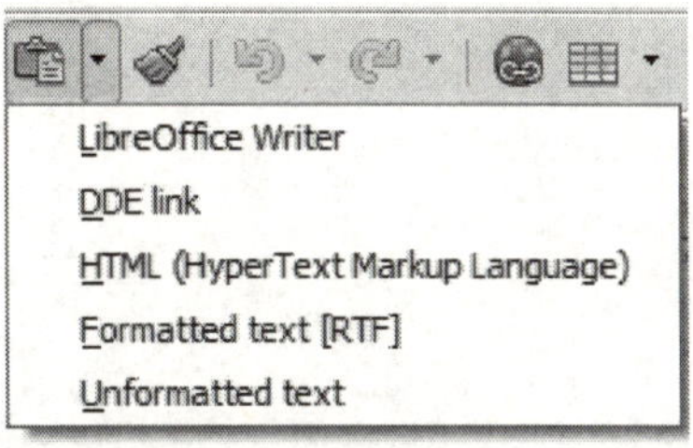

Figure 69: Paste Special menu

Finding and replacing text and formatting

Writer has two ways to find text within a document: the Find toolbar for fast searching and the Find & Replace dialog. In the dialog, you can:

- Find and replace words and phrases
- Use wildcards and regular expressions to fine-tune a search
- Find and replace specific formatting
- Find and replace paragraph styles

Using the Find toolbar

If the Find toolbar is not visible, you can display it by choosing **View > Toolbars > Find** from the menu bar or by pressing *Ctrl+F*. The Find toolbar is shown docked at the bottom of the LibreOffice window (just above the Status Bar) in Figure 70, but you can float it or dock it in another location. For more information on floating and docking toolbars, see Chapter 1, Introducing LibreOffice.

Figure 70: Docked position of Find toolbar

To use the Find toolbar, click in the box and type your search text, then press *Enter* to find the next occurrence of that term. Click the **Find Next** or **Find Previous** buttons as needed. Clicking the binocular icon opens the Find and Replace dialog.

Using the Find & Replace dialog

To display the Find & Replace dialog, use the keyboard shortcut *Ctrl+H* or choose **Edit > Find & Replace** from the menu bar. Optionally, click the **More Options** button to expand the dialog; the button changes to **Fewer Options**.

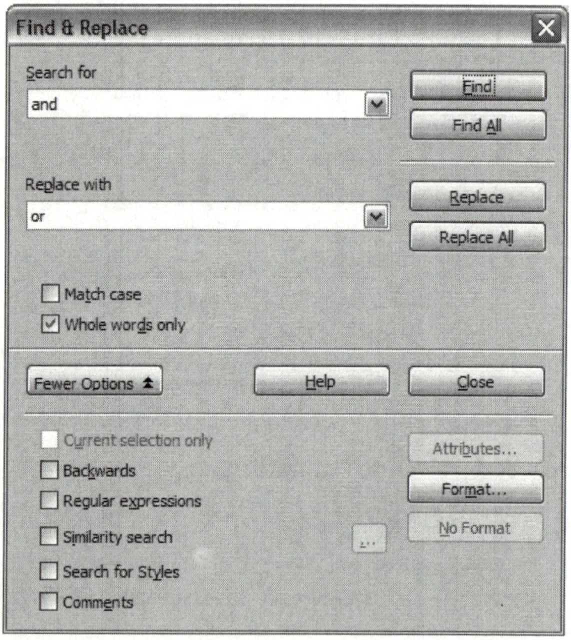

Figure 71: Expanded Find & Replace dialog

To use the Find & Replace dialog:

1) Type the text you want to find in the **Search for** box.
2) To replace the text with different text, type the new text in the **Replace with** box.
3) You can select various options such as matching the case, matching whole words only, or doing a search for similar words.

4) When you have set up your search, click **Find**. To replace the found text, click **Replace**.

For more information on using Find & Replace, see the *Writer Guide*.

Tip	If you click **Find All**, LibreOffice selects all instances of the search text in the document. Similarly, if you click **Replace All**, LibreOffice replaces all matches.

Caution	Use **Replace All** with caution; otherwise, you may end up with some hilarious (and highly embarrassing) mistakes. A mistake with **Replace All** might require a manual, word-by-word, search to fix.

Inserting special characters

A *special character* is one not found on a standard English keyboard. For example, © ¾ æ ç ñ ö ø ¢ are all special characters. To insert a special character:

1) Place the cursor where you want the character to appear.
2) Choose **Insert > Special Character** to open the Special Characters dialog.
3) Select the characters (from any font or mixture of fonts) you wish to insert, in order, then click **OK**. The characters selected for insertion are shown in the lower left of the dialog. As you select a character, it is shown on the right, along with its numerical code.

Note	Different fonts include different special characters. If you do not find a particular special character, try changing the *Font* selection.

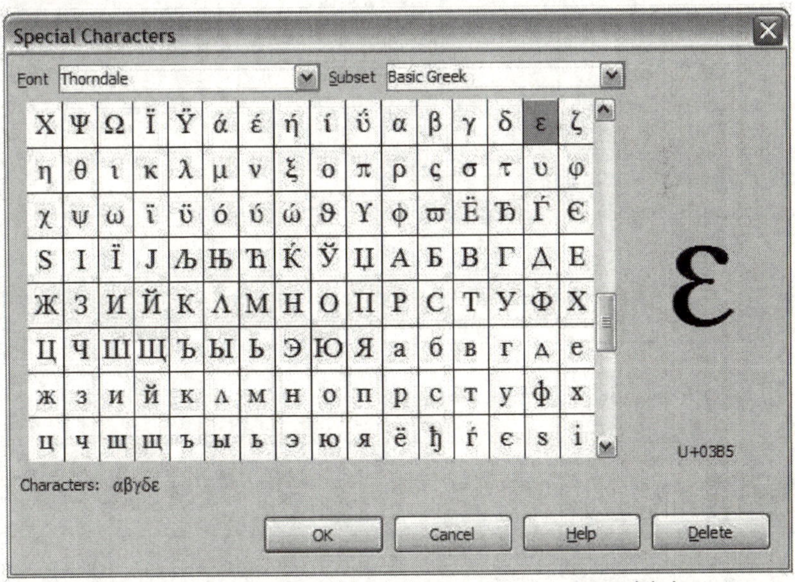

Figure 72: The Special Characters dialog, where you can insert special characters

Inserting dashes and non-breaking spaces and hyphens

To prevent two words from being separated at the end of a line, press *Ctrl+Shift* when you type the space between the two words.

In cases where you do not want the hyphen to appear at the end of a line, for example in a number such as 123-4567, you can press *Shift+Ctrl+minus sign* to insert a non-breaking hyphen.

To enter en and em dashes, you can use the *Replace dashes* option on the Options tab under **Tools > AutoCorrect Options**. This option replaces two hyphens, under certain conditions, with the corresponding dash.

– is an en-dash; that is, a dash the width of the letter "n" in the font you are using. Type at least one character, a space, one or two hyphens, another space, and at least one more letter. The one or two hyphens will be replaced by an en-dash.

— is an em-dash; that is, a dash the width of the letter "m" in the font you are using. Type at least one character, two hyphens, and at least one more character. The two hyphens will be replaced by an em-dash.

See the Help for more details. For other methods of inserting dashes, see the *Writer Guide Chapter 3*.

Setting tab stops and indents

The horizontal ruler shows the tab stops. Any tab stops that you have defined will overwrite the default tab stops. Tab settings affect indentation of full paragraphs (using the **Increase Indent** and **Decrease Indent** icons on the Formatting toolbar) as well as indentation of parts of a paragraph (by pressing the *Tab* key on the keyboard).

Using the default tab spacing can cause formatting problems if you share documents with other people. If you use the default tab spacing and then send the document to someone else who has chosen a different default tab spacing, tabbed material will change to use the other person's settings. Instead of using the defaults, define your own tab settings, as described in this section.

To define indents and tab settings for one or more selected paragraphs, double-click on a part of the ruler that is not between the left and right indent icons to open the *Indents & Spacing* page of the Paragraph dialog. Double-click anywhere between the left and right indent icons on the ruler to open the *Tabs* page of the Paragraph dialog.

A better strategy is to define tabs for the paragraph *style*. See Chapters 6 and 7 in the *Writer Guide* for more information.

Tip	Using tabs to space out material on a page is not recommended. Depending on what you are trying to accomplish, a table is usually a better choice.

Changing the default tab stop interval

Note	Any changes to the default tab setting will affect the existing default tab stops in any document you open afterward, as well as tab stops you insert after making the change.

To set the measurement unit and the spacing of default tab stop intervals, go to **Tools > Options > LibreOffice Writer > General**.

Figure 73: Selecting a default tab stop interval

You can also set or change the measurement unit for rulers in the current document by right-clicking on the ruler to open a list of units. Click on one of them to change the ruler to that unit. The selected setting applies only to that ruler.

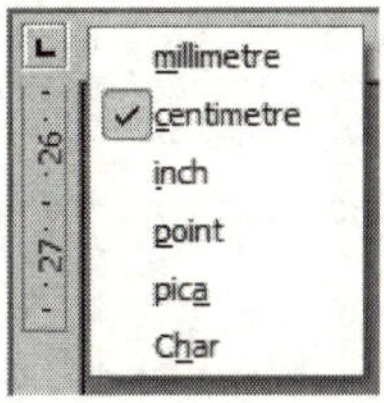

Figure 74: Changing the measurement unit for a ruler

Checking spelling and grammar

Writer provides a spelling checker, which can be used in two ways.

AutoSpellcheck checks each word as it is typed and displays a wavy red line under any unrecognised words. When the word is corrected, the line disappears.

To perform a combined spelling and grammar check on the document (or a text selection) click the **Spelling and Grammar** button. This checks the document or selection and opens the Spelling and Grammar dialog if any unrecognized words are found. In order to use this, the appropriate dictionaries must be installed. By default, four dictionaries are installed: a spellchecker, a grammar checker, a hyphenation dictionary, and a thesaurus.

Here are some more features of the spelling checker:

- You can right-click on a word with a wavy underline to open a context menu. If you select from the suggested words on the menu, the selection will replace the unrecognised word in your text. Other menu options are discussed below.
- You can change the dictionary language (for example, Spanish, French or German) on the Spelling and Grammar dialog.
- You can add a word to the dictionary. Click **Add** in the Spelling and Grammar dialog and pick the dictionary to add it to.
- Click the **Options** button on the Spelling and Grammar dialog to open a dialog similar to the one in **Tools > Options > Language Settings > Writing Aids** described in Chapter 2. There you can choose whether to check uppercase words and words with numbers, and you can manage custom dictionaries, that is, add or delete dictionaries and add or delete words in a dictionary.
- On the Font tab of the Paragraph Styles dialog, you can set paragraphs to be checked in a specific language (different from the rest of the document). See Chapter 7, Working with Styles, in the *Writer Guide* for more information.

See *Writer Guide, Chapter 3* for a detailed explanation of the spelling and grammar checking facility.

Using built-in language tools

Writer provides some tools that make your work easier if you mix multiple languages within the same document or if you write documents in various languages.

The main advantage of changing the language for a text selection is that you can then use the correct dictionaries to check spelling and apply the localized versions of Autocorrect replacement tables, thesaurus, and hyphenation rules.

You can also set the language for a paragraph or a group of characters as **None (Do not check spelling)**. This option is especially useful when you insert text such as web addresses or programming language snippets that you do not want to check for spelling.

Specifying the language in character and paragraph styles is the preferred method, because styles allow a greater level of control and make changing the language much faster. On the Font tab of the Paragraph Styles dialog, you can specify that certain paragraphs be checked in a language that is different from the language of the rest of the document. See Chapter 7, Working with Styles, in the *Writer Guide* for information on how to manage the language settings of a style.

You can also set the language for the whole document, for individual paragraphs, or even for individual words and characters, from **Tools > Language** on the menu bar.

Another way to change the language of a whole document is to use **Tools > Options > Language Settings > Languages**. In the *Default languages for documents* section, you can choose a different language for all the text that is not explicitly marked as a different language.

The spelling checker works only for those languages in the list that have the symbol  next to them. If you do not see the symbol next to your preferred language, you can install the additional dictionary using **Tools > Languages > More dictionaries online**.

The language used for checking spelling is also shown in the status bar, next to the page style in use.

Using AutoCorrect

Writer's AutoCorrect function has a long list of common misspellings and typing errors, which it corrects automatically. For example, "hte" will be changed to "the".

AutoCorrect is turned on when Writer is installed. To turn it off, uncheck **Format > AutoCorrect > While Typing**.

Choose **Tools > AutoCorrect Options** to open the AutoCorrect dialog. There you can define which strings of text are corrected and how. In most cases, the defaults are fine.

To stop Writer replacing a specific spelling, go to the **Replace** tab, highlight the word pair, and click **Delete**.

To add a new spelling to the list, type it into the *Replace* and *With* boxes on the Replace tab, and click **New**.

See the different tabs of the dialog for the wide variety of other options available to fine-tune AutoCorrect.

Tip	AutoCorrect can be used as a quick way to insert special characters. For example, (c) will be changed to ©. You can add your own special characters.

Using word completion

If Word Completion is enabled, Writer tries to guess which word you are typing and offers to complete the word for you. To accept the suggestion, press *Enter*. Otherwise, continue typing.

To turn off Word Completion, select **Tools > AutoCorrect Options > Word Completion** and deselect **Enable word completion**.

You can customize word completion from the *Word Completion* page of the AutoCorrect dialog:

- Add (append) a space automatically after an accepted word
- Show the suggested word as a tip (hovering over the word) rather than completing the text as you type
- Collect words when working on a document, and then either save them for later use in other documents or select the option to remove them from the list when closing the document.
- Change the maximum number of words remembered for word completion and the length of the smallest words to be remembered
- Delete specific entries from the word completion list
- Change the key that accepts a suggested entry—the options are *Right arrow*, *End* key, *Return* (*Enter*), and *Space bar*

Note	Automatic word completion only occurs after you type a word for the second time in a document.

Using AutoText

Use AutoText to store text, tables, graphics and other items for reuse and assign them to a key combination for easy retrieval. For example, rather than typing "Senior Management" every time you use that phrase, you can set up an AutoText entry to insert those words when you type "sm" and press *F3*.

AutoText is especially powerful when assigned to fields. See Chapter 14, Working with Fields, in the *Writer Guide* for more information.

Creating AutoText

To store some text as AutoText:

1) Type the text into your document.
2) Select the text.
3) Choose **Edit > AutoText** (or press *Ctrl+F3*).
4) In the AutoText dialog box, type a name for the AutoText in the *Name* box. Writer will suggest a one-letter shortcut, which you can change.
5) In the large box to the left, choose the category for the AutoText entry, for example *My AutoText*.
6) Click the **AutoText** button on the right and select **New (text only)** from the menu.
7) Click **Close** to return to your document.

Tip	If the only option under the AutoText button is Import, either you have not entered a name for your AutoText or there is no text selected in the document.

Inserting AutoText

To insert AutoText, type the shortcut and press *F3*.

Formatting text

Using styles is recommended

Styles are central to using Writer. Styles enable you to easily format your document consistently, and to change the format with minimal effort. A style is a named set of formatting options. When you apply a style, you apply a whole group of formats at the same time. In addition, styles are used by LibreOffice for many processes, even if you are not aware of them. For example, Writer relies on heading styles (or other styles you specify) when it compiles a table of contents.

> **Caution**
>
> Manual formatting (also called *direct formatting*) overrides styles, and you cannot get rid of the manual formatting by applying a style to it.

Writer defines several types of styles, for different types of elements: characters, paragraphs, pages, frames, and lists. See Chapter 3, Using Styles and Templates, in this book and Chapters 6 and 7 in the *Writer Guide*.

Formatting paragraphs

You can apply many formats to paragraphs using the buttons on the Formatting toolbar. Figure 75 shows the Formatting toolbar as a floating toolbar, customized to show only the icons for paragraph formatting. The appearance of the icons may vary with your operating system and the selection of icon size and style in **Tools > Options > LibreOffice > View**.

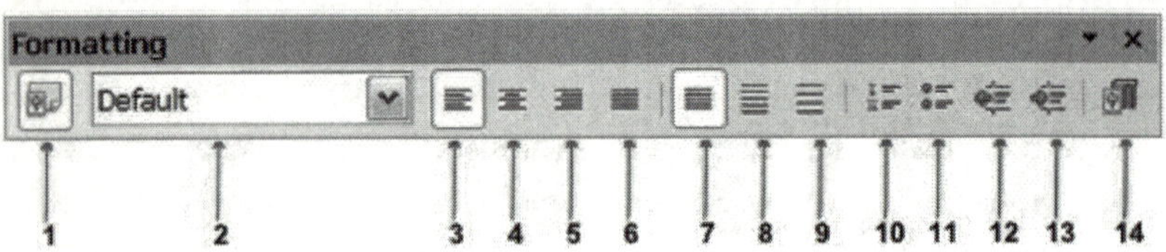

- **1** Open Styles and Formatting Window
- **2** Apply Style
- **3** Align Left
- **4** Centered
- **5** Align Right
- **6** Justified
- **7** Line Spacing: 1
- **8** Line Spacing: 1.5
- **9** Line Spacing: 2
- **10** Numbering On/Off
- **11** Bullets On/Off
- **12** Decrease Indent
- **13** Increase Indent
- **14** Paragraph format dialog

Figure 75: Formatting toolbar, showing icons for paragraph formatting

Formatting characters

You can apply many formats to characters using the buttons on the Formatting toolbar. Figure 76 shows the Formatting toolbar, customized to include only the icon for character formatting.

The appearance of the icons may vary with your operating system and the selection of icon size and style in **Tools > Options > LibreOffice > View**.

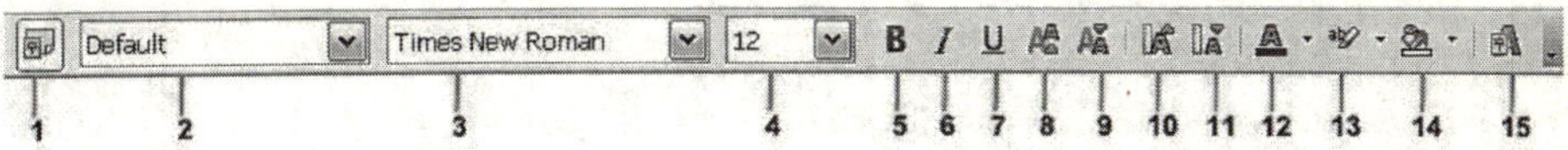

1 Open Styles and Formatting Window
2 Apply Style
3 Font Name
4 Font Size
5 Bold
6 Italic
7 Underline
8 Superscript
9 Subscript
10 Increase Font
11 Reduce Font
12 Font Color
13 Highlighting
14 Background Color
15 Open Character Format Dialog

Figure 76: Formatting toolbar, showing icons for character formatting

Tip	To remove manual formatting, select the text and choose **Format > Clear Direct Formatting** from the menu bar, or right-click and choose **Clear Direct Formatting** from the context menu, or use *Ctrl+M* from the keyboard.

Autoformatting

You can set Writer to automatically format parts of a document according to the choices made on the Options page of the AutoCorrect dialog (**Tools > AutoCorrect Options**).

Tip	If you notice unexpected formatting changes occurring in your document, this is the first place to look for the cause.

The Help describes each of these choices and how to activate the autoformats. Some common unwanted or unexpected formatting changes include:

- Horizontal lines. If you type three or more hyphens (---), underscores (___) or equal signs (===) on a line and then press *Enter*, the paragraph is replaced by a horizontal line as wide as the page. The line is actually the lower border of the preceding paragraph.
- Bulleted and numbered lists. A bulleted list is created when you type a hyphen (-), star (*), or plus sign (+), followed by a space or tab at the beginning of a paragraph. A numbered list is created when you type a number followed by a period (.), followed by a space or tab at the beginning of a paragraph. Automatic numbering is only applied to paragraphs formatted with the *Default*, *Text body* or *Text body indent* paragraph styles.

To turn autoformatting on or off, choose **Format > AutoCorrect** and select or deselect the items on the list.

Creating numbered or bulleted lists

There are several ways to create numbered or bulleted lists:

- Use autoformatting, as described above.
- Use list (numbering) styles, as described in Chapter 6, Introduction to Styles, and Chapter 7, Working with Styles, in the *Writer Guide*.
- Use the **Numbering** and **Bullets** icons on the paragraph formatting toolbar (see Figure 75): select the paragraphs in the list, and then click the appropriate icon on the toolbar.

Note	It is a matter of personal preference whether you type your information first, then apply Numbering/Bullets, or apply them as you type.

Using the Bullets and Numbering toolbar

You can create nested lists (where one or more list items has a sub-list under it, as in an outline) by using the buttons on the Bullets and Numbering toolbar (Figure 77). You can move items up or down the list, or create sub-points, and even change the style of bullets. Use **View > Toolbars > Bullets and Numbering** to see the toolbar.

Note	If numbering or bullets are being applied automatically in a way that you find inappropriate, you can switch them off temporarily by unchecking F**ormat > AutoCorrect > While Typing**.

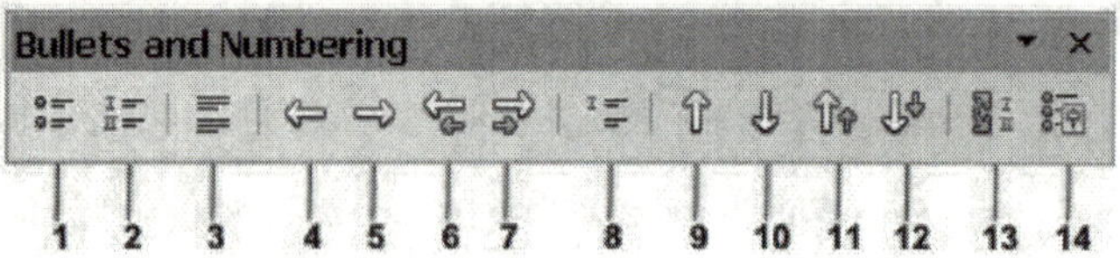

1 Bullets On/Off
2 Numbering On/Off
3 Numbering Off
4 Promote One Level
5 Demote One Level
6 Promote One Level with Subpoints
7 Demote One Level with Subpoints
8 Insert Unnumbered Entry
9 Move Up
10 Move Down
11 Move Up with Subpoints
12 Move Down with Subpoints
13 Restart Numbering
14 Bullets and Numbering

Figure 77: Bullets and Numbering toolbar

Hyphenating words

You have several choices regarding hyphenation: let Writer do it automatically (using its hyphenation dictionaries), insert conditional hyphens manually where necessary, or don’t hyphenate at all.

Automatic hyphenation

To turn automatic hyphenation of words on or off:

1) Press *F11* (⌘+*T* on Mac) to open the Styles and Formatting window.
2) On the Paragraph Styles page (Figure 78), right-click on **Default** and select **Modify**.

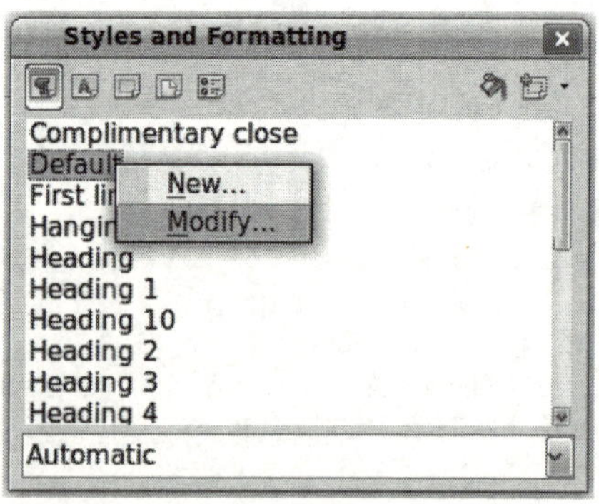

Figure 78: Modifying a style

3) On the Paragraph Style dialog (Figure 79), go to the *Text Flow* page.
4) Under Hyphenation, select or deselect the **Automatically** option. Click **OK** to save.

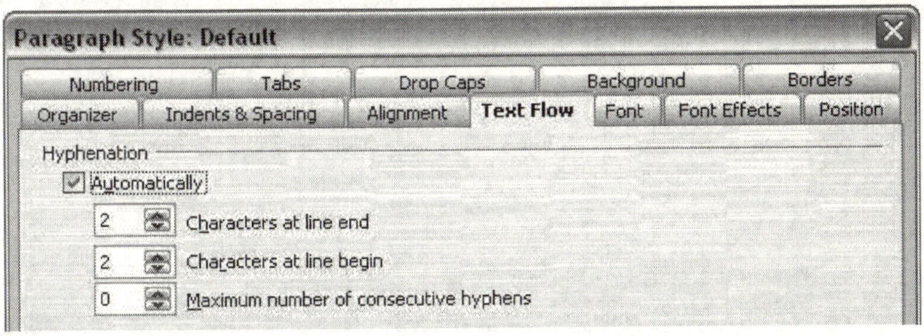

Figure 79: Turning on automatic hyphenation

Note	Turning on hyphenation for the Default paragraph style affects all other paragraph styles that are based on Default. You can individually change other styles so that hyphenation is not active; for example, you might not want headings to be hyphenated. Any styles that are not based on Default are not affected. See Writer Guide Chapter 3, Styles and Templates, for more about styles based on other styles.

You can also set hyphenation choices through **Tools > Options > Language Settings > Writing Aids**. In Options, near the bottom of the dialog, scroll down to find the hyphenation settings.

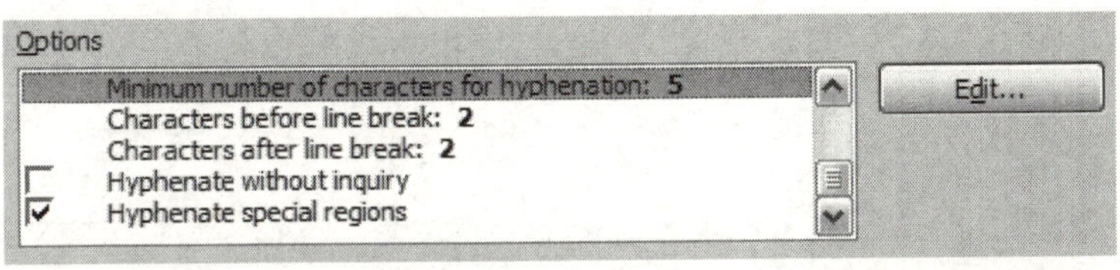

Figure 80: Setting hyphenation options

To change the minimum number of characters for hyphenation, the minimum number of characters before a line break, or the minimum number of characters after a line break, select the item, and then click the **Edit** button in the Options section.

Hyphenation options set on the Writing Aids dialog are effective only if hyphenation is turned on through paragraph styles.

Manual hyphenation

To manually hyphenate words, *do not* use a normal hyphen, which will remain visible even if the word is no longer at the end of a line when you add or delete text or change margins or font size. Instead, use a *conditional hyphen*, which is visible only when required.

To insert a conditional hyphen inside a word, click where you want the hyphen to appear and press *Ctrl+hyphen*. The word will be hyphenated at this position when it is at the end of the line, even if automatic hyphenation for this paragraph is switched off.

Formatting pages

Writer provides several ways for you to control page layouts: page styles, columns, frames, tables, and sections. For more information, see Chapter 4, Formatting Pages, in the *Writer Guide*.

Tip	Page layout is usually easier if you show text, object, table, and section boundaries in **Tools > Options > LibreOffice > Appearance**, and paragraph end, tabs, breaks, and other items in **Tools > Options > LibreOffice Writer > Formatting Aids**.

Which layout method to choose?

The best layout method depends on what the final document should look like and what sort of information will be in the document. Here are some examples.

For a book similar to this user guide, with one column of text, some figures without text beside them, and some other figures with descriptive text, use page styles for basic layout, and tables to place figures beside descriptive text when necessary.

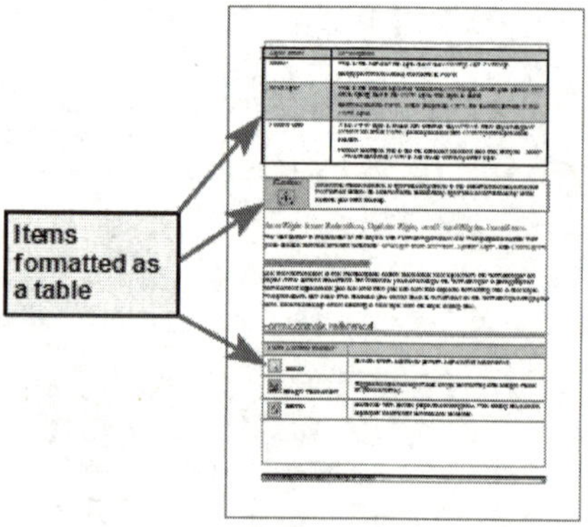

For an index or other document with two columns of text, where the text continues from the left-hand column to the right-hand column and then to the next page, all in sequence (also known as “snaking columns” of text), use page styles (with two columns). If the title of the document (on the first page) is full-page width, put it in a single-column section.

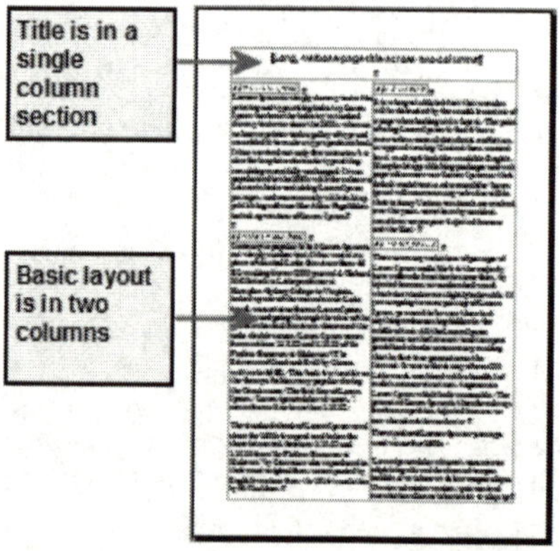

For a newsletter with complex layout, two or three columns on the page, and some articles that continue from one page to some place several pages later, use page styles for basic layout. Place articles in linked frames and anchor graphics to fixed positions on the page if necessary.

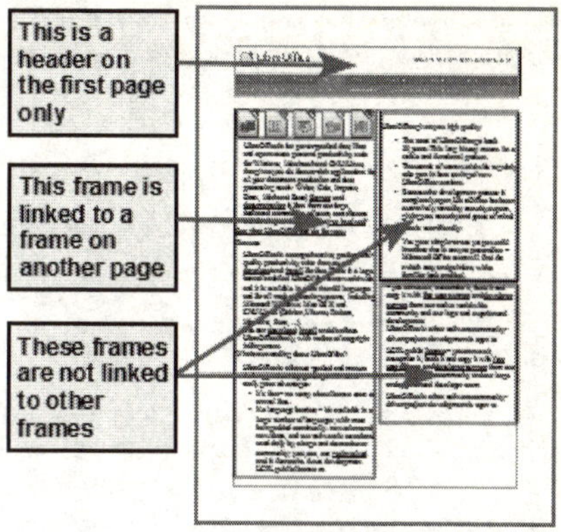

For a document with terms and translations to appear side-by-side in what appear to be columns, use a table to keep items lined up, and so you can type in both "columns".

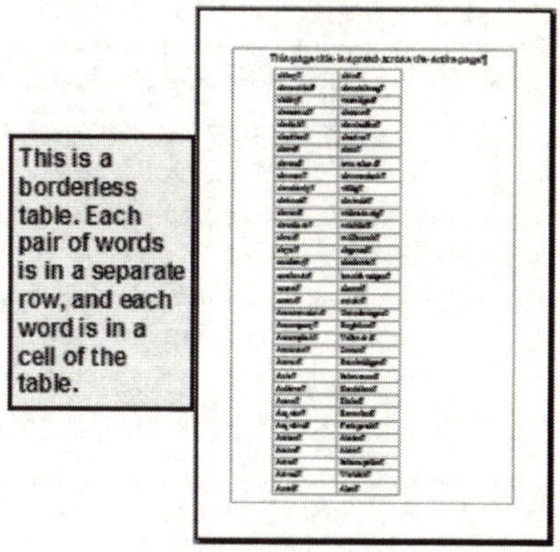

Creating headers and footers

A header is an area that appears at the top of a page. A footer appears at the bottom of the page. Information such as page numbers inserted into a header or footer displays on every page of the document with that page style.

Inserting a header or footer

To insert a header, you can either:

- Choose **Insert > Header > Default** (or the page style, if not Default), or
- Hover the mouse over the top of the text area until the Header marker appears (Figure 81), and then click on the **+**.

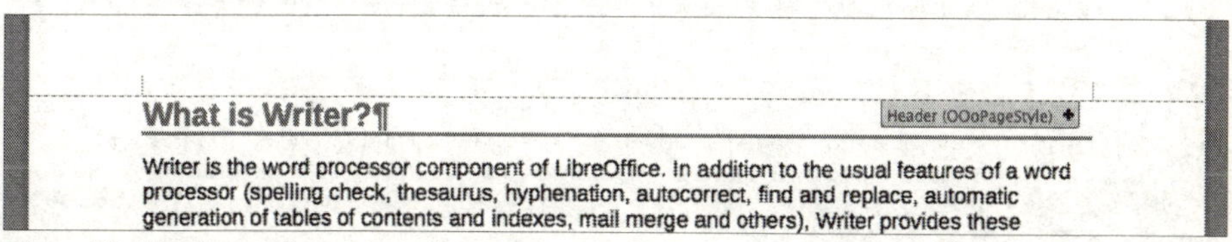

Figure 81: Header marker at top of text area

After a header has been created, a down-arrow appears on the header marker. Click on this arrow to drop down a menu of choices for working with the header (Figure 82).

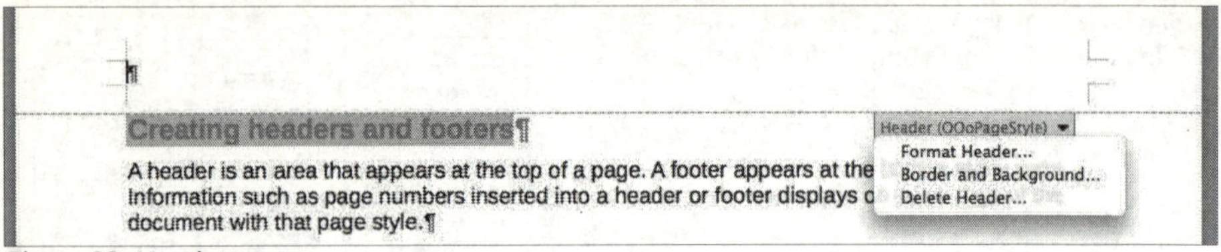

Figure 82: Header menu

To format a header, you can use either the menu item shown in Figure 82 or **Format > Page > Header**. Both methods take you to the same tab on the Page Style dialog.

Inserting header and footer contents

Other information such as document titles and chapter titles is often put into the header or footer. These items are best added as fields. That way, if something changes, the headers and footers are updated automatically. Here is one common example.

To insert the document title into the header:

1) Choose **File > Properties > Description** and type a title for your document.
2) Add a header (**Insert > Header > Default**).
3) Place the cursor in the header part of the page.
4) Choose **Insert > Fields > Title**. The title should appear on a gray background (which does not show when printed and can be turned off).
5) To change the title for the whole document, go back to **File > Properties > Description**.

Fields are covered in detail in Chapter 14, Working with Fields, in the *Writer Guide*.

For more about headers and footers, see Chapter 4, Formatting Pages, and Chapter 6, Introduction to Styles, in the *Writer Guide*.

Numbering pages

Displaying the page number

To automatically display page numbers:

1) Insert a header or footer, as described in "Creating headers and footers" above.
2) Place the cursor in the header or footer where you want the page number to appear and choose **Insert > Fields > Page Number**.

Including the total number of pages

To include the total number of pages (as in "page 1 of 12"):

1) Type the word "page" and a space, then insert the page number as above.
2) Press the space bar once, type the word "of" and a space, then choose **Insert > Fields > Page Count**.

Note	The Page Count field inserts the total number of pages in the document, as shown on the Statistics tab of the document's Properties window (**File > Properties**). If you restart page numbering anywhere in the document, then the total page count may not be what you want. See Chapter 4, Formatting Pages, in the *Writer Guide* for more information.

Restarting page numbering

Often you will want to restart the page numbering at 1, for example on the page following a title page or a table of contents. In addition, many documents have the "front matter" (such as the table of contents) numbered with Roman numerals and the main body of the document numbered in Arabic numerals, starting with 1.

You can restart page numbering in two ways.

Method 1:

1) Place the cursor in the first paragraph of the new page.
2) Choose **Format > Paragraph**.
3) On the Text Flow tab of the Paragraph dialog (Figure 79 on page 99), select **Breaks**.
4) Select **Insert** and then **With Page Style** and specify the page style to use.
5) Specify the page number to start from, and then click **OK**.

Tip	Method 1 is also useful for numbering the first page of a document with a page number greater than 1. For example, you may be writing a book, with each chapter in a separate file. Chapter 1 may start with page 1, but Chapter 2 could begin with page 25 and Chapter 3 with page 51.

Method 2:

1) **Insert > Manual break**.
2) By default, **Page break** is selected on the Insert Break dialog (Figure 83).
3) Choose the required page **Style**.
4) Select **Change page number.**
5) Specify the page number to start from, and then click **OK**.

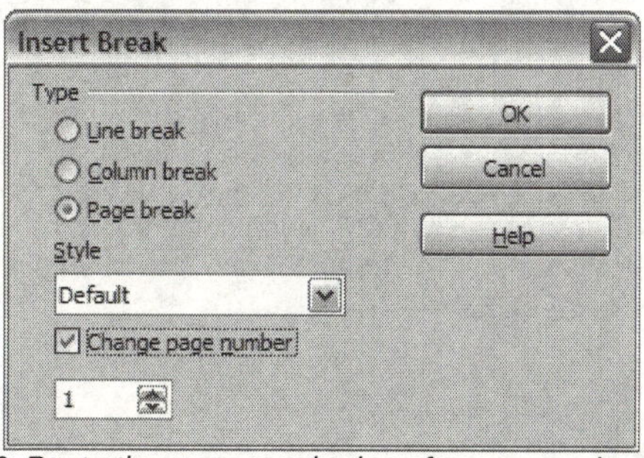

Figure 83: Restarting page numbering after a manual page break

Changing page margins

You can change page margins in two ways:

- Using the page rulers—quick and easy, but does not have fine control
- Using the Page Style dialog—can specify margins to two decimal places

Note	If you change the margins using the rulers, the new margins affect the page style and will be shown in the Page Style dialog the next time you open it. Because the page style is affected, the changed margins apply to **all** pages using that style.

To change margins using the rulers:

1) The gray sections of the rulers are the margins. Put the mouse cursor over the line between the gray and white sections. The pointer turns into a double-headed arrow.
2) Hold down the left mouse button and drag the mouse to move the margin.

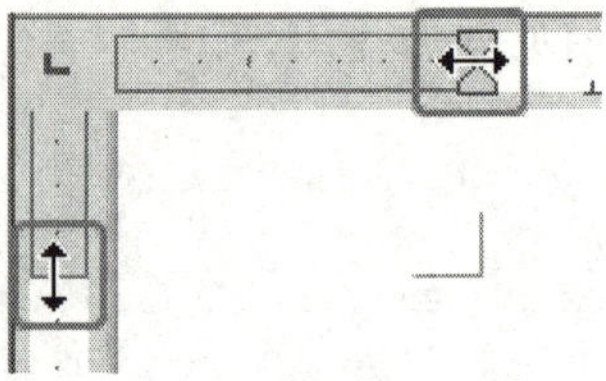

Figure 84: Moving the margins

> **Caution** The small arrowheads on the ruler (the gray triangles) are used for indenting paragraphs. They are often in the same place as the page margins, so you need to be careful to move the margin marker, not the arrows. The double-headed arrows shown in Figure 84 are actual mouse cursors placed in the correct position.

To change margins using the Page Style dialog:

1) Right-click anywhere in the text area on the page and select **Page** from the pop-up menu.
2) On the **Page** tab of the dialog, type the required distances in the Margins boxes.

Adding comments to a document

Authors and reviewers often use comments (formerly called "notes") to exchange ideas, ask for suggestions, or mark items needing attention.

A block of text may be selected for a comment, or a single point may be selected at which the comment will be inserted. To insert a comment select the text, or place the cursor in the place the comment refers to and choose **Insert > Comment** or press *Ctrl+Alt+C*. The anchor point of the comment is connected by a dotted line to a box on the right-hand side of the page where you can type the text of the comment. Writer automatically adds at the bottom of the comment the author's name and a time stamp indicating when the comment was created. Figure 85 shows an example of text with comments from two different authors.

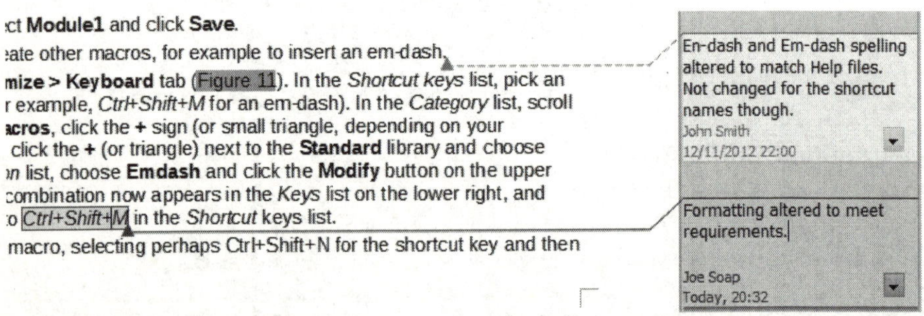

Figure 85: Example of comments

Choose **Tools > Options > User Data** to configure the name you want to appear in the Author field of the comment, or to change it.

If more than one person edits the document, each author is automatically allocated a different background color.

Right-clicking on a comment pops up a menu where you can delete the current comment, all the comments from the same author, or all the comments in the document. From this menu, you can also apply some basic formatting to the text of the comment. You can also change the font type, size, and alignment from the main menu.

To navigate from one comment to another, open the Navigator (*F5*), expand the Comments section, and click on the comment text to move the cursor to the anchor point of the comment in the document. Right-click on the comment to quickly edit or delete it.

You can also navigate through the comments using the keyboard. Use *Ctrl+Alt+Page Down* to move to the next comment and *Ctrl+Alt+Page Up* to move to the previous comment.

Creating a table of contents

Writer's table of contents feature lets you build an automated table of contents from the headings in your document. Before you start, make sure that the headings are styled consistently. For example, you can use the *Heading 1* style for chapter titles and the *Heading 2* and *Heading 3* styles for chapter subheadings.

Although tables of contents can be customized extensively in Writer, often the default settings are all you need. Creating a quick table of contents is simple:

1) When you create your document, use the following paragraph styles for different heading levels (such as chapter and section headings): *Heading 1*, *Heading 2*, *Heading 3*, and so on. These are what will appear in your table of contents.
2) Place the cursor where you want the table of contents to be inserted.
3) Choose **Insert > Indexes and Tables > Indexes and Tables**.
4) Change nothing in the Insert Index/Table dialog. Click **OK**.

If you add or delete text (so that headings move to different pages) or you add, delete, or change headings, you need to update the table of contents.

To do this:

1) Place the cursor within the table of contents.
2) Right-click and choose **Update Index/Table** from the pop-up menu.

Note	If you cannot place your cursor in the table of contents, choose **Tools > Options > LibreOffice Writer > Formatting Aids**, and then select **Enable** in the **Cursor in protected areas** section.

You can customize an existing table of contents at any time. Right-click anywhere in it and choose **Edit Index/Table** from the pop-up menu. Chapter 12, Creating Tables of Contents, Indexes and Bibliographies, of the *Writer Guide* describes in detail all the customizations you can choose.

Creating indexes and bibliographies

Indexes and bibliographies work in a similar way to tables of contents. Chapter 12, Creating Tables of Contents, Indexes and Bibliographies, in the *Writer Guide* describes the process in detail.

In addition to alphabetical indexes, other types of indexes supplied with Writer include those for illustrations, tables, and objects, and you can even create a user-defined index. For example, you might want an index containing only the scientific names of species mentioned in the text, and a separate index containing only the common names of species. Before creating some types of indexes, you first need to create index entries embedded in your Writer document.

Working with graphics

Graphics in Writer are of three basic types:

- Image files, including photos, drawings, scanned images, and others
- Diagrams created using LibreOffice's drawing tools
- Charts created using LibreOffice's Chart component

See Chapter 11, Graphics, the Gallery, and Fontwork, in this book and Chapter 8, Working with Graphics, in the *Writer Guide*.

Printing

See Chapter 10, Printing, Exporting, and E-mailing, in this book and Chapter 5, Printing, Exporting, Faxing, and E-mailing, in the *Writer Guide* for details on previewing pages before printing, selecting print options, printing in black and white on a color printer, printing brochures, and other printing features.

Using mail merge

Writer provides very useful features to create and print:

- Multiple copies of a document to send to a list of different recipients (form letters)
- Mailing labels
- Envelopes

All these facilities use a registered data source (a spreadsheet or database containing the name and address records and other information). Chapter 11, Using Mail Merge, in the *Writer Guide* describes the process.

Tracking changes to a document

You can use several methods to keep track of changes made to a document.

1) Make your changes to a copy of the document (stored in a different folder, or under a different name, or both), then use Writer to combine the two files and show the differences. Choose **Edit > Compare Document**. This technique is particularly useful if you are the only person working on the document, as it avoids the increase in file size and complexity caused by the other methods.
2) Save versions that are stored as part of the original file. However, this method can cause problems with documents of non-trivial size or complexity, especially if you save a lot of versions. Avoid this method if you can.
3) Use Writer's change marks (often called "redlines" or "revision marks") to show where you have added or deleted material, or changed formatting. Choose **Edit > Changes > Record** before starting to edit. Later, you or another person can review and accept or reject each change. Choose **Edit > Changes > Show**. Right-click on an individual change and choose **Accept Change** or **Reject Change** from the pop-up menu, or choose **Edit > Changes > Accept or Reject** to view the list of changes and accept or reject them. Details are in the *Writer Guide*.

Tip	Not all changes are recorded. For example, changing a tab stop from align left to align right, and changes in formulas (equations) or linked graphics are not recorded.

Using fields

Fields are extremely useful features of Writer. They are used for data that changes in a document (such as the current date or the total number of pages) and for inserting document properties such as name, author, and date of last update. Fields are the basis of cross-referencing (see below); automatic numbering of figures, tables, headings, and other elements; and a wide range of other functions—far too many to describe here. See Chapter 14, Working with Fields, in the *Writer Guide* for details.

Linking to another part of a document

If you type in cross-references to other parts of a document, those references can easily get out of date if you reorganize the order of topics, add or remove material, or reword a heading. Writer provides two ways to ensure that your references are up to date, by inserting links to other parts of the same document or to a different document:

- Hyperlinks
- Cross-references

The two methods have the same result if you *Ctrl+click* the link when the document is open in Writer: you are taken directly to the cross-referenced item. However, they also have major differences:

- The text in a hyperlink does **not** automatically update if you change the text of the linked item (although you can change it manually), but changed text does automatically update in a cross-reference.
- When using a hyperlink, you do not have a choice of the content of the link (for example text or page number), but when using a cross-reference, you have several choices, including bookmarks.
- To hyperlink to an object such as a graphic, and have the hyperlink show useful text such as *Figure 6*, you need to give such an object a useful name (instead of a default name like *Graphics6)*, or use the Hyperlink dialog to modify the visible text. In contrast, cross-references to figures with captions automatically show useful text, and you have a choice of several variations of the name.
- If you save a Writer document to HTML, hyperlinks remain active but cross-references do not. (Both remain active when the document is exported to PDF.)

Using hyperlinks

The easiest way to insert a hyperlink to another part of the same document is by using the Navigator:

1) Open the document containing the items you want to cross-reference.
2) Open the Navigator by clicking its icon, choosing **View > Navigator**, or by pressing *F5*.
3) Click the arrow next to the **Drag Mode** icon, and choose **Insert as Hyperlink**.
4) In the list at the bottom of the Navigator, select the document containing the item that you want to cross-reference.
5) In the Navigator list, select the item that you want to insert as a hyperlink.

6) Drag the item to where you want to insert the hyperlink in the document. The name of the item is inserted in the document as an active hyperlink.

You can also use the Hyperlink dialog to insert and modify hyperlinks within and between documents. See Chapter 12, Creating Web Pages.

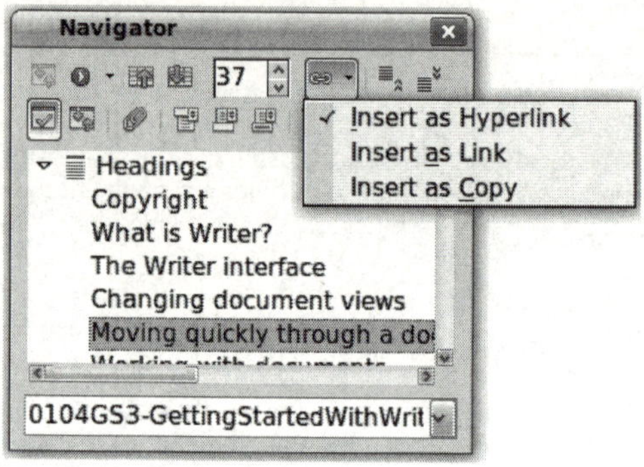

Figure 86: Inserting a hyperlink using the Navigator

Using cross-references

If you type in references to other parts of the document, those references can easily get out of date if you reword a heading, add or remove figures, or reorganize topics. Replace any typed cross-references with automatic ones and, when you update fields, all the references will update automatically to show the current wording or page numbers. The *Cross-references* tab of the Fields dialog lists some items, such as headings, bookmarks, figures, tables, and numbered items such as steps in a procedure. You can also create your own reference items; see "Setting References" in Chapter 14, Working with Fields, in the *Writer Guide* for instructions.

To insert a cross-reference to a heading, figure, bookmark, or other item:

1) In your document, place the cursor where you want the cross-reference to appear.
2) If the Fields dialog is not open, click **Insert > Cross-reference**. On the *Cross-references* tab (Figure 87), in the *Type* list, select the type of item to be referenced (for example, *Heading* or *Figure*). You can leave this page open while you insert many cross-references.
3) Click on the required item in the *Selection* list, which shows all the items of the selected type. In the *Insert reference to* list, choose the format required. The list varies according to the Type. The most commonly used options are **Reference** (to insert the full text of a heading or caption), **Category and Number** (to insert a figure number preceded by the word *Figure* or *Table*, but without the caption text), **Numbering** (to insert only the figure or table number, without the word "Figure" or "Table"), or **Page** (to insert the number of the page the referenced text is on). Click **Insert**.

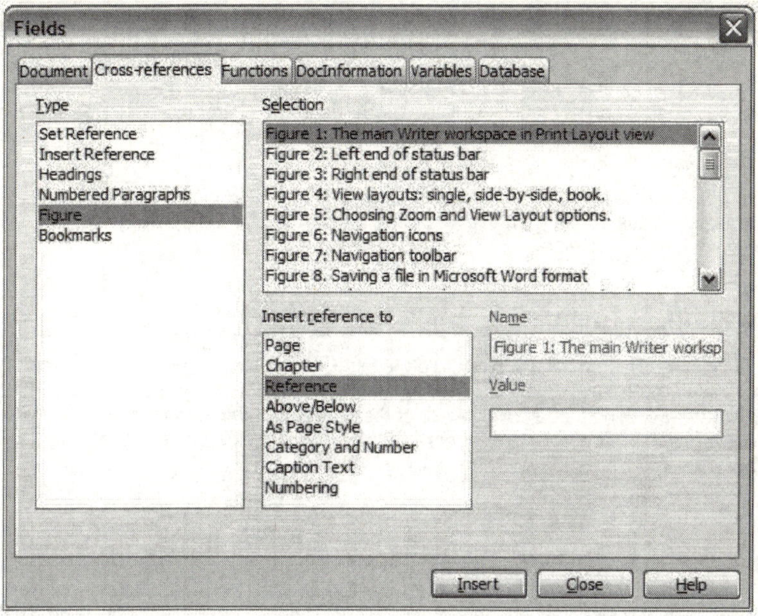

Figure 87: The Cross-references tab of the Fields dialog

Using bookmarks

Bookmarks are listed in the Navigator and can be accessed directly from there with a single mouse click. You can cross-reference to bookmarks and create hyperlinks to bookmarks, as described above.

1) Select the text you want to bookmark. Click **Insert > Bookmark**.
2) On the Insert Bookmark dialog, the larger box lists any previously defined bookmarks. Type a name for this bookmark in the top box, and then click **OK**.

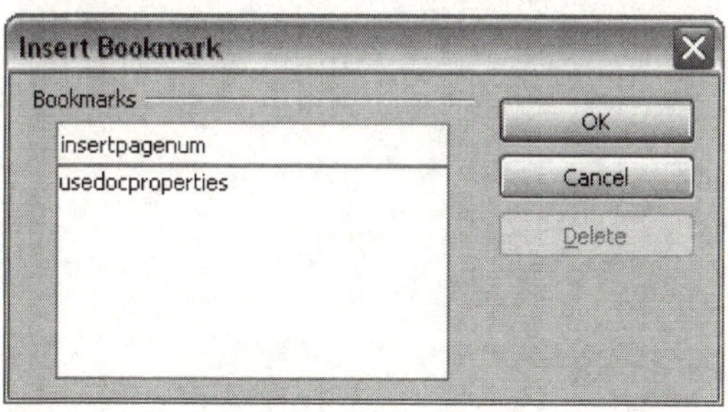

Figure 88: Inserting a bookmark

Using master documents

Master documents are typically used for producing long documents such as a book, a thesis, or a long report; or when different people are writing different chapters or other parts of the full document, so you don't need to share files. A master document joins separate text documents into one larger document, and unifies the formatting, table of contents (TOC), bibliography, index, and other tables or lists.

Yes, master documents do work in Writer. However, until you become familiar with them, you may think that master documents are unreliable or difficult to use. See Chapter 13, Working with Master Documents, in the *Writer Guide*.

Creating fill-in forms

A standard text document displays information: a letter, report, or brochure, for example. Typically the reader may either edit everything or nothing in any way. A form has sections that are not to be edited, and other sections that are designed for the reader to make changes. For example, a questionnaire has an introduction and questions (which do not change) and spaces for the reader to enter answers.

Forms are used in three ways:

- To create a simple document for the recipient to complete, such as a questionnaire sent out to a group of people who fill it in and return it.
- To link into a database or data source and allow the user to enter information. Someone taking orders might enter the information for each order into a database using a form.
- To view information held in a database or data source. A librarian might call up information about books.

Writer offers several ways to fill information into a form, including check boxes, option buttons, text boxes, pull-down lists and spinners. See Chapter 15, Using Forms in Writer, in the *Writer Guide*.

Chapter 5
Getting Started with Calc

Using Spreadsheets in LibreOffice

What is Calc?

Calc is the spreadsheet component of LibreOffice. You can enter data (usually numerical) in a spreadsheet and then manipulate this data to produce certain results.

Alternatively, you can enter data and then use Calc in a 'What if...' manner by changing some of the data and observing the results without having to retype the entire spreadsheet or sheet.

Other features provided by Calc include:

- Functions, which can be used to create formulas to perform complex calculations on data.
- Database functions, to arrange, store, and filter data.
- Dynamic charts; a wide range of 2D and 3D charts.
- Macros, for recording and executing repetitive tasks; scripting languages supported include LibreOffice Basic, Python, BeanShell, and JavaScript.
- Ability to open, edit, and save Microsoft Excel spreadsheets.
- Import and export of spreadsheets in multiple formats, including HTML, CSV, PDF, and PostScript.

Note	If you want to use macros written in Microsoft Excel using the VBA macro code in LibreOffice, you must first edit the code in the LibreOffice Basic IDE editor. See *Chapter 13 Getting Started with Macros* and *Calc Guide Chapter 12 Calc Macros*.

Spreadsheets, sheets and cells

Calc works with elements called *spreadsheets*. Spreadsheets consist of a number of individual *sheets*, each sheet containing cells arranged in rows and columns. A particular cell is identified by its row number and column letter.

Cells hold the individual elements – text, numbers, formulas, and so on – that make up the data to display and manipulate.

Each spreadsheet can have several sheets, and each sheet can have several individual cells. In Calc, each sheet can have a maximum of 1,048,576 rows (65,536 rows in Calc 3.2 and earlier) and a maximum of 1024 columns.

Calc main dialog

When Calc is started, the main window opens (Figure 89) and the various parts of this dialog are explained below.

Title bar

The Title bar, located at the top, shows the name of the current spreadsheet. When the spreadsheet is newly created, its name is *Untitled X*, where *X* is a number. When you save a spreadsheet for the first time, you are prompted to enter a name of your choice.

Menu bar

The Menu bar is where you select one of the menus and various sub-menus appear giving you more options. You can also customize the Menu bar; see *Chapter 14 Customizing LibreOffice* for more information.

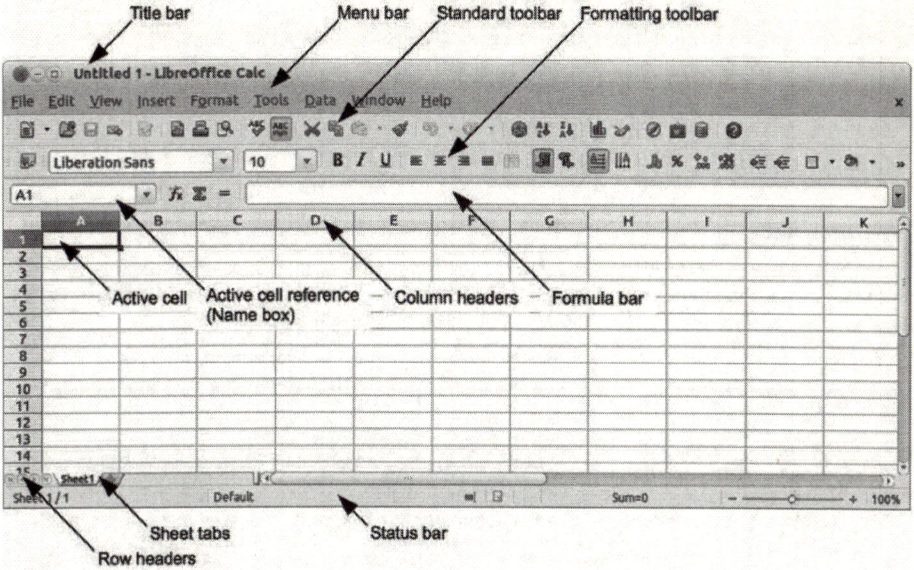

Figure 89: Calc main dialog

- **File** – contains commands that apply to the entire document; for example *Open*, *Save*, *Wizards*, *Export as PDF*, *Print, Digital Signatures* and so on.
- **Edit** – contains commands for editing the document; for example *Undo*, *Copy*, *Changes*, *Fill*, *Plug-in* and so on.
- **View** – contains commands for modifying how the Calc user interface looks; for example *Toolbars*, *Column & Row Headers*, *Full Screen*, *Zoom* and so on.
- **Insert** – contains commands for inserting elements into a spreadsheet; for example *Cells*, *Rows*, *Columns*, *Sheets*, *Picture* and so on.
- **Format** – contains commands for modifying the layout of a spreadsheet; for example *Cells*, *Page*, *Styles and Formatting*, *Alignment* and so on.
- **Tools** – contains various functions to help you check and customize your spreadsheet, for example *Spelling*, *Share Document*, *Gallery*, *Macros* and so on.
- **Data** – contains commands for manipulating data in your spreadsheet; for example *Define Range*, *Sort*, *Consolidate* and so on.
- **Window** – contains commands for the display window; for example *New Window*, *Split* and so on.
- **Help** – contains links to the help system included with the software and other miscellaneous functions; for example *Help*, *License Information*, *Check for Updates* and so on.

Toolbars

The default setting when Calc opens is for the Standard and Formatting toolbars to be docked at the top of the workspace (Figure 89).

Calc toolbars can be either docked and fixed in place, or floating allowing you to move a toolbar into a more convenient position on your workspace. Docked toolbars can be undocked and moved to different docked position on the workspace or undocked to become a floating toolbar. Toolbars that are floating when opened can be docked into a fixed position on your workspace.

The default set of icons (sometimes called buttons) on toolbars provide a wide range of common commands and functions. You can also remove or add icons to toolbars, see *Chapter 14 Customizing LibreOffice* for more information.

Formula bar

The **Formula Bar** is located at the top of the sheet in your Calc workspace. The Formula Bar is permanently docked in this position and cannot be used as a floating toolbar. If the Formula Bar is not visible, go to **View** on the main menu bar and select **Formula Bar**.

Figure 90: Formula bar

Going from left to right and referring to Figure 90, the Formula Bar consists of the following:

- **Name Box** – gives the cell reference using a combination of a letter and number, for example A1. The letter indicates the column and the number indicates the row of the selected cell.
- **Function Wizard** – opens a dialog from which you can search through a list of available functions. This can be very useful because it also shows how the functions are formatted.
- **Sum** – clicking on the Sum icon totals the numbers in the cells above the selected cell and then places the total in the selected cell. If there are no numbers above the selected cell, then the cells to the left are totaled.
- **Function** – clicking on the Function icon inserts an equals (=) sign into the selected cell and the **Input line** allowing a formula to be entered.
- **Input line** – displays the contents of the selected cell (data, formula, or function) and allows you to edit the cell contents.
- You can also edit the contents of a cell directly in the cell itself by double clicking on the cell. When you enter new data into a cell, the Sum and Function icons change to **Cancel** and **Accept** icons .

Note	In a spreadsheet the term function covers much more than just mathematical functions. See the *Calc Guide Chapter 7 Using Formulas and Functions* in for more information.

Spreadsheet layout

Individual cells

The main section of the workspace in Calc displays the cells in the form of a grid. Each cell is formed by the intersection of the columns and rows in the spreadsheet.

At the top of the columns and the left end of the rows are a series of header boxes containing letters and numbers. The column headers use an alpha character starting at A and go on to the right. The row headers use a numerical character starting at 1 and go down.

These column and row headers form the cell references that appear in the Name Box on the Formula Bar (Figure 90). If the headers are not visible on your spreadsheet, go to **View** on the main menu bar and select **Column & Row Headers**.

Sheet tabs

In Calc you can have more than one sheet in a spreadsheet. At the bottom of the grid of cells in a spreadsheet are sheet tabs indicating how many sheets there are in your spreadsheet. Clicking on a tab enables access to each individual sheet and displays that sheet. An active sheet is indicated with a white tab (default Calc setup). You can also select multiple sheet by holding down the *Ctrl* key while you click on the sheet tabs.

To change the default name for a sheet (Sheet1, Sheet2, and so on), right click on a sheet tab and select **Rename Sheet** from the context menu. A dialog opens allowing you to type in a new name for the sheet. Click **OK** when finished to close the dialog.

To change the color of a sheet tab, right click on the tab and select **Tab Color** from the context menu to open the **Tab Color** dialog (Figure 91). Select your color and click **OK** when finished to close the dialog. To add new colors to this color palette, see *Chapter 14 Customizing LibreOffice* for more information.

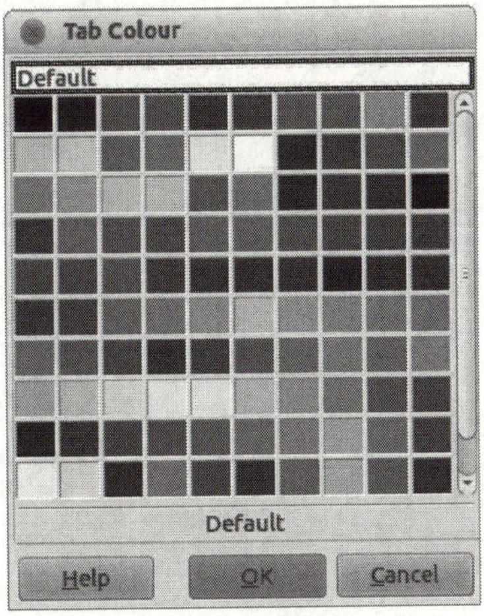

Figure 91: Tab color dialog

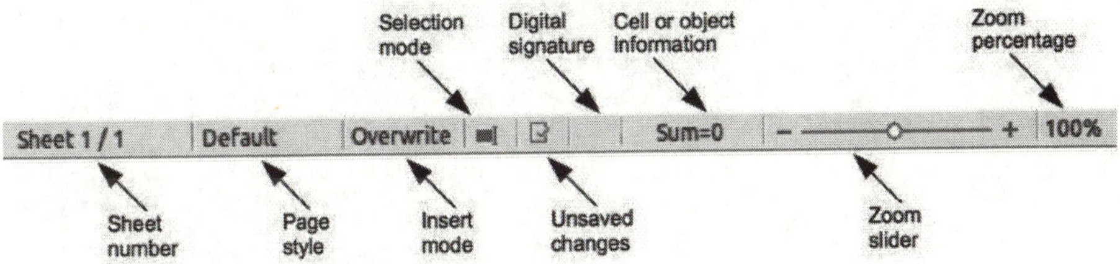

Figure 92: Calc status bar

Status bar

The Calc status bar (Figure 92) provides information about the spreadsheet and convenient ways to quickly change some of its features. Most of the fields are similar to those in other components of LibreOffice; see *Chapter 1 Introducing LibreOffice* in this guide and the *Calc Guide Chapter 1 Introducing Calc* for more information.

Opening a CSV file

Comma-separated-values (CSV) files are spreadsheet files in a text format where cell contents are separated by a character, for example comma, semi-colon, and so on. Each line in a CSV text file represents a row in a spreadsheet. Text is entered between quotation marks; numbers are entered without quotation marks.

To open a CSV file in Calc:

1) Choose **File > Open** on the main menu bar and locate the CSV file that you want to open.
2) Select the file and click **Open**. By default, a CSV file has the extension `.csv`. However, some CSV files may have a `.txt` extension.
3) The **Text Import** dialog (Figure 93) opens allowing you to select the various options available when importing a CSV file into a Calc spreadsheet.
4) Click **OK** to open and import the file.

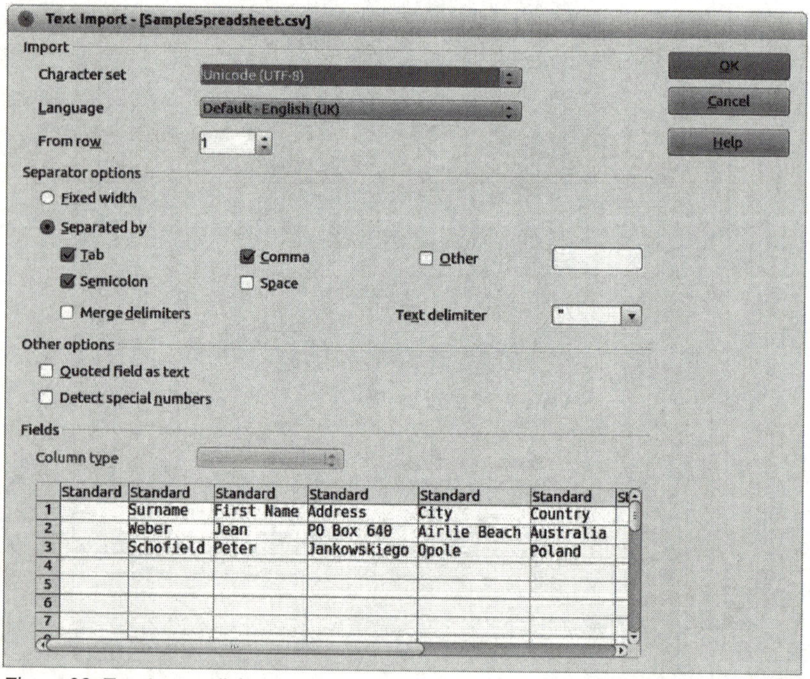

Figure 93: Text Import dialog

The various options for importing CSV files into a Calc spreadsheet are as follows:

- **Import**
  - *Character Set* – specifies the character set to be used in the imported file.
  - *Language* – determines how the number strings are imported.

    If Language is set to Default for CSV import, Calc will use the globally set language. If Language is set to a specific language, that language will be used when importing numbers.
  - *From Row* – specifies the row where you want to start the import. The rows are visible in the preview window at the bottom of the dialog.
- **Separator Options** – specifies whether your data uses separators or fixed widths as delimiters.
  - *Fixed width* – separates fixed-width data (equal number of characters) into columns. Click on the ruler in the preview window to set the width.
  - *Separated by* – select the separator used in your data to delimit the data into columns. When you select *Other*, you specify the character used to separate data into columns. This custom separator must also be contained in your data.
  - *Merge delimiters* – combines consecutive delimiters and removes blank data fields.
  - *Text delimiter* – select a character to delimit text data.
- **Other options**
  - *Quoted fields as text* – when this option is enabled, fields or cells whose values are quoted in their entirety (the first and last characters of the value equal the text delimiter) are imported as text.
  - *Detect special numbers* – when this option is enabled, Calc will automatically detect all number formats, including special number formats such as dates, time, and scientific notation.

    The selected language also influences how such special numbers are detected, since different languages and regions many have different conventions for such special numbers.

    When this option is disabled, Calc will detect and convert only decimal numbers. The rest, including numbers formatted in scientific notation, will be imported as text. A decimal number string can have digits 0-9, thousands separators, and a decimal separator. Thousands separators and decimal separators may vary with the selected language and region.
- **Fields** – shows how your data will look when it is separated into columns.
  - *Column type* – select a column in the preview window and select the data type to be applied to the imported data.
  - *Standard* – Calc determines the type of data.
  - *Text* – imported data are treated as text.
  - *US English* – numbers formatted in US English are searched for and included regardless of the system language. A number format is not applied. If there are no US English entries, the *Standard* format is applied.
  - *Hide* – the data in the column are not imported.

Saving spreadsheets

To save a spreadsheet, see *Chapter 1 Introducing LibreOffice* for more details on how to save files manually or automatically. Calc can also save spreadsheets in a range of formats and also export spreadsheets to PDF, HTML and XHTML file formats, see the *Calc Guide Chapter 6 Printing, Exporting, and E-mailing* for more information.

Saving in other spreadsheet formats

If you need to exchange files with users who are unable to receive spreadsheet files in Open Document Format (ODF) (`*.ods`), which Calc uses as default format, you can save a spreadsheet in an another format.

1) Save your spreadsheet in Calc spreadsheet file format (`*.ods`).
2) Select **File > Save As** on the main menu bar to open the **Save As** dialog (Figure 94).
3) In **File name**, if you wish, enter a new file name for the spreadsheet.
4) In **File type** drop-down menu, select the type of spreadsheet format you want to use.
5) If **Automatic file name extension** is selected, the correct file extension for the spreadsheet format you have selected will be added to the file name.
6) Click **Save**.
7) Each time you click **Save**, the **Confirm File Format** dialog opens (Figure 95). Click **Use [xxx] Format** to continue saving in your selected spreadsheet format or click **Use ODF Format** to save the spreadsheet in Calc ODS format.
8) If you select **Text CSV** format (`*.csv`) for your spreadsheet, the **Export Text File** dialog (Figure 96) opens allowing you to select the character set, field delimiter, text delimiter and so on to be used for your CSV file.

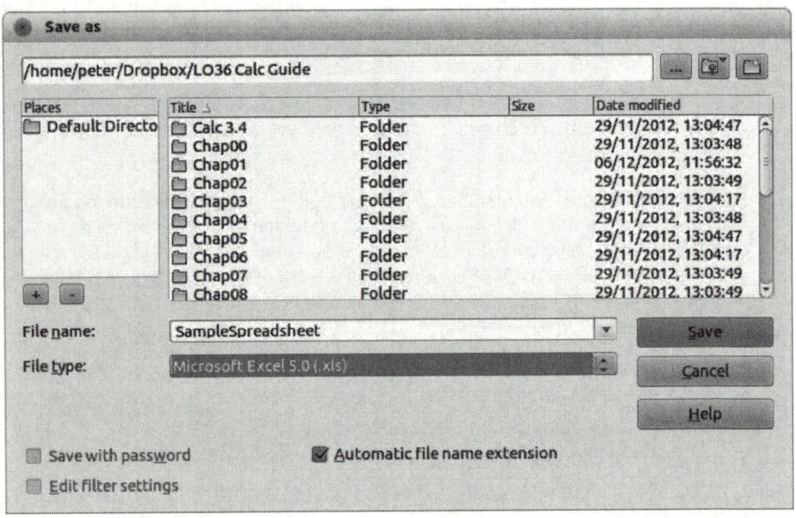

Figure 94: Save As dialog

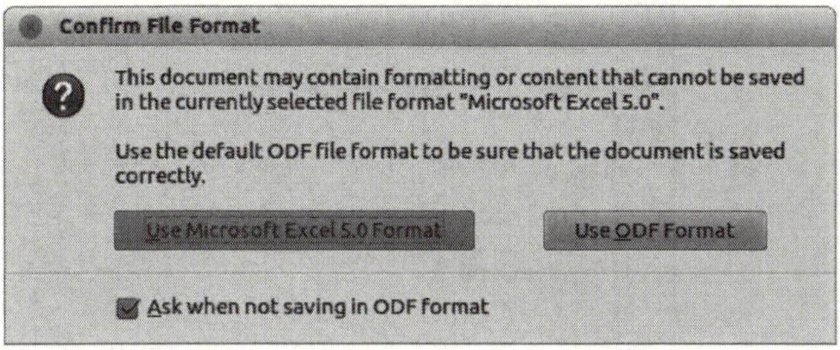

Figure 95: Confirm File Format dialog

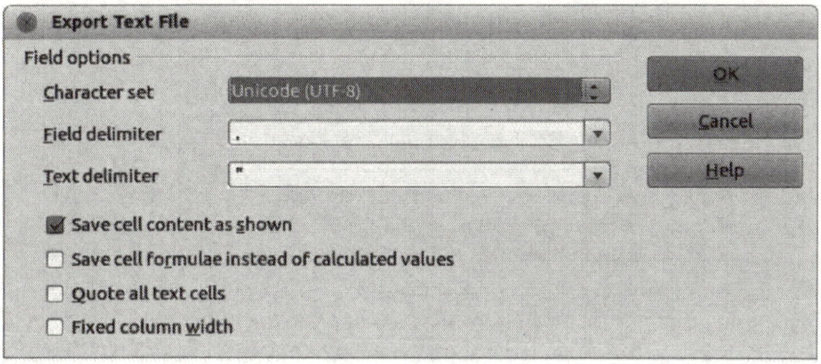

Figure 96: Export Text File dialog for CSV files

Tip	To have Calc save documents by default in a file format other than the default ODF format, go to **Tools > Options > Load/Save > General**. In *Default file format and ODF settings > Document type*, select **Spreadsheet**, then in *Always save as*, select your preferred file format.

Navigating within spreadsheets

Calc provides many ways to navigate within a spreadsheet from cell to cell and sheet to sheet. You can generally use the method you prefer.

Cell navigation

When a cell is selected or in focus, the cell borders are emphasized. When a group of cells is selected, the cell area is colored. The color of the cell border emphasis and the color of a group of selected cells depends on the operating system being used and how you have set up LibreOffice.

- **Using the mouse** – place the mouse pointer over the cell and click the left mouse button. To move the focus to another cell using the mouse, simply move the mouse pointer to the cell where you want the focus to be and click the left mouse button.
- **Using a cell reference** – highlight or delete the existing cell reference in the Name Box on the Formula Bar (Figure 90 on page 114). Type the new cell reference of the cell you want to move to and press *Enter* key. Cell references are case insensitive: for example, typing a3 or A3 will move the focus to cell A3.

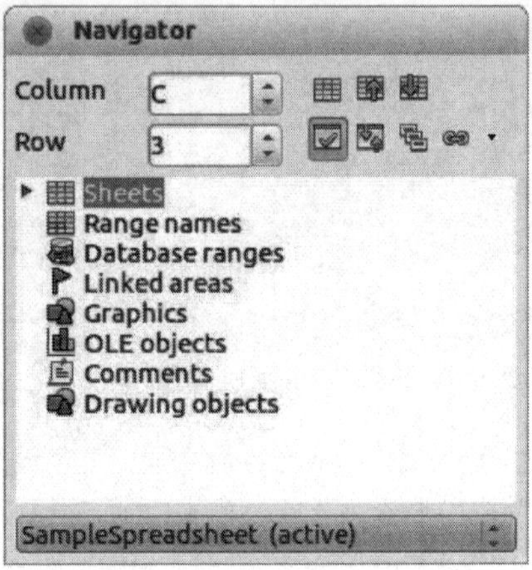

Figure 97: Navigator dialog in Calc

- **Using the Navigator** – click on the **Navigator** icon  on the Standard toolbar or press the *F5* key to open the **Navigator** dialog (Figure 97). Type the cell reference into the Column and Row fields and press the *Enter* key.
- **Using the Enter key** – pressing *Enter* moves the cell focus down in a column to the next row. Pressing *Shift+Enter* moves the focus up in a column to the next row.
- **Using the Tab key** – pressing *Tab* moves the cell focus right in a row to the next column. Pressing *Shift+Tab* moves the focus to the left in a row to the next column.
- **Using the arrow keys** – pressing the arrow keys on the keyboard moves the cell focus in the direction of the arrow pressed.
- **Using Home, End, Page Up and Page Down**
  - *Home* moves the cell focus to the start of a row.
  - *End* moves the cell focus to the last cell on the right in the row that contains data.
  - *Page Down* moves the cell focus down one complete screen display.
  - *Page Up* moves the cell focus up one complete screen display.

Sheet navigation

Each sheet in a spreadsheet is independent of the other sheets, though references can be linked from one sheet to another. There are three ways to navigate between different sheets in a spreadsheet.

- **Using the Navigator** – when the Navigator is open (Figure 97), double-clicking on any of the listed sheets selects the sheet.
- **Using the keyboard** – using key combinations *Ctrl+Page Down* moves one sheet to the right and *Ctrl+Page Up* moves one sheet to the left.
- **Using the mouse** – clicking on one of the sheet tabs at the bottom of the spreadsheet selects that sheet.

If there are a lot of sheets in your spreadsheet, then some of the sheet tabs may be hidden behind the horizontal scroll bar at the bottom of the screen. If this is the case, using the four buttons to the left of the sheet tabs can move the tabs into view (Figure 98).

Note	The sheet tab arrows that appear in Figure 98 are only active if there are sheet tabs that cannot be seen.

Note	When you insert a new sheet into your spreadsheet, Calc automatically uses the next number in the numeric sequence as a name. Depending on which sheet is open when you insert a new sheet, your new sheet may not be in numerical order. It is recommended to rename sheets in your spreadsheet to make them more recognizable.

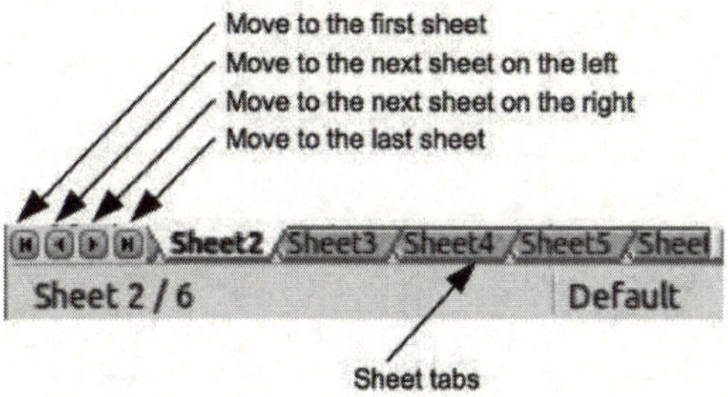

Figure 98. Navigating sheet tabs

Keyboard navigation

Pressing a key or a combination of keys allows you to navigate a spreadsheet using the keyboard. A key combination is where you press more than one key together, for example *Ctrl+Home* key combination to move to cell A1. Table 4 lists the keys and key combinations you can use for spreadsheet navigation in Calc.

Table 4. Keyboard cell navigation

Keyboard shortcut	*Cell navigation*
→	Moves cell focus right one cell
←	Moves cell focus left one cell
↑	Moves cell focus up one cell
↓	Moves cell focus down one cell
Ctrl+→	Moves cell focus to the first column on the right containing data in that row if cell focus is on a blank cell. Moves cell focus to the last column on the right containing data in that row if cell focus is on a cell containing data. Moves cell focus to the last column on the right in the spreadsheet if there are no more cells containing data.
Ctrl+←	Moves cell focus to the last column on the left containing data in that row if cell focus is on a blank cell. Moves cell focus to the first column on the left containing data in the spreadsheet if cell focus is on a cell containing data. Moves cell focus to the first column in that row if there are no more cells containing data.

Keyboard shortcut	*Cell navigation*
Ctrl+↑	Moves cell focus from a blank cell to the first cell above containing data in the same column. Moves cell focus from a cell containing data to the cell in Row 1 in the same column.
Ctrl+↓	Moves cell focus from a blank cell to the first cell below containing data in the same column. Moves cell focus from a cell containing data to the last cell containing data in the same column. Moves cell focus from the last cell containing data to the cell in the same column in the last row of the spreadsheet.
Ctrl+Home	Moves cell focus from anywhere on the spreadsheet to Cell A1 on the same sheet.
Ctrl+End	Moves cell focus from anywhere on the spreadsheet to the last cell in the lower right-hand corner of the rectangular area of cells containing data on the same sheet.
Alt+Page Down	Moves cell focus one screen to the right (if possible).
Alt+Page Up	Moves cell focus one screen to the left (if possible).
Ctrl+Page Down	Moves cell focus to the same cell on the next sheet to the right in sheet tabs if the spreadsheet has more than on sheet.
Ctrl+Page Up	Moves cell focus to the same cell on the next sheet to the left in sheet tabs if the spreadsheet has more than on sheet.
Tab	Moves cell focus to the next cell on the right
Shift+Tab	Moves cell focus to the next cell on the left
Enter	Down one cell (unless changed by user)
Shift+Enter	Up one cell (unless changed by user)

Customizing the Enter key

You can choose the direction in which the *Enter* key moves the cell focus by going to **Tools > Options > LibreOffice Calc > General**. Select the direction cell focus moves from the drop-down list. Depending on the file being used or the type of data being entered, setting a different direction can be useful. The *Enter* key can also be used to switch into and out of editing mode. Use the first two options under *Input settings* in Figure 99 to change the *Enter* key settings.

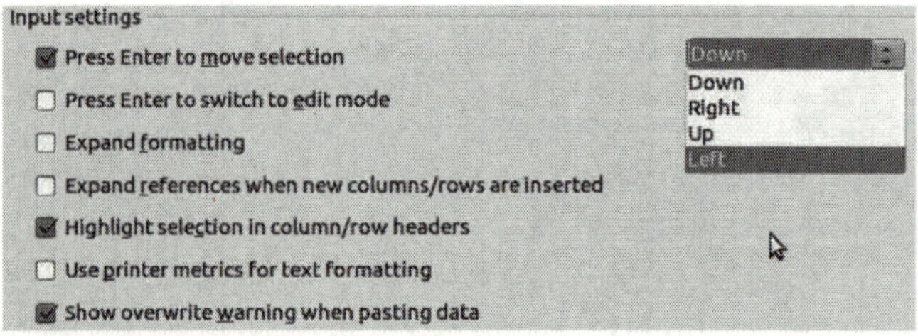

Figure 99: Customizing the Enter key

Selecting items in a spreadsheet

Selecting cells

Single cell

Left-click in the cell. You can verify your selection by looking in the Name Box on the Formula Bar (Figure 90 on page 114).

Range of contiguous cells

A range of cells can be selected using the keyboard or the mouse.

To select a range of cells by dragging the mouse cursor:

1) Click in a cell.
2) Press and hold down the left mouse button.
3) Move the mouse around the screen.
4) Once the desired block of cells is highlighted, release the left mouse button.

To select a range of cells without dragging the mouse:

1) Click in the cell which is to be one corner of the range of cells.
2) Move the mouse to the opposite corner of the range of cells.
3) Hold down the *Shift* key and click.

Tip	You can also select a contiguous range of cells by first clicking in the **Selection mode** field on the Status Bar (Figure 92 on page 115) and selecting **Extending selection** before clicking in the opposite corner of the range of cells. Make sure to change back to **Standard selection** or you may find yourself extending a cell selection unintentionally.

To select a range of cells without using the mouse:

1) Select the cell that will be one of the corners in the range of cells.
2) While holding down the *Shift* key, use the cursor arrows to select the rest of the range.

Tip	You can also directly select a range of cells using the Name Box. Click into the Name Box on the Formula Bar (Figure 90 on page 114). To select a range of cells, enter the cell reference for the upper left-hand cell, followed by a colon (:), and then the lower right-hand cell reference. For example, to select the range that would go from A3 to C6, you would enter *A3:C6*.

Range of non-contiguous cells

1) Select the cell or range of cells using one of the methods above.
2) Move the mouse pointer to the start of the next range or single cell.
3) Hold down the *Ctrl* key and click or click-and-drag to select another range of cells to add to the first range.
4) Repeat as necessary.

Selecting columns and rows

Single column or row

To select a single column, click on the column header (Figure 89 on page 113).

To select a single row, click on the row header.

Multiple columns or rows

To select multiple columns or rows that are contiguous:

1) Click on the first column or row in the group.
2) Hold down the *Shift* key.
3) Click the last column or row in the group.

To select multiple columns or rows that are not contiguous:

1) Click on the first column or row in the group.
2) Hold down the *Ctrl* key.
3) Click on all of the subsequent columns or rows while holding down the *Ctrl* key.

Entire sheet

To select the entire sheet, click on the small box between the column headers and the row headers (Figure 100), or use the key combination *Ctrl+A* to select the entire sheet, or go to **Edit** on the main menu bar and select **Select All**.

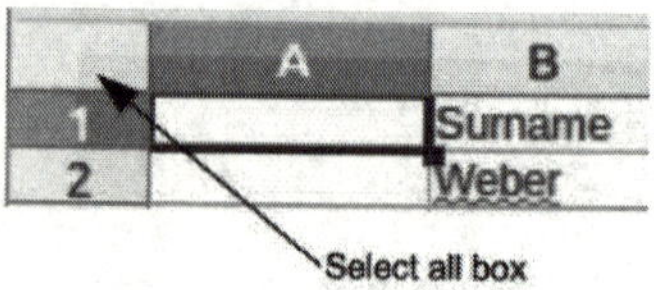

Figure 100. Select All box

Selecting sheets

You can select either one or multiple sheets in Calc. It can be advantageous to select multiple sheets, especially when you want to make changes to many sheets at once.

Single sheet

Click on the sheet tab for the sheet you want to select. The tab for the selected sheet becomes white (default Calc setup).

Multiple contiguous sheets

To select multiple contiguous sheets:

1) Click on the sheet tab for the first desired sheet.
2) Move the mouse pointer over the sheet tab for the last desired sheet.
3) Hold down the *Shift* key and click on the sheet tab.
4) All tabs between these two selections will turn white (default Calc setup). Any actions that you perform will now affect all highlighted sheets.

Multiple non-contiguous sheets

To select multiple non-contiguous sheets:

1) Click on the sheet tab for the first desired sheet.
2) Move the mouse pointer over the sheet tab for the second desired sheet.
3) Hold down the *Ctrl* key and click on the sheet tab.
4) Repeat as necessary.
5) The selected tabs will turn white (default Calc setup). Any actions that you perform will now affect all highlighted sheets.

All sheets

Right-click a sheet tab and choose **Select All Sheets** from the context menu.

Working with columns and rows

Inserting columns and rows

Note	When you insert a column, it is inserted to the *left* of the highlighted column. When you insert a row, it is inserted *above* the highlighted row. When you insert columns or rows, the cells take the formatting of the corresponding cells in the next column to left or the row above.

Single column or row

Using the **Insert** menu:

1) Select a cell, column, or row where you want the new column or row inserted.
2) Go to **Insert** on the main menu bar and select either **Insert > Columns** or **Insert > Rows**.

Using the mouse:

1) Select a column or row where you want the new column or row inserted.
2) Right-click the column or row header.
3) Select **Insert Columns** or **Insert Rows** from the context menu.

Multiple columns or rows

Multiple columns or rows can be inserted at once rather than inserting them one at a time.

1) Highlight the required number of columns or rows by holding down the left mouse button on the first one and then dragging across the required number of identifiers.
2) Proceed as for inserting a single column or row above.

Deleting columns and rows

Single column or row

To delete a single column or row:

1) Select a cell in the column or row you want to delete,.
2) Go to **Edit** on the main menu bar and select **Delete Cells** or right click and select **Delete** from the context menu.

3) Select the option you require from the **Delete Cells** dialog (Figure 101).

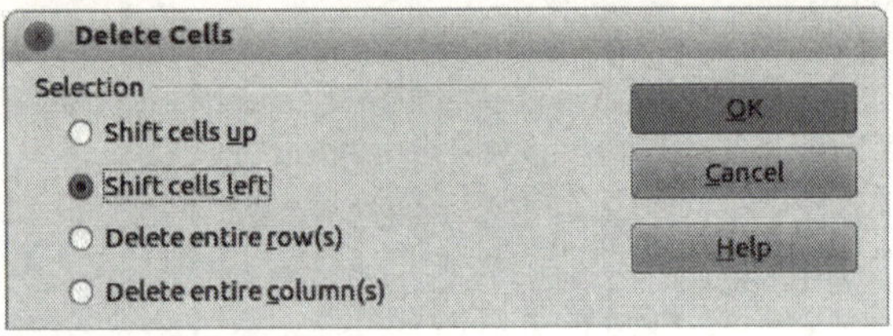

Figure 101: Delete Cells dialog

Alternatively:

1) Click in the column or header to select the column or row.
2) Go to **Edit** on the main menu bar and select **Delete Cells** or right click and select **Delete Columns** or **Delete Rows** from the context menu.

Multiple columns or rows

To delete multiple columns or rows:

1) Select the columns or rows, see “Multiple columns or rows” on page 124 for more information.
2) Go to **Edit** on the main menu bar and select **Delete Cells** or right click and select **Delete Columns** or **Delete Rows** from the context menu.

Working with sheets

Inserting new sheets

Click on the **Add Sheet** icon . This inserts a new sheet after the last sheet in the spreadsheet without opening the **Insert Sheet** dialog. The following methods open the **Insert Sheet** dialog (Figure 102) where you can position the new sheet, create more than one sheet, name the new sheet, or select a sheet from a file.

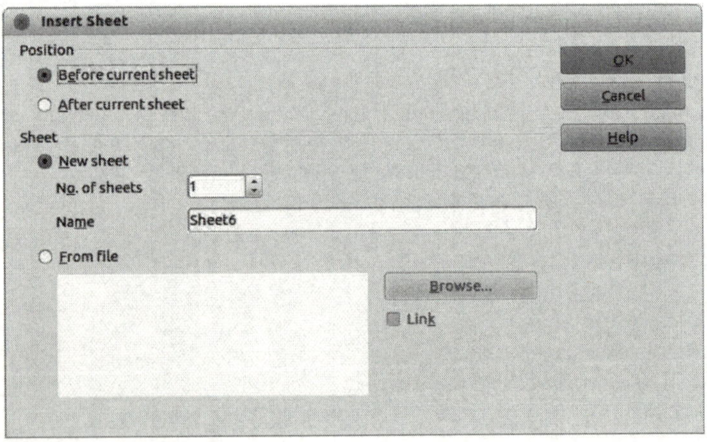

Figure 102: Insert Sheet dialog

- Select the sheet where you want to insert a new sheet, then go to **Insert > Sheet** on the main menu bar.
- Right-click on the sheet tab where you want to insert a new sheet and select **Insert Sheet** from the context menu.
- Click in the empty space at the end of the sheet tabs.
- Right-click in the empty space at the end of the sheet tabs and select **Insert Sheet** from the context menu.

Moving and copying sheets

You can move or copy sheets within the same spreadsheet by dragging and dropping or using the **Move/Copy Sheet** dialog. To move or copy a sheet into a different spreadsheet; you have to use the **Move/Copy Sheet** dialog.

Dragging and dropping

To move a sheet to a different position within the same spreadsheet, click on the sheet tab and drag it to its new position before releasing the mouse button.

To *copy* a sheet within the same spreadsheet, hold down the *Ctrl* key (*Option* key on Mac) then click on the sheet tab and drag it to its new position before releasing the mouse button. The mouse pointer may change to include a plus sign depending on the setup of your operating system.

Using a dialog

The **Move/Copy Sheet** dialog (Figure 103) allows you to specify exactly whether you want the sheet in the same or a different spreadsheet, its position within the spreadsheet, the sheet name when you move or copy the sheet.

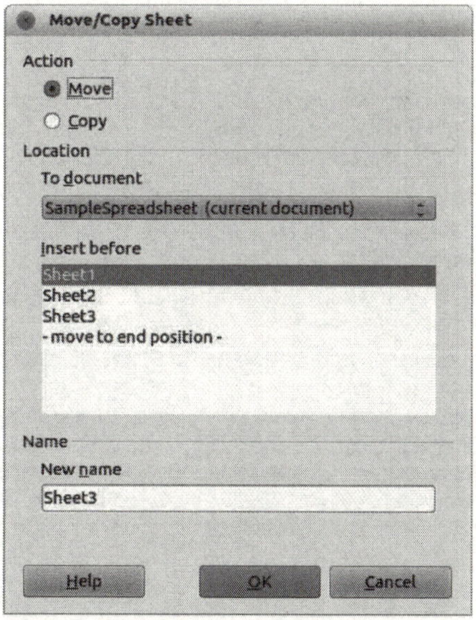

Figure 103: Move/Copy Sheet dialog

1) In the current document, right-click on the sheet tab you wish to move or copy and select **Move/Copy Sheet** from the context menu or go to **Edit > Sheet > Move/Copy** on the main menu bar.
2) Select **Move** to move the sheet or **Copy** to copy the sheet.
3) Select the spreadsheet where you want the sheet to be placed from the drop-down list in **To document**. This can be the same spreadsheet, another spreadsheet already open, or you can create a new spreadsheet.
4) Select the position in **Insert before** where you want to place the sheet.
5) Type a name in the **New name** text box if you want to rename the sheet when it is moved or copied. If you do not enter a name, Calc creates a default name (Sheet 1, Sheet 2, and so on).
6) Click **OK** to confirm the move or copy and close the dialog.

Caution	When you move or copy to another spreadsheet or a new spreadsheet, a conflict may occur with formulae linked to other sheets in the previous location.

Deleting sheets

To delete a single sheet, right-click on the sheet tab you want to delete and select **Delete Sheet** from the context menu, or go to **Edit > Sheet > Delete** from on the main menu bar. Click **Yes** to confirm the deletion.

To delete multiple sheets, select the sheets (see "Selecting sheets" on page 124), then right-click one of the sheet tabs and select **Delete Sheet** from the context menu, or go to **Edit > Sheet > Delete** from on the main menu bar. Click **Yes** to confirm the deletion.

Renaming sheets

By default, the name for each new sheet added is *SheetX*, where *X* is the number of the next sheet to be added. While this works for a small spreadsheet with only a few sheets, it can become difficult to identify sheets when a spreadsheet contains many sheets..

You can rename a sheet using one of the following methods:

- Enter the name in the **Name** text box when you create the sheet using the Insert Sheet dialog (Figure 102 on page 126).
- Right-click on a sheet tab and select **Rename Sheet** from the context menu to replace the existing name with a different one.
- Double-click on a sheet tab to open the **Rename Sheet** dialog.

Note	Sheet names must start with either a letter or a number; other characters including spaces are not allowed. Apart from the first character of the sheet name, permitted characters are letters, numbers, spaces, and the underscore character. Attempting to rename a sheet with an invalid name will produce an error message.

Viewing Calc

Changing document view

Use the zoom function to show more or fewer cells in the window when you are working on a spreadsheet. For more about zoom, see *Chapter 1 Introducing LibreOffice* in this guide.

Freezing rows and columns

Freezing locks a number of rows at the top of a spreadsheet or a number of columns on the left of a spreadsheet or both rows and columns. Then, when moving around within a sheet, the cells in frozen rows and columns always remain in view.

Figure 104 shows some frozen rows and columns. The heavier horizontal line between rows 3 and 23 and the heavier vertical line between columns F and Q indicate that rows 1 to 3 and columns A to F are frozen. The rows between 3 and 23 and the columns between F and Q have been scrolled off the page.

	A	B	C	D	E	F	Q	R
1		Surname	First Name	Address	City	Country		
2		Weber	Jean	PO Box 640	Airlie Beach	Australia		
3		Schofield	Peter	Jankowskiego	Opole	Poland		
23								
24								

Figure 104. Frozen rows and columns

Freezing rows or columns

1) Click on the row header below the rows you want the freeze or click on the column header to the right of the columns where you want the freeze.
2) Go to **Window** on the main menu bar and select **Freeze**. A heavier line appears between the rows or columns indicating where the freeze has been placed.

Freezing rows and columns

1) Click into the cell that is immediately below the rows you want frozen and immediately to the right of the columns you want frozen.
2) Go to **Window** on the main menu bar and select **Freeze**. A heavier line appears between the rows or columns indicating where the freeze has been placed.

Unfreezing

To unfreeze rows or columns, go to **Window** on the main menu bar and uncheck **Freeze**. The heavier lines indicating freezing will disappear.

Splitting the screen

Another way to change the view is by splitting the screen your spreadsheet is displayed in (also known as splitting the window). The screen can be split horizontally, vertically, or both, giving you up to four portions of the spreadsheet in view at any one time. An example of splitting the screen is shown in Figure 105 where a split is indicated by a black line.

Why would you want to do this? For example, a large spreadsheet in which one cell has a number in it that is used by three formulas in other cells. Using the split-screen technique, you can position the cell containing the number in one section and each of the cells with formulas in the other sections. This allows you to change the number in one cell and watch how it affects each of the formulas.

Splitting horizontally or vertically

1) Click on the row header below the rows where you want to split the screen horizontally or click on the column header to the right of the columns where you want to split the screen vertically.
2) Go to **Window** on the main menu bar and select **Split**. A heavy black line appears between the rows or columns indicating where the split has been placed.

Alternatively for a horizontal split, click on the thick black line at the top of the vertical scroll bar (Figure 106) and drag the split line below the row where you want the horizontal split positioned.

Alternatively for a vertical split, click on the thick black line at the right of the horizontal scroll bar (Figure 106) and drag the split line to the right of the column where you want the vertical split positioned.

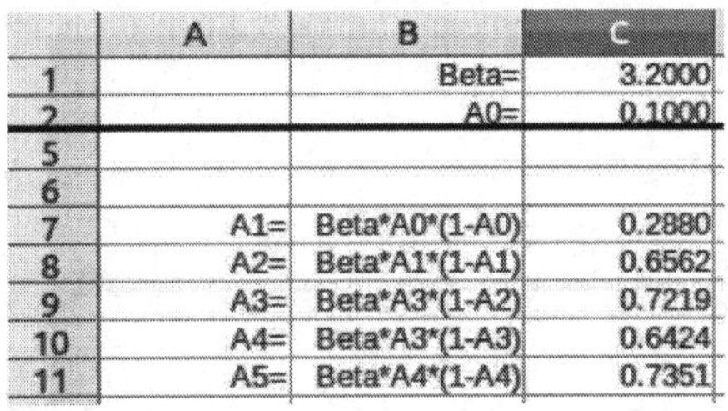

	A	B	C
1		Beta=	3.2000
2		A0=	0.1000
5			
6			
7	A1=	Beta*A0*(1-A0)	0.2880
8	A2=	Beta*A1*(1-A1)	0.6562
9	A3=	Beta*A3*(1-A2)	0.7219
10	A4=	Beta*A3*(1-A3)	0.6424
11	A5=	Beta*A4*(1-A4)	0.7351

Figure 105. Split screen example

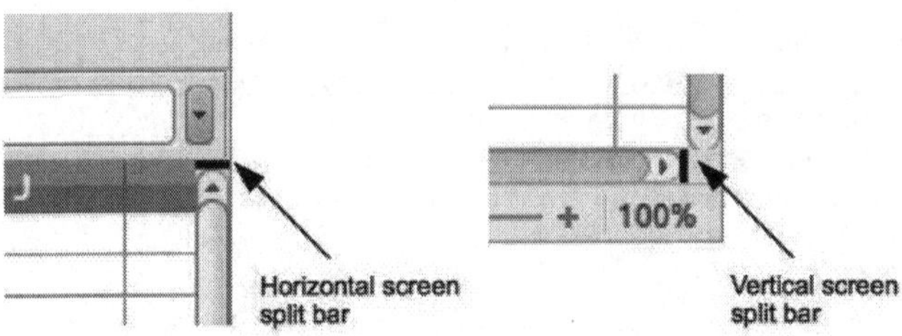

Figure 106. Split screen bars

Splitting horizontally and vertically

1) Click into the cell that is immediately below the rows where you want to split the screen horizontally and immediately to the right of the columns where you want to split the screen vertically.
2) Go to **Window** on the main menu bar and select **Split**. A heavy black line appears between the rows or columns indicating where the split has been placed.

Removing split views

To remove a split view, do any of the following:

- Double-click on each split line.
- Click on and drag the split lines back to their places at the ends of the scroll bars.
- Go to **Window** on the main menu bar and uncheck **Split**.

Using the keyboard

Most data entry in Calc can be accomplished using the keyboard.

Numbers

Click in the cell and type in a number using the number keys on either the main keyboard or numeric keypad. By default, numbers are right aligned in a cell.

Minus numbers

To enter a negative number, either type a minus (–) sign in front of the number or enclose the number in parentheses (), for example (1234). The result for both methods of entry will be the same, for example -1234.

Leading zeroes

To retain a minimum number of characters in a cell when entering numbers and retain the number format, for example 1234 and 0012, leading zeroes have to be added as follows:

1) With the cell selected, right click on the cell select **Format Cells** from the context menu or go to **Format > Cells** on the main menu bar or use the keyboard shortcut *Ctrl+1* to open the **Format Cells** dialog (Figure 107).
2) Make sure the **Numbers** page is selected then select *Number* in the *Category* list.
3) In *Options > Leading Zeros*, enter the minimum number of characters required. For example, for four characters, enter 4. Any number less than four characters will have leading zeroes added, for example 12 becomes 0012.
4) Click **OK**. The number entered retains its number format and any formula used in the spreadsheet will treat the entry as a number in formula functions.

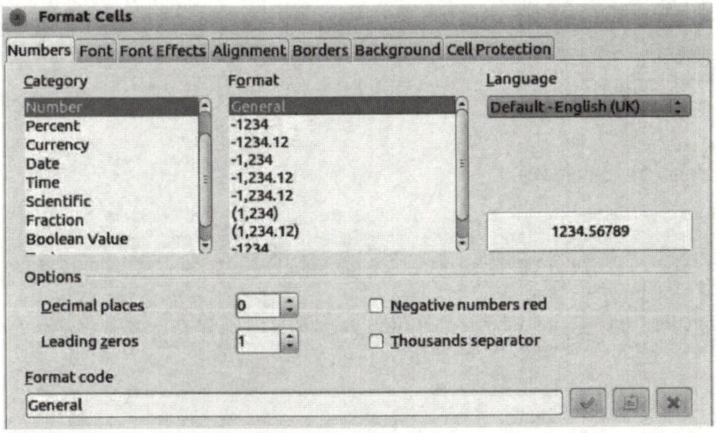

Figure 107: Format Cells dialog – Numbers page

If a number is entered with leading zeroes, for example 01481, by default Calc will automatically drop the leading 0. To preserve leading zeroes in a number:

1) Type an apostrophe (') before the number, for example '01481.
2) Move the cell focus to another cell. The apostrophe is automatically removed, the leading zeroes are retained and the number is converted to text left aligned.

Numbers as text

Numbers can also be converted to text as follows:

1) With the cell selected, right click on the cell select **Format Cells** from the context menu or go to **Format > Cells** on the main menu bar or use the keyboard shortcut *Ctrl+1* to open the **Format Cells** dialog (Figure 107).
2) Make sure the **Numbers** page is selected, then select *Text* from the *Category* list.
3) Click **OK** and the number is converted to text and, by default, left aligned.

Note	Any numbers that have been formatted as text in a spreadsheet will be treated as a zero by any formulas used in the spreadsheet. Formula functions will ignore text entries.

Text

Click in the cell and type the text. By default, text is left-aligned in a cell.

Date and time

Select the cell and type the date or time.

You can separate the date elements with a slash (/) or a hyphen (–) or use text, for example 10 Oct 2012. The date format automatically changes to the selected format used by Calc.

When entering a time, separate time elements with colons, for example 10:43:45. The time format automatically changes to the selected format used by Calc.

To change the date or time format used by Calc:

1) With the cell selected, right click on the cell select **Format Cells** from the context menu or go to **Format > Cells** on the main menu bar or use the keyboard shortcut *Ctrl+1* to open the **Format Cells** dialog (Figure 107).
2) Make sure the **Numbers** page is selected, then select *Date* or *Time* from the *Category* list.
3) Select the date or time format you want to use from the *Format* list.
4) Click **OK**.

Autocorrection options

Calc automatically applies many changes during data input using autocorrection, unless you have deactivated any autocorrect changes. You can also undo any autocorrection changes by using the keyboard shortcut *Ctrl+Z* or manually by going back to the change and replacing the autocorrection with what you want to actually see.

To change the autocorrect options, go to **Tools > AutoCorrect Options** on the main menu bar to open the **AutoCorrect** dialog (Figure 108).

Replace

Edits the replacement table for automatically correcting or replacing words or abbreviations in your document.

Exceptions

Specify the abbreviations or letter combinations that you do not want LibreOffice to correct automatically.

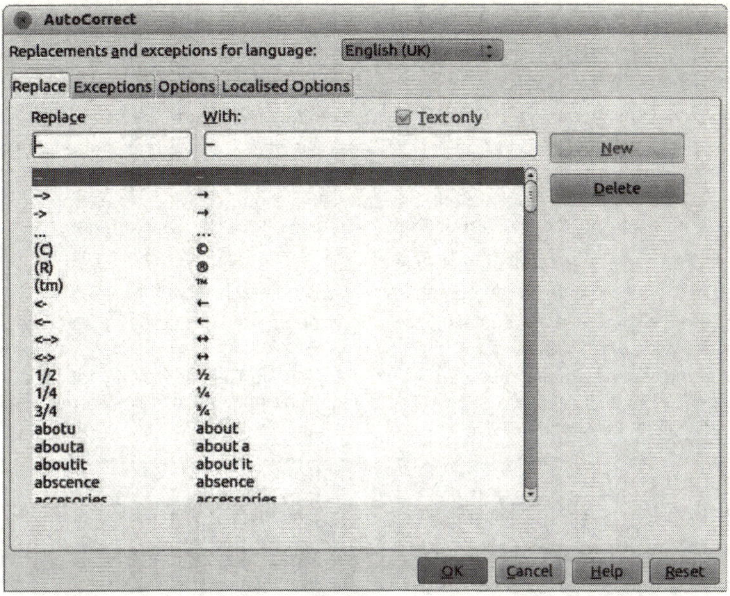

Figure 108: AutoCorrect dialog

Options

Select the options for automatically correcting errors as you type and then click **OK**.

Localized options

Specify the AutoCorrect options for quotation marks and for options that are specific to the language of the text.

Reset

Resets modified values back to the LibreOffice default values.

Deactivating automatic changes

Some AutoCorrect settings are applied when you press the spacebar after you enter data. To turn off or on Calc AutoCorrect, go to **Tools > Cell Contents** on the main menu bar and deselect or select **AutoInput**.

Speeding up data entry

Entering data into a spreadsheet can be very labor-intensive, but Calc provides several tools for removing some of the drudgery from input.

The most basic ability is to drop and drag the contents of one cell to another with a mouse. Many people also find AutoInput helpful. Calc also includes several other tools for automating input, especially of repetitive material. They include the fill tool, selection lists, and the ability to input information into multiple sheets of the same document.

Using the Fill tool

The Calc Fill tool is used to duplicate existing content or create a series in a range of cells in your spreadsheet (Figure 109).

1) Select the cell containing the contents you want to copy or start the series from.
2) Drag the mouse in any direction or hold down the *Shift* key and click in the last cell you want to fill.
3) Go to **Edit > Fill** on the main menu bar and select the direction in which you want to copy or create data (**Up**, **Down**, **Left** or **Right**) or **Series** from the context menu.

Alternatively, you can use a shortcut to fill cells.

1) Select the cell containing the contents you want to copy or start the series from.
2) Move the cursor over the small square in the bottom right corner of the selected cell. The cursor will change shape.
3) Click and drag in the direction you want the cells to be filled. If the original cell contained text, then the text will automatically be copied. If the original cell contained a number, a series will be created.

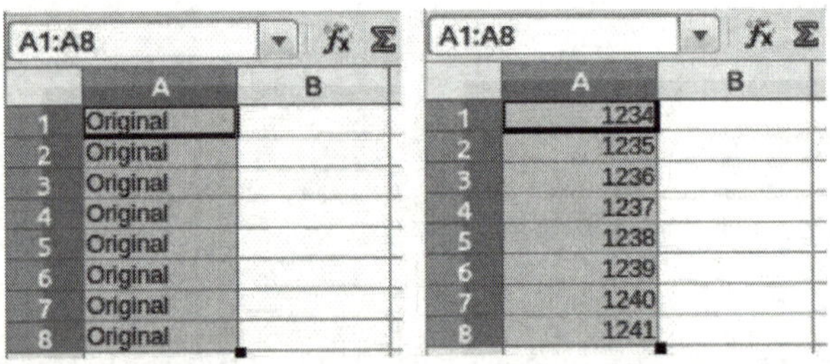

Figure 109: Using the Fill tool

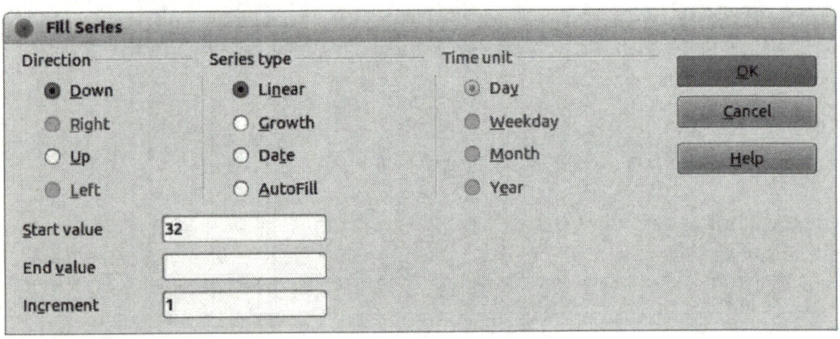

Figure 110: Fill Series dialog

Using a fill series

When you select a series fill from **Edit > Fill > Series**, the **Fill Series** dialog (Figure 110) opens allowing you to select the type of series you want.

- **Direction** – determines the direction of series creation.
  - *Down* – creates a downward series in the selected cell range for the column using the defined increment to the end value.

- *Right* – creates a series running from left to right within the selected cell range using the defined increment to the end value.
- *Up* – creates an upward series in the cell range of the column using the defined increment to the end value.
- *Left* – creates a series running from right to left in the selected cell range using the defined increment to the end value.

- **Series Type** – defines the series type.
  - *Linear* – creates a linear number series using the defined increment and end value.
  - *Growth* – creates a growth series using the defined increment and end value.
  - *Date* – creates a date series using the defined increment and end date.
  - *AutoFill* – forms a series directly in the sheet. The AutoFill function takes account of customized lists. For example, by entering January in the first cell, the series is completed using the list defined in **LibreOffice > Tools > Options > LibreOffice Calc > Sort Lists**. AutoFill tries to complete a value series by using a defined pattern. For example, a numerical series using 1,3,5 is automatically completed with 7,9,11,13; a date and time series using 01.01.99 and 15.01.99, an interval of fourteen days is used.
- **Unit of Time** – in this area you specify the desired unit of time. This area is only active if the Date option has been chosen in the Series type area.
  - *Day* – use the Date series type and this option to create a series using seven days.
  - *Weekday* – use the Date series type and this option to create a series of five day sets.
  - *Month* – use the Date series type and this option to form a series from the names or abbreviations of the months.
  - *Year* – use the Date series type and this option to create a series of years.
- **Start Value** – determines the start value for the series. Use numbers, dates or times.
- **End Value** – determines the end value for the series. Use numbers, dates or times.
- **Increment** – determines the value by which the series of the selected type increases by each step. Entries can only be made if the linear, growth or date series types have been selected.

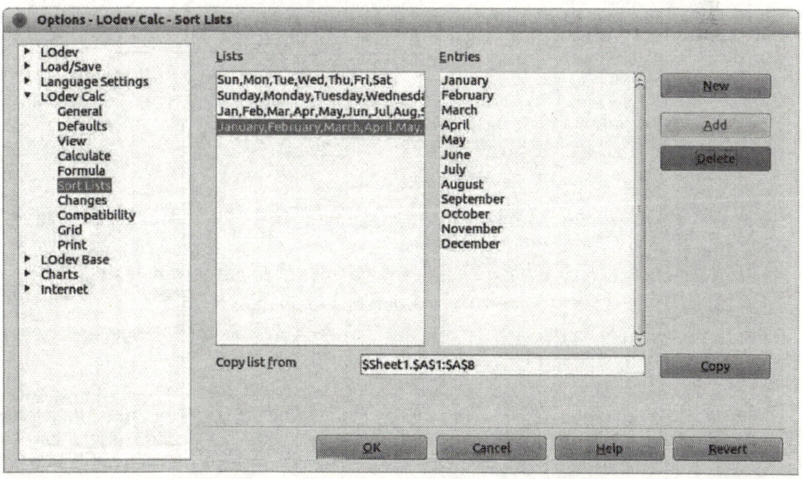

Figure 111: Sort Lists dialog

Defining a fill series

To define your own fill series:

1) Go to **Tools > Options > LibreOffice Calc > Sort Lists** to open the **Sort Lists** dialog (Figure 111). This dialog shows the previously-defined series in the *Lists* box on the left and the contents of the highlighted list in the *Entries* box.
2) Click **New** and the *Entries* box is cleared.
3) Type the series for the new list in the *Entries* box (one entry per line).
4) Click **Add** and the new list will now appear in the *Lists* box.
5) Click **OK** to save the new list.

Using selection lists

Selection lists are available only for text and are limited to using only text that has already been entered in the same column.

1) Select a blank cell in a column that contains cells with text entries.
2) Right click and select **Selection Lists** from the context menu. A drop-down list appears listing any cell in the same column that either has at least one text character or whose format is defined as text.
3) Click on the text entry you require and it is entered into the selected cell.

Sharing content between sheets

You might want to enter the same information in the same cell on multiple sheets, for example to set up standard listings for a group of individuals or organizations. Instead of entering the list on each sheet individually, you can enter the information in several sheets at the same time.

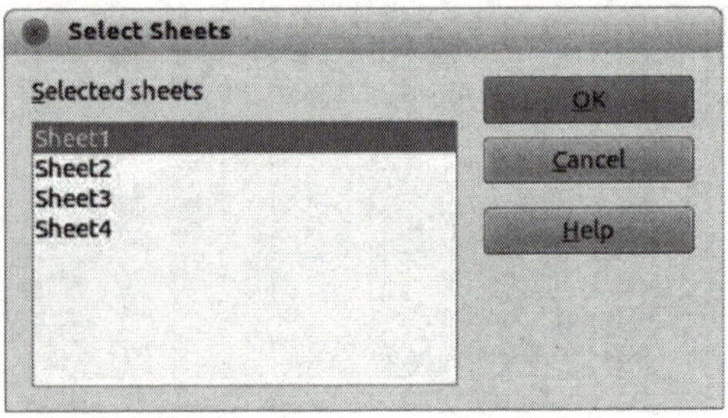

Figure 112: Select Sheets dialog

1) Go to **Edit > Sheet > Select** on the main menu bar to open the **Select Sheets** dialog (Figure 112).
2) Select the individual sheets where you want the information to be repeated.
3) Click **OK** to select the sheets and the sheet tabs will change color.
4) Enter the information in the cells on the sheet where you want the information to first appear and the information will repeated in the selected sheets.

Caution	This technique automatically overwrites, without any warning, any information that is already in the cells on the selected sheets. Make sure you deselect the additional sheets when you are finished entering information that is going to be repeated before continuing entering data into your spreadsheet.

Validating cell contents

When creating spreadsheets for other people to use, validating cell contents makes sure they enter data that is valid or appropriate for the cell. You can also use validation in your own work as a guide to entering data that is either complex or rarely used.

Fill series and selection lists can handle some types of data, but are limited to predefined information. To validate new data entered by a user, select a cell and go to **Data > Validity** on the main menu bar to define the type of contents that can be entered in that cell. For example, a cell may require a date or a whole number with no alphabetic characters or decimal points, or a cell may not be left empty.

Depending on how validation is set up, validation can also define the range of contents that can be entered, provide help messages explaining the content rules set up for the cell and what users should do when they enter invalid content. You can also set the cell to refuse invalid content, accept it with a warning, or start a macro when an error is entered. See the *Calc Guide Chapter 2 Entering, Editing and Formatting Data* for more information on validating cell contents.

Editing data

Deleting data

Deleting data only

Data can be deleted from a cell without deleting any of the cell formatting. Click in the cell to select it and then press the *Delete* key.

Deleting data and formatting

Data and cell formatting can be deleted from a cell at the same time.

1) Click in the cell to select it.
2) Press the *Backspace* key, or right-click in the cell and select **Delete Contents** from the context menu, or go to **Edit > Delete Contents**) on the main menu bar to open the **Delete Contents** dialog (Figure 113). This dialog allows you to delete the different aspects of the data in the cell or to delete everything in the cell.

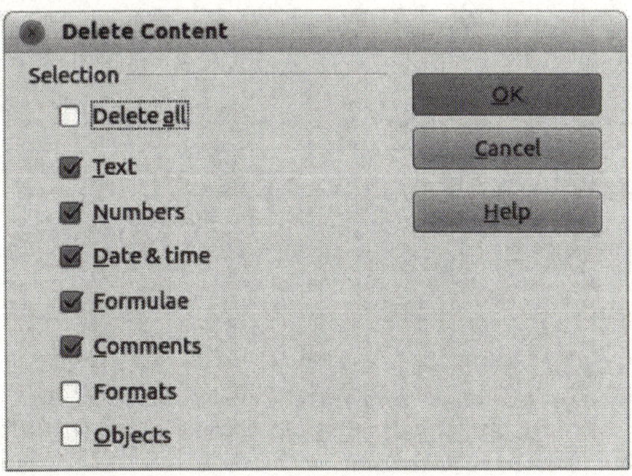

Figure 113: Delete Contents dialog

Replacing data

To completely replace data in a cell and insert new data, select the cell and type in the new data. The new data will replace the data already contained in the cell and will retain the original formatting used in the cell.

Alternatively, click in the Input Line on the Formula Bar (Figure 90 on page 114) then double click on the data to highlight it completely and type the new data.

Editing data

Sometimes it is necessary to edit the contents of cell without removing all of the data from the cell. For example, changing the phrase "Sales in Qtr. 2" to "Sales rose in Qtr" can be done as follows.

Using the keyboard

1) Click in the cell to select it.
2) Press the *F2* key and the cursor is placed at the end of the cell.
3) Use the keyboard arrow keys to reposition the cursor where you want to start entering the new data in the cell.
4) When you have finished, press the *Enter* key and your editing changes are saved.

Using the mouse

1) Double-click on the cell to select it and place the cursor in the cell for editing.
2) Reposition the cursor to where you want to start entering the new data in the cell.

Alternatively:

1) Single-click to select the cell.
2) Move the cursor to the Input Line on the Formula Bar (Figure 90 on page 114) and click at the position where you want to start entering the new data in the cell.

When you have finished, click away from the cell to deselect it and your editing changes are saved.

Formatting data

Note	All the settings discussed in this section can also be set as a part of the cell style. See the *Calc Guide Chapter 4 Using Styles and Templates in Calc* for more information.

Multiple lines of text

Multiple lines of text can be entered into a single cell using automatic wrapping or manual line breaks. Each method is useful for different situations.

Automatic wrapping

To automatically wrap multiple lines of text in a cell:

1) Right-click on the cell and select **Format Cells** from the context menu, or go to **Format > Cells** on the main menu bar, or press *Ctrl+1* to open the Format Cells dialog.
2) Click on the *Alignment* tab (Figure 114).
3) Under **Properties**, select *Wrap text automatically* and click **OK**.

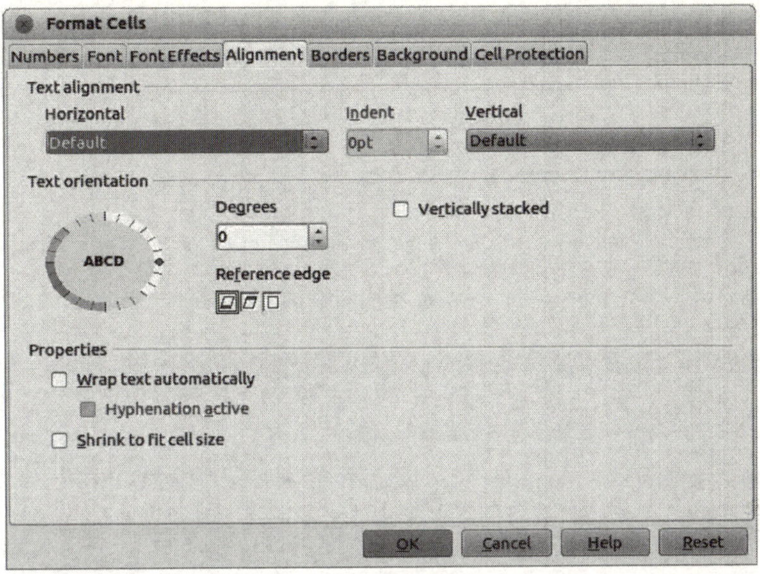

Figure 114: Format Cells dialog – Alignment page

Manual line breaks

To insert a manual line break while typing in a cell, press *Ctrl+Enter*. This method does not work with the cursor in the input line. When editing text, double-click the cell, then reposition the cursor to where you want the line break.

When a manual line break is entered, the cell width does not change and your text may still overlap the end of the cell. You have to change the cell width manually or reposition your line break so that your text does not overlap the end of the cell.

Shrinking text to fit the cell

The font size of the data in a cell can automatically adjust to fit inside cell borders. To do this, select the *Shrink to fit cell size* option under **Properties** in the Format Cells dialog (Figure 114).

Formatting numbers

Several different number formats can be applied to cells by using icons on the Formatting toolbar (highlighted in Figure 115). Select the cell, then click the relevant icon to change the number format.

Figure 115: Number icons on Formatting toolbar

For more control or to select other number formats, use the *Numbers* page of the Format Cells dialog (Figure 107 on page 131):

- Apply any of the data types in the **Category** list to the data.
- Control the number of decimal places and leading zeros in **Options**.

- Enter a custom format code.
- The **Language** setting controls the local settings for the different formats such as the date format and currency symbol.

Formatting font

To quickly select a font and format it for use in a cell:

1) Select the cell.
2) Click the small triangle on the right of the Font Name box on the Formatting toolbar (highlighted in Figure 116) and select a font from the drop-down list.
3) Click on the small triangle on the right of the Font Size on the Formatting toolbar and select a font size from the drop down list.

Figure 116: Font Name and Size on Formatting toolbar

4) To change the character format, click on the **Bold**, *Italic*, or Underline icons.
5) To change the paragraph alignment of the font, click on one of the four alignment icons (Left, Center, Right, Justified) .
6) To change the font color, click the arrow next to the Font Color icon to display the color palette, then select the desired color.

To specify the language used in the cell, open the *Font* page on the Format Cells dialog. Changing language in a cell allows different languages to exist within the same document. Use the *Font Effects* tab on the Format Cells dialog to set other font characteristics. See the *Calc Guide Chapter 4 Using Styles and Templates in Calc* for more information.

Formatting cell borders

To format the borders of a cell or a group of selected cells, click on the Borders icon on the Formatting toolbar, and select one of the border options displayed in the palette.

To format the line style and line color for the borders of a cell, click the small arrows next to the Line Style and Line Color (Border Color) icons on the Formatting toolbar. A line style palette or a border color palette is displayed.

For more control, including the spacing between cell borders and any data in the cell, use the *Borders* page of the Format Cells dialog (Figure 107 on page 131), where you can also define a shadow style. See the *Calc Guide Chapter 4 Using Styles and Templates in Calc* for more information.

Note	Cell border properties apply only to the selected cells and can be changed only if you are editing those cells. For example, if cell C3 has a top border, that border can be removed only by selecting C3. It cannot be removed in C2 although it appears to be the bottom border for cell C2.

Formatting cell background

To format the background color for a cell or a group of cells, click the small arrow next to the Background Color icon on the Formatting toolbar. A color palette, similar to the Font Color palette, is displayed. You can also use the *Background* tab of the Format Cells dialog (Figure 107 on page 131). See the *Calc Guide Chapter 4 Using Styles and Templates in Calc* for more information.

AutoFormat of cells

Using AutoFormat

You can use Calc's AutoFormat feature to format a group of cells quickly and easily.

1) Select the cells in at least three columns and rows, including column and row headers, that you want to format.
2) Go to **Format > AutoFormat** on the main menu bar to open the **AutoFormat** dialog (Figure 117).
3) Select the type of format and format color from the list.
4) If necessary, click **More** to open **Formatting** if Formatting is not visible.
5) Select the formatting properties to be included in the AutoFormat function.
6) Click **OK**.

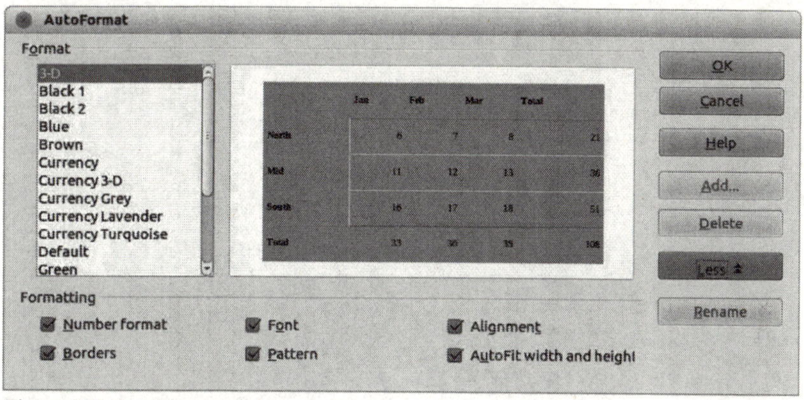

Figure 117: AutoFormat dialog

Defining a new AutoFormat

You can define a new AutoFormat so that it becomes available for use in all spreadsheets.

1) Format the data type, font, font size, cell borders, cell background and so on for a group of cells.
2) Go to **Edit > Select All** on the main menu bar to select the whole spreadsheet.
3) Go to **Format > AutoFormat** to open the AutoFormat dialog and the **Add** button is now active.
4) Click **Add**.
5) In the *Name* box of the Add AutoFormat dialog that opens, type a meaningful name for the new format.
6) Click **OK** to save. The new AutoFormat is now available in the *Format* list in the AutoFormat dialog.

Using themes

Calc comes with a predefined set of formatting themes that you can apply to spreadsheets. It is not possible to add themes to Calc and they cannot be modified. However, you can modify their styles after you apply them to a spreadsheet and the modified styles are only available for use for that spreadsheet when you save the spreadsheet.

To apply a theme to a spreadsheet:

1) Click the **Choose Themes** icon in the **Tools** toolbar. If this toolbar is not visible, go to **View > Toolbars** on the main menu bar and select **Tools** and the **Theme Selection** dialog (Figure 118) opens. This dialog lists the available themes for the whole spreadsheet.
2) Select the theme that you want to apply. As soon as you select a theme, the theme styles are applied to the spreadsheet and are immediately visible.
3) Click **OK**.
4) If you wish, you can now open the Styles and Formatting window to modify specific styles. These modifications do not modify the theme; they only change the appearance of the style in the specific spreadsheet you are creating.

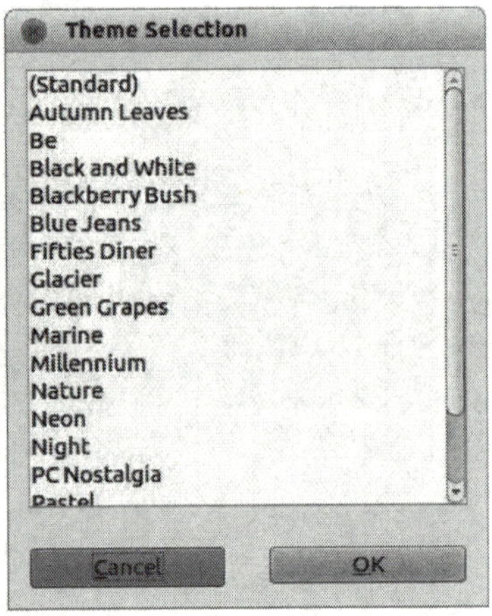

Figure 118: Theme Selection dialog

Using conditional formatting

You can set up cell formats to change depending on conditions that you specify. For example, in a table of numbers, you can show all the values above the average in green and all those below the average in red.

Conditional formatting depends upon the use of styles and the AutoCalculate feature must be enabled. Go to **Tools > Cell Contents > AutoCalculate** on the main menu bar to enable this feature. See the *Calc Guide Chapter 2 Entering, Editing, and Formatting Data* for more information.

Hiding and showing data

In Calc you can hide elements so that they are neither visible on a computer display nor printed when a spreadsheet is printed. However, hidden elements can still be selected for copying if you select the elements around them. For example, if column B is hidden, it is copied when you select columns A and C.

For more information on how to hide and show data, including how to use outline groups and filtering, see the *Calc Guide Chapter 2 Entering, Editing, and Formatting Data*.

Hiding data

To hide sheets, rows, and columns:

1) Select the sheet, row or column you want to hide.
2) Go to **Format** on the main menu bar and select **Sheet**, **Row** or **Column**.
3) Select **Hide** from the menu and the sheet, row or column can no longer viewed or printed.
4) Alternatively, right-click on the sheet tab, row header or column header and select **Hide** from the context menu.

To hide and protect data in selected cells:

1) Go to **Tools > Protect Document** and select **Sheet** from the menu options. The **Protect Sheet** dialog dialog will open (Figure 119).
2) Select *Protect this sheet and the contents of protected cells.*
3) Create a password and then confirm the password.
4) Select or deselect the user selection options for cells.
5) Click **OK**.
6) Select the cells you want to hide.
7) Go to **Format > Cells** on the main menu bar, or right-click and select **Format Cells** from the context menu, or use the keyboard shortcut *Ctrl+1* to open the **Format Cells** dialog.
8) Click the *Cell Protection* tab (Figure 120) and select an option to hide the cells.
9) Click **OK**.

Note	When data in cells are hidden, it is only the data contained in the cells that is hidden and the protected cells cannot be modified. The blank cells remain visible in the spreadsheet.

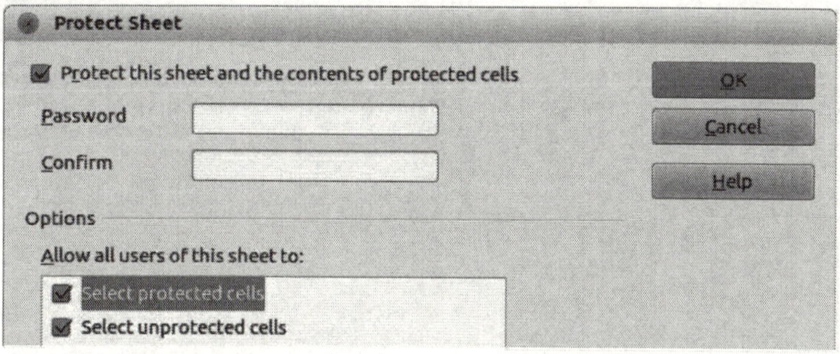

Figure 119: Protect Sheet dialog

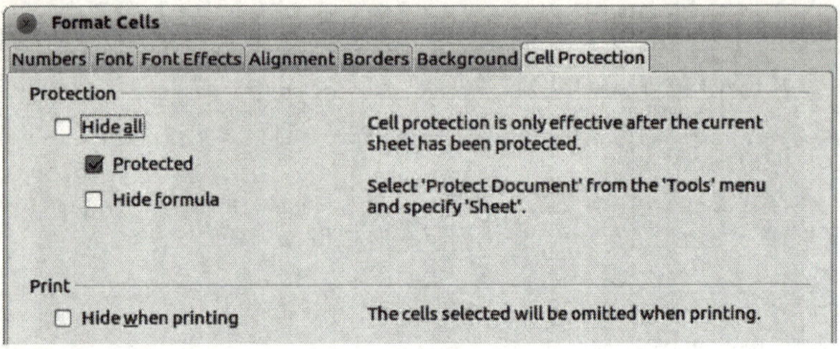

Figure 120: Cell Protection page in Format Cells dialog

Showing data

To show hidden sheets, rows, and columns:

1) Select the sheets, rows or columns each side of the hidden sheet, row or column.
2) Go to **Format** on the main menu bar and select **Sheet**, **Row** or **Column**.
3) Select **Show** from the menu and the sheet, row or column will be displayed and can be printed.
4) Alternatively, right-click on the sheet tabs, row headers or column headers and select **Show** from the context menu.

To show hidden data in cells:

1) Go to **Tools > Protect Document** and select **Sheet** from the menu options.
2) Enter the password to unprotect the sheet and click **OK**.
3) Go to **Format > Cells** on the main menu bar, or right-click and select **Format Cells** from the context menu, or use the keyboard shortcut *Ctrl+1* to open the **Format Cells** dialog.
4) Click the *Cell Protection* tab (Figure 120) and deselect the hide options for the cells.
5) Click **OK**.

Sorting records

Sorting within Calc arranges the cells in a sheet using the sort criteria that you specify. Several criteria can be used and a sort applies each criteria consecutively. Sorts are useful when you are searching for a particular item and become even more useful after you have filtered data.

Also, sorting is useful when you add new information to your spreadsheet. When a spreadsheet is long, it is usually easier to add new information at the bottom of the sheet, rather than adding rows in their correct place. After you have added information, you then carry out a sort to update the spreadsheet.

For more information on how to sort records and the sorting options available, see the *Calc Guide Chapter 2 Entering, Editing, and Formatting Data*.

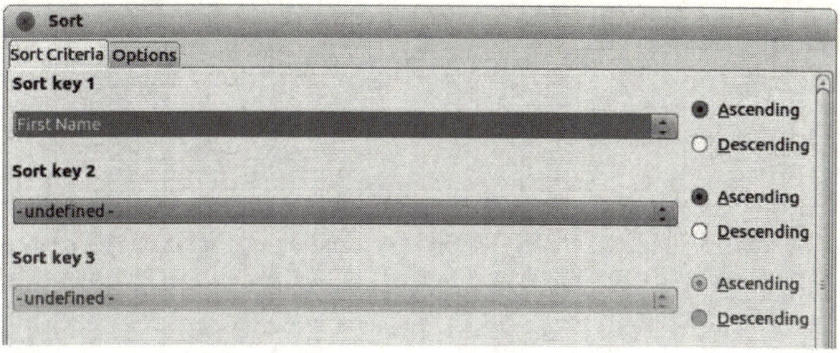

Figure 121: Sort Criteria dialog

To sort cells in your spreadsheet:

1) Select the cells to be sorted.
2) Go to **Data > Sort** on the main menu bar to open the **Sort** dialog (Figure 121).
3) Select the sort criteria from the drop down lists. The selected lists are populated from the selected cells.
4) Select either ascending order (A-Z, 1-9) or descending order (Z-A, 9-1).
5) Click **OK** and the sort is carried out on your spreadsheet.

Using formulas and functions

You may need more than numbers and text on your spreadsheet. Often the contents of one cell depend on the contents of other cells. Formulas are equations that use numbers and variables to produce a result. Variables are placed in cells to hold data required equations.

A function is a predefined calculation entered in a cell to help you analyze or manipulate data. All you have to do is enter the arguments and the calculation is automatically made for you. Functions help you create the formulas required to get the results that you are looking for.

See the *Calc Guide Chapter 7 Using Formulas and Functions* for more information.

Analyzing data

Calc includes several tools to help you analyze the information in your spreadsheets, ranging from features for copying and reusing data, to creating subtotals automatically, to varying information to help you find the answers you need. These tools are divided between the Tools and Data menus.

One of the most useful of these tools is the PivotTable, which is used for combining, comparing, and analyzing large amounts of data easily. Using the PivotTable, you can view different summaries of the source data, display the details of areas of interest, and create reports, whether you are a beginner, an intermediate or advanced user.

See the *Calc Guide Chapter 8 Using Pivot Tables* and *Chapter 9 Data Analysis* for more information on pivot tables and other tools available in Calc to analyze your data.

Printing

Printing from Calc is much the same as printing from other LibreOffice components (see *Chapter 10 Printing, Exporting, and Emailing* in this guide). However, some details for printing in Calc are different, especially regarding preparation for printing.

Print ranges

Print ranges have several uses, including printing only a specific part of the data or printing selected rows or columns on every page. For more information about using print ranges, see the *Calc Guide Chapter 6 Printing, Exporting, and E-mailing*.

Defining a print range

To define a new print range or modify an existing print range:

1) Select the range of cells to be included in the print range.
2) Go to **Format > Print Ranges > Define** on the main menu bar. Page break lines are displayed on screen.
3) To check the print range, go to **File > Page Preview** on the main menu bar or click on the **Page Preview** icon . LibreOffice will display the cells in the print range.

Adding to a print range

After defining a print range, you can add more cells to it by creating another print range. This allows multiple, separate areas of the same sheet to be printed while not printing the whole sheet.

1) After defining a print range, select an extra range of cells for adding to the print range.
2) Go to **Format > Print Ranges > Add** on the main menu bar to add the extra cells to the print range. The page break lines are no longer displayed on the screen.
3) To check the print ranges, go to **File > Page Preview** on the main menu bar or click on the **Page Preview** icon . LibreOffice will display the print ranges as separate pages.

Note	The additional print range will print as a separate page, even if both ranges are on the same sheet.

Removing a print range

It may become necessary to remove a defined print range, for example, if the whole sheet needs to be printed later.

To remove all the defined print ranges, go to **Format > Print Ranges > Remove** on the main menu bar. After the print ranges have been removed, the default page break lines will appear on the screen.

Editing a print range

At any time, you can directly edit the print range, for example to remove or resize part of the print range. Go to **Format > Print Ranges > Edit** on the main menu bar to open the **Edit Print Ranges** dialog where you can define the print range.

Printing options

To select the printing options of page order, details, and scale to be used when printing a spreadsheet:

1) Go to **Format > Page** on the main menu to open the **Page Style** dialog ().
2) Select the **Sheet** tab and make your selections from the available options.
3) Click **OK**.

For more information on printing options, see the *Calc Guide Chapter 6 Printing, Exporting, and E-mailing*.

Repeat printing of rows or columns

If a sheet is printed on multiple pages, you can set up certain rows or columns to repeat on each printed page. For example, if the top two rows of the sheet as well as column A need to be printed on all pages, do the following:

1) Go to **Format > Print Ranges > Edit**. on the main menu bar to open the **Edit Print Ranges** dialog (Figure 122).
2) Type the row identifiers in the *Rows to repeat* box. For example, to repeat rows 1 and 2, type **$1:$2**. This automatically changes *Rows to repeat* from, **- none -** to **- user defined -**.
3) Type the column identifiers in the *Columns to repeat* box. For example, to repeat column A, type **$A**. In the *Columns to repeat* list, **- none -** changes to **- user defined -**.
4) Click **OK**.

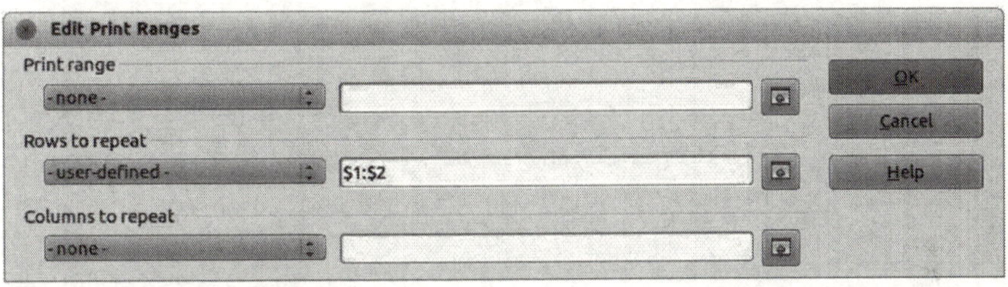

Figure 122: Edit Print Ranges dialog

For more information on editing print ranges, see the *Calc Guide Chapter 6 Printing, Exporting, and E-mailing*.

Page breaks

While defining a print range can be a powerful tool, it may sometimes be necessary to manually adjust the Calc printout manually using a *manual or page break*. A page break helps to ensure that your data prints properly according to your page size and page orientation. You can insert a horizontal page break above or a vertical page break to the left of the active cell.

For more information on manual breaks, see the *Calc Guide Chapter 6 Printing, Exporting, and E-mailing*.

Inserting a break

To insert a page break:

1) Navigate to the cell where the page break will begin.
2) Go to **Insert > Page Break** on the main menu bar.

3) Select **Row Break** to create a page break above the selected cell.
4) Select **Column Break** to create a page break to the left of the selected cell.

Deleting a page break

To remove a page break:

1) Navigate to a cell that is next to the break you want to remove.
2) Go to **Edit > Delete Page Break** on the main menu bar.
3) Select **Row Break** or **Column Break** depending on your need and break is removed.

Note	Multiple manual row and column breaks can exist on the same page. When you want to remove them, you have to remove each break individually.

Headers and footers

Headers and footers are predefined pieces of text that are printed at the top or bottom of a printed page when a spreadsheet is printed. Headers and footers are set and defined using the same method. For more information on setting and defining headers and footers, see the *Calc Guide Chapter 6 Printing, Exporting, and E-mailing*.

Headers and footers are also assigned to a page style. You can define more than one page style for a spreadsheet and assign different page styles to different sheets within a spreadsheet. For more information on page styles, see the *Calc Guide Chapter 4 Using Styles and Templates*.

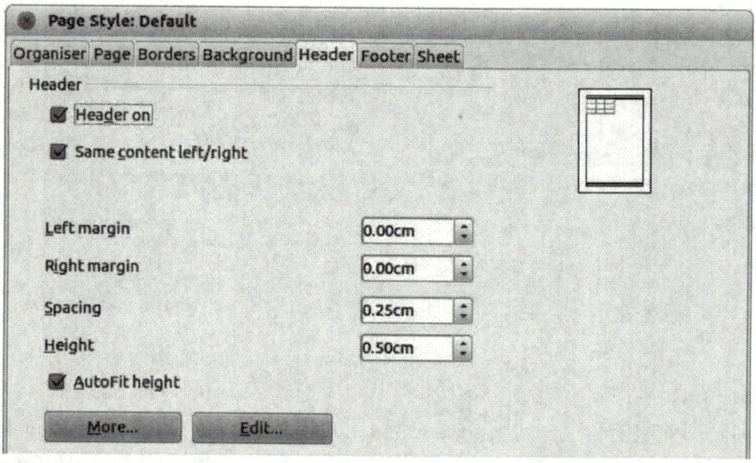

Figure 123: Header dialog

Setting a header or footer

To set a header or footer:

1) Navigate to the sheet that you want to set the header or footer for.
2) Go to **Format > Page** on the main menu bar to open the **Page Style** dialog (Figure 123).
3) On the Page Style dialog, select **Header** or **Footer** tab.
4) Select the **Header on** or **Footer on** option.

5) Select **Same content left/right** option if you want the same header or footer to appear on all the printed pages.
6) Set the margins, spacing, and height for the header or footer. You can also select **AutoFit height** box to automatically adjust the height of the header or footer.
7) To change the appearance of the header or footer, click on **More** to open the borders and background dialog.
8) To set the contents, for example page number, date and so on, that appears in the header or footer, click on **Edit** to open the style dialog.

LibreOffice
The Document Foundation

Chapter 6
Getting Started with Impress

Presentations in LibreOffice

What is Impress?

Impress is the presentation (slide show) program included in LibreOffice. You can create slides that contain many different elements, including text, bulleted and numbered lists, tables, charts, and a wide range of graphic objects such as clipart, drawings and photographs. Impress also includes a spelling checker, a thesaurus, text styles, and background styles.

This chapter includes instructions, screenshots, and hints to guide you through the Impress environment while designing your presentations. Although more difficult designs are mentioned throughout this chapter, explanations for creating them are in the *Impress Guide*. If you have a working knowledge of how to create slide shows, we recommend you use the *Impress Guide* for your source of information.

To use Impress for more than very simple slide shows requires some knowledge of the elements which the slides contain. Slides containing text use styles to determine the appearance of that text. Creating drawings in Impress is similar to the Draw program included in LibreOffice. For this reason, we recommend that you also see *Chapter 3 Using Styles and Templates*, and *Chapter 7 Getting Started with Draw* in this guide. You may also wish to consult the *Draw Guide* for more details on how to use the drawing tools.

Starting Impress

You can start Impress in several ways:

- From the LibreOffice Start Center, if no component is open, click on the Presentation icon.
- From the system menu, the standard menu from which most applications are started. On Windows, it is called the Start menu. On Gnome, it is called the Applications menu. On KDE it is identified by the KDE logo. On Mac OS X, it is the Applications menu. Details vary with your operating system; see *Chapter 1 Introducing LibreOffice.*
- On Windows, use the Presentation selection in the LibreOffice Quickstarter. Similar functions exist for Mac and Linux; see *Chapter 1 Introducing LibreOffice*.
- From any open component of LibreOffice. Click the triangle to the right of the **New** icon on the main menu bar and select *Presentation* from the drop-down menu or choose **File > New > Presentation** on the main menu bar.

Note	When LibreOffice was installed on your computer, in most cases a menu entry for each component was added to your system menu. The exact name and location of these menu entries depend on the operating system and graphical user interface.

When you start Impress for the first time, the Presentation Wizard is shown. Here you can choose from the following options:

- **Empty presentation** gives you a blank document
- **From template** is a presentation designed with a template of your choice
- **Open existing presentation**
- Click **Create** to open the main Impress window.

For detailed instructions about how to use the Presentation Wizard, see “Creating a new presentation” on page 160.

If you prefer not to use the Presentation Wizard in future, you can select **Do not show this wizard again**. You can enable the wizard again later in **Tools > Options > LibreOffice Impress > General > New document** and select the **Start with wizard** option.

Main Impress window

The main Impress window (Figure 124) has three parts: the *Slides pane*, *Workspace*, and *Tasks pane*. Additionally, several toolbars can be displayed or hidden during the creation of a presentation.

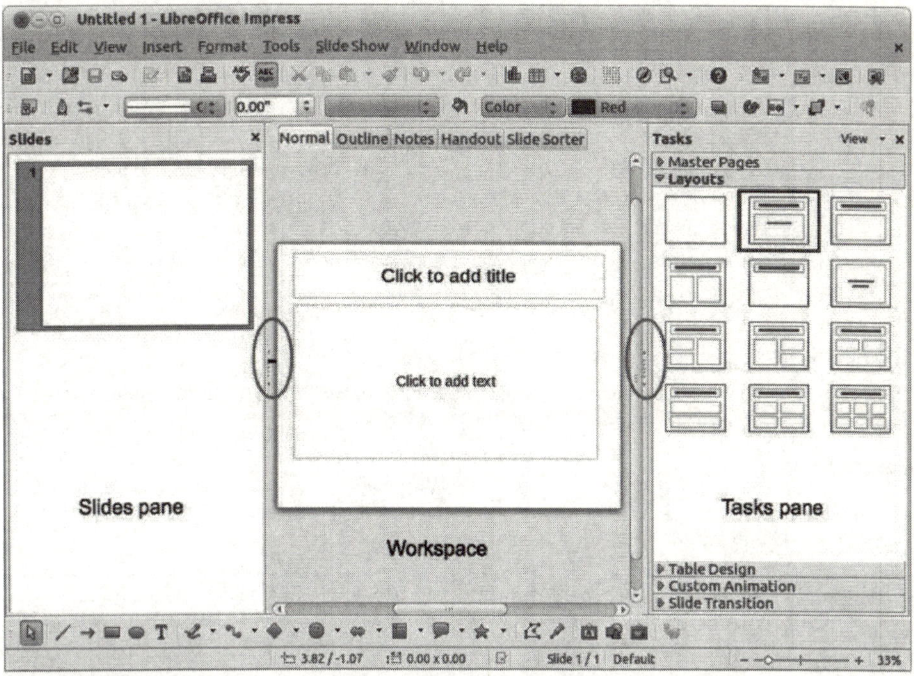

Figure 124: Main window of Impress; ovals indicate the Hide/Show markers

Tip	
	You can close the *Slides pane* or the *Tasks pane* by clicking the *X* in the upper right corner of the pane or go to **View > Slide Pane** or **View > Tasks Pane** on the main menu bar to deselect the pane. To reopen a pane, go to **View** on the main menu bar and select **Slide Pane** or **Tasks Pane** again. You can also maximize the Workspace area by clicking on the Hide/Show marker in the middle of the vertical separator line (highlighted in Figure 124). Using the Hide/Show marker hides, but does not close, the Slides or Tasks panes. To restore the pane, click again on its Hide/Show marker.

Slides pane

The *Slides pane* contains thumbnail pictures of the slides in your presentation, in the order they will be shown unless you change the slide show order. Clicking a slide in this pane selects it and places it in the *Workspace*. When a slide is in the Workspace, you can make changes any way you like.

Several additional operations can be performed on one or more slides simultaneously in the Slides pane:

- Add new slides to the presentation.
- Mark a slide as hidden so that it will not be shown as part of the presentation.
- Delete a slide from the presentation if it is no longer needed.
- Rename a slide.
- Duplicate a slide (copy and paste) or move it to a different position in the presentation (cut and paste).

It is also possible to perform the following operations, although there are more efficient methods than using the Slides pane:

- Change the slide transition following the selected slide or after each slide in a group of slides.
- Change the sequence of slides in the presentation.
- Change the slide design.
- Change slide layout for a group of slides simultaneously.

Tasks pane

The *Tasks pane* has five sections. To expand the section you wish to use, click on the title bar of each section. Only one section at a time can be expanded.

Master Pages
Here you define the page (slide) style for your presentation. Impress includes several designs of Master Pages (slide masters). One of them - Default - is blank, and the rest have background and styled text.

Tip	Press *F11* to open the Styles and Formatting dialog, where you can modify the styles used in any master page to suit your purpose. This can be done at any time.

Layout
The layouts included in Impress are shown here. You can choose the one you want and use it as it is, or you can modify it to meet your own requirements. However, it is not possible to save custom layouts.

Table Design
The standard table styles are provided in this section. You can further modify the appearance of a table with the options to show or hide specific rows and columns, or to apply a banded appearance to the rows and columns.

Custom Animation
A variety of animations can be used to emphasize or enhance different elements of each slide. The Custom Animation section provides an easy way to add, change, or remove animations.

Slide Transition
The Slide Transition section provides access to a number of slide transition options. The default is set to *No Transition*, in which the following slide simply replaces the existing one. However, many additional transitions are available. You can also specify the transition speed (slow, medium, fast), choose between an automatic or manual transition, and choose how long the selected slide should be shown (automatic transition only).

Workspace

The *Workspace* (normally in the center of the main window) has five tabs: **Normal**, **Outline**, **Notes**, **Handout**, and **Slide Sorter** (Figure 125). These five tabs are called View buttons. The Workspace below the View buttons changes depending on the chosen view. The workspace views are described in detail on page 156.

Figure 125: Workspace tabs

Toolbars

Many toolbars can be used during slide creation; they can be displayed or hidden by going to **View > Toolbars** on the main menu bar and selecting from the context menu.

You can also select the icons that you wish to appear on each toolbar. For more information, refer to *Chapter 1 Introducing LibreOffice*.

Many of the toolbars in Impress are similar to the toolbars in Draw. Refer to the *Draw Guide* for details on the functions available and how to use them.

Status bar

The *Status bar* (Figure 126), located at the bottom of the Impress window, contains information that you may find useful when working on a presentation. For details on the contents and use of these fields, see *Chapter 1 Introducing LibreOffice* in this guide and the *Impress Guide Chapter 1 Introducing Impress*.

Note	The sizes are given in the current measurement unit (not to be confused with the ruler units). This unit is defined in **Tools > Options > LibreOffice Impress > General**.

Figure 126: Status bar

From left to right, you will find:

- **Information area** – changes depending on the selection. For example:

Example selection	Examples of information shown
Text area	Text Edit: Paragraph x, Row y, Column z
Charts, spreadsheets	Embedded object (OLE) “ObjectName” selected
Graphics	Bitmap with transparency selected

- **Cursor position** – the position of the cursor or of the top left corner of the selection measured from the top left corner of the slide, followed by the width and height of the selection or text box where the cursor is located.
- **Unsaved changes** – a flag indicating that the file needs saving. Double clicking on this flag opens the file save dialog.

- **Digital signature** – a flag indicating whether the document is digitally signed. After the file has been saved, double clicking on this flag opens the digital signatures dialog.
- **Slide number** – the slide number currently displayed in the Workspace and the total number of slides in the presentation.
- **Page (slide) style** – the style associated with the slide, handout, or notes page currently in the Workspace. Double clicking on the style name opens the slide design dialog.
- **Zoom slider** – adjusts the zoom percentage of the Workspace displayed.
- **Zoom percentage** – indicates the zoom percentage of the Workspace displayed. Double clicking on zoom percentage opens the zoom and layout dialog.
- You can hide the Status Bar and its information by going to **View** on the main menu bar and deselecting **Status Bar**.

Workspace views

Each of the workspace views is designed to ease the completion of certain tasks; it is therefore useful to familiarize yourself with them in order to quickly accomplish those tasks.

Note	Each Workspace view displays a different set of toolbars when selected. These toolbar sets can be customized by going to **View > Toolbars** on the main menu bar, then check or uncheck the toolbar you want to add or remove.

Normal view

Normal view is the main view for working with individual slides. Use this view to format and design and to add text, graphics, and animation effects.

To place a slide in the slide design area (Normal view) (Figure 124 on page 153), click the slide thumbnail in the Slides pane or double-click it in the Navigator (see *Chapter 1 Introducing LibreOffice* and the *Impress Guide* for more information on the Navigator).

Outline view

Outline view (Figure 127) contains all the slides of the presentation in their numbered sequence. It shows topic titles, bulleted lists, and numbered lists for each slide in outline format. Only the text contained in the default text boxes in each slide is shown, so if your slide includes other text boxes or drawing objects, the text in these objects is not displayed. Slide names are also not included.

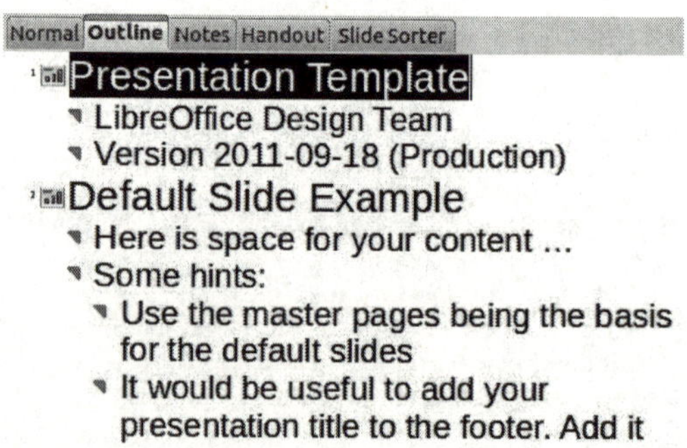

Figure 127: Outline view

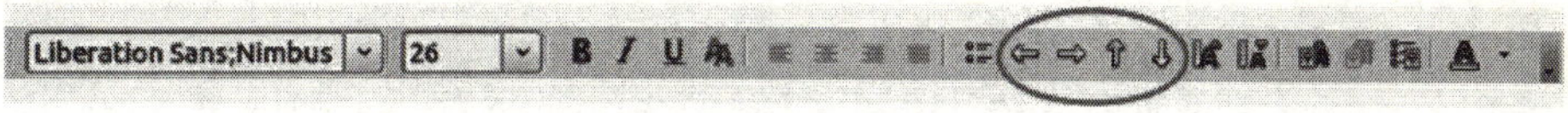

Figure 128: Outline level and movement arrows in Text Formatting toolbar

Use Outline view for the following purposes.

1) Making changes in the text of a slide:
   a) Add and delete the text in a slide just as in the Normal view.
   b) Move the paragraphs of text in the selected slide up or down by using the up and down arrow buttons (Move Up or Move Down) on the Text Formatting toolbar (highlighted in Figure 128).
   c) Change the outline level for any of the paragraphs in a slide using the left and right arrow buttons (Promote or Demote) on the Text Formatting toolbar.
   d) Both move a paragraph and change its outline level using a combination of these four arrow buttons.
2) Compare slides with your outline (if you have prepared one in advance). If you notice from your outline that another slide is needed, you can create it directly in the Outline view or you can return to the Normal view to create it.

Notes view

Use the *Notes view* (Figure 129) to add notes to a slide. These notes are not seen when the presentation is shown.

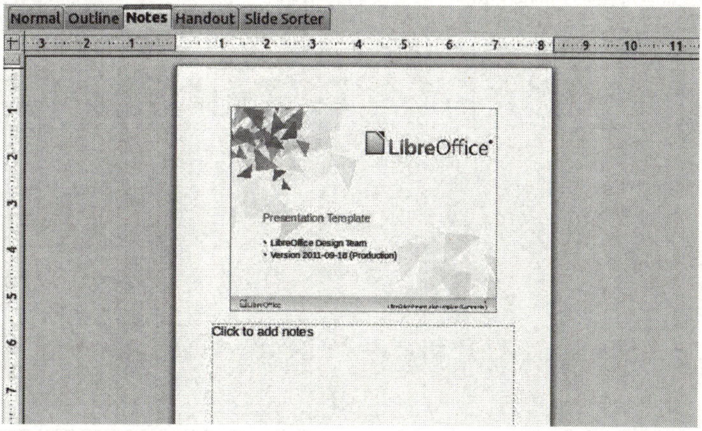

Figure 129: Notes view

1) Click the **Notes** tab in the Workspace.
2) Select the slide to which you want to add notes.
3) Click the slide in the Slides pane, or double-click the slide name in the Navigator.
4) In the text box below the slide, click on the words *Click to add notes* and begin typing.

You can resize the Notes text box using the colored resizing handles which appear when you click on the edge of the box. You can also move the box by placing the pointer on the border, then clicking and dragging. To make changes in the text style, press the *F11* key to open the Styles and Formatting dialog.

Handout view

Handout view is for setting up the layout of your slide for a printed handout. Click the *Handout* tab in the workspace, then choose **Layouts** in the Tasks pane (Figure 130) where you can then choose to print 1, 2, 3, 4, 6, or 9 slides per page.

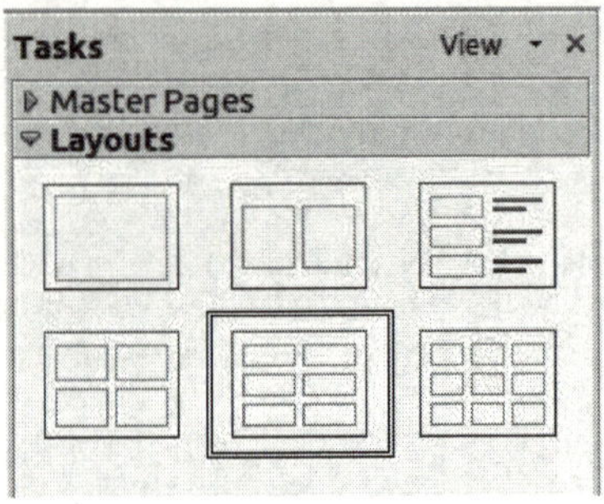

Figure 130: Handout layouts

Use this view also to customize the information printed on the handout. Refer to the *Impress Guide Chapter 10 Printing, E-mailing, Exporting, and Saving Slide Shows* for instructions on printing slides, handouts, and notes.

Go to **Insert > Page Number** or **Insert > Date and Time** on the main menu bar and the Header and Footer dialog opens. Click on the *Notes and Handouts* tab (Figure 131) and use this page to select the elements you want to appear on each handout page and their contents. More details on how to use this dialog are provided in the *Impress Guide*.

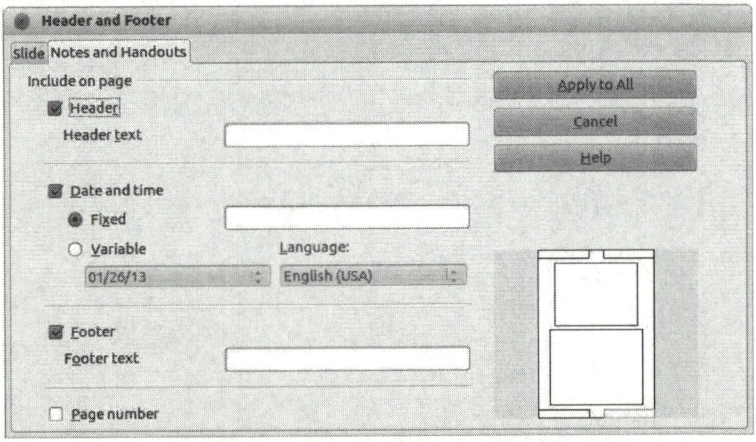

Figure 131: Header and Footer dialog – Handouts and Notes page

Slide Sorter view

Slide Sorter view (Figure 132) contains all of the slide thumbnails. Use this view to work with a group of slides or with only one slide.

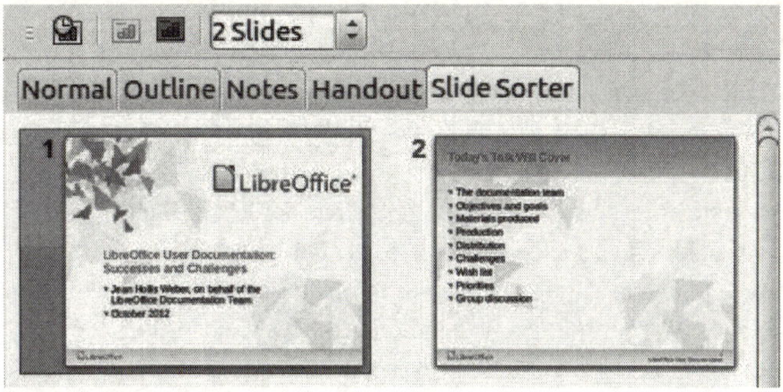

Figure 132: Slide Sorter view

Customizing Slide Sorter view

To change the number of slides per row:

1) Go to **View > Toolbars** and select **Slide Sorter** and **Slide View** to show or hide the Slide Sorter and Slide View toolbars (Figure 133).
2) Adjust the number of slides (up to a maximum of 15).

Figure 133: Slide Sorter and Slide View toolbars

Moving a slide using Slide Sorter

To move a slide in a presentation in the Slide Sorter:

1) Click the slide and the slide is highlighted (Figure 132).
2) Drag and drop it to the location you want.

Selecting and moving groups of slides

To select a group of slides, use one of these methods:

- Using the *Ctrl* key – click on the first slide and, while pressing the *Ctrl* key, select the other desired slides.
- Using the *Shift* key – click on the first slide, and while pressing the *Shift* key, select the final slide in the group. This selects all of the other slides between the first and the last slide selected.
- Using the mouse – click slightly to one side (left or right) of the first slide to be selected. Hold down the left mouse button and drag the cursor until all of the slides you want selected are highlighted.

To move a group of slides:

1) Select a group of slides.
2) Drag and drop the group to their new location.

Working in Slide Sorter view

You can work with slides in the Slide Sorter view just as you can in the Slide pane. To make changes, right-click a slide and choose any of the following from the context menu:

- **New Slide** – adds a new slide after the selected slide (see "New slide" on page 162).

- **Duplicate Slide** – creates a duplicate of the selected slide and places the new slide immediately after the selected slide (see "Duplicate slide" on page 163).
- **Delete Slide** – deletes the selected slide.
- **Rename Slide** – allows you to rename the selected slide.
- **Slide Layout** – allows you to change the layout of the selected slide.
- **Slide Transition** – allows you to change the transition of the selected slide.
  - For one slide, select a slide and add the desired transition.
  - For more than one slide, select a group of slides and add the desired transition.
- **Hide Slide** – any slides that are hidden are not shown in the slide show.
- **Cut** – removes the selected slide and saves it to the clipboard.
- **Copy** – copies the selected slide to the clipboard without removing it.
- **Paste** – inserts a slide from the clipboard after the selected slide.

Creating a new presentation

This section describes how to start a new presentation using the Presentation Wizard.

Tip	The first thing to do is decide on the purpose of the presentation and plan the presentation. Although you can make changes as you go, having an idea of who the audience will be, the structure, the content, and how the presentation will be delivered, will save you a lot of time from the start.

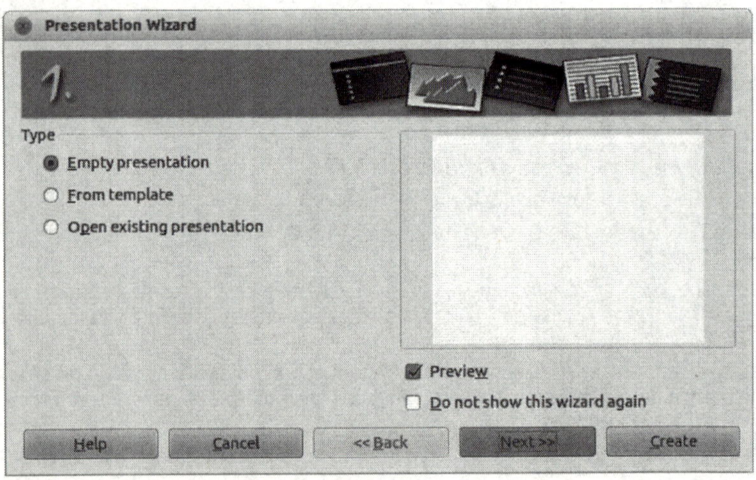

Figure 134. Choosing the type of presentation

When you start Impress, the Presentation Wizard appears (Figure 134).

1) Under **Type**, choose one of the options. These options are covered in the *Impress Guide*.
   a) *Empty presentation* creates a blank presentation.
   b) *From template* uses a template design already created as the basis for a new presentation. The wizard changes to show a list of available templates. Choose the template you want.

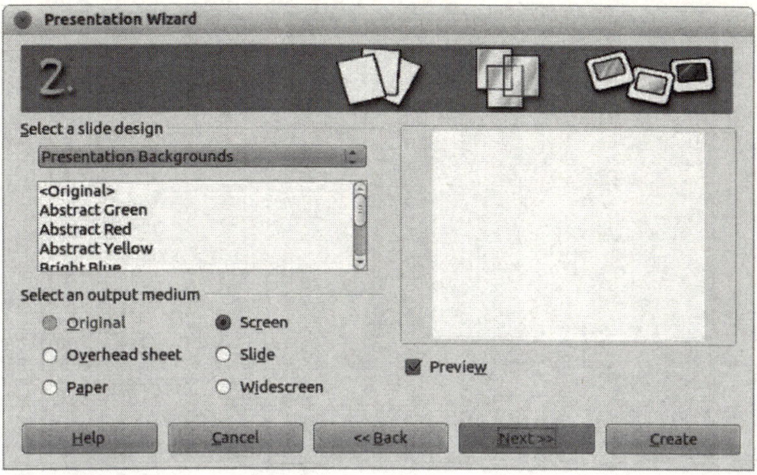

Figure 135. Selecting a slide design

   c) *Open existing presentation* continues work on a previously created presentation. The wizard changes to show a list of existing presentations. Choose the presentation you want.

2) Click **Next**. Figure 135 shows the Presentation Wizard step 2 as it appears if you selected *Empty Presentation* at step 1. If you selected *From template*, an example slide is shown in the Preview box.
3) Choose a design under **Select a slide design**. The slide design section gives you two main choices: *Presentation Backgrounds* and *Presentations*. Each one has a list of choices for slide designs. If you want to use one of these other than <Original>, click it to select it.
   a) The types of *Presentation Backgrounds* are shown in Figure 135. When you select a presentation background, you will see a preview of the slide design in the Preview window.
   b) <Original> is for a blank presentation slide design.
4) Select how the presentation will be used under **Select an output medium.** The majority of presentations are created for computer screen display. It is recommended to select *Screen*. You can change the page format at any time.

Note	The Screen page is optimized for a 4:3 display (28cm x 21cm) so it is not suitable for modern widescreen displays. You can change the slide size at any time by switching to Normal view and selecting **Format > Page**.

5) Click **Next**. The **Presentation** Wizard step 3 appears (Figure 136).
   a) Choose the desired slide transition from the *Effect* drop-down menu.
   b) Select the desired speed for the transition between the different slides in the presentation from the **Speed** drop-down menu. *Medium* is a good choice for now.
6) Click **Create.** A new presentation is created.

Note	If you selected *From template* on step 1 of the Wizard, the **Next** button will be active on step 3 and other pages will be available. These pages are not described here.

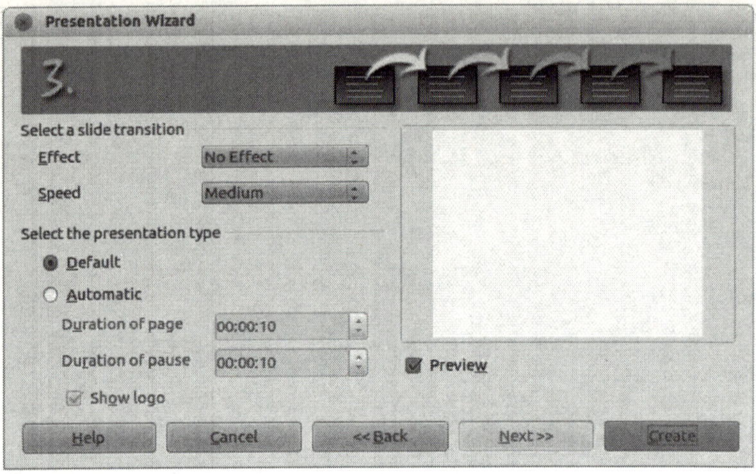

Figure 136: Selecting a slide transition effect

Tip	You can accept the default values for both *Effect* and *Speed* unless you are skilled at creating presentations. Both of these values can be changed later while working with slide transitions and animations. These two features are explained in more detail in the *Impress Guide Chapter 9 Slide Shows*.

Caution ⚠	Remember to save frequently while working on the presentation, to prevent any loss of information should something unexpected occur. You might also want to activate the AutoRecovery function (**Tools > Options > Load/Save > General)**. Select **Save AutoRecovery information every** and enter the number of minutes to be used as the frequency for auto recovery.

Formatting a presentation

A new presentation contains only one empty slide. In this section we will start adding new slides and preparing them for the intended contents.

Inserting slides

New slide

A new slide can be inserted into a presentation as follows:.

1) Go to **Insert** on the main menu bar and select **Slide**.
2) Or right-click on a slide in the Workspace, Slides Pane or Slide Sorter view and select **Slide > New Slide** from the context menu.
3) Or click the **Slide** icon in the Presentation toolbar. If the Presentation toolbar is not visible, go to **View > Toolbars** on the main menu bar and select **Presentation** from the list.

A new slide is inserted after the selected slide in the presentation.

Duplicate slide

Sometimes, rather than starting from a new slide you may want to duplicate a slide already included in your presentation. To duplicate a slide:

1) Select the slide you want to duplicate from the Slides Pane.
2) Right-click on the slide in the Slides Pane or Workspace and select **Duplicate Slide** from the context menu.

   Or, go to Slide Sorter view, right-click on a slide and select **Duplicate Slide** from the context menu.

   Alternatively, go to **Insert** on the main menu bar and select **Duplicate Slide**.
3) A duplicate slide is inserted after the selected slide in the presentation.

Selecting slide layout

In the Tasks Pane, select **Layouts** by clicking on the title to display the available layouts (Figure 137). The layouts included in LibreOffice range from a blank slide to a slide with six contents boxes and a title.

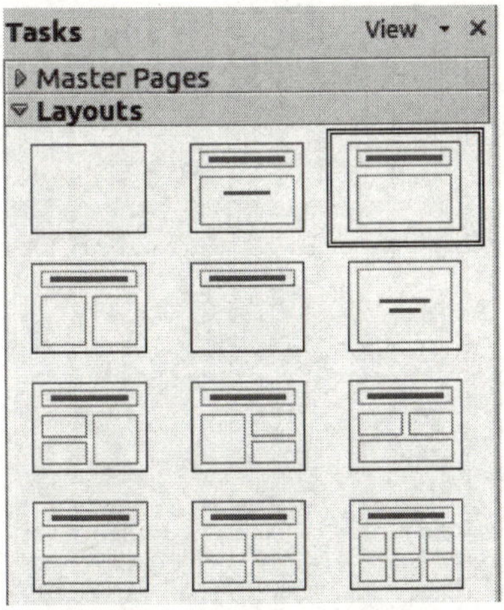

Figure 137: Available slide layouts

The first slide in a presentation is normally a title slide. You can use either a blank layout or one of the title layouts as your title slide.

To create a title, if one of the title layouts has been selected, click on *Click to add title* and then type the title text. To add a subtitle or text content, depending on the slide layout selected, click on *Click to add text* and type your subtitle or text. To adjust the formatting of the title, subtitle, or content, modify the presentation style; see the *Impress Guide Chapter 2 Using Slide Masters, Styles, and Templates* for more information.

Note	Text and graphic elements can be readjusted at any time during the preparation of the presentation, but changing the layout of a slide that already contains some contents can have an effect on the content format. Therefore, it is recommended that you pay particular attention to the layout you select to prevent any loss of content.

Tip	To view the names for the included layouts, use the Tooltip feature: position the cursor on an icon in the Layout section (or on any toolbar icon) and its name will be displayed in a small rectangle. If tooltips are not enabled, choose **Tools > Options > LibreOffice > General > Help** and select the **Tips** option. If the **Extended tips** option is also selected, you will get more detailed tooltip information, but the tooltip names themselves will not be provided.

To select or change the layout of a slide, select the slide in the Slides Pane so that it appears in the Workspace and select the desired layout from Layouts in the Tasks Pane. Several layouts contain one or more content boxes. Each of these content boxes can be configured to contain text, movies, pictures, charts or tables.

You can choose the type of contents by clicking on the corresponding icon that is displayed in the middle of the contents box as shown in Figure 138. If you intend to use the contents box for text, click on *Click to add text*.

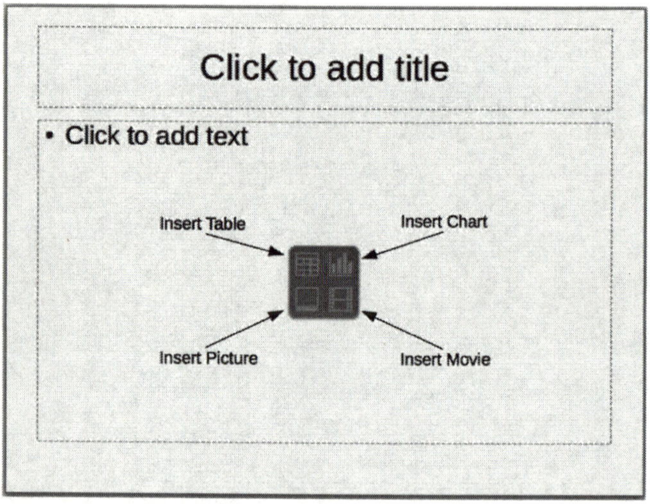

Figure 138: Selecting contents type

Modifying slide elements

A slide contains elements that were included in the slide master, as well as those elements included in the selected slide layout. However, it is unlikely that the predefined layouts will suit all your needs for your presentation. You may want to remove elements that are not required or insert objects such as text and graphics.

Although Impress does not have the functionality to create new layouts, it allows you to resize and move the layout elements. It is also possible to add elements without being limited to the size and position of the layout boxes.

To resize a contents box, click on the outer frame so that the resizing handles are displayed. To move it, place the mouse cursor on the frame so that the cursor changes shape. You can now click and drag the contents box to a new position on the slide.

To remove any unwanted elements:

1) Click the element to highlight it. The resizing handles show it is selected.
2) Press the *Delete* key to remove it.

Caution	Changes to any of the layouts included in Impress can only be made using **View > Normal**, which is the default. Attempting any changes by modifying a slide master, although possible, may result in unpredictable results and requires extra care as well as a certain amount of trial and error.

Adding text

To add text to a slide that contains a text frame, click on *Click to add text* in the text frame and then type your text. The Outline styles are automatically applied to the text as you insert it. You can change the outline level of each paragraph as well as its position within the text by using the arrow buttons on the *Text Formatting* toolbar (see Figure 128 and "Outline view" on page 156). For more information on text, see "Adding and formatting text" on page 166.

Adding objects

To add any objects to a slide, for example a picture, clipart, drawing, photograph, or spreadsheet, click on **Insert** then select from the drop down menu what type of insert you require. For more information, see "Adding pictures, tables, charts and media" on page 170.

Modifying appearance of all slides

To change the background and other characteristics of all slides in the presentation, you need to modify the master page or choose a different master page as explained in "Working with slide masters and styles" on page 173.

A *Slide Master* is a slide with a specified set of characteristics that acts as a template and is used as the starting point for creating other slides. These characteristics include slide background, objects in the background, formatting of any text used, and any background graphics.

Note	LibreOffice uses three interchangeable terms for this one concept: *Master slide*, *slide master*, and *master page.* These terms all refer to a slide that is used to create other slides. This guide, however, uses only the term *slide master,* except when describing the user interface.

Impress has a range of slide masters and these are found in the **Master Pages** section of the Tasks Pane. You can also create and save additional slide masters or add more from other sources. See the *Impress Guide Chapter 2 Using Slide Masters, Styles, and Templates* for more information on creating and modifying slide masters.

If all you need to do is to change the background, you can use a shortcut:

1) Select **Format > Page** and go to the *Background* tab on the **Page Setup** dialog that opens.
2) Select the desired background between solid color, gradient, hatching and bitmap.
3) Click **OK** to apply it.

A dialog will open asking if the background should be applied to all the slides. If you click **Yes**, Impress will automatically modify the master page for you.

Note	Inserting and correctly formatting a background is beyond the scope of this chapter, but you can find all the information you need in the *Draw Guide Chapter 4 Changing Object Attributes* or in the *Impress Guide Chapter 6 Formatting Graphic Objects*.

Modifying the slide show

By default the slide show will display all the slides in the same order as they appear in the slide sorter, without any transition between slides. You need to use keyboard input or mouse interaction to move from one slide to the next.

You can use **Slide Show** on the main menu bar to change the order of the slides, choose which ones are shown, automate moving from one slide to the next, and other settings. To change the slide transition, animate slides, add a soundtrack to the presentation, and make other enhancements, you need to use functions in the Tasks Pane. See the *Impress Guide* for details on how to use all of these features.

Adding and formatting text

Many of your slides are likely to contain some text. This section gives you some guidelines on how to add text and how to change its appearance. Text used in slides is contained in *text boxes*. For more information on adding and formatting text, see the *Impress Guide Chapter 3 Adding and Formatting Text* .

There are two types of text boxes that you can add to a slide:

- Choose a predefined layout from the *Layouts* section of the Tasks pane and do not select any special contents type. These text boxes are called **AutoLayout** text boxes.
- Create a text box using the **Text** icon on the Drawing toolbar (Figure 139) or the Text toolbar (Figure 140), or use the keyboard shortcut *F2*.

Figure 139: Drawing toolbar

Figure 140: Text toolbar

Using AutoLayout text boxes

1) Make sure Normal view is selected.
2) Click in the text box that reads **Click to add text**.
3) Type or paste your text in the text box.

Using text boxes

1) Make sure Normal view is selected.
2) Click on the **Text** icon on the Drawing or Text toolbar or use the keyboard shortcut *F2*. If the Drawing or Text toolbar is not visible, go to **View > Toolbars** on the main menu bar and select **Drawing** or **Text**.
3) Click and drag to draw a box for the text on the slide. Do not worry about the vertical size and position as the text box will expand if needed as you type.
4) Release the mouse button when finished. The cursor appears in the text box, which is now in edit mode (a hashed border shown in Figure 141).

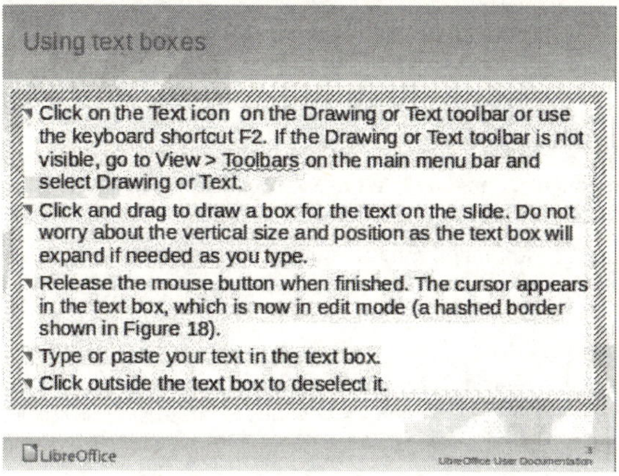

Figure 141: Creating and editing text boxes

5) Type or paste your text in the text box.
6) Click outside the text box to deselect it.

You can move, resize, and delete text boxes. For more information, see the *Impress Guide Chapter 3 Adding and Formatting Text*.

Vertical text

In addition to the normal text boxes where text is horizontally aligned, it is possible to insert text boxes where the text is aligned vertically. Vertical text is available only when Asian languages are enabled in **Tools > Options > Language Settings > Languages**. Click the **Vertical Text** icon in the Drawing toolbar or Text toolbar to create a vertical text box.

Quick font resizing

Impress has an **Increase Font** icon and a **Decrease Font** icon on the Text Formatting toolbar (highlighted in Figure 142) to increase or decrease font size of selected text. The amount by which the font size changes depends on the standard sizes available for the font in use.

Figure 142: Quick font resizing on Text Formatting toolbar

Pasting text

Text may be inserted into the text box by copying it from another document and pasting it into Impress. However, pasted text will probably not match the formatting of the surrounding text on the slide or that of the other slides in the presentation. This may be what you want on some occasions; however, in most cases you want to make sure that the presentation style is consistent and does not become a patchwork of different paragraph styles, font types, bullet points and so on. There are several ways to ensure consistency in your presentation.

Pasting unformatted text

It is normally good practice to paste text without formatting and apply the formatting later. To paste text without formatting:

- Use the keyboard shortcut *Ctrl+Shift+V* and select **Unformatted text** from the Paste Special dialog that opens.
- Or, click on the small triangle next to the **Paste** icon in the Standard toolbar and select **Unformatted text** from the context menu.

The unformatted text will be formatted with the outline or paragraph style at the cursor position in an AutoLayout text box or with the default graphic style in a normal text box.

Formatting pasted text

If you are pasting the text into an **AutoLayout** text box, you need to apply the appropriate *outline style* to the text to give it the same look and feel as the rest of the presentation.

1) Paste the text in the desired position.
2) Select the text you have just pasted.
3) Select **Format > Default formatting** on the main menu bar.
4) Use the four arrow buttons on the Text Formatting toolbar (highlighted in Figure 128) to move the text to the appropriate position and give it the appropriate outline level.
   - Left arrow promotes the list entry by one level (for example from Outline 3 to Outline 2).
   - Right arrow button demotes the list entry by one level.
   - Up arrow moves the list entry up in the list order.
   - Down arrow moves the list entry down in the list order.
5) Apply any necessary manual formatting to the text to change font attributes, tabs, and so on.

If you are pasting text in a **text box**, you can still use styles to quickly format the text. Only one graphic style can be applied to the pasted text as follows:

1) Paste the text in the desired position.
2) Select the text you have just pasted.
3) Select the desired graphic style to format the text.
4) Apply any necessary manual formatting to the text to change font attributes, tabs, and so on.

Creating bulleted and numbered lists

The procedure to create a bulleted or numbered list is quite different depending on the type of text box used, although the tools to manage the list and customize the appearance are the same. In AutoLayout text boxes, the outline styles available are, by default, bulleted lists. For normal text boxes an additional step is required to create a bulleted list.

AutoLayout text boxes

AutoLayout text boxes included in the available layouts are already formatted as a bulleted list. Create a bulleted list as follows:

1) From the Layout pane, choose a slide design that contains a text box.
2) In the text box, click on **Click to add text.**
3) Type your text and press the *Enter* key to start a new bulleted point.
4) The default list type is a bulleted list. Methods for changing the appearance of a list are explained in “Changing list appearance” on page 169.

Tip	Press *Shift+Enter* to start a new line without creating a new bullet point. The new line will have the same indentation as the previous line. To switch off bullets altogether, click the **Bullets On/Off** icon on the Text Formatting toolbar. If the Text Formatting toolbar is not displayed, go to **View > Toolbar > Text Formatting** on the main menu bar.

Text boxes

Create a bulleted list in a text box as follows:

1) Click the **Text** icon on the Drawing toolbar and draw a text box on your slide.
2) Click the **Bullets On/Off** icon on the Text Formatting toolbar.
3) Type the text and press *Enter* to start a new bulleted line.

The default list type is a bulleted list. Methods for changing the appearance of a list are explained in "Changing list appearance" below.

Creating a new outline level

In AutoLayout text boxes, a new outline level is created as follows:

1) If necessary, press *Enter* to begin a new list entry.
2) To demote a list entry (move it to the right). press the *Tab* key, or click the Demote (right arrow) icon on the Text Formatting toolbar or use the keyboard shortcut *Alt+Shift+Right*. The list entry moves to the right and is indented to the next outline level.

   Pressing *Enter* again creates a new list entry at the same level as the previous one.
3) To promote a list entry (move it to the left), press *Shift+Tab* or click the Promote (left arrow) icon on the Text Formatting toolbar or use the keyboard shortcut *Alt+Shift+Left*. The list entry moves to the left and is indented at the next higher level.

   Pressing *Enter* again creates a new list entry at the same level as the previous one.

In the AutoLayout text boxes, promoting or demoting an item in the list corresponds to applying a different outline style. The second outline level corresponds to Outline 2 style, the third outline level to Outline 3 style, and so on. With a change in level and style produces other changes, for example, to font size, bullet type, and so on.

In text boxes, a new outline level can only be created using the *Tab* key to demote the list entry and the *Shift+Tab* key combination to promote the list entry.

Note	Do not try to change the outline level by selecting the text and then clicking the desired outline style as you would in Writer. Due to the way that presentation styles work in Impress, it is not possible to change the level in this way.

Changing list appearance

You can fully customize list appearance by changing the bullet type or numbering for the entire list or for only a single entry. All of the changes can be made using the Bullets and Numbering dialog (Figure 143), which is accessed by going to **Format > Bullets and Numbering** on the main menu bar or by clicking on the **Bullets and Numbering** icon on the Text Formatting toolbar.

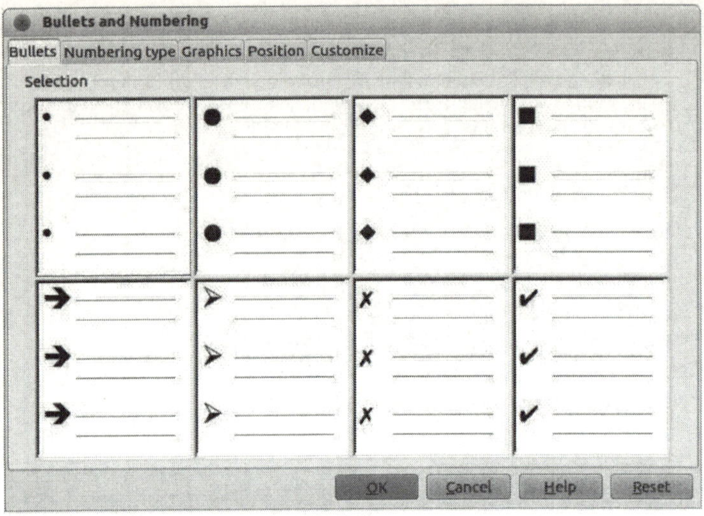

Figure 143: Bullets and Numbering dialog

For the entire list:

1) Select the entire list or click on the border of the text box so that the resizing handles are displayed.
2) Select **Format > Bullets and Numbering** on the main menu bar or click on the **Bullets and Numbering** icon  on the Text Formatting toolbar.
3) The Bullets and Numbering dialog (Figure 143) contains five pages: Bullets, Numbering type, Graphics, Position, and Customize.
   a) If a bullet list is needed, select the desired bullet style from the default styles available on the *Bullets* page.
   b) If a graphics style is needed, select one from those available on the *Graphics* page.
   c) If a numbered list is needed, select one of the default numbering styles on the *Numbering type* page.
   d) The *Position* page allows you to set the indent and numbering spacing and alignment of your list.
   e) The *Customize* page allows you to customize the numbering, color, relative size and character used for your list.

For a single list entry, click anywhere in the text and then follow steps 2 and 3 above.

If the list was created in an AutoLayout text box, then an alternative way to change the entire list is to modify the Outline styles. Changes made to the outline style will apply to all the slides using them.

Adding pictures, tables, charts and media

A contents box can also contain pictures, tables, charts or media as well as text and this section provides a quick overview of how to work with these objects. For more information on adding pictures, tables, charts or media, please refer to the *Impress Guide*.

Adding pictures

To add a picture to a contents box:

1) Go to **Insert > Picture** on the main menu bar and then select either **From file** or **Scan**.

   Alternatively, after inserting a new slide, click the **Insert Picture** icon (Figure 138 on page 164) on the new slide and select the file from the Insert Picture dialog that opens. To see a preview of the picture, check **Preview** at the bottom of the Insert Picture dialog.

2) Move the picture to the desired location.

The picture will automatically resize to fill the area of the contents box. Follow the directions in the note below when manually resizing a graphic.

Note	When resizing a graphic, right-click the picture. Select **Position and Size** from the context menu and make sure that **Keep ratio** is selected. Then adjust the height or width to the size you need. As you adjust one dimension. both dimensions will change to keep the width and height ratio the same. Failure to do so will cause the picture to become distorted. Remember also that resizing a bitmap image will reduce its quality; it is better to create an image of the desired size outside of Impress.

Adding tables

To add basic tables to a slide:

1) Go to **Insert > Table** on the main menu bar, or click the **Table** icon on the Standard toolbar.

2) If there is a table already on the slide and it is selected, click the **Table** icon on the Table toolbar. The Table toolbar is only visible after selecting **View > Toolbars > Table** on the main menu bar and when a table is selected.

   Alternatively, and after inserting a new slide into your presentation, click the **Insert Table** icon (Figure 138 on page 164).

3) Select the number of rows and columns required from the Insert Table dialog that opens.

   Alternatively, click the small triangle to the right of the the **Table** icon and select the number of rows and columns by dragging the cursor.

4) Click on the Table Design section in the Tasks Pane and select a design style from the available options.

   Alternatively, click on the **Table Design** icon on the Table toolbar to open the Table Design section on the Tasks Pane and then select a design style.

Note	Selecting from any of the styles in the Table Design section on the Tasks Pane creates a table based on that style. If you create a table by another method, you can still apply a style of your choice later.

The Table toolbar in Impress offers the same functions as the Table toolbar in Writer, with the exception of the calculation functions Sort and Sum. To use Sum and Sort in your presentation you have to insert a Calc spreadsheet.

After the table is created, you can modify it by adding and deleting rows and columns, adjusting width and spacing, adding borders, background colors and so on. For more information on working with tables see the *Impress Guide Chapter 3 Adding and Formatting Text* and the *Writer Guide Chapter 9 Working with Tables*.

Entering data into table cells is similar to working with text box objects. Click in the cell you wish to add data to and begin typing. To move around cells quickly, use the following keyboard options:

- Press the *arrow keys to* move the cursor to another cell if the cell is empty, or to the next character if the cell already contains text.
- Press the *Tab* key to move to the next cell on the right and press *Shift+Tab* to move to the next cell on the left..

Adding charts

To insert a chart in a slide:

1) Go to **Insert > Chart** on the main menu bar or click on the **Chart** icon in the Standard toolbar.

   Alternatively, and after inserting a new slide, click on the **Insert Chart** icon (Figure 138 on page 164).
2) Impress will insert a default chart and open the Chart dialog. To modify the chart type, insert your own data and change the formatting, refer to the *Impress Guide*.

Adding media files

To insert media files, such as music and movie clips, in a slide:

1) Go to **Insert > Movie and Sound** on the main menu bar.

   Alternatively, and after inserting a new slide, click on the **Insert Movie** icon (Figure 138 on page 164).
2) A media player will open at the bottom of the screen and you can preview the media.
3) When an audio file is inserted, the contents box will show a loudspeaker image.

Caution	In Linux-based systems such as Ubuntu, media files do not immediately work. You have to download the Java Media Framework API (JMF) and add the path `jmf.jar` to the Class Path in **Tools > Options > LibreOffice > Java**.

Adding graphics, spreadsheets, and other objects

Graphics, such as shapes, callouts, arrows, and so on, are often useful to complement the text on a slide. These objects are handled much the same way as graphics in Draw. For more information, see the *Draw Guide Chapter 7 Getting Started with Draw*, or the *Impress Guide Chapters 4, 5,* and *6*.

Spreadsheets embedded in Impress include most of the functionality of Calc spreadsheets and are capable of performing extremely complex calculations and data analysis. If you need to analyze your data or apply formulas, these operations are best performed in a Calc spreadsheet and the results displayed in an embedded Calc spreadsheet or even better in an Impress table.

Alternatively, go to **Insert > Object > OLE Object** on the main menu bar. This opens a spreadsheet in the middle of the slide and the menus and toolbars change to those used in Calc. You can start adding data, though you may have to resize the visible area on the slide. You can also insert an existing spreadsheet and use the viewport to select the data that you want to display on your slide.

Impress offers the capability of inserting into a slide various other types of objects such Writer documents, Math formulae, or another presentation. For details on using these objects, refer to the *Impress Guide Chapter 7 Including Spreadsheets, Charts, and Other Objects.*

Working with slide masters and styles

A slide master is a slide that is used as the starting point for other slides. It is similar to a page style in Writer and it controls the basic formatting of all slides based on it. A slide show can have more than one slide master.

Note	LibreOffice uses three terms for a slide that is used to create other slides: *master slide*, *slide master*, and *master page*. This book uses the term *slide master,* except when describing the user interface.

A slide master has a defined set of characteristics, including background colors, graphics, gradients; and other objects (such as logos, decorative lines and so on), headers and footers, placement and size of text frames, and text format.

Styles

All of the characteristics of slide masters are controlled by styles. New slides that you create using a slide master have styles that are inherited from the slide master from which was used. Changing a style in a slide master results in changes to all slides based on that slide master, but you can modify individual slides without affecting the slide master.

Note	Although it is highly recommended to use the slide masters whenever possible, there are occasions where manual changes are needed for a particular slide, for example to enlarge the chart area when the text and chart layout is used.

Slide masters have two types of styles associated with them: *presentation styles* and *graphic styles*. The prepackaged presentation styles can be modified, but new presentation styles cannot be created. For graphic styles, you can modify the prepackaged styles and also create new styles.

Presentation styles affect three elements of a slide master: background, background objects (such as icons, decorative lines, and text frames), and text placed on the slide. Text styles are further divided into *Notes*, *Outline 1* through *Outline 9*, *Subtitle*, and *Title*. The outline styles are used for the different levels of the outline to which they belong. For example, Outline 2 is used for the sub-points of Outline 1, and Outline 3 is used for the sub-points of Outline 2, and so on.

Graphic styles are not restricted and can affect many of the elements of a slide. Note that text styles exist in both the presentation and graphic style selections.

Slide masters

Impress comes with a collection of slide masters. These slide masters are shown in the Master Pages section of the Tasks Pane (Figure 144) and has three subsections: *Used in This Presentation*, *Recently Used*, and *Available for Use*. Click the + sign next to the name of a subsection to expand it to show thumbnails of the slides, or click the – sign to collapse the subsection to hide the thumbnails.

Each of the slide masters shown in the *Available for Use* list is from a template of the same name. If you have created your own templates, or added templates from other sources, slide masters from those templates will also appear in this list.

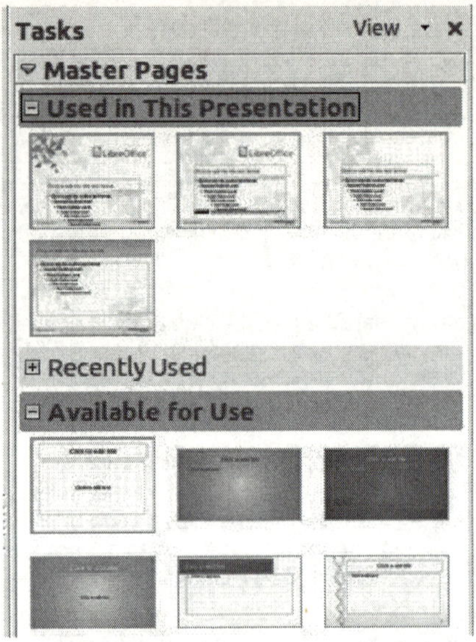

Figure 144: Slide (page) masters in Tasks Pane

Figure 145: Master View toolbar

Creating a slide master

Creating a new slide master is similar to modifying the default slide master.

1) Enable editing of slide masters by selecting **View > Master > Slide Master** on the main menu bar and the **Master View** toolbar opens (Figure 145). If the Master View toolbar does not appear, go to **View > Toolbars** and select **Master View**.

   Alternatively, right-click on a slide master in the Master Pages section of the tasks pane that you want to use and select **Edit Master** to open the Master View toolbar.

2) On the Master View toolbar, click the **New Master** icon .
3) A new slide master appears in the Slides pane. Modify this slide master to suit your requirements.
4) It is also recommended that you rename this new slide master. Right-click on the slide in the Slides pane and select **Rename master** from the context menu.
5) When finished creating a slide master, click **Close Master View** on the Master View toolbar and return to normal slide editing mode.

Applying a slide master

To apply a slide master to all the slides in your presentation:

1) In the Tasks Pane, make sure the Master Pages section is showing (Figure 144).

2) To apply one of the slide masters to *all slides* in your presentation, right-click on it from the available selection and select **Apply to All Slides** on the context menu.

To apply a different slide master to one or more selected slides:

1) In the Slide Pane, select the slide or slides where you want to use a new slide master.
2) In the Tasks Pane, right-click on the slide master you want to apply to the selected slides, and select **Apply to Selected Slides** on the context menu.

Loading additional slide masters

Sometimes, in the same set of slides, you may need to mix multiple slide masters that may belong to different templates. For example, you may need a completely different layout for the first slide of the presentation, or you may want to add to your presentation a slide from a different presentation (based on a template available on the hard disk).

1) Go to **Format > Slide Design** on the main menu bar or right-click on a slide in the Slides Pane and select **Slide Design** from the context menu to open the Slide Design dialog (Figure 146). This dialog shows the slide masters already available for use.
2) To add more slide masters, click the **Load** button to open the Load Slide Design dialog (Figure 147).
3) Select in the Load Slide Design dialog the template from which to load the slide master and click **OK.**
4) Click **OK** again to close the Slide Design dialog.
5) The slide masters in the template you selected to use are now shown in the *Available for use* subsection of Master Pages.

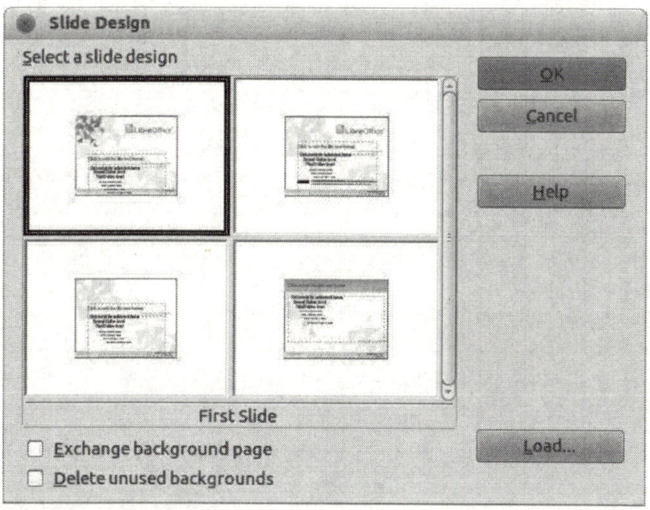

Figure 146: Slide Design

Note	The slide masters you have loaded will also be available the next time you load the presentation. If you want to delete the unused slide masters, click the corresponding checkbox in the Slide Design dialog. If the slide master was not used in the presentation, it is removed from the list of available slide masters.

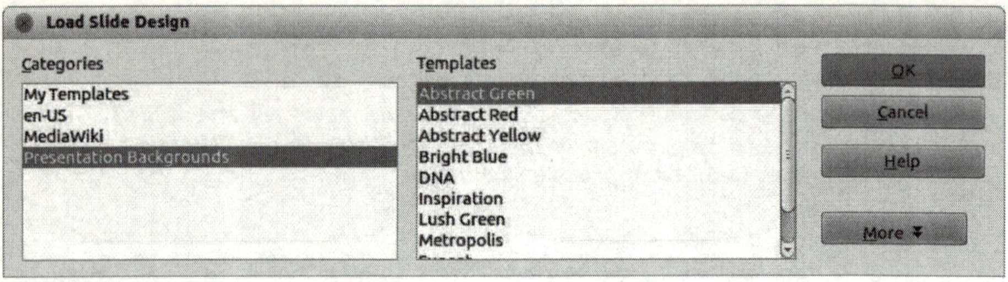

Figure 147: Load Slide Design dialog

Tip	To limit the size of the presentation file, you may want to minimize the number of slide masters used.

Modifying a slide master

The following items can be changed on a slide master:

- Background (color, gradient, hatching, or bitmap)
- Background objects (for example, a logo or decorative graphics)
- Size, placement, and contents of header and footer elements to appear on every slide
- Size and placement of default frames for slide titles and content

Before working on the slide master, make sure that the Styles and Formatting dialog is open.

To select the slide master for modification. For more information on modifying slide masters, see the *Impress Guide Chapter 2 Using Slide Masters, Styles, and Templates*.

1) Select **View > Master > Slide Master** from the menu bar. This unlocks the properties of a slide master so you can edit it.
2) Select a slide master in *Master Pages* in the Tasks pane.
3) Right-click on the slide master you want to modify and select **Edit Master** from the context menu.
4) Make changes as required to the slide master, then click the **Close Master View** icon on the Master View toolbar or go to **View > Normal** on the main menu bar to exit from editing slide masters.
5) Save your presentation file before continuing.

Caution	Any changes made to one slide when in Master View mode will appear on *all* slides using this slide master. Always make sure you Close Master View and return to Normal view before working on any of the presentation slides.

Note	The changes made to one of the slides in Normal view (for example, changes to the bullet point style, the color of the title area, and so on) will not be overridden by subsequent changes to the slide master. There are cases, however, where it is desirable to revert a manually modified element of the slide to the style defined in the slide master. To revert back to default formatting, select the element and select **Format > Default Formatting** from the main menu bar.

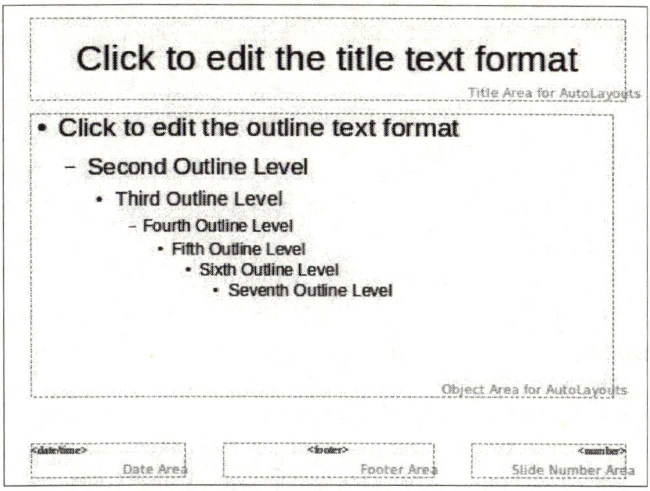

Figure 148: Example master view

Adding text, footers, and fields to all slides

A slide master can have text, footers, or fields added so that they appear on every slide in your presentation. Due to the layout of slides in Impress, headers are not normally added to slides.

Text

1) Go to **View > Master > Slide Master** on the main menu bar to open Master View (Figure 148).
2) On the Drawing toolbar, select the **Text** icon or press the *F2* key.
3) Click and drag in the master page to draw a text object and then type or paste your text into the text object.
4) Go to **View > Normal** on the main menu bar or click on **Close Master View** on the Master View toolbar when you are finished entering text objects that you want to appear on every slide in your presentation.

Footers

To add a footer to your slides:

1) Go to **View > Master > Slide Master** on the main menu bar to open Master View (Figure 148).
2) Go to **Insert > Date** or **Insert > Page Number** on the main menu bar and time to open the Header and Footer dialog (Figure 149).
3) Select the type of date and time, type in the footer text and slide number from the available options in the dialog.
4) Click **Apply to All** to apply your changes to all the slides in your presentation, or click **Apply** to apply your changes to the selected slide in your presentation.

   Alternatively, you can add the date/time, footer text and slide number directly into their respective areas as shown in Figure 148.

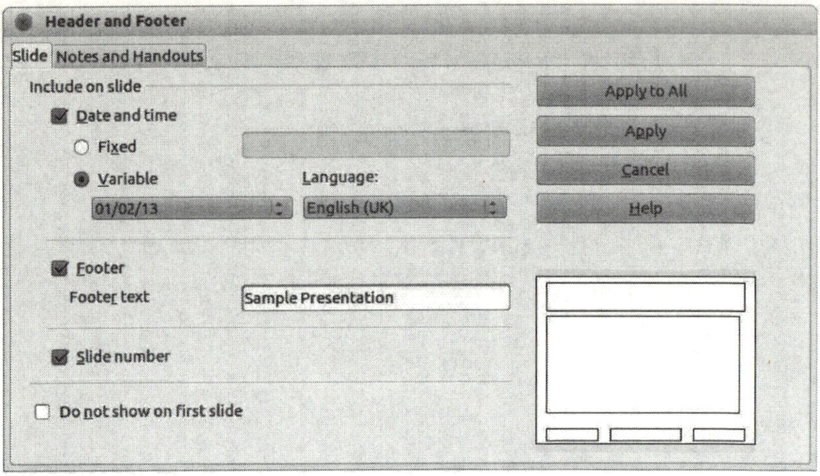

Figure 149: Header and Footer dialog in Impress

Note	Normally only footers are used on a slide. To create a header, you can use a text box as explained in "Text" on page 177.

Fields

To add a field into an object or as a separate object on a slide, select **Insert > Fields** on the main menu bar and select the required field from the submenu. If you want to edit this field in your slide, see the *Impress Guide Chapter 3 Adding and Formatting Text* for more information.

The fields you can use in Impress are as follows:

- Date (fixed)
- Date (variable): updates automatically when you reload a file
- Time (fixed)
- Time (variable): updates automatically when you reload a file
- Author: first and last names listed in the LibreOffice user data
- Page Number: this is the slide number in Impress.
- Page Count: this is the number of slides in your presentation.
- File Name

Tip	To change the author information, go to **Tools > Options > LibreOffice > User Data** on the main menu bar. To change the number format (1,2,3 or a,b,c or i,ii,iii, and so on) for the number field, go to **Format > Page** on the main menu bar and then select a format from the *Format* list in the **Layout Settings** area. To change a paragraph style throughout your presentation, open the Styles and Formatting dialog and modify the appropriate presentation style.

Adding comments to a presentation

Impress supports comments similar to those in Writer and Calc.

In Normal View, go to **Insert > Comment** on the main menu bar to open a blank comment (Figure 150). A small box containing your initials appears in the upper left-hand corner of the slide, with a larger text box beside it. Impress automatically adds your name and the current date at the bottom of the text box.

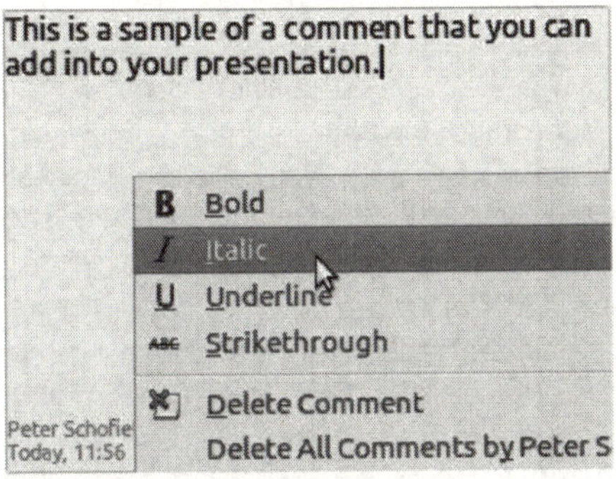

Figure 150: Inserting comments

Type or paste your comment into the text box. You can optionally apply some basic formatting to the comment by selecting it, right-clicking, and choosing from the context menu that opens. This menu allows you to apply formatting to selected text, delete the current comment, delete all comments from the same author, or delete all comments in the presentation.

You can move the small comment markers to anywhere you wish on the slide. Typically you might place it on or near an object you refer to in the comment.

To show or hide the comment markers, choose **View > Comments**.

Select **Tools > Options > User Data** to configure the name you want to appear in the comment.

If more than one person edits the document, each author is automatically allocated a different background color for their comments.

Setting up a slide show

As mentioned in “Modifying the slide show” on page 166, Impress allocates reasonable default settings for slide shows, while at the same time allowing you to customize many aspects of the slide show experience. This section covers only some aspects and more advanced techniques are explained in the *Impress Guide Chapter 9 Slide Shows*.

Most of the tasks are best done in Slide Sorter view where you can see most of the slides simultaneously. Go to **View > Slide Sorter** on the main menu bar or click the Slide Sorter tab at the top of the Workspace.

One slide set – multiple presentations

In many situations, you may find that you have more slides than the time available to present them or you may want to provide a rapid overview without dwelling on the details. Rather than having to create a new presentation, you can use two tools that Impress offers: hiding slides and custom slide shows.

Hiding slides

1) Select the slide you want to hide in the Slide Pane or Slide Sorter view on the Workspace area.
2) Go to **Slide Show > Hide Slide** on the main menu bar or right-click on the slide thumbnail and select **Hide Slide** from the context menu. Hidden slides are marked by a diagonal bars across the slide.

Custom slide shows

If you want to create a custom slide show from the same presentation:

1) Select the slides you want to use in your custom slide show.
2) Go to **Slide Show > Custom Slide Show** on the main menu bar.
3) Click on the **New** button to create a new sequence of slides and save it with a different name. You can have as many slide shows as you want from a single presentation.

Slide transitions

Slide transition is the animation that is played when a slide is changed for the next slide in your presentation. You can configure the slide transition from the Slide Transition section in the Tasks Pane.

1) Select the desired transition, the speed of the animation, and whether the transition should happen when you click the mouse (preferred) or automatically after a certain number of seconds.
2) Click **Apply to All Slides** to apply the transition for all of your presentation or continue selecting transitions to place between each slide in your presentation.

Tip	The Slide Transition section has a very useful choice: *Automatic preview*. Select its checkbox and when you make any changes in a slide transition, the new slide is previewed in the Slide Design area, including its transition effect.

Slide advance

You can set the presentation to automatically advance to the next slide after a set amount of time from the Slide Transition section in the Task pane.

1) Go to **Advance slide** and select the **Automatically after** option.
2) Enter the required amount of time in seconds that each slide will be displayed.
3) Click on the **Apply to All Slides** button to apply the same display time to all slides.

To apply a different display time to each slide in your presentation:

1) Go to **Slide Show > Rehearse Timings** on the main menu bar and the slide show starts.
2) When you are ready to advance to the next slide, mouse click on the display background or press the right arrow or spacebar on your keyboard.
3) Impress will memorize the timings for each slide and advance to next the slide automatically using the timings when you run the slide show.

To automatically restart a slide show after the last slide has been displayed:

1) Go to **Slide Show > Slide Show Settings** on the main menu bar.
2) Select **Auto** and the timing of the pause between slide shows.
3) Click **OK** when you have finished.

Running a slide show

To run a slide show, do one of the following:

- Click **Slide Show > Slide Show** on the menu bar.
- Click the **Slide Show** icon on the Presentation toolbar.
- Press *F5* on the keyboard.

If the slide transition is *Automatic after x seconds*, let the slide show run by itself.

If the slide transition is *On mouse click*, do one of the following to move from one slide to the next:

- Use the arrow keys on the keyboard to go to the next slide or to go back to the previous one.
- Click the mouse to move to the next slide.
- Press the spacebar on the keyboard to advance to the next slide.

Right-click anywhere on the screen to open a context menu where you can navigate through the slides and set other options.

To exit the slide show at any time including when the slide show has ended, press the *Esc* key.

Using the Presenter Console

LibreOffice Impress has a Presenter Console function that can be used when an extra display for presentation has been connected to your computer. The Presenter Console (Figure 151) provides extra control over slide shows by using different views on your computer display and on the display that the audience sees. The view you see on your computer display includes the current slide, the upcoming slide, any slide notes, and a presentation timer.

For more information and details about using the Presenter Console, see the *Impress Guide Chapter 9 Slide Shows*.

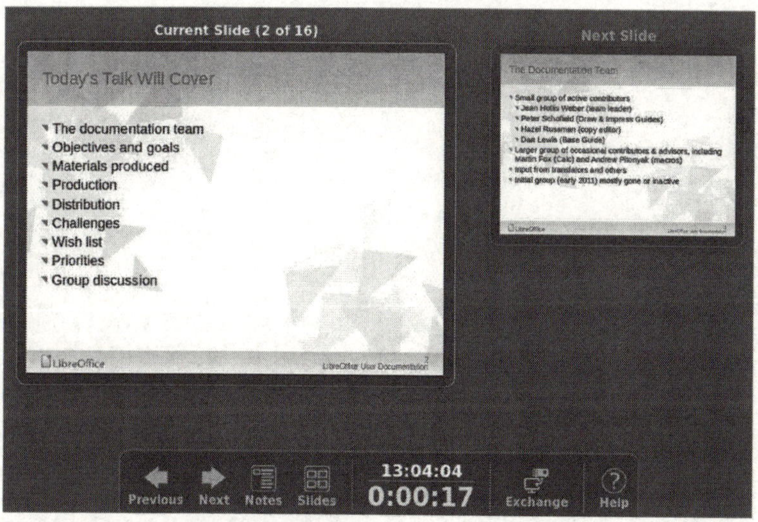

Figure 151: Impress Presenter Console

LibreOffice
The Document Foundation

Chapter 7
Getting Started with Draw

Vector Drawing in LibreOffice

What is Draw?

Draw is a vector graphics drawing program, although it can also perform some operations on raster graphics (pixels). Using Draw, you can quickly create a wide variety of graphical images.

Vector graphics store and display an image as simple geometric elements such as lines, circles, and polygons rather than a collections of pixels (points on the screen). Vector graphics allow for easier storage and scaling of the image.

Draw is fully integrated into the LibreOffice suite, and this simplifies exchanging graphics with all components of the suite. For example, if you create an image in Draw, reusing it in a Writer document is as simple as copying and pasting the image. You can also work with drawings directly from within Writer or Impress, using a subset of the functions and tools from Draw.

The functionality of LibreOffice Draw is extensive and, even though it was not designed to rival high-end graphics applications, it possesses more functionality than the drawing tools that are generally integrated with most office productivity suites.

A few examples of the drawing functions are: layer management, magnetic grid-point system, dimensions and measurement display, connectors for making organization charts, 3D functions that enable small three-dimensional drawings to be created (with texture and lighting effects), drawing and page-style integration, and Bézier curves.

This chapter introduces some features of Draw and does not attempt to cover all of the Draw features. See the *Draw Guide* and the application help for more information.

Draw workspace

The main components of the Draw workspace are shown in Figure 152.

The large area in the center of the window is where you make the drawings. You can surround the drawing area with toolbars and information areas. The number and position of the visible tools vary with the task in hand and user preferences. Therefore your setup may look different. For example, many users put the main Drawing toolbar on the left-hand side of the workspace and not at the bottom, as shown in Figure 152.

You can split drawings in Draw over several pages. Multi-page drawings are used mainly for presentations. The *Pages* pane, on the left side of the Draw window in Figure 152 gives an overview of the pages that you create. If the Pages pane is not visible on your setup, you can enable it from the View menu on the main menu bar (**View > Page Pane**). To make changes to the page order, just drag and drop one or more pages.

In LibreOffice Draw, the maximum size of a drawing page is 300 cm by 300 cm.

Rulers

You should see rulers (bars with numbers) on the upper and left-hand sides of the workspace. If they are not visible, you can enable them by selecting **View > Ruler** in the main menu bar. The rulers show the size of a selected object on the page using double lines (highlighted in Figure 153). When no object is selected, they show the location of the mouse pointer, which helps to position drawing objects more accurately.

You can also use the rulers to manage object handles and guide lines, making it easier to position objects.

The page margins in the drawing area are also represented on the rulers. You can change the margins directly on the rulers by dragging them with the mouse. The margin area is indicated by the grayed out area on the rulers as shown in Figure 153.

To change the measurement units of the rulers, which can be defined independently, right-click on a ruler, as illustrated for the horizontal ruler in Figure 154.

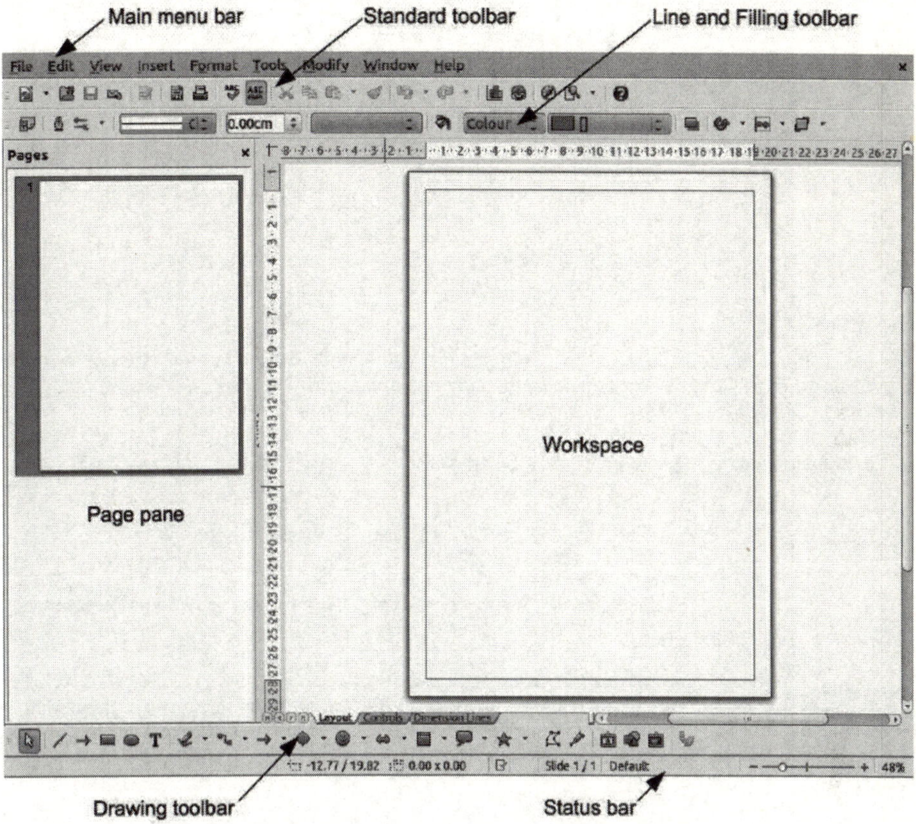

Figure 152: LibreOffice Draw workspace

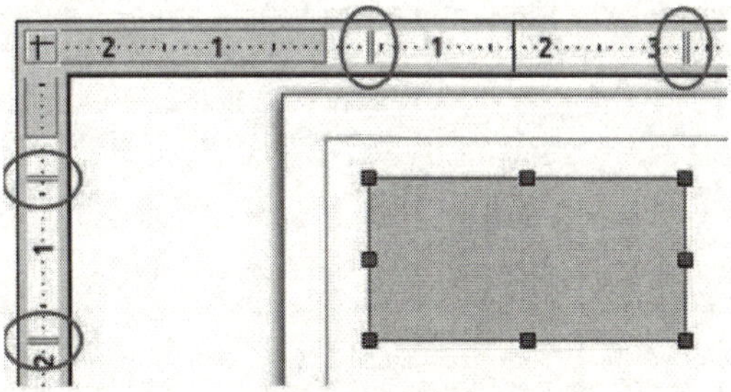

Figure 153: Rulers showing size of a selected object

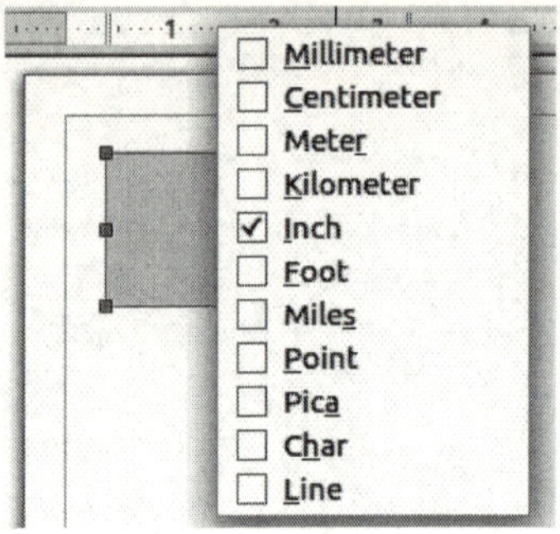

Figure 154: Ruler units

Status bar

The Status bar is located at the bottom of the screen in all LibreOffice components; it includes several Draw-specific fields. For details on the contents and use of these fields, see *Chapter 1 Introducing LibreOffice* in this guide and in the *Draw Guide Chapter 1 Introducing Draw*.

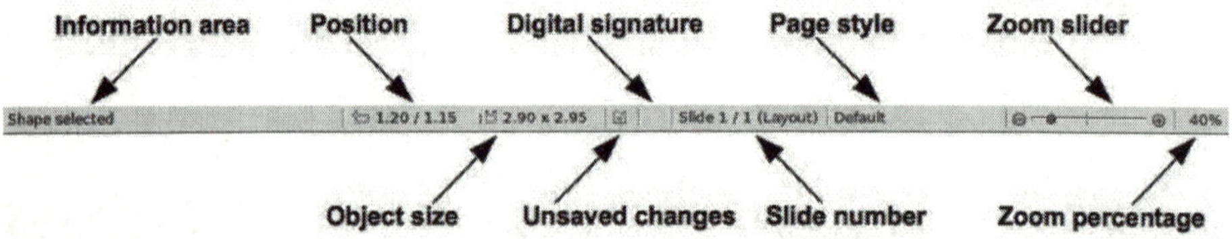

Figure 155: Draw status bar

Note	The sizes are given in the current measurement unit and are not to be confused with the ruler units. This current measurement unit is defined in **Tools > Options > LibreOffice Draw > General**, where you can also change the scale of the page.

Toolbars

To display or hide the various Draw toolbars. choose **View > Toolbars**. On the menu that appears, select which toolbars you want to display. For more about working with toolbars, see *Chapter 1 Introducing LibreOffice* in this guide.

The tools available in the Draw toolbars are explained in the following sections. The appearance of the toolbar icons may vary depending on your operating system and the selection of icon size and style in **Tools > Options > LibreOffice > View**.

Standard toolbar

The **Standard** toolbar is the same for all LibreOffice components and is not described in detail in this chapter.

Figure 156: Standard toolbar

Drawing toolbar

The **Drawing** toolbar is the most important toolbar in Draw. It contains all the necessary functions for drawing various geometric and freehand shapes and for organizing them on the page.

Figure 157: Drawing toolbar

Line and Filling toolbar

The **Line and Filling** toolbar lets you modify the main properties of a drawing object. The icons and pull-down lists vary, according to the type of object selected. For example, to change the style of a line, click on the up and down arrows for Line Style and select the required style.

Figure 158: Line and Filling toolbar

Text Formatting toolbar

If the selected object is text, the Line and Filling toolbar changes to the **Text Formatting** toolbar, which is similar to the Formatting toolbar in Writer. For more information, see *Chapter 4 Getting Started with Writer* in this guide.

Figure 159: Text Formatting toolbar

Options toolbar

Use the **Options** toolbar to activate or deactivate various drawing aids. The Options toolbar is not one of the toolbars displayed by default. To display the Options toolbar, select **View > Toolbars > Options**.

Figure 160: Options toolbar

Choosing and defining colors

To display the **Color bar**, select **View > Toolbars > Color Bar**. The toolbar appears at the bottom of the workspace and displays the current color palette. This toolbar lets you rapidly choose the color of the various objects (lines, areas, and 3D effects). The first box in the panel corresponds to invisible (no color).

Figure 161: Color bar

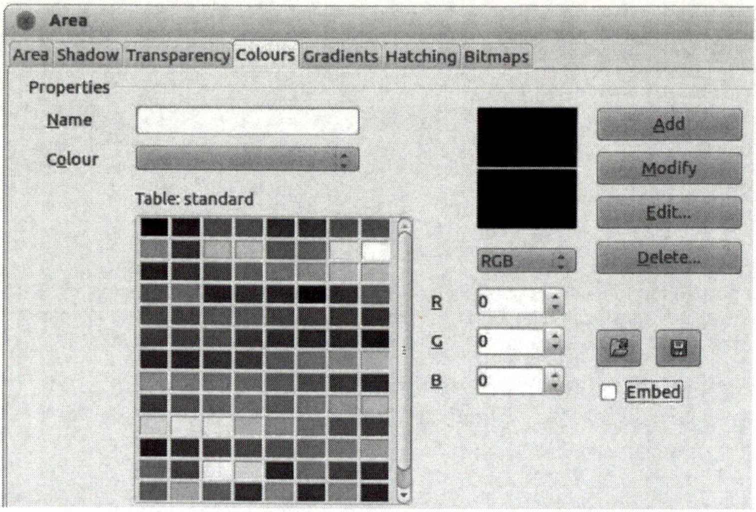

Figure 162. Changing the color palette

You can access several specialized color palettes in Draw, as well as change individual colors to your own taste. This is done using the Area dialog by selecting **Format > Area** on the main menu bar or clicking the *Area* icon  on the Line and Filling toolbar, then selecting the **Colors** tab (Figure 162).

To load another palette, click on the **Load Color List** icon . The file selector dialog asks you to choose one of the standard LibreOffice palettes (files with the file extension `*.soc`). For example, `web.soc` is a color palette that is adapted to creating drawings for placing in web pages. These colors will display correctly on workstations with screens capable of at least 256 colors.

The color selection box also lets you individually change any color by modifying the numerical values in the fields provided to the right of the color palette. You can use the color schemes known as CMYK (Cyan, Magenta, Yellow, Black) or RGB (Red, Green, Blue).

Click on the **Edit** button to open the Color dialog, where you can set individual colors. See "Color options" in *Chapter 2 Setting Up LibreOffice* in this guide.

For a more detailed description of color palettes and their options, see the *Draw Guide Chapter 10 Advanced Draw Techniques*.

Drawing basic shapes

Draw provides a wide range of shapes, located in palettes accessed from the Drawing toolbar (Figure 157) and a full list of these various tools is shown in Figure 163. The icons or buttons that already installed on the Drawing toolbar are highlighted in Figure 163. This may differ from the tools that are installed on your Drawing toolbar.

This section describes only a few of the basic shapes, which are treated as objects in Draw, including text. See the *Draw Guide* for a complete description of the shapes available.

Please note that some of the icons on the Drawing toolbar will change according to the shape that has been selected from the choice available. Icons with tool palettes available are indicated by a small triangle to the right of the icon.

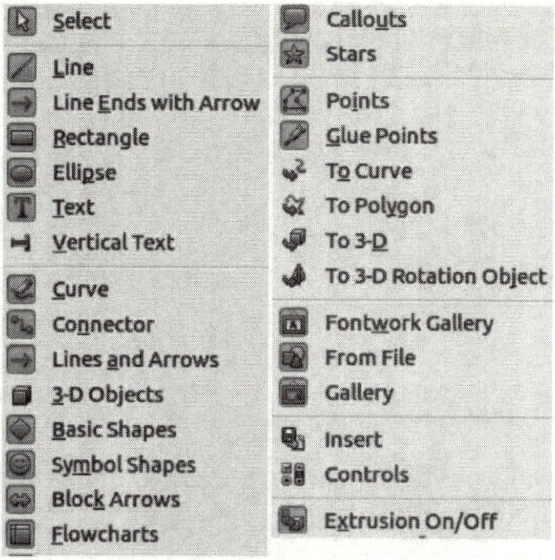

Figure 163: Tools available for Drawing toolbar

Note	When you draw a basic shape or select one for editing, the *Info* field at the left side in the status bar changes to reflect the present action: for example *Line created*, *Text frame xxyy selected*, and so on.

Drawing a straight line

Click on the **Line** icon  and place the mouse pointer at the point where you want to start the line (Figure 164). Drag the mouse while keeping the mouse button pressed. Release the mouse button at the point where you want to end the line. A selection handle appears at each end of the line, showing that this object is the currently selected object. The selection handle at the starting point of the line is slightly larger than the other selection handle.

Keeping the *Shift* key pressed while you draw a line restricts the drawing angle of the line to a multiple of 45 degrees (0, 45, 90, 135, and so on).

Note	This is the default behavior of the *Shift* key. However, if the option *When creating or moving objects* in the *Snap position* section of **Tools > Options > LibreOffice Draw > Grid** has been selected, the action of the *Shift* key is the opposite. Lines will automatically be drawn at a multiple of 45 degrees *unless* the *Shift* key is pressed.

Keeping the *Ctrl* key pressed while drawing a line enables the end of the line to snap to the nearest grid point.

Note	This is the default behavior of the *Ctrl* key. However, if the **Snap to Grid** option on the **View > Grid** menu has been selected, the *Ctrl* key deactivates the snap to grid activity.

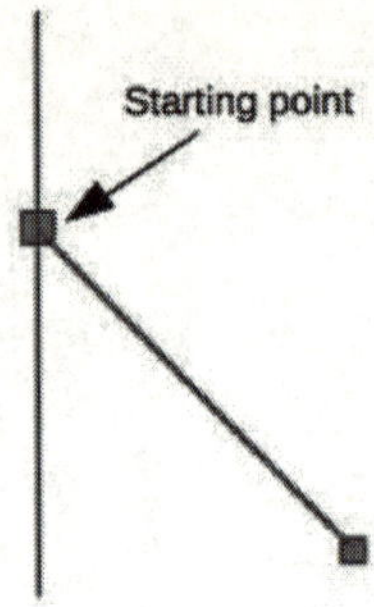

Figure 164: Drawing a straight line

Holding down the *Alt* key while drawing a line results in the line extending outwards symmetrically in both directions from the start point. This lets you draw lines by starting from the middle of the line.

When a line is drawn, it uses default attributes. To change any of these attributes, select the line by clicking on it, then *right-click* and select **Line** from the context menu or got to **Format > Line** on the main menu bar to open the **Line** dialog (Figure 165). Line style, line width and line color can also be changed using the controls in the Line and Filling toolbar at the top of the workspace.

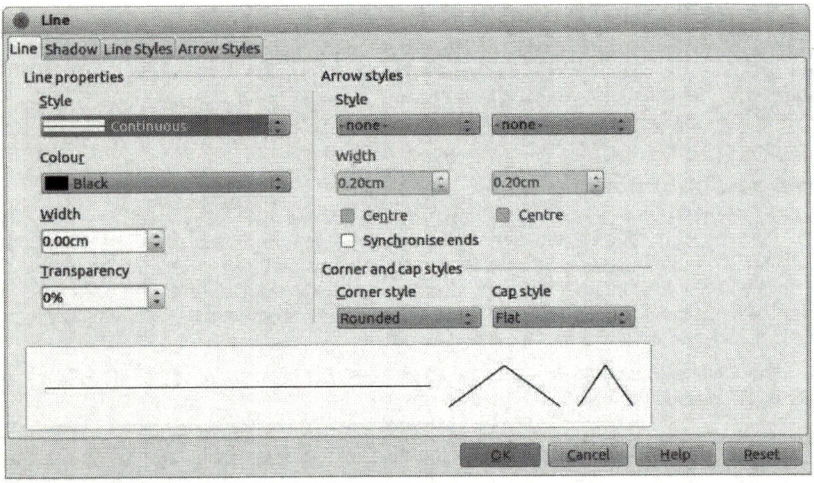

Figure 165: Line dialog

Drawing an arrow

Arrows are drawn like lines. In fact Draw classifies *arrows* as a subgroup of lines: lines with arrowheads. The information field on the status bar shows them only as lines. Click on the **Line Ends with Arrow** icon to draw an arrow. The arrow head is drawn at the end point of the arrow when you release the mouse button.

Choosing line endings

Several types of line endings (arrows, circles, squares, and others) are available in Draw. Click on the small triangle to the right of the **Lines and Arrows** icon on the Drawing toolbar to open a tool palette containing tools for drawing lines and arrows. Alternatively, go to **View > Toolbars > Arrows** to open the Arrows toolbar as a floating toolbar (Figure 166). The icon for the tool used most recently will be shown on the Drawing toolbar to make it easier to use the same tool again.

After drawing the line, you can change the arrow style by clicking on the **Arrowheads** icon in the Line and Filling toolbar and select the arrow start and end options.

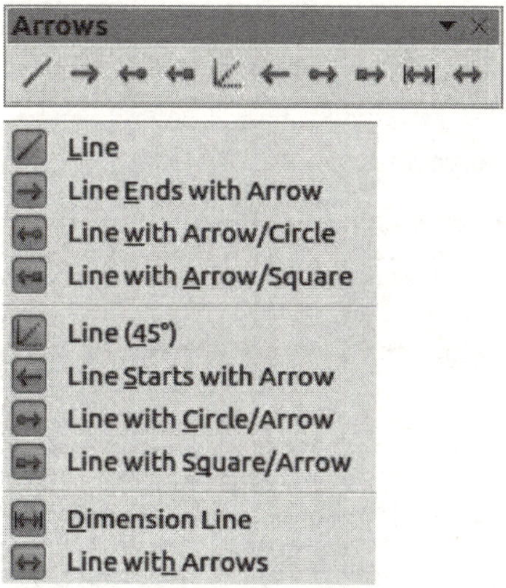

Figure 166: Arrows toolbar and available tools

Drawing rectangles or squares

Drawing a rectangle is similar to drawing a straight line. Click on the **Rectangle** icon in the Drawing toolbar. As you draw the rectangle with the mouse cursor, the rectangle appears with the bottom right corner of the rectangle attached to the cursor.

Squares are rectangles with all sides of equal length. To draw a square, click on the **Rectangle** icon and hold down the *Shift* key whilst you draw a square.

Note	If the option *When creating or moving objects* has been selected in **Tools > Options > LibreOffice Draw > General**, the action of the *Shift* key is reversed. When the Rectangle tool is selected, a square is drawn. To draw a rectangle, you have to press the *Shift* key when drawing. This *Shift* key reversal also applies when drawing ellipses and circles.

To draw a rectangle or square from its center rather than the bottom right corner, position your cursor on the drawing, press the mouse button and then hold down the *Alt* key while dragging with the cursor. The rectangle or square uses the start point (where you first clicked the mouse button) as the center.

Drawing circles or ellipses

To draw an ellipse (also called an oval), click on the **Ellipse** icon on the Drawing toolbar. A circle is an ellipse with both axes the same length. To draw a circle, click on the **Ellipse** icon and hold down the *Shift* key whilst you draw a circle.

To draw an ellipse or circle from its center, position your cursor on the drawing, press the mouse button and then hold down the *Alt* key while dragging with the cursor. The ellipse or circle uses the start point (where you first clicked the mouse button) as the center.

Note	If you first press and hold down the *Ctrl* key and then click on one of the icons for Line, Rectangle, Ellipse, or Text, a standard sized object is drawn automatically in the work area; the size, shape, and color are all standard values. These attributes can be changed later, if desired. See the *Draw Guide* for more information.

Drawing curves or polygons

To draw a curve or polygon click the **Curve** icon on the Drawing toolbar. Click on the triangle to the right of the icon to open the tool palette containing tools that are available for drawing curves and polygons (Figure 167). The icon for the tool used most recently will be shown on the Drawing toolbar to make it easier to use the same tool again.

If you move the mouse cursor over one of the icons, a tooltip pops up with a description of the function.

Note	Hovering the mouse pointer over this icon gives a tooltip of *Curve*. If you open the floating toolbar, the title is *Lines*, as shown in Figure 167. Holding down the *Shift* key when drawing lines with the Curve or Polygon tools will restrict the angles between the lines to 45 or 90 degrees.

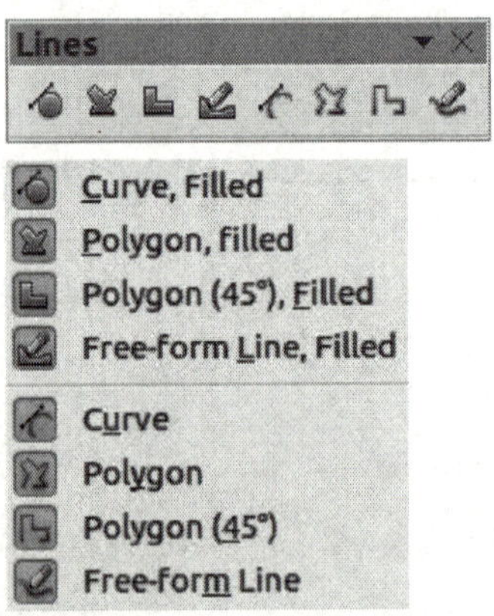

Figure 167: Curves (Lines) toolbar and available tools

Curves

Click and hold the left mouse button to create the starting point of your curve, then, while holding down the left mouse button, drag from the starting point to draw a line. Release the left mouse button and continue to drag the cursor to bend the line into a curve. Click to set the end point of the curve and fix the line on the page. To continue with your line, drag the mouse cursor to draw a straight line. Each mouse click sets a corner point and allows you to continue drawing another straight line from the corner point. A double click ends the drawing of your line.

A filled curve automatically joins the last point to the first point to close off the figure and fills it with the current standard fill color. A curve without filling will not be closed at the end of the drawing.

Polygons

Click and draw the first line from the start point with the left mouse button held down. As soon as you release the mouse button, a line between the first and second points is drawn. Move the cursor to draw the next line. Each mouse click sets a corner point and allows you to draw another line. A double-click ends the drawing.

A filled polygon automatically joins the last point to the first point to close off the figure and fills it with the current standard fill color. A polygon without filling will not be closed at the end of the drawing.

Polygons 45°

Like ordinary polygons, these are formed from lines, but the angles between lines are restricted to 45 or 90 degrees.

Freeform lines

Using the freeform line tools is similar to drawing with a pencil on paper. Press and hold the left mouse button and drag the cursor to the line shape you require. It is not necessary to end the drawing with a double-click, just release the mouse button and the drawing is completed.

If Freeform Line Filled is selected, the end point is joined automatically to the start point and the object is filled with the appropriate color.

Adding text

To activate the text tool, click on the **Text** icon for horizontal text or the **Vertical Text** icon for vertical script. If the Vertical Text icon is not visible, check that the option *Enabled for Asian languages* has been selected in **Tools > Options > Language Settings > Languages**. The Text Formatting toolbar appears (Figure 159 on page 187) when the Text icon is selected; from this toolbar you can select font type, font size, and other text properties before you start typing your text.

After activating the Text command, click at the location where you want to position the text. A small text frame appears, containing only the cursor. This frame can be moved like any other object. A text frame is also dynamic and grows as you enter text.

Observe the information field in the status bar: it shows that you are editing text and also provides details about the current cursor location using paragraph, row, and column numbers (Figure 168).

You can insert a line break with the *Shift+Enter* key combination or start a new paragraph with the *Enter* key. The insertion of line breaks or new paragraphs does not terminate text editing or deselect the text frame. When you have finished typing text, click outside the text frame to cancel adding or editing text.

If you want to edit text, double-click on the text to open the Text Formatting toolbar and highlight the text to start editing.

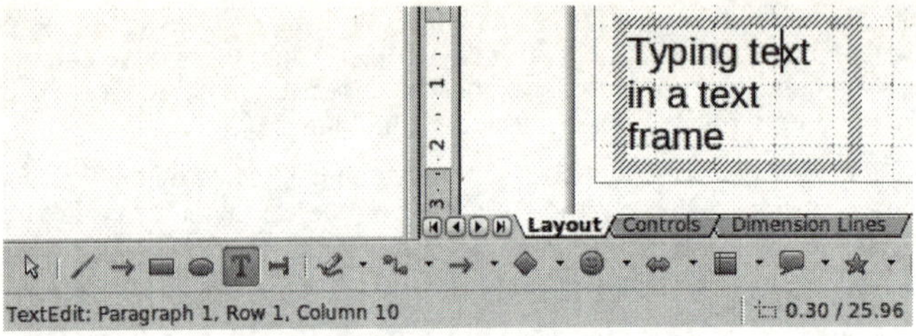

Figure 168: Text information on the Status Bar

Text properties can also be changed during text input, with any changes taking effect from the cursor position onwards. To change the properties for all of the text in the text frame, you have to highlight all text in the text frame.

You can create Graphics styles that you can reuse for other text frames. Select **Format > Styles and Formatting** or press *F11* to open the Styles and Formatting dialog. Graphics styles affect all of the text within a text frame. To only format parts of the text, use direct formatting with the toolbar.

Text frames can also have fill colors, shadows, and other attributes, just like any other Draw object. You can rotate the frame and write the text at any angle. These options are available by right-clicking on the text frame itself.

If you double-click on a graphic object, or press *F2* or click on the **Text** icon when an object is selected, you can add text to the graphic object. This text then becomes part of the graphic object.

A graphic object is not dynamic and does not behave like a text frame. To keep text within the borders of the object, you have to use paragraphs, line breaks, or smaller text size, increase the object size, or combine all four methods.

For more information about text, see the *Draw Guide Chapter 2 Drawing Basic Shapes* and *Chapter 9 Adding and Formatting Text*.

Glue points and connectors

Glue points

All Draw objects have glue points, which are not normally displayed. Glue points become visible when the **Connectors** icon on the Drawing toolbar is selected. Most objects have four glue points (Figure 169). You can add more glue points and customize glue points, using the **Glue Points** toolbar (Figure 170). Go to **View > Toolbars > Glue Points** on to open the toolbar.

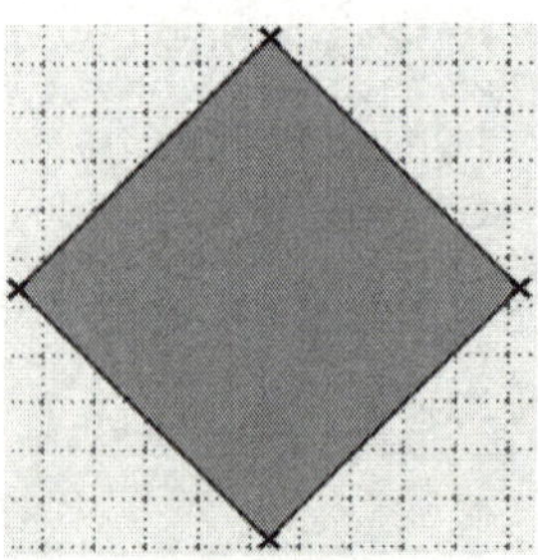

Figure 169: Glue points

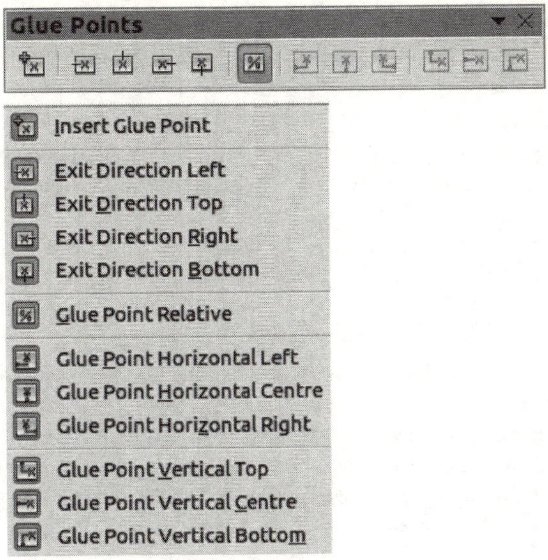

Figure 170: Glue Points toolbar and available tools

Glue points are not the same as the selection handles of an object. The handles are for moving or changing the shape of an object. Glue points are used to fix or glue a connector to an object so that when the object moves, the connector stays fixed to the object. For a more detailed description on the use of glue points, see the *Draw Guide Chapter 3 Working with Objects and Object Points* and *Chapter 8 Connections, Flowcharts and Organization Charts*.

Connectors

Connectors are lines or arrows whose ends automatically snap to a glue point of an object. Connectors are especially useful in drawing organization charts, flow diagrams, and mind-maps. When objects are moved or reordered, the connectors remain attached to a glue point. Figure 171 shows an example of two objects and a connector.

Draw offers a range of different connectors and connector functions. Click on the triangle next to the **Connector** icon 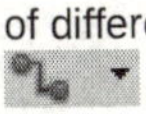 to open the **Connectors** toolbar (Figure 172). For a more detailed description of the use of connectors, see the *Draw Guide Chapter 8 Connections, Flowcharts and Organization Charts*.

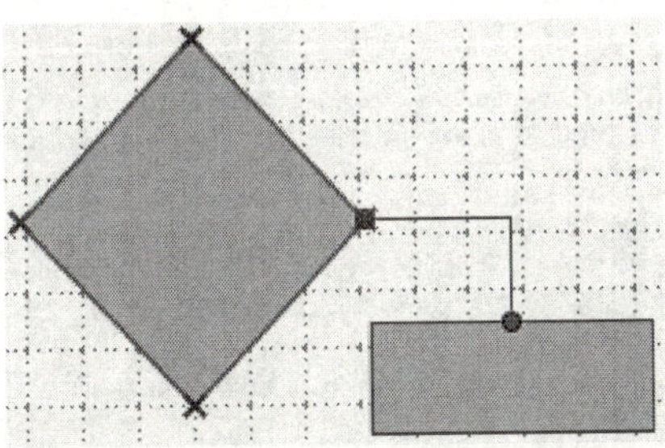

Figure 171: A connector between two objects

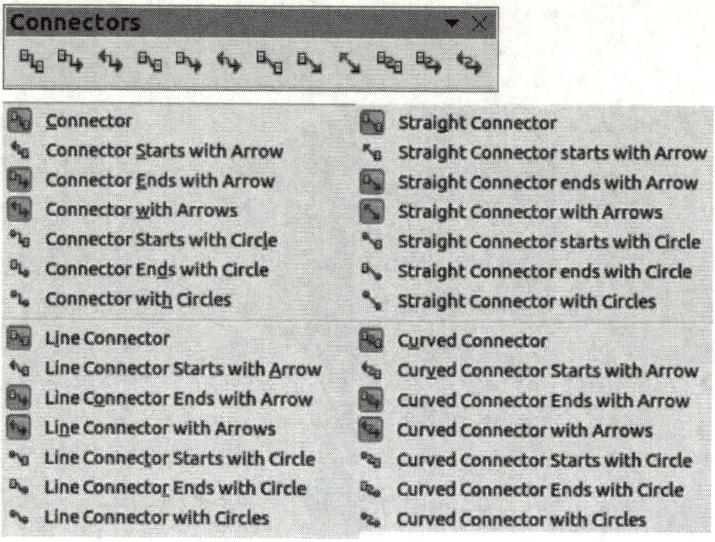

Figure 172: Connectors toolbar and available tools

Drawing geometric shapes

The icons for drawing geometric shapes are located on the Drawing toolbar and each geometric shape is explained in the following sections. Clicking on the triangle to the right of the icon opens a floating toolbar giving access to the tools for that geometric shape.

Tip	The use of these tools for geometric shapes is similar to the tool used for drawing rectangles and squares. For more information, see "Drawing basic shapes" on page 188 and the *Draw Guide Chapter 2 Drawing Basic Shapes*.

Note	The icons for geometric shapes displayed on the Drawing toolbar will change shape according to the last tool selected and used to draw an object.

Basic shapes

Click on the triangle to the right of the **Basic Shapes** icon  to open the **Basic Shapes** toolbar for drawing basic shapes. This toolbar also includes a rectangle tool identical to the one already displayed on the Drawing toolbar.

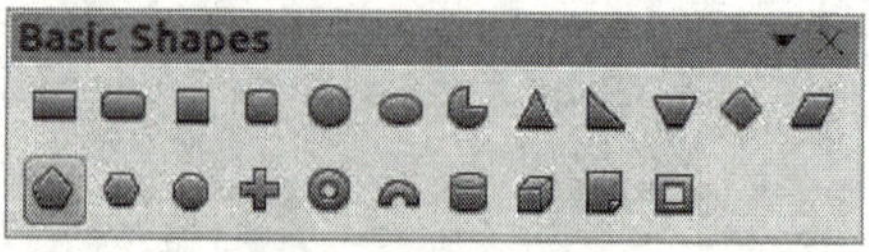

Figure 173: Basic Shapes toolbar

Symbol shapes

Click on the triangle to the right of the **Symbol Shapes** icon  to open the **Symbol Shapes** toolbar for drawing symbols.

Figure 174: Symbol Shapes toolbar

Block arrows

Click on the triangle to the right of the **Block Arrows** icon  to open the **Block Arrows** toolbar for drawing block arrows.

Figure 175: Block Arrows toolbar

Flowcharts

Click on the triangle to the right of the **Flowcharts** icon  to open the **Flowchart** toolbar for symbols used in drawing flowcharts. The creation of flowcharts, organization charts, and similar planning tools are further described in the *Draw Guide Chapter 8 Connections, Flowcharts and Organization Charts.*

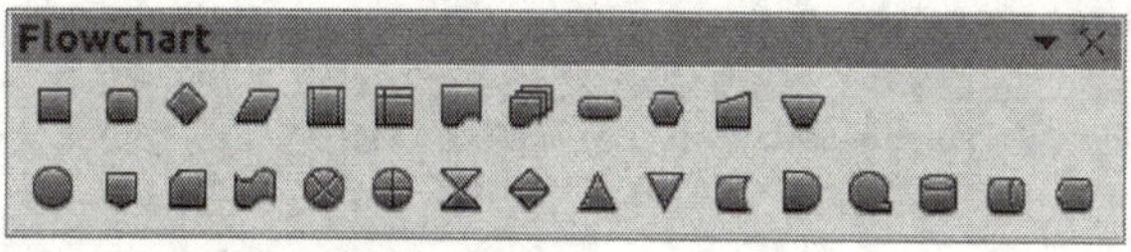

Figure 176: Flowcharts toolbar

Callouts

Click on the triangle to the right of the **Callouts** icon  to open the **Callouts** toolbar for drawing callouts.

Figure 177: Callouts toolbar

Stars and banners

Click on the triangle to the right of the **Stars** icon to open the **Stars and Banners** toolbar for drawing stars and banners.

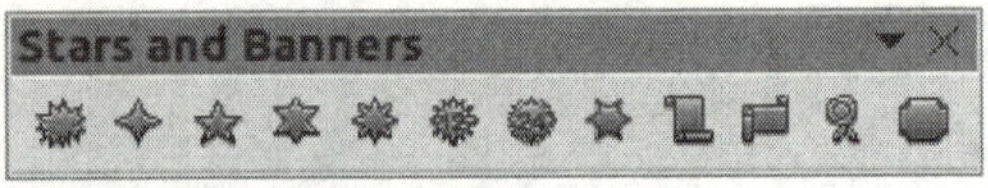

Figure 178: Stars and Banners toolbar

Note	You can add text to all these geometric shapes. For more information, see the *Draw Guide Chapter 2 Drawing Basic Shapes* and *Chapter 10 Advanced Draw Techniques*.

Selecting objects

Direct selection

The easiest way to select an object is to click directly on it. For objects that are not filled, click on the object outline to select it. One click selects; a second click deselects. To select or deselect more than one object, hold the shift button down while clicking.

Selection by framing

You can also select several objects at once by dragging the mouse cursor around the objects. This cursor dragging draws a rectangle around the objects and only objects that lie entirely within the rectangle will be selected.

To select multiple objects by framing, the **Select** icon on the Drawing toolbar must be active.

Note	When dragging the mouse cursor to select multiple objects, the selection rectangle being drawn is also known as a marquee.

Selecting hidden objects

Even if objects are located behind others and not visible, they can still be selected. Hold down the *Alt* key and click on the object at the front of where the hidden object is located, then click again to select the hidden object. If there are several hidden objects, keep holding down the *Alt* key and clicking until you reach the object you want. To cycle through the objects in reverse order, hold down the *Alt+Shift* keys and click.

When you click on the selected object, its outline will appear briefly through the objects covering it.

Note	Using the *Alt* key method works on computers using a Windows or Mac operating systems. On a computer using a Linux operating system the *Tab* key method, described below, has to be used.

To select an object that is covered by another object using the keyboard, use the *Tab* key to cycle through the objects, stopping at the object you want to select. To cycle through the objects in reverse order, press *Shift+Tab*. This is a very quick way to reach an object, but it may not be practical if there a large number of objects in a drawing.

Arranging objects

In a complex drawing, several objects may be stacked on top of one another. To rearrange the stacking order by moving an object forward or backward, select an object, click **Modify > Arrange** on the main menu bar and select **Bring Forward** or **Send Backward**. Alternatively, right-click the object, select **Arrange** from the context menu, then **Bring Forward** or **Send Backward**.

The arrange options are also available by clicking on the small triangle to the right of the **Arrange** icon  on the Line and Filling toolbar. This opens the **Position** toolbar giving access to the various arrangement options (Figure 179).

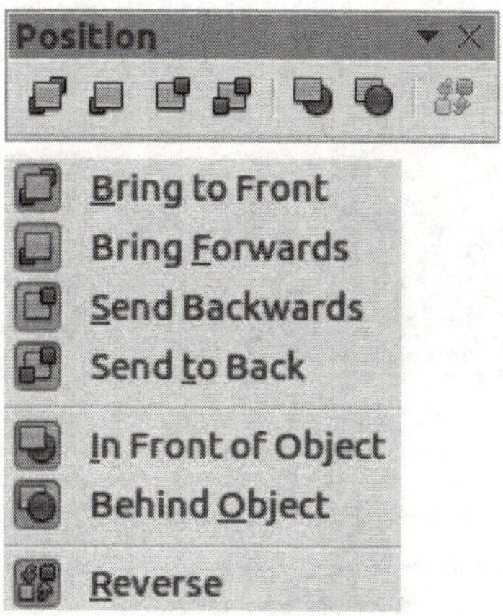

Figure 179: Position toolbar and available tools

Moving and adjusting object size

When moving an object or changing its size, check the left-hand area of the status bar at the bottom of the Draw window (Figure 180). The area on the left of the Drawing toolbar, from left to right, shows what object is selected, its position on the drawing in X/Y coordinates and dimensions of the object. The units of measurement are those selected in **Tools > Options > LibreOffice Draw > General**.

For more information on moving and adjusting object size, see the *Draw Guide Chapter 3 Working with Objects and Object Points*.

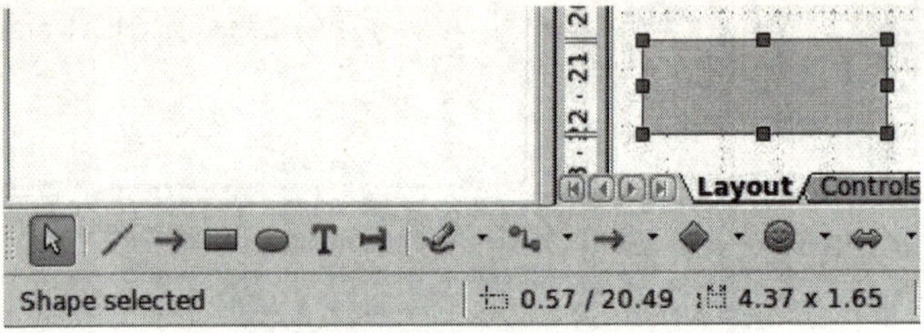

Figure 180: Left end of status bar when moving or adjusting an object

Moving objects

To move an object (or a group of objects), select it and then click within the object borders and hold down the left mouse button while dragging the mouse. During movement, the ghost image of the object appears to help with repositioning (Figure 181). To locate the object at its new location, release the mouse button.

Figure 181: Moving an object

Adjusting object size

To change the size of a selected object (or a group of selected objects), move the mouse cursor to one of the selection handles. The mouse cursor will change shape to indicate the direction of movement for that selection handle. As you change the size of the object, a ghosted outline of the object appears (Figure 182). When you have reached the desired size of the object, release the mouse button.

The results depend on which selection handle you use. To resize an object along one axis, use a side handle. To resize along both axes, use a corner handle.

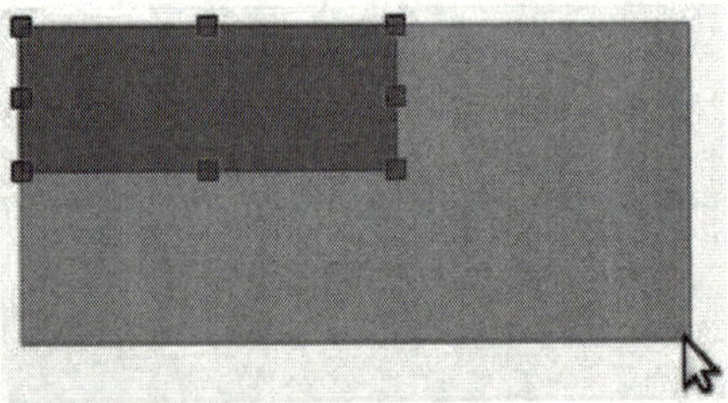
Figure 182: Adjusting object size

Note

If you press the *Shift* key while resizing an object, the change in size will be carried out symmetrically with respect to the two axes so that the aspect ratio of the object remains the same. This *Shift* key behavior works on all selection handles.

This is the default behavior of the *Shift* key. However, if *When creating or moving objects* has been selected in **Tools > Options > LibreOffice Draw > Grid**, the action of the *Shift* key is reversed: that is the aspect ratio will be preserved *unless* the *Shift* key is pressed.

Rotating and slanting an object

For more information on rotating and slanting an object, see the *Draw Guide Chapter 3 Working with Objects and Object Points*.

Rotating an object

To rotate an object (or a group of objects), select the object, then go to rotation mode using one of the following methods:

- Click on the object again. Do not double click as this will cancel object selection.
- Click on the Rotate icon on the Drawing toolbar.
- Go to **View > Toolbars > Mode** and select the Rotate icon.

The selection handles will change shape and color (Figure 183). Also a center of rotation point will appear in the center of the object. As you move the mouse cursor over the handles the cursor changes shape. The corner handles are for rotating an object and the top, bottom and side handles are to slant an object.

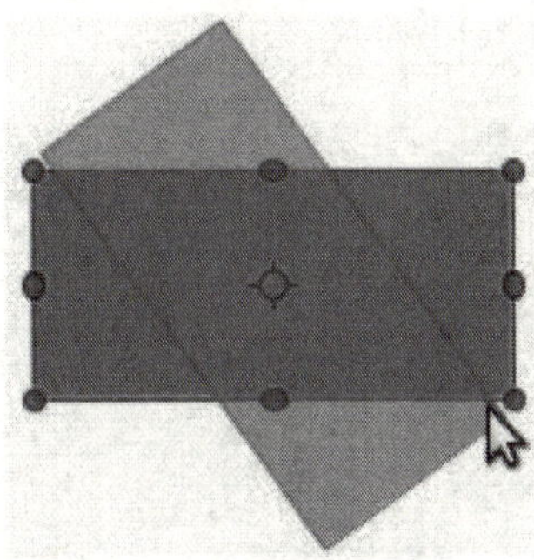

Figure 183: Rotating an object

Move the mouse cursor to one of the corner handles and it normally changes to an arc with an arrow at each end. Click and hold the mouse button, then start to move the cursor to rotate the object. A ghost image of the object being rotated appears and the current angle of rotation is shown in the status bar.

Note

Rotation works differently for 3D objects because rotation occurs in global axes and not in a single axis. See the *Draw Guide Chapter 7 Working with 3D Objects* for more information.

The rotation point is normally located at the center of an object. To change the position of the rotation point, click on the object with the mouse cursor and drag the object until the rotation point is at the desired position. This rotation point can even be outside of the object.

Note	If you press the *Shift* key while rotating an object, rotation will be restricted to 15° of movement. This is the default behavior of the *Shift* key. However, if *When creating or moving objects* has been selected in **Tools > Options > LibreOffice Draw > Grid**, the action of the *Shift* key is reversed: that is rotation will be restricted to 15° of movement *unless* the *Shift* key is pressed.

Slanting an object

To slant an object, use the handles located at the midpoints on the top, bottom and sides of a selected object. The mouse cursor changes when it hovers over one of these midpoint handles. The axis used for slanting an object is the object edge directly opposite the midpoint handle being used to slant the object. This axis stays fixed in location while the other sides of the object move in relation to it as you drag the mouse cursor.

Click and hold the mouse button, then start to move the cursor to shear the object. A ghost image of the object being slanted appears (Figure 184) and the current angle of slanting is shown in the status bar.

Note	If you press the *Shift* key while slanting an object, slanting will be restricted to 15° of movement. This is the default behavior of the *Shift* key. However, if *When creating or moving objects* has been selected in **Tools > Options > LibreOffice Draw > Grid**, the action of the *Shift* key is reversed: that is slanting will be restricted to 15° of movement *unless* the *Shift* key is pressed.

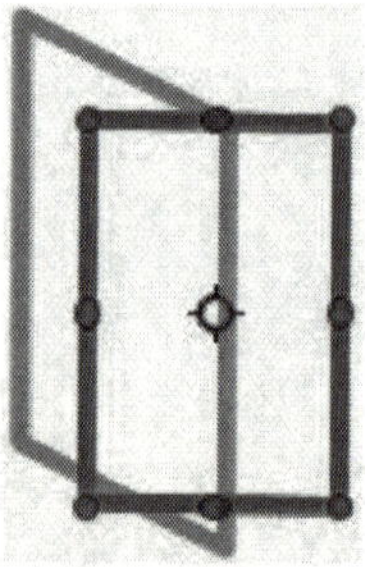

Figure 184: Slanting an object

Editing objects

To edit an object or change its attributes, such as color or border width, and so on, the Line and Filling toolbar, the Text Formatting toolbar, or the context menu can be used. More information on editing objects and changing attributes can be found in the *Draw Guide Chapter 4 Changing Object Attributes*.

Line and Filling toolbar

By default, the **Line and Filling** toolbar in Draw is placed at the top of the workspace. However, if the Line and Filling toolbar is not displayed, go to **View > Toolbars > Line and Filling** on the main menu bar to open the toolbar (Figure 185). The most common object attributes can be edited using this toolbar. You can also open the Line dialog by clicking on the **Line** icon and the Area dialog by clicking on the **Area** icon for access to more formatting options.

Text Formatting toolbar

When you select text, the Line and Filling toolbar automatically changes to show the **Text Formatting** toolbar (Figure 186). You can also open the Text Formatting toolbar by selecting **View > Toolbars > Text Formatting** on the main menu bar. The tools on this toolbar will not become active until text has been selected.

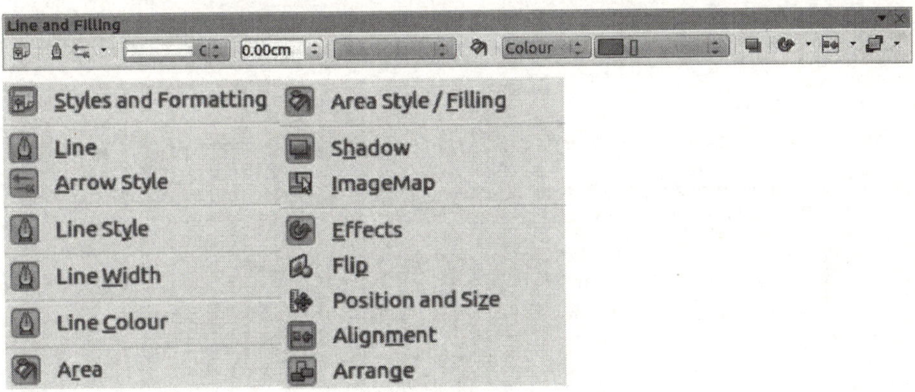

Figure 185: Line and Filling toolbar and its available tools

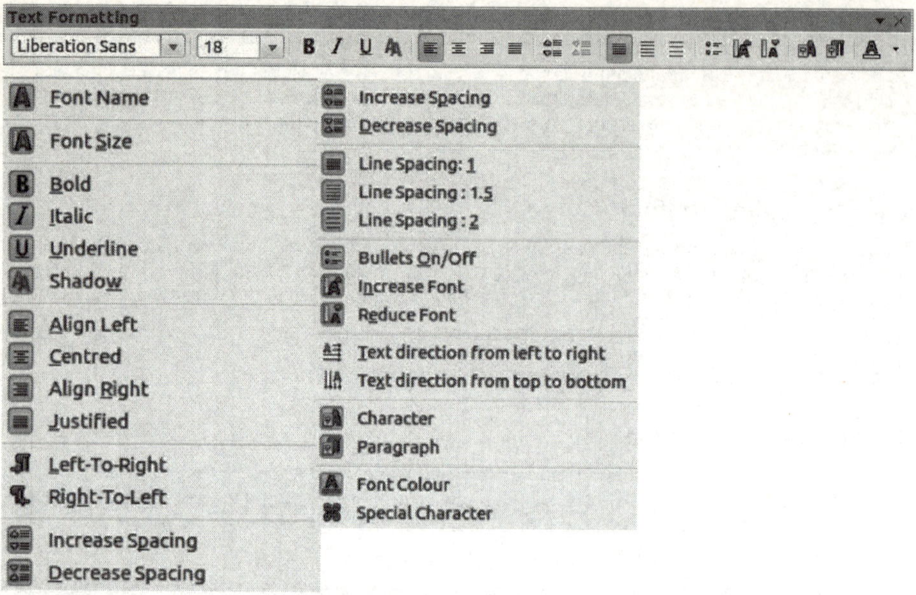

Figure 186: Text Formatting toolbar and its available tools

Context menu

When an object is selected and you right-click on the object, a context menu (Figure 187) opens that applies to the selected object. This context menu provides access to the options available and allows you to change object attributes without having to open a dialog. Menu entries with a small arrow on the right-hand side contain a submenu.

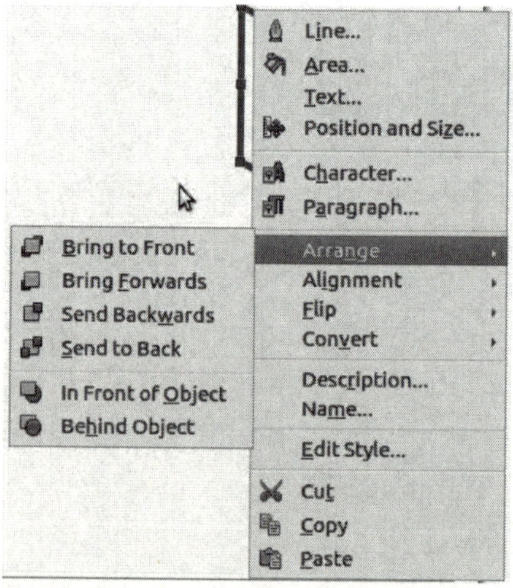

Figure 187: Example of a context menu

Formatting lines and borders

In LibreOffice the term *line* indicates both a freestanding segment (line), outer edge of a shape (border), or an arrow. In most cases the properties of the line you can modify are its style (solid, dashed, invisible, and so on), its width and its color.

Select the line you need to format and then use the controls on the Line and Filling toolbar to change the most common options (highlighted in Figure 188).

Figure 188: Common line properties (style, color, width)

If you need to fine tune the appearance of a line, choose **Format > Line** from the main menu bar, or right-click on the line and select **Line** from the context menu, or select the **Line** icon from the Line and Filling toolbar. All of these methods open the **Line** dialog (Figure 165 on page 190), where you can set line properties. This dialog consists of three pages: *Line*, *Line Styles*, and *Arrow Styles*.

Arrows, arrowheads and line endings

Arrows, arrowheads and other line endings are usually referred to as arrows and can be treated the same as lines when editing and changing attributes. Select a line and click on the **Arrow Style** icon from the Line and Filling toolbar to open the **Arrowheads** menu (Figure 189).

Several types of arrowheads are available. Each end of a line can have a different arrowhead or no arrowhead). Arrowheads are only applicable to lines and they have no effect on the border of an object.

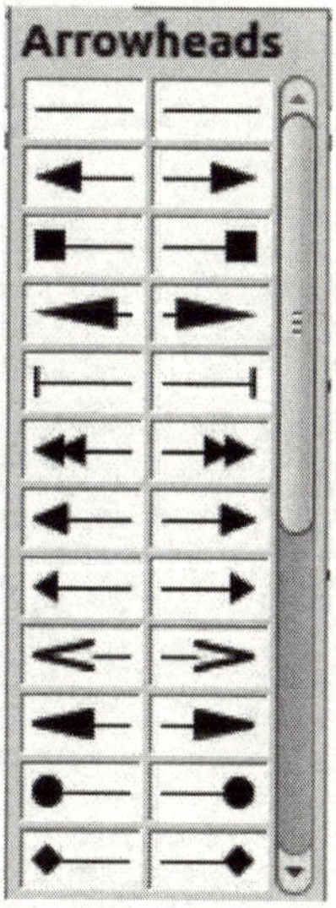

Figure 189: Arrowheads menu

Formatting area fill

The term **area fill** refers to the inside of an object, which can be a uniform color, gradient, hatching pattern, or bitmap (Figure 190). An area fill can be made partly or wholly transparent. In most cases, you will choose one of the standard fill options, which are all available from the Line and Filling toolbar. You can also define your own area fills. For more information on formatting area fill, see the *Draw Guide Chapter 4 Changing Object Attributes*.

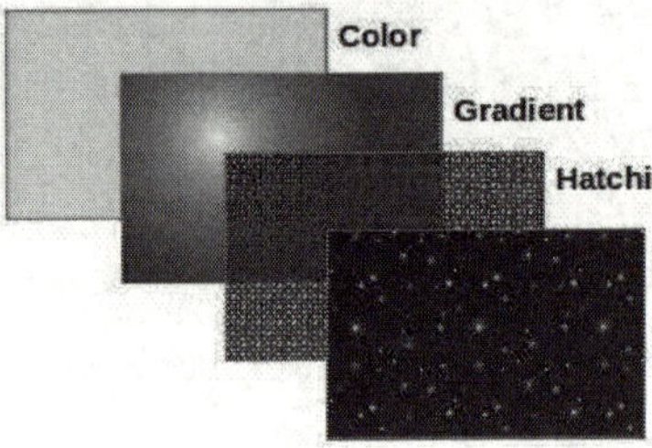

Figure 190: Different types of area fill

Using styles

Suppose that you want to apply the same area fill, line thickness, and border to a set of objects. This repetitive process can be greatly simplified by the use of styles. Styles allow you to define a formatting template (a style) and then to apply that style to multiple objects. For more information on styles, see *Chapter 3 Using Styles and Templates* in this guide, the *Writer Guide Chapter 6 Introduction to Styles* and the *Draw Guide Chapter 4 Changing Object Attributes.*

Positioning objects

Snap function

In Draw, objects can be accurately and consistently positioned using the snap function. Grid points, snap points and lines, object frames, individual points on objects, or page edges can all be used with the snap function.

Snap function is easier to work with at the highest zoom values that are practical for your display. Two different snap functions can be used at the same time; for example snapping to a guide line and to the page edge. It is recommended, however, to activate only the functions that you really need.

For more detailed information about the snap function, see the *Draw Guide Chapter 3 Working with Objects and Object Points* and *Chapter 10 Advanced Draw Techniques*.

Snap to grid

Snap to grid allows you to position an object to a grid point (Figure 191). Go to **View > Grid > Snap to Grid** on the main menu bar or click on the **Snap to Grid** icon  on the **Options** toolbar to turn on or off the snap to grid function. If the Options toolbar is not displayed, go to **View > Toolbars > Options** on the main menu bar.

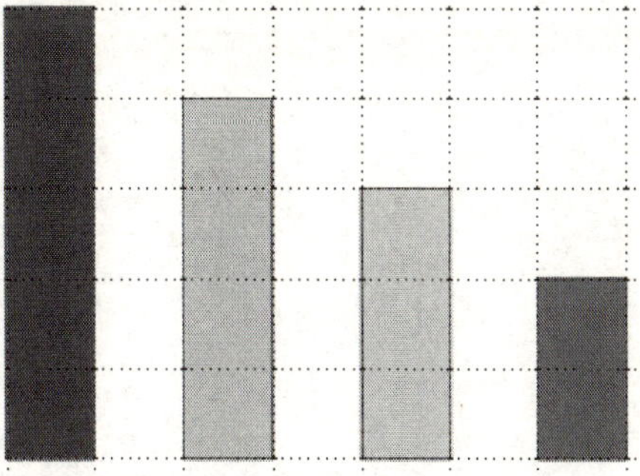

Figure 191: Positioning with snap to grid

Displaying the grid

To display the grid in Draw or to switch off the grid, go to **View > Grid > Display Grid** on the main menu bar or click on the **Display Grid** icon on the Options toolbar.

Configuring the grid

The resolution, snap and snap position of the grid points can be configured. Go to **Tools > Options > LibreOffice Draw > Grid** on the main menu bar to open the options dialog for the grid (Figure 192).

- Vertical and horizontal spacing of the dots in the grid. You can also change the unit of measurement used in the general Draw options by going to **Tools > Options > LibreOffice Draw > General**.
- The resolution is the size of the squares or rectangles in the grid. If the resolution is 1 cm horizontal and 2 cm vertical, the grid consists of rectangles 2 cm high and 1 cm wide.
- Subdivisions are additional points that appear along the sides of each rectangle or square in the grid. Objects snap to subdivisions as well as to the corners of the grid.
- The pixel size of the snap area defines how close you need to bring an object to a snap point or line before it will snap to it.
- The default color of the grid is light gray. To change the color of the grid points, go to **Tools > Options > LibreOffice > Appearance** on the main menu bar.

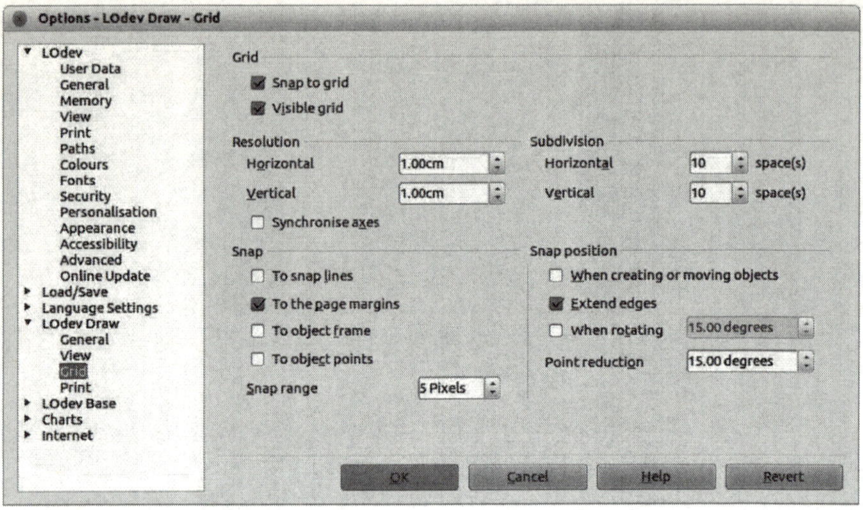

Figure 192: Configuring the grid

Help lines

Draw has help lines to easily allow you to position an object using the rulers at the top and left side of the workspace. To turn on or off the help lines, go to **Tools > Options > LibreOffice Draw > View** on the main menu bar and select **Snap Lines when moving** option, or go to the Options toolbar and click on the **Helplines While Moving** icon .

Applying special effects

With Draw, you can apply many special effects to objects and groups of objects and this section is an introduction to some of these effects. For more information on special effects can be found in the *Draw Guide Chapter 4 Changing Object Attributes*..

To access the tools used for special effects, go to **View > Toolbars > Mode** (Figure 193). **Rotate** and **Flip** can also be accessed by going to **Modify** on the main menu bar or by right clicking on the object and using the context menu.

Flipping objects

The quickest and easiest method to flip an object horizontally or vertically is as follows:

1) Click on a graphic object and the selection handles will show.
2) Right-click and select **Flip > Vertically** or **Horizontally**, or got to **Modify > Flip > Vertically** or **Horizontally** on the main menu bar and the selected object will be flipped to face the other direction.

However, the **Flip** tool on the Mode or Drawing toolbar can be used to give you greater control over the flipping process. Using the Flip tool allows you to change the position and angle that the object flips over and this is described in the *Draw Guide Chapter 4 Changing Object Attributes*.

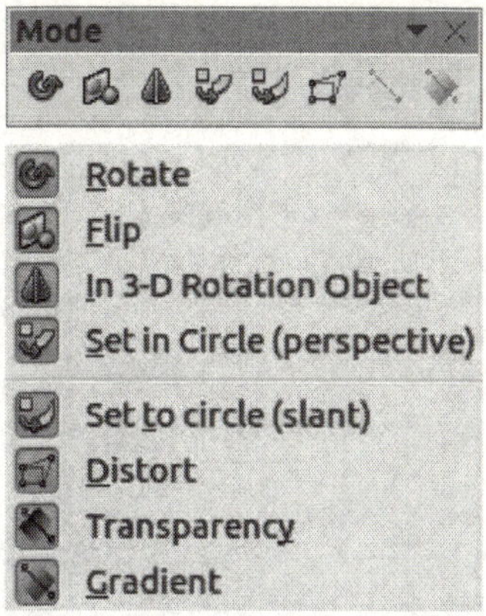

Figure 193: Mode toolbar and its available tools

Mirror copies

At the moment there is no mirror command existing in Draw. However, mirroring an object can be emulated by using the **Flip** tool and this is described in the *Draw Guide Chapter 4 Changing Object Attributes*.

Distorting an object

Three tools on the Mode toolbar let you drag the corners and edges of an object to distort the image.

- **Distort tool**  distorts an object in perspective.
- **Set to Circle (slant)**  creates a pseudo three-dimensional effect.
- **Set in Circle (perspective)**  creates a pseudo three-dimensional effect.

In all three cases you are initially asked if you want to transform the object to a curve. This is a necessary first step, so click **Yes**. Then you can move the object handles to produce the desired effect. See the *Draw Guide Chapter 4 Changing Object Attributes* for more information on how to distort an object.

Dynamic transparency gradients

You can control transparency gradients in the same manner as color gradients. Both types of gradient can be used together. With a transparency gradient, the direction and degree of object fill color changes from opaque to transparent. In a regular gradient, the fill changes from one color to another, but the degree of transparency remains the same.

The **Transparency** and **Gradient** tools on the Mode toolbar dynamically control transparency and color gradients. See the *Draw Guide Chapter 4 Changing Object Attributes* for more information on how to create transparencies and gradients in an object.

Duplication

Duplication makes copies of an object while applying a set of changes such as color or rotation to the duplicates that are created.

1) Click on an object or group of objects and go to **Edit > Duplicate** on the main menu bar or use the keyboard shortcut *Shift+F3* to open the **Duplicate** dialog (Figure 194).
2) Select the required options chosen from the options available. For example, when the options in the dialog are applied to a rectangle, they produce the result shown in Figure 195.

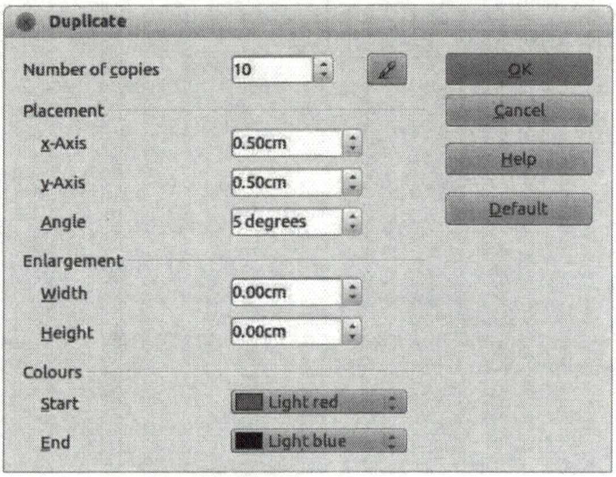

Figure 194: Duplicate dialog

Figure 195: Duplication result

Cross-fading

Cross-fading transforms one object shape to another object shape and only works when two objects are selected.

1) Select two differently shaped objects.
2) Go to **Edit > Cross-fading** on the main menu bar to open the **Cross-fading** dialog (Figure 196).
3) Select **Increments** to determine the number of shapes between the two objects.

4) Select **Cross-fading attributes** to apply a gradual change of line and fill properties between the two objects.
5) Select **Same orientation** to apply a smooth transition between the two objects.
6) Click on **OK** and the result is a new group of objects with the first object selected as the start object and the second object selected as the end object. For example, when the options in the dialog are applied to a rectangle and a triangle, the cross fade produces the result shown in Figure 197.

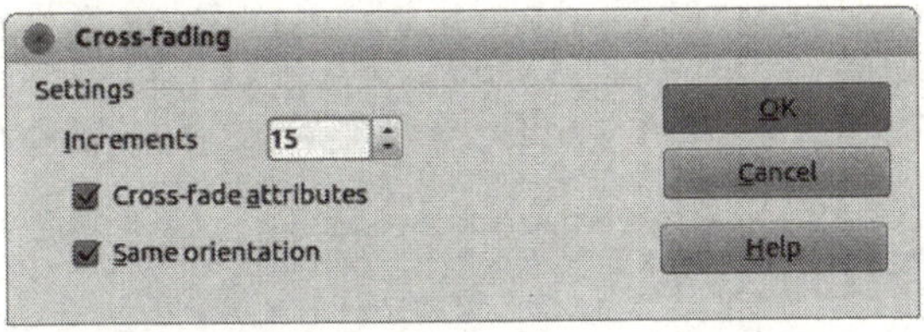

Figure 196: Cross-fading dialog

Figure 197: Cross-fading result

Combining multiple objects

Using Draw, you can group or combine objects together allowing you to treat multiple objects as one unit, or to merge objects to form a new shape. For more information, see the Draw Guide *Chapter 5 Combining Multiple Objects*.

Grouping of objects is similar to putting objects into a container. You can move the objects as a group and apply global changes to the objects within the group. A group can always be undone and the objects that make up the group can always be manipulated separately. The objects within a group also retain their own individual properties.

Combining objects is a permanent merging of objects that creates a new object. The original objects are no longer available as individual entities and cannot be edited as individual objects. Any editing of a combined object affects all the objects that were used when combination was carried out.

Grouping

Temporary grouping

A temporary grouping is when several objects are selected using the Select icon on the Drawing toolbar or using the mouse to drag a rectangle around the objects (also known as a marquee). Any changes to object parameters you carry out are applied to all of the objects within the temporary group. For example, you can rotate a temporary group of objects in its entirety.

To cancel a temporary grouping of objects simply click outside of the selection handles displayed around the objects.

Permanent grouping

A permanent grouping of objects is created after you have selected your objects. Go to **Modify > Group** on the main menu bar, or right-click on the selection and select **Group** from the context menu, or use the keyboard shortcut *Ctrl+Shift+G*. When you deselect your selection, the objects remain grouped together.

When objects are permanently grouped, any editing operations carried out on that group are applied to all members of the group. If you click on one member of the group, the whole group is selected.

You can edit an individual member of a group without ungrouping or breaking the group. Select the group and go to **Modify > Enter Group**, or right click and select **Enter Group** from the context menu, or use the keyboard shortcut *F3*, or double click on the group.

When you have finished editing an individual member of a group, go to **Modify > Exit Group**, or right click and select **Exit Group** from the context menu, or use the keyboard shortcut *Shift+F3*.

Ungrouping

To ungroup or break apart a group of objects, select the group then go to **Modify > Ungroup** on the main menu bar, or right click and select **Ungroup** from the context menu or use the keyboard shortcut *Ctrl+Alt+Shift+G*.

Combining objects

Combining objects is a permanent merging of objects that creates a new object. The original objects are no longer available as individual entities and cannot be edited as individual objects. Any editing of a combined object affects all the objects that were used when combination was carried out.

Select several objects, then go to **Modify > Combine** on the main menu bar, or right click on the objects and select **Combine** from the context menu, or use the keyboard shortcut *Ctrl+Shift+K*.

After you have selected your objects, the **Merge**, **Subtract**, and **Intersect** functions also become available so that you can create a new object from your selected objects. See the *Draw Guide Chapter 5 Combining Multiple Objects* for more information on these functions.

Arranging, aligning and distributing objects

In Draw you can arrange, align and distribute selected objects in relation to each other:

- Arrange the position of an object by moving it either forward or backward in relation to the order of objects.
- Align objects with respect to each other using **Left**, **Centered**, or **Right** for horizontal alignment and **Top**, **Center** or **Bottom** for vertical alignment.
- Distribute objects so that the space between each of the objects is the same.

See the *Draw Guide Chapter 5 Combining Multiple Objects* for more information on arranging and aligning objects in relation to each other.

Inserting and editing pictures

Draw contains a number of functions for editing pictures or raster graphics (bitmaps); for example, photos and scanned images. This includes the import and export of graphics, and the conversion of one graphic format to another.

Draw includes a large range of graphic filters so that it can read and display several graphic file formats. It also includes several tools for working with raster graphics, but does not have the same functionality as specialized graphic programs like Gimp or Adobe Photoshop. See the *Draw Guide Chapter 6 Editing Pictures* for more information.

You can add pictures from several sources:

- Directly from a scanner (**Insert > Picture > Scan**)
- Images created by another program, including photographs from a digital camera (**Insert > Picture > From File**)
- The Draw Gallery; see *Chapter 11 Graphics, the Gallery, and Fontwork* in this guide for more information.

Working with 3D objects

Although Draw does not match the functionality of the leading drawing or picture editing programs, it is capable of producing and editing very good 3D drawings.

Draw offers two types of 3D objects: *3D bodies* and *3D shapes*. Depending on which type you choose, there are different methods of editing of a 3D object (rotation, illumination, perspective, and so on) with 3D shapes being simpler to set up and edit than 3D bodies. However, 3D bodies currently allow for more customization.

See the *Draw Guide Chapter 7 Working with 3D Objects* for more information.

Exporting graphics

Draw saves graphics and images in the open source format *.odg. To save a graphic or the entire file in another format, use **File > Export** and select a format from the list displayed. The graphic formats that Draw can export and save to are listed in *Appendix B Open Source, Open Standards, OpenDocument* in this guide.

You can also export Draw files to HTML, XHTML, PDF, or Flash. PDF export for modules of LibreOffice is described in *Chapter 10 Printing, Exporting, and E-mailing* of this guide.

HTML export uses a conversion wizard that creates as many web pages as there are pages in your Draw document. You can optionally choose to display pages in frames with a navigator and set an index page. For more information, see *Chapter 12 Creating Web Pages* in this guide.

Inserting comments in a drawing

You can insert comments into your drawing using a similar process to the one used in Writer and Calc.

1) Go to **Insert > Comment** on the menu bar. A small box containing your initials appears in the upper left-hand corner of your drawing with a larger text box beside it (Figure 198). Draw automatically adds your name and the date at the bottom of this text box.
2) Type or paste your comment into the text box. You can apply basic formatting to parts of the text by selecting it, right-clicking, and choosing from the context menu. From this menu,

you can also delete the current comment, all the comments from the same author, or all the comments in the document.

3) You can move the small comment markers to anywhere you wish on the drawing. Typically you might place it on or near an object you refer to in the comment.

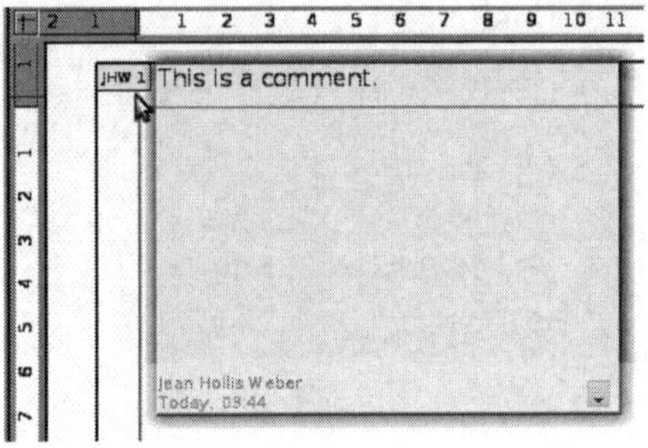

Figure 198: Inserting comments

4) To show or hide the comment markers, go to **View > Comments** on the main menu bar.
5) Go to **Tools > Options > User Data** to enter the name you want to appear in the Author field of the comment.
6) If more than one person edits the document, each author is automatically allocated a different background color.

LibreOffice
The Document Foundation

Chapter 8
Getting Started with Base

LibreOffice's Database Component

What is Base?

A data source, or database, is a collection of pieces of information that can be accessed or managed by LibreOffice. For example, a list of names and addresses is a data source that could be used for producing a mail merge letter. A shop stock list could be a data source managed through LibreOffice.

Note	LibreOffice uses the terms "Data Source" and "Database" to refer to the same thing, which could be a database such as MySQL or dBase or a spreadsheet or text document holding data.

This chapter covers creating a database, showing what is contained in a database and how the different parts are used by LibreOffice. It also covers using the Base component of LibreOffice to register other data sources. A data source can be a database, spreadsheet, or text document.

Note	LibreOffice Base uses the HSQL database engine. All of the files created by this engine, including the database forms, are kept in one zipped file.

A *database* consists of a number of *fields* that contain the individual pieces of data. Each *table* of the database is a group of fields. When creating a table, you also determine the characteristics of each field within it. *Forms* are for data entry into the fields of one or more tables which have been associated with the form. They can also be used for viewing fields from one or more tables associated with the form. A *query* creates a new table from the existing tables based upon how you create the query. A *report* organizes the information from the fields of a query into a document according to your requirements.

Caution	The database in LibreOffice requires Java Runtime Environment (JRE). If you do not have it on your computer, you can download it from www.java.com and install it following the instructions on the site. It should be Java 6.0 or higher and 7.0 is preferred. In LibreOffice, use **Tools > Options > LibreOffice > Java** to register Java. Windows' version of JRE can **not** be used, while there are other versions that can.

Base creates *relational databases*. This makes it fairly easy to create a database in which the fields of the database have relationships with each other.

For example: Consider a database for a library. It will contain a field for the names of the authors and another field for the names of the books. There is an obvious relationship between the authors and the books they have written. The library may contain more than one book by the same author. This is what is known as a one-to-many relationship: one author and more than one book. Most if not all the relationships in such a database are one-to-many relationships.

Consider an employment database for the same library. One of the fields contains the names of the employees while others contain the social security numbers, and other personal data. The relationship between the names and social security numbers is one-to-one: only one social security number for each name.

If you are acquainted with mathematical sets, a relational database can easily be explained in terms of sets: elements, subsets, unions, and intersections. The fields of a database are the elements. The tables are subsets. Relationships are defined in terms of unions and intersections of the subsets (tables).

To explain how a database works and how to to use it, we will create one for automobile expenses.

Planning a database

The first step in creating a database is to ask yourself many questions. Write them down, and leave some space between the questions to write the answers later. At least some of the answers should seem obvious after you take some time to think.

You may have to go through this process a few times before everything becomes clear in your mind and on paper. Using a text document for these questions and answers makes it easier to move the questions around, add additional questions, or change the answers.

Here are some of the questions and answers I developed before I created a database for automobile expenses. I had an idea of what I wanted before I started, but as I began asking questions and listing the answers, I discovered that I needed additional tables and fields.

What are the fields going to be? My expenses divided into three broad areas: fuel purchases, maintenance, and vacations. The annual cost for the car's license plate and driver's license every four years did not fit into any of these. It will be a table of its own: license fees.

What fields fit the fuel purchases area? Date purchased, odometer reading, fuel cost, fuel quantity, and payment method fit. (Fuel economy need not be included, as it can be calculated using a query.)

What fields fit the maintenance area? Date of service, odometer reading, type of service, cost of service, and next scheduled service of this type (for example, for oil changes list when the next oil change should be). But it would be nice if there was a way to write notes. So a field for notes was added to the list.

What fields fit the vacations area? Date, odometer reading, fuel (including all the fields of the fuel table), food (including meals and snacks), motel, total tolls, and miscellaneous. Since these purchases are made by one of two bank cards or with cash, I want a field to state which payment type was used for each item.

What fields fit into the food category? Breakfast, lunch, supper, and snacks seem to fit. Do I list all the snacks individually or list the total cost for snacks for the day? I chose to divide snacks into two fields: number of snacks and total cost of snacks. I also need a payment type for each of these: breakfast, lunch, supper, and total cost of snacks.

What are the fields that are common to more than one area? Date appears in all of the areas as does odometer reading and payment type.

How will I use this information about these three fields? While on vacation, I want the expenses for each day to be listed together. The date fields suggest a relationship between the vacation table and the dates in each of these tables: fuel and food, This means that the date fields in these tables will be linked as we create the database.

The type of payment includes two bank cards and cash. So we will create a table with a field for the type of payment and use it in list boxes in the forms.

Tip	While we have listed fields we will create in the tables of the database, there is one more field that may be needed in a table: the field for the primary key. In some tables, the field for the primary key has already been listed. In other tables such as the payment type, an additional field for the primary key must be created.

Creating a new database

To create a new database, choose **File > New > Database** from the menu bar, or click the arrow next to the **New** icon on the Standard toolbar and select **Database** from the drop down menu. Both methods open the Database Wizard.

On the first page of the Database Wizard, select **Create a new database** and then click **Next**.

The second page has two questions. Make sure the choice for the first question is **Yes, register the database for me** and the choice for the second question is **Open the database for editing**. Click **Finish**.

Note

The *F4* key opens and closes the Data Source window containing the list of registered databases. You can access this window and its data while using Writer and Calc. If the database is not registered, this window does not contain it. So, you can not access the database to use in Writer or Calc.

Save the new database with the name *Automobile.* This opens the Automobile – LibreOffice Base window. Figure 199 shows part of this window.

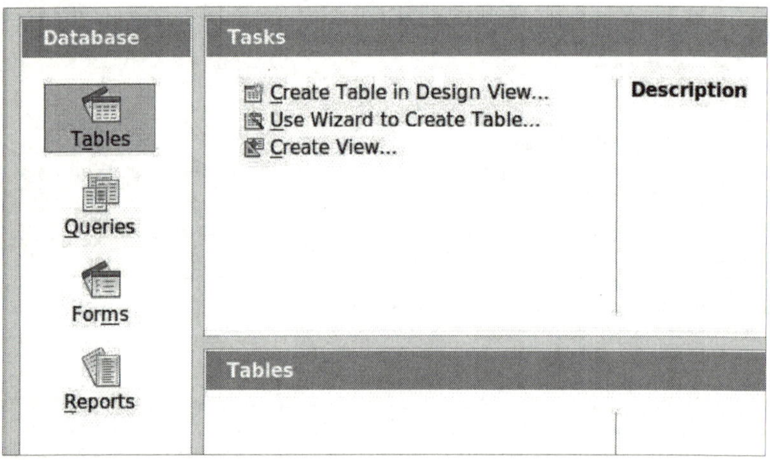

Figure 199: Creating database tables

Tip

Every time the *Automobile* database is opened, the Automobile – LibreOffice Base window opens. Changes can then be made to the database. The title for this window is always <database name> – LibreOffice Base.

Caution

As you create a database, you should save your work regularly. This means more than saving what you have just created. You must save the whole database as well.

For example, when you create your first table, you must save it before you can close it. When the table is first saved, it is also made part of the database in memory. Only when you save the database file do you write the table in the database file.

Creating database tables

In a database, a table stores information for a group of things we call fields. For example, a table might hold an address book, a stock list, a phone book or a price list. A database must have at least one table and may have several.

To work with tables, click the *Tables* icon in the *Database* list, or press *Alt+a*. The three tasks that you can perform on a table are in the *Tasks* list (see Figure 199).

Using the Wizard to create a table

Wizards are designed to do the basic work. Sometimes this is not sufficient for what we want; in those cases we can use a wizard as a starting point and then build upon what it produces.

The Table Wizard in Base contains two categories of suggested tables: business and personal. Each category contains sample tables from which to choose. Each table has a list of available fields. We can delete some of these fields and add other fields.

A field in a table is one bit of information. For example, a price list table might have one field for item name, one for the description, and a third for the price.

Since none of the fields we need for our Automobile database are contained in any of the sample wizard tables, we will create a simple table using the wizard that has nothing to do with our database. This section is merely an exercise in explaining how the Wizard works.

The Wizard permits the fields of the table to come from more than one suggested table. We will create a table with fields from three different suggested tables in the Wizard.

Caution	Every table requires a *Primary key field*. (What this field does will be explained later.) We will use this field to number our entries and want that number to automatically increase as we add each entry.

Click *Use Wizard to Create Table*. This opens the Table Wizard (Figure 200).

Step 1: Select fields.

We will use the *CD-Collection* Sample table in the Personal category to select the fields we need.

1) *Category*: Select *Personal*. The *Sample Tables* drop down list changes to a list of personal sample tables.
2) *Sample tables*: Select *CD-Collection*. The *Available fields* box changes to a list of available fields for this table.
3) *Selected fields*: Using the **>** button, move the following fields from the *Available fields* window to the *Selected fields* window in this order: *CollectionID, AlbumTitle, Artist, DatePurchased, Format, Notes,* and *NumberofTracks.*
4) *Selected Fields from another sample* table. Click Business as the Category. Select *Employees* from the drop down list of sample tables. Use the **>** button to move the *Photo* field from the *Available fields* window to the *Selected fields* window. It will be at the bottom of the list directly below the *NumberofTracks* field.
5) If you make a mistake in selecting fields, click on the field name in the *Selected fields* list and use the **<** button to move it from the *Selected fields* list back to the *Available fields* list.
6) If you make a mistake in the order of the selected fields, click on the field name that is in the wrong order and use the **Up** or **Down** arrow on the right side of the *Selected fields* list to move the field name to the correct position.
7) Click **Next**.

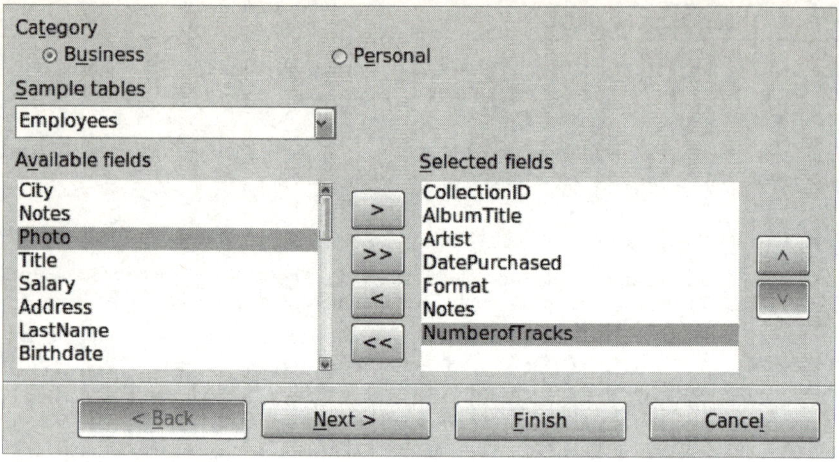

Figure 200: Selecting fields for the table

Step 2: Set field types and formats.

In this step you give the fields their properties. When you click a field, the information on the right changes. (See Figure 201.) You can then make changes to meet your needs. Click each field, one at a time, and make the changes listed below.

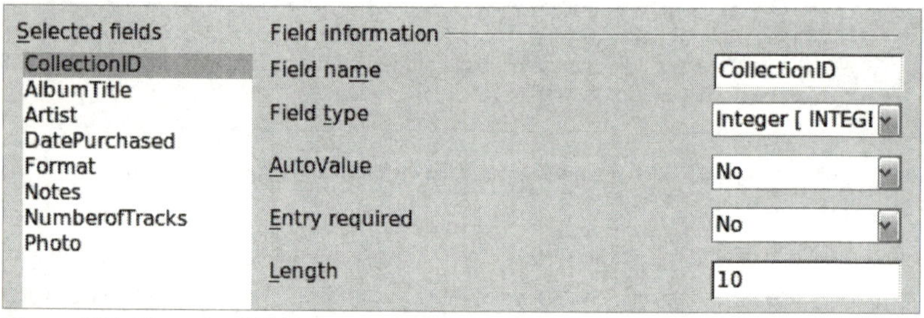

Figure 201: Changing field types

Note	If any of these fields requires a mandatory entry, set *Entry required* to **Yes**. A blank field will then not be allowed. In general, only set *Entry required* to **Yes** if something must always be put in that field. By default, *Entry required* is set to **No**.

- *CollectionID:* Change *AutoValue* from **No** to **Yes**. (example of a mandatory entry)
- *AlbumTitle*:
  - *Entry required*: Leave *Entry required* as *No*, unless all of your music is in albums.
  - *Length*: Unless you have an album title that exceeds 100 characters counting the spaces, do not change the length.
- *Artist*: Use the Default setting. And since music has artists, set *Entry Required* to *Yes.*
- *Date Purchased*: *Field type*: default date setting. *Entry required* should be *No.* (You may not know the date.)

Note	In Base the maximum length of each field must be specified on creation. It is not easy to change this later, so if in doubt specify a greater length. Base uses VCHAR as the field format for text fields. This format uses only the actual number of characters in a field up to the limit set, so a field containing 20 characters will occupy only 20 characters even if the limit is set at 100. Two album titles containing 25 and 32 characters respectively will use space for 25 and 32 characters and not 100 characters.

- *Format*: Only change the *Entry Required* setting: from *No* to *Yes*.
- *Notes*: No changes are required.
- *NumberofTracks*: Change the *Field Type* to *Tiny Integer [TINYINT]*. Your allowable number of tracks will be 999. Small Integer [SMALLINT] would allow 99999 tracks if you needed more than 999 tracks.
- *Photo:* Use the default settings.

When you have finished, click **Next**.

Note	Each field has a *Field Type*, which must be specified. Types include text, integer, date, and decimal. If the field is going to have general information in it (for example, a name or a description), use text. If the field will always contain a number (for example, a price), the type should be decimal or another numerical field. The wizard picks the right field type, so to get an idea of how this works, see what the wizard has chosen for different fields.

Step 3: Set primary key.

1) *Create a primary key* should be checked.
2) Select option *Use an existing field as a primary key*.
3) In the *Fieldname drop down* list, select *CollectionID*.
4) Check *Auto value* if it is not already checked.
5) Click **Next**.

Note	A primary key uniquely identifies an item (or record) in the table. For example, you might know two people called "Randy Herring" or three people living at the same address and the database needs to distinguish between them. The simplest method is to assign a unique number to each one: number the first person 1, the second 2, and so on. Each entry has one number and every number is different, so it is easy to say "record ID 172". This is the option chosen here: CollectionID is just a number assigned automatically by Base to each record of this table.

Step 4: Create the table.

1) If desired, rename the table at this point. If you rename it, make the name meaningful to you. For this example, make no changes.
2) Leave the option *Insert data immediately* checked.
3) Click **Finish** to complete the table wizard. Close the window created by the table wizard. You are now back to the main window of the database with the listing of the tables, queries, forms, and reports. Notice that a table named "CD-Collection" is now listed in the Tables portion of the window.

Creating a table by copying an existing table

If you have a large collection of music, you might want to create a table for each type of music you have. Rather than creating each table from the wizard, you can make copies of the original table, naming each according to the type of music contained in it.

1) Click on the **Tables** icon in the Database pane to see the existing tables.
2) Right-click on the *CD-Collection* table icon. Choose **Copy** from the pop-up menu.
3) Move the mouse pointer below this table, right-click, and select **Paste**. The Copy table dialog opens.
4) Change the table name to *Pop* and click **Next**.
5) Click the **>>** button to move all the fields from the left box to the right box and click **Next**.
6) Since all the fields already have the proper Field type, no changes should be needed. However, this is the time and place to make any changes if they are needed. (See Caution below for the reason why.) Click **Create**. The new table is created.

Caution

Once tables have been created using the wizard, and data has been entered, editing them should be very limited. Fields can be added or deleted, but adding a field requires you to enter the data for that one field for every existing record with an entry for that field.

Deleting a field deletes **all the data** once contained in that field. Changing the field type of a field can lead to data being lost either partially or completely. When creating a new table, it pays to create the fields with the correct names, length, and format before you add any data.

Deleting a table removes all of the data contained in every field of the table. Unless you are sure, do not delete a table.

Creating tables in Design View

Design View is a more advanced method for creating a new table, in which you directly enter information about each field in the table. We will use this method for the tables of our database.

Note

While the *Field type* and *formatting* are different in *Design View*, the concepts are the same as in the Wizard.

The first table to be created is *Fuel*. Its fields are *FuelID, Date, FuelCost, FuelQuantity, Odometer*, and *PaymentType*.

1) Click Create Table in Design View.
2) *FuelID* field: Type *FuelID* as the first Field Name. Press the *Tab* key to move to the Field Type column. Select *Integer [INTEGER]* as the Field Type from the drop down list. (The default setting is Text [VARCHAR].)

Tip

A shortcut for selecting from the Field Type drop down list: press the key for the first letter of the choice. You can cycle through the choices for a given letter by repeatedly pressing that key.

a) Change the Field Properties in the bottom section.

Change *AutoValue* from *No* to *Yes.*

b) Set *FuelID* as the *Primary key*.

Right-click on the green triangle to the left of *FuelID* (Figure 202) and choose *Primary Key* from the menu. This places a key icon in front of *FuelID*.

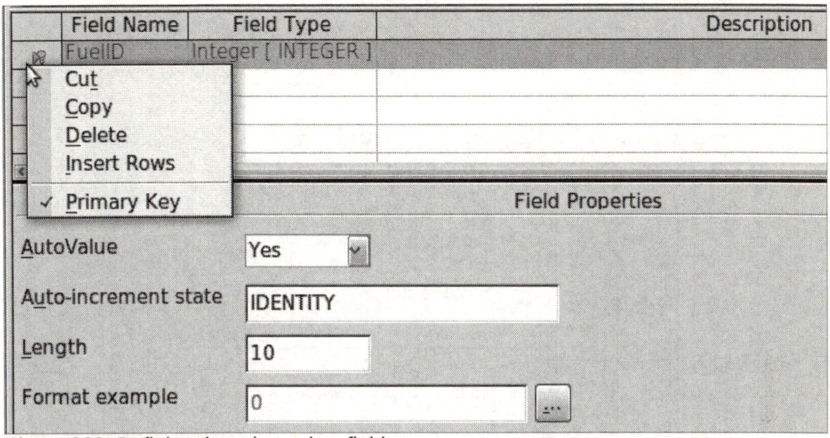

Figure 202: Defining the primary key field

Note	The primary key serves only one purpose: to identify the record uniquely. Any name can be used for this field. We have used *FuelID* for convenience, so we know to which table it belongs.

3) All other fields (*Date, FuelCost, FuelQuantity, Odometer*, and *PaymentType*):
   a) Type the next field name in the Field Name column.
   b) Select the Field Type for each field.
      - For *Date* use Date[DATE]. (Press the *D* key to select it.)
      - *PaymentType* uses Text [VARCHAR], the default setting.
      - All other fields use Number [NUMERIC]. (Press the *N* key once to select it.)
   c) *FuelCost*, *FuelQuantity*, and *Odometer* need changes in the Field Properties section (Figure 203).
      - *FuelQuantity*: Change *Length* to 6 and *Decimal places* to 3. (Many fuel pumps measure fuel to thousandths of a gallon in the USA, where I live.)
      - *Odometer*: Change the *Length* to 10 and the *Decimal places* to 1.
      - *FuelCost*: Change the Length to 5 and Decimal places to 2. Click the *Format example* button (Figure 203). This opens the Field Format window (Figure 204). Use *Currency* as the Category and your currency as the Format. My currency has two decimal places. Use what is appropriate for yours.

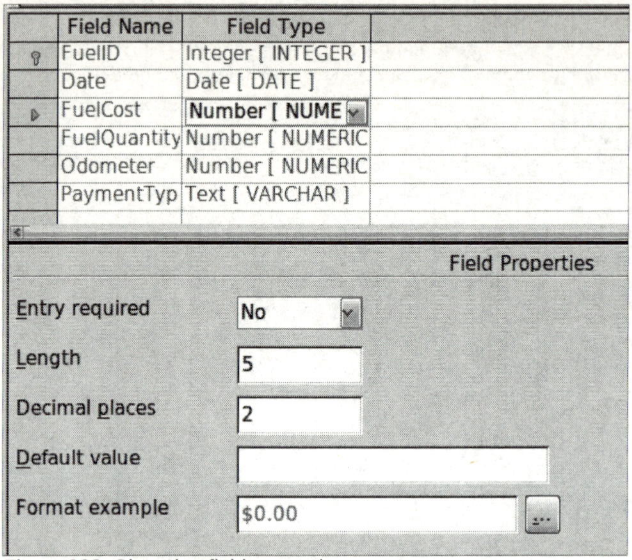

Figure 203: Changing field properties

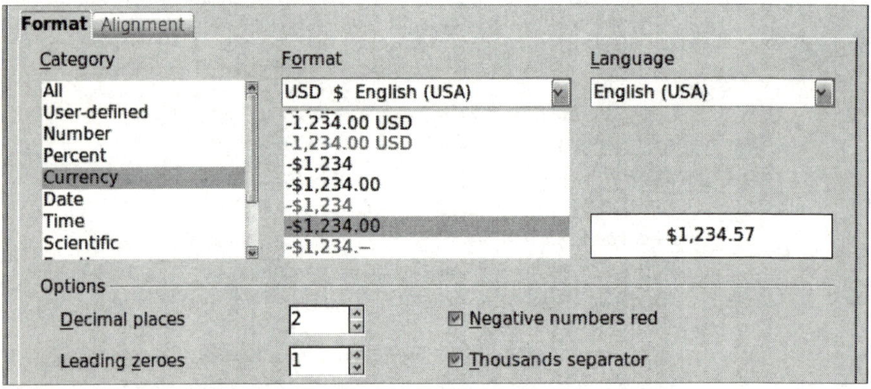

Figure 204: Field Format options

4) To access additional formatting options, click the button to the right of the Format example field.
5) *Description* can be anything, or can be left blank.
6) To save and close the table, choose **File > Save**. Name the table *Fuel*. Close the Fuel table.

Follow the same steps to create the *Vacations* table. The fields and their field types are listed in Figure 205. Make sure you make the Date field the primary key before closing. (Right-click the gray box to the left of Date and select **Primary key** from the menu.) Save the table and name it *Vacations*. Close the Vacations table.

	Field Name	Field Type	
🔑	Date	Date [DATE]	
	Odometer	Number [NUMERIC]	Odometer reading
	Motel	Number [NUMERIC]	
	Tolls	Number [NUMERIC]	total tolls
	Breakfast	Number [NUMERIC]	
	BPayment	Text [VARCHAR]	payment type
	Lunch	Number [NUMERIC]	
	LPayment	Text [VARCHAR]	payment type
	Supper	Number [NUMERIC]	
	SPayment	Text [VARCHAR]	payment type
	SnackNo	Number [NUMERIC]	
	SnackCost	Number [NUMERIC]	
	SnPayment	Text [VARCHAR]	payment type for snacks
	Miscellaneous	Number [NUMERIC]	misc. costs
	MPayment	Text [VARCHAR]	payment type for motel
	MiscNotes	Memo [LONGVARCH.	
	MiscPayment	Text [VARCHAR]	payment type for miscellaneous

Figure 205: Fields in Vacations table

Defining relationships

Now that the tables have been created, what are the relationships between our tables? This is the time to define them based upon the questions we asked and answered in the beginning.

When on vacation, we want to enter all of our expenses at once each day. Most of these expenses are in the Vacations table, but the fuel we buy is not. So we will link these two tables using the Date fields. Since the Fuel table may have more than one entry per date, this relationship between the Vacations and Fuel tables is one to many (it is designated 1:n.)

The Fuel and Maintenance tables do not really have a relationship even though they share similar fields: Date and Odometer.

Tip	As you create your own databases, you will also need to determine where tables are related and how.

1) To begin defining relationships, choose **Tools > Relationships**. The Automobile – LibreOffice Base: Relation Design window opens and the Add Tables dialog pops up. (You can also open it by clicking the Add Tables icon on the Relation Design window.)
2) On the Add Tables dialog, use either of these ways to add a table to the Relation Design window:
   - Double-click the name of the table. In our case, do this for both *Vacations* and *Fuel*.
   - Or, click the name of the table and then click **Add** for each table.
3) Click **Close** to close the Add Tables dialog when you have added the tables you want.

4) You can define the relationship between the Vacations and Fuel tables in two ways:
   - Click and drag the *Date* field in the Fuel table to the *Date* field in the Vacations table. When you release the mouse button, a connecting line forms between the two date fields.
   - Or, click the **New Relation** icon. This opens the Relations window (Figure 207). Our two tables are listed in the *Tables involved* section.
     a) In the *Fields involved* section, click the drop down list under the Fuel label.
     b) Select *Date* from the Fuel table list.
     c) Click in the cell to the right of this drop down list. This opens a drop down list for the Vacations table.
     d) Select *Date* from the Vacations table list. It should now look like Figure 207.
     e) Click **OK**.

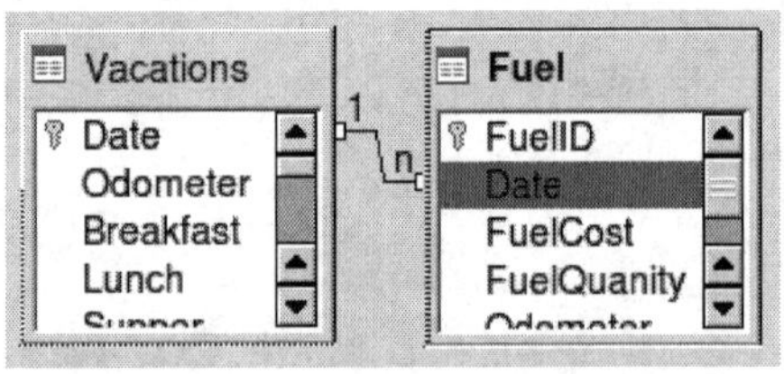

Figure 206: Designation for a 1:n relationship

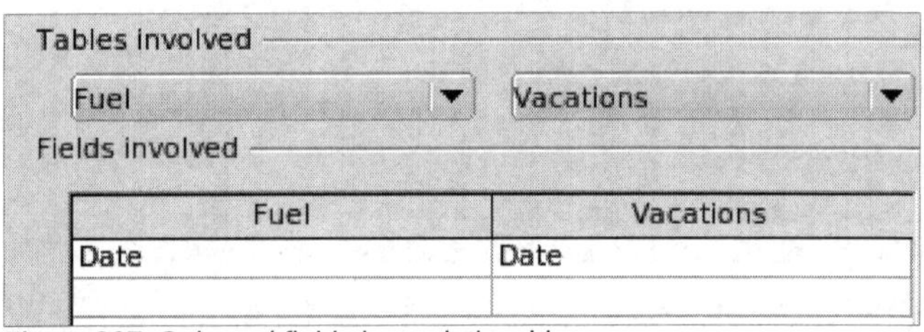

Figure 207: Selected fields in a relationship

5) Modifying the *Update options* and *Delete options* section of the Relation window.
   a) Right-click the line connecting the Date fields in the two table lists to open a menu.
   b) Select **Edit** to open the Relations dialog (Figure 208).

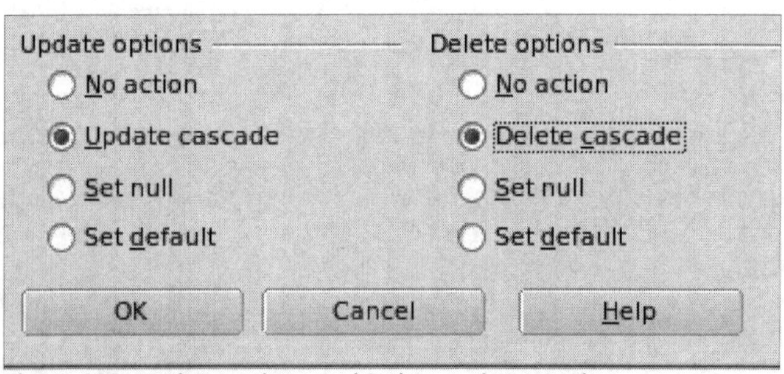

Figure 208: Update options and Delete options section

   c) Select **Update cascade**.

d) Select **Delete cascade**.

e) Click **OK** to close the Relations dialog and choose **File > Save** to save the Relation Design window.

While these options are not strictly necessary, they do help. Having them selected permits you to update a table that has a relationship defined with another table which has been modified. It also permits you to delete a field from the table without causing inconsistencies.

Creating a database form

Databases are used to store data. But, how is the data put into the database? Forms are used to do this. In the language of databases, a form is a front end for data entry and editing.

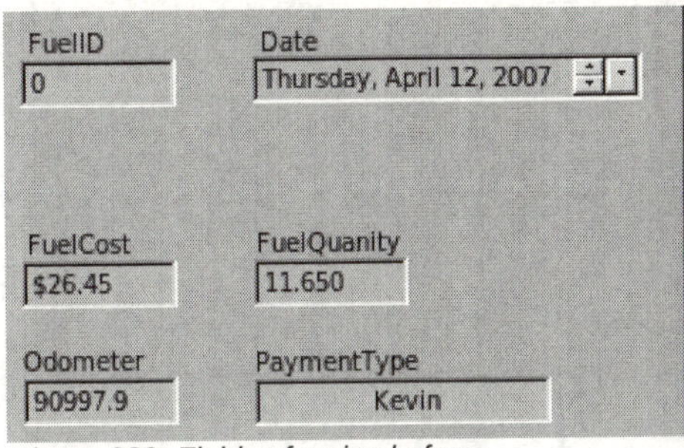

Figure 209: Fields of a simple form

Figure 210: Simple form with additions

A simple form consists of the fields from a table (Figure 209). More complex forms can contain much more, including additional text, graphics, selection boxes, and many other elements. Figure 210 is made from the same table with a text label (Fuel Purchases), a list box placed in PaymentType, and a graphic background.

A list box is useful when a field contains a fixed choice of options. It saves you from having to type in data by hand, and ensures that invalid options are not entered.

In our database, payments for food or fuel might be made from one of two credit cards (Dan or Kevin) or in cash, so these would be the available options for all boxes that contain payments.

To create a list box, we first need to create a small, separate table containing the options. This is then linked to the corresponding field in the form. The topic is dealt with in detail in the Base User Guide and will not be pursued further here.

Using the Wizard to create a form

We will use the Form Wizard to create a Vacations form, which will contain a form and a subform

In the main database window (Figure 199), click the **Forms** icon in the left column. In the Tasks list, double-click **Use Wizard to Create Form** to open the Form Wizard (Figure 211). Simple forms require only some of these steps, while more complex forms may use all of them.

Step 1: Select fields.

1) Under Tables or queries, select Table: Vacations. *Available fields* lists the fields for the Vacations table.

2) Click the right double arrow to move all of these fields to the *Fields in the form* list. Click **Next**.

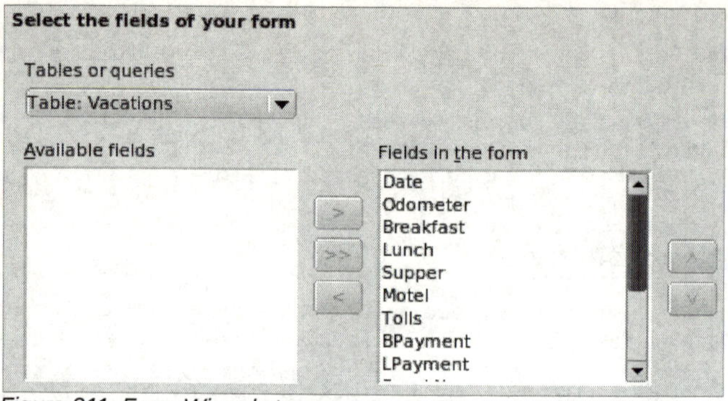

Figure 211: Form Wizard steps

Step 2: Set up a subform

Since we have already created a relationship between the Fuel and Vacations tables, we will use that relationship. If no relationship had been defined, this would need to be done in step 4.

1) Click the box labeled *Add* Subform
2) Click Sub form *based upon existing relation*.
3) Fuel is listed as a relation we want to add. So click Fuel to highlight it, as in Figure 212. Click **Next**.

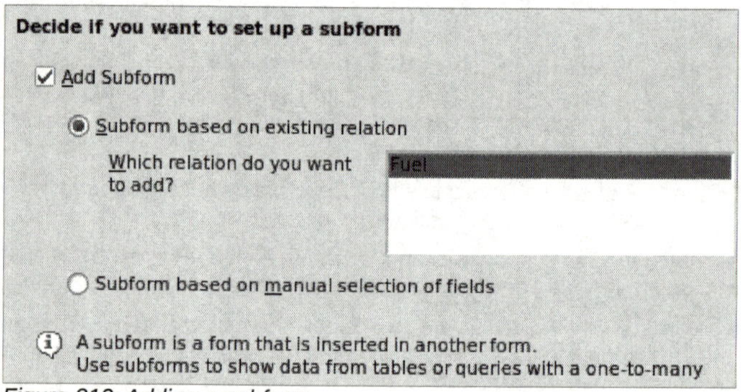

Figure 212: Adding a subform

Step 3: Add subform fields.

This step is similar to step 1. The only difference is that not all of the fields will be used in the subform.

1) Fuel is preselected under *Tables or queries*.
2) Use the **>>** button to move all the fields to the right.
3) Click the FuelID field to highlight it.
4) Use the **<** button to move the FuelID to the left (Figure 213).
5) Click **Next**.

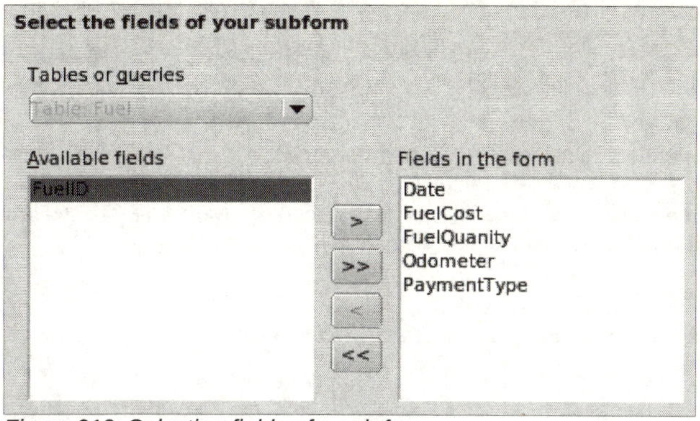

Figure 213: Selecting fields of a sub form

Step 4: Get joined fields.

This step is for tables or queries for which no relationship has been defined. Because we have already defined the relationship, the wizard skips this step.

Note	It is possible to create a relationship between two tables that is based upon more than one pair of fields. How to do that and why is discussed in the *Base Guide*.

Caution

When selecting a pair of fields from two tables to use as a relationship, they have to have the same field type. That is why we used the Date field from both tables: both their field types are Date[DATE].

Whether a single pair of fields from two tables are chosen as the relationship or two or more pairs are chosen, certain requirements must be met for the form to work.

- No field from the subform can be the Primary key for its table. (FuelID cannot be used.)
- Each pair of joined fields must have the same file type.
- One of the fields from the main form must be the Primary key for its table. (Date would have to be used.)

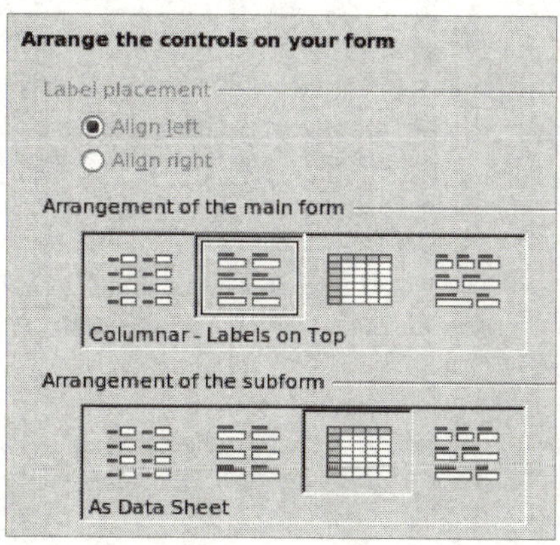

Step 5: Arrange controls.

A control in a form consists of two parts: label and field. This step in creating the form determines where a control's label and field are placed relative to each other. The four choices from left to right are *Columnar left*, *Columnar - Labels on top*, As *Data Sheet*, and *In Blocks - Labels Above*.

1) Arrangement of the main form: Click the second icon (*Columnar - Labels on top*). The labels will be placed above their field.
2) Arrangement of the sub form: Click the third icon (*As Data Sheet*). (The labels are column headings and the field entries are in spreadsheet format.) Click **Next**.

Step 6: Set data entry.

Unless you have a need for any of these entries to be checked, accept the default settings. Click **Next**.

Step 7: Apply styles.

1) Select the color you want in the *Apply Styles* list. (I chose the beige which is Orange 4 in the Color table.)
2) Select the Field border you want. (I prefer the 3D look. You might want to experiment with the different possible settings.)
3) Click **Next**.

Step 8: Set name.

1) Enter the name for the form. In this case, it is *Fuel*.
2) Click *Modify the form*.
3) Click **Finish**. The form opens in Edit mode.

Modifying a form

We will be moving the controls to different places in the form and changing the background to a picture. We will also modify the label for the PaymentType field as well as change the field to a list box.

First, we must decide what we want to change. The discussion will follow this outline of our planned changes.

- Provide a drop-down capability for the Date field in the main form, and lengthen the field to show the day of the week, month, day, and year.
- Shorten the length of the payment fields (all fields containing the word Payment).
- Move the controls into groups: food, fuel subform, and miscellaneous.
- Change the wording of some of the labels. Some single words should be two words. Some abbreviations should be used if possible (Misc. for miscellaneous).
- Change the lengths of several fields and labels. Only Lunch, Supper, Motel, and Tolls have acceptable lengths. But for a better appearance, changes will be made to these as well.
- Lengthen the Note field vertically, add a scroll bar, and move it.
- Make changes in the Date and PaymentType columns of the subform to match the changes in the main form.
- Add headings for each group in the main form.
- Change the background to a picture, then modify some of the labels so that they can be read clearly against this background.
- Change the font color of the headings.

Here are some methods that we will be using in these steps. The controls in the main form consist of a label and its field. Sometimes we want to work with the entire control, sometimes with only the label or the field, and there are times when we want to work with a group of controls.

- Clicking a label or field selects the entire control. A border appears around the control with eight green handles. You can then drag and drop it where you want.

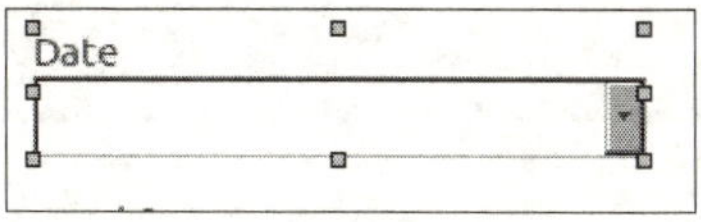

Figure 214: A selected control

- *Control+click* a label or field selects only the label or the field. You can press the *Tab* key to change the selection from the field to the label or the label to the field.

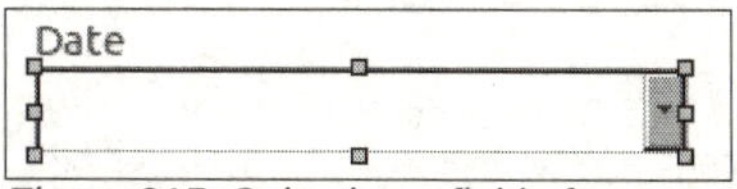

Figure 215: Selecting a field of a control

- Moving a group of controls is almost as easy as moving one of them.
  1) Click the field of the top left control to be moved, to select it.
  2) Move the cursor to just above and to the left of the selected control.
  3) Drag the cursor to the bottom right of the group of controls and release the mouse button.

As you drag the cursor, a dashed box appears, showing what is contained in your selection. Make sure it is big enough to include the entire length of all the controls.

When you release the mouse button, a border with its green handles appears around the controls you selected.

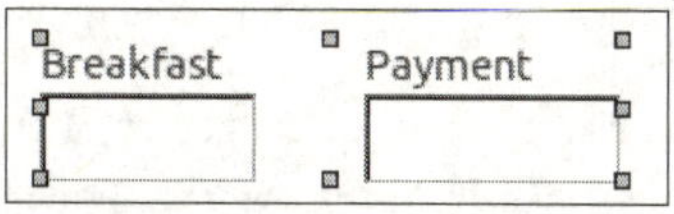

Figure 216: Selecting multiple controls

Move the cursor over one of the fields. It changes to a drag icon. Drag the group of controls to where you want them.

- Click the Tolls control to select it. Then drag it to the right close to the Lunch control.

Tip	When either changing size or moving a control, two properties of the Form Design toolbar should be selected: *Snap to Grid*, and *Guides when Moving*. Your controls will line up better, and an outline of what you are moving moves as the cursor moves. You should also have both rulers active (**View > Ruler**).

Step 1: Change the Date field.

1) *Control+click* the Date field to select it.
2) Move the cursor over the middle green handle on the right side. It should change to a double-headed arrow.

3) Hold the left mouse button down as you drag the cursor to the right until the length is 6 cm. The vertical dashed line is lined up with the 6. Release the mouse button.
4) Click the Control icon in the Form Controls toolbar. If it is not visible, choose **View > Toolbars > Form Controls.** The *Properties: Date Field* window opens. Each line contains a property of the field.

Figure 217: Form Controls toolbar

- Scroll down to the *Date format* property. This is a drop down list with Standard (short) as the default setting. Click it to open the list. Select the *Standard (long)* entry.
- Scroll down to the *Drop down* property. Its default setting is No. It is also a drop down list. Click to open the list. Select *Yes*.

Tip	To see what the Date field will look like, click the **Form Mode On/Off** icon (the second icon from the left in Figure 217). You can do this any time you want to see the form with the changes you have made.

Step 2: Shorten the width of some fields.

All of the fields with a label containing the word payment are too wide. They need to be shortened before the controls are moved.

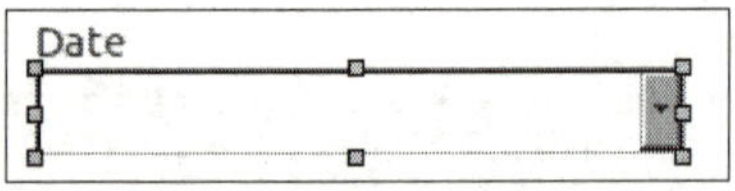

Figure 218: Selecting a field

1) *Control+click* the BPayment field.
2) Move the cursor over the middle green handle on the right. The cursor becomes a double-headed arrow.
3) Drag the cursor to the left until the field is 2.5 cm (1 inch) wide.
4) Repeat these steps to shorten these fields: Lpayment, SPayment, SnPayment, Mpayment, and MiscPayment.

Tip	If you have the *Snap to Grid* and *Guides when moving* icons selected in the Design Format toolbar, you will see how wide the field is as you shorten it.

Step 3: Move the controls to group them by category.

We want to move the controls so that they look like Figure 219.

1) Click the first control you want to move. A border appears around the control with eight green handles.
2) Move the cursor over the label or field of the control. It changes shape to a drag icon.
3) Drag and drop the control to where you want it.
4) Use the same steps to move the rest of the controls to where they belong.

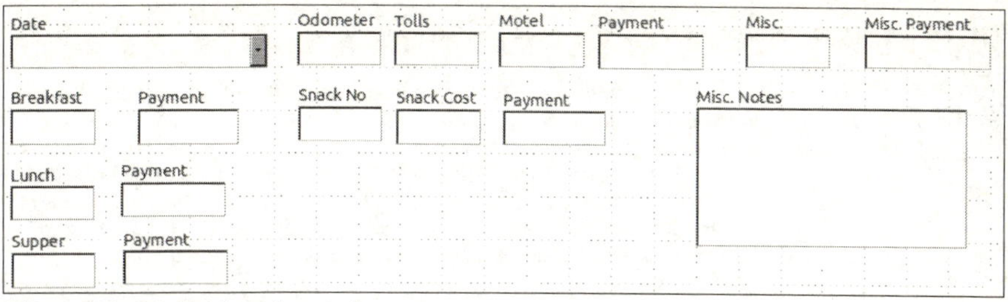

Figure 219: Positioning of controls

Caution	Do not use *Control+click* when moving a field. It moves either the field or the label but not both. To move both, use a plain *mouse click* and drag to the desired spot.

Step 4: Change the label wording.

Field names have been required to be single words for some time. However, the labels for the fields in a form can be more than one word. So we will change them by editing the text in the label.

1) *Control+click* the SnackNo label. Do one of the following:
   - Right-click the SnackNo label and select **Control** from the pop-up menu.
   - Or click the Control icon in the Form Control toolbar (Figure 217).
2) The dialog that opens is labeled Properties: Label Field. It contains all the properties of the selected label.
   - In the Label selection, edit the label to Snack No.
   - Close the Properties dialog.
3) Use the same procedure to change these labels as well: BPayment to Payment, LPayment to Payment, SPayment to Payment, Miscellaneous to Misc., SnackCost to Snack Cost, MPayment to Payment, MiscPayment to Misc. Payment, and MiscNotes to Misc. Notes.

Tip	You can modify all of the listings in the Properties window. For example, if you change the Alignment from Left to Center, the word or words in the label are centered within the label. When you have some time, you might want to experiment with different settings just to see the results you get.

Step 5: Change the widths of the labels and fields.

We want the following controls to be 2 cm wide (0.8 inches): Breakfast, Lunch, Supper, Odometer, Snack No., Tolls, Snack Cost, Motel, and Misc. All of the payment fields were changed in step 2, but Misc. Payment needs to be changed to 3 cm (1.2 inches).

1) Right-click Breakfast and choose **Position and Size**. On the Position and Size dialog, change Width to 2 cm.
2) Repeat for the other listed controls, using 3 cm for Misc.Payment.

Caution	When changing the position or size of an entire control, use the Position and Size dialog or the drag and drop method. When working with either the label or the field (but not both at the same time), you can use the Properties dialog to make these changes when you want to be exact. However, you need to be careful not to accidentally select the entire control for use with the Properties dialog or you will apply exactly the same values to both the label and field. For example, if you enter the values for a new position, both the field and the label moves to the same position and the field is positioned on top of the label. Then you will have to move each of them to where you really want them.

Note	To open the Properties window, right-click a control and select **Control** from the pop-up menu. Or, you can click the Control icon in the *Form Controls* toolbar. Just be careful, and use *Control+Z* to undo any mistakes you may make. Detailed instructions on how to use the Properties window are given in the *Base Guide*.

Step 6: Change the Misc. Notes field.

We want the Misc. Notes control, which has a field type of Memo, to have a vertical scroll bar for additional text space if desired.

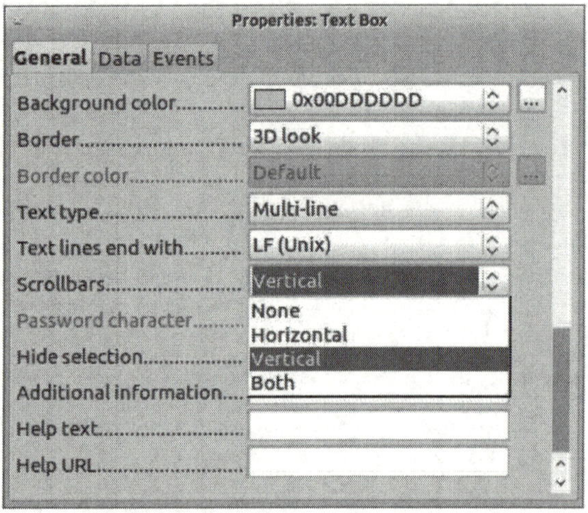

Figure 220: Scroll bar selections in the Properties window

1) *Control+click* the *Misc. Notes* field. The green handles should surround the field but not its label.
2) Click the **Control** icon to open the Properties window (Figure 220).
3) Scroll down to the Text type property with single-line as the default value.
   - Change it to Multi-line.
4) Scroll down to the *Scrollbars* setting. Change the selection from *None* to *Vertical* in this list.
5) Close the Properties window. (*Esc* key)
6) Lengthen the Misc. Notes field by moving the cursor over the middle green handle at the bottom of the field and dragging down until the length is 6 cm (2.4 inches).

Step 7: Change labels and fields in the subform

The subform is located at the bottom of the form. We want to widen the Date column, and change the label for the PaymentType column to two words.

- To widen the Date column, move the mouse pointer over the dividing line between the Date and FuelCost columns. When the pointer changes shape, click and drag to move the divider to the right.
- To change the PaymentType column:
  - Right-click the label PaymentType to open the menu.
  - Select **Column** to open the Properties dialog. In the *Label* property, change PaymentType to Payment Type.
  - Close the Properties dialog.

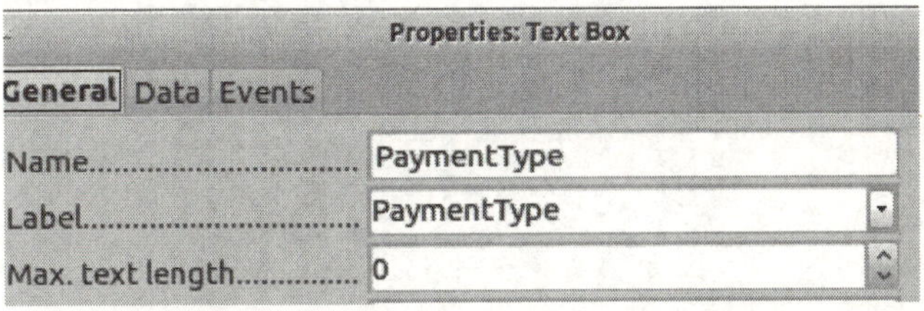

Step 8: Add headings to groups.

This step is easier to do if you have end-of-paragraph markers visible. Choose **View > Non printing Characters** to turn them on.

Figure 221: Apply Styles list

1) Make sure the cursor is in the upper left corner. If it is not, click in that corner to move it there.
2) Press the *Enter* key to move the cursor down to the space between the Date field and the Breakfast field.
3) Change the *Apply Styles* drop down list from *Default* to *Heading 2*.
4) Use the spacebar to move the cursor to where you want the heading to start.
5) Type the heading *Meals*.
6) Use the spacebar to move the cursor to the center of snack area.
7) Type the heading *Snacks*.
8) Use the *Enter* key to move the cursor between the Supper control and the subform.
9) Use the spacebar to move the cursor to the center of the subform.
10) Type the heading *Fuel Data*.

Note	If you know how to use styles, you can open the Styles and Formatting window using *F11*. Right-clicking the Heading 2 paragraph style allows you to modify the appearance of all three headings. See Chapter 6 of the *Writer Guide* for details.

Step 9: Change the background of a form.

The background for a form can be a color, or a graphic (picture). You can use any of the colors in the Color Table at **Tools > Options > LibreOffice > Colors**. If you know how to create custom colors, you can use them. You can also use a picture (graphic file) as the background.

1) Right-click the form to open a context menu.
2) Select **Page**.
3) Make sure the *Background* tab has been selected. (It will be in bold type while the other tabs will be in default type.)

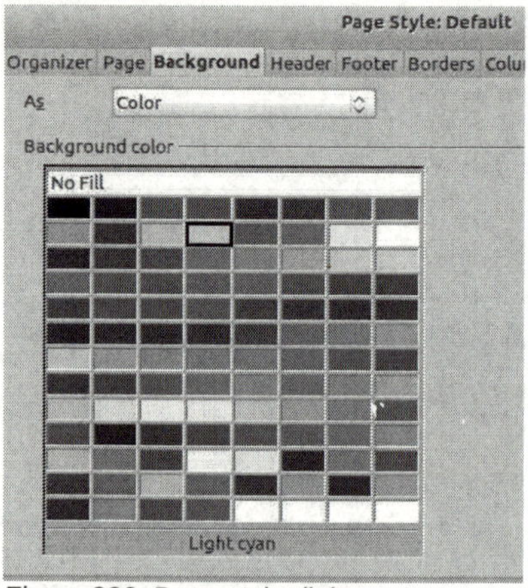

Figure 222: Page style dialog

4) Click *Light cyan*. (Second row, fourth column from the left.)
5) Click **Apply** to see the effects of adding the color. OR, click **OK** to close the dialog.

Tip	Learning how to use styles can be very helpful at times. By using styles, we changed the font color for all three headings at one time. There are other methods of changing the font color, but they require repeating the same steps for each heading.

6) To add a graphic to the background:
   a) Click the Gallery tool (circled in red). The gallery window opens.

   b) Select the graphic you want to use. (I have done these steps selecting pebble-light.)
      i) Browse through the choices.
      ii) Right-click your choice.
      iii) **Insert > Background > Page**
   c) Click the Gallery tool to close the gallery window.
   d) The form should look like Figure 223.

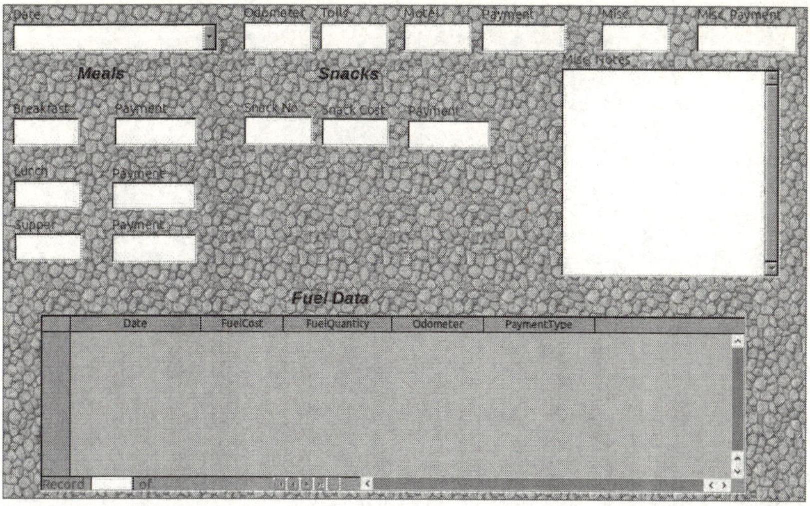

Figure 223: Finished form

Step 10: Change the tab order.

The *Tab* key moves the cursor from field to field. This is much easier to do than to click each field to enter data into it. It also permits us to group our expenses into areas before we begin entering data. For example, all of our meal receipts can be grouped together as can our snacks and also our fuel purchases.

Figure 224: Form Design toolbar with Activation Order icon circled

1) *Control+click* the Date field.
2) Click the **Form Design** icon in the Form Controls toolbar to open the Form Design toolbar (Figure 224), or choose **View > Toolbar > Form Design** to open this toolbar.
3) Click the **Activation Order** icon (circled).
4) Rearrange the order of the fields in the Tab Order window.
   a) Find the txtMPayment listing near the bottom of the list and click it.
   b) Click the **Move Up** button until txtPayment is just below fmtMotel.
   c) Use the same two steps to put the fields in the same order as in Figure 225. Click **OK**.
5) Save and close the form.
6) Save the database.

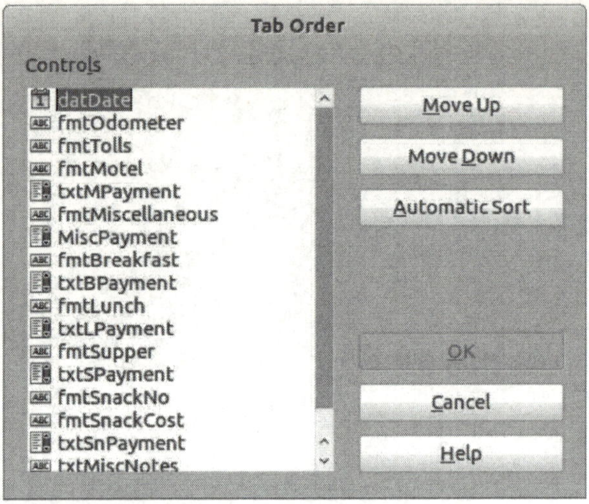

Figure 225: Tab order for the main form

Creating forms and sub forms in Design View

This method requires using the *Form Controls* and *Form Design* toolbars extensively. These techniques are beyond the scope of this document. Instructions for creating forms using Design view will be described in the *Database Guide*.

Accessing other data sources

LibreOffice allows data sources to be accessed and then linked into LibreOffice documents. For example, a mail merge links an external document containing a list of names and addresses into a letter, with one copy of the letter being generated for each entry.

To access a data source that is not a *.odb file:

1) **File > New > Database** opens the *Database Wizard* window.
2) Select **Connect to an existing database**. Click the arrow next to the *Database type* field and select the database type from the drop down list. Click **Next.**
3) Click *Browse* and select the database. Click **Next**.
4) Accept the default settings: *Register the database for me,* and *Open the database for editing*. Click **Finish**. Name and save the database in the location of your choice.

Caution	
⚠	One of the choices available when you select *Connect to an existing database* is *LDAP Address Book*. Beginning with LibreOffice 4.0.0, this option no longer works.

Accessing a spreadsheet as a data source

Accessing a spreadsheet is similar to accessing other databases:

1) Choose **File > New > Database**.
2) Select *Connect to an existing database*. Select *Spreadsheet* as the *Database type*.

3) Click **Browse** to locate the spreadsheet you want to access. If the spreadsheet is password protected, check the *Password required* box. Click **Next**.
4) If the spreadsheet requires a user's name, enter it. If a password is also required, check its box. Click **Next**.

Note	Using this method of accessing a spreadsheet, you cannot change anything in the spreadsheet. You can only view the contents of the spreadsheet, run queries, and create reports based upon the data already entered into the spreadsheet. All changes in a spreadsheet must be made in the spreadsheet itself, using Calc. After modifying the spreadsheet and saving it, you will see the changes in the database. If you create and save an additional sheet in your spreadsheet, the database will have a new table the next time you access it.

Registering *.odb databases

Databases created by LibreOffice are in the *.odb (OpenDocument Base) format. Other programs can also produce databases in this format. Registering a *.odb database is simple:

1) Choose **Tools > Options > LibreOffice Base > Databases**.
2) Under *Registered databases*, click **New.**
3) Browse to where the database is located.
4) Make sure the registered name is correct.
5) Click **OK.**

Note	Sometimes when updating LibreOffice to a newer version, your list of registered database files disappears. When that happens, you need to use these steps to register your database files with your latest version of LibreOffice.

Using data sources in LibreOffice

Having registered the data source, whether a spreadsheet, text document, external database or other accepted data source, you can use it in other LibreOffice components including Writer and Calc.

Viewing data sources

Open a document in Writer or Calc. To view the data sources available, press *F4* or select **View > Data Sources** from the pull-down menu. This brings up a list of registered databases, which will include Bibliography and any other database registered, such as the Automobile database created earlier in this chapter.

To view each database, click on the ‖▶ to the left of the database's name (see Figure 226). This brings up Tables and Queries. Click on the ‖▶ next to Tables to view the individual tables created. Now click on a table to see all the records held in it.

Figure 226: Databases

Editing data sources

Some data sources (but not spreadsheets) can be edited in the Data View window. A record can be edited, added, or deleted.

View a table's data

If you click on a table its rows and columns of data appear on the right side of the Data Source window. Editing this data requires only a click in the cell whose data should be changed, change the data, and click in the row above or below it to save the new data.

Beneath the records are five tiny buttons. The first four move backwards or forwards through the records, or to the beginning or end. The fifth button, with a small star, inserts a new record.

Figure 227: View Data Sources navigation buttons

To delete a record, right-click on the gray box to the left of a row to highlight the entire row, and select **Delete Rows** to remove the selected row.

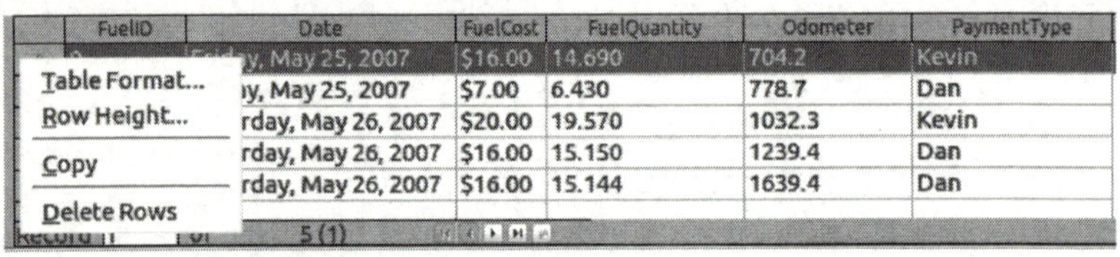

Figure 228: Deleting a row in the Data View window

Launching Base to work on data sources

You can launch LibreOffice Base at any time from the Data Source window. Just right-click on a database or its Tables or Queries icons and select **Edit Database File**. Once in Base, you can edit, add, and delete tables, queries, forms, and reports.

Using data sources in Writer and Calc

Data can be placed into Writer and Calc documents from the tables in the data source window. In Writer, values from individual fields can be inserted. Or a complete table can be created in the Writer document. One common way to use a data source is to perform a mail merge.

Figure 229: Toolbar for the Data Sources window

Tip	Choosing **Tools > Mail Merge Wizard** or clicking on the Mail Merge icon (circled in red) in the Data Sources window launches the Mail Merge wizard which steps you through creating a mail merge document. See Chapter 11 in the *Writer Guide*.

Writer documents

To insert a field from a table opened in the data source window into a Writer document, click on the field name (the gray square at the top of the field list) and, with the left mouse button held down, drag the field onto the document. In a Writer document, it will appear as <FIELD> (where FIELD is the name of the field you dragged).

For example, to enter the cost of meals and who paid for them on a certain date of a vacation:

1) Open the list of data sources (*F4*) and select the Vacations table in the Automobile database.
2) Use this sentence: "On (date), our breakfast cost (amount) paid by (name), our lunch cost (amount) paid by (name), and our supper cost (amount) paid by (name)." But only type "On , our breakfast cost paid by , our lunch cost paid by , and our supper cost paid by ."
3) To replace (date), click the field name Date in the data source window and drag it to the right of the word *On*. The result: On <Date>. If you have Field shadings turned on (**View > Field shading**), <Date> has a gray background. Otherwise it does not.
4) To replace first (amount), click the Breakfast field name and drag it to the right of *our breakfast cost*. Make sure you have the proper spacing between the field names and the words before and after them. Result: breakfast cost <Breakfast>.
5) To replace the first (name), click the Bpayment field name and drag it to the right of *paid by*. Result: paid by <Bpayment>.
6) In the same way, fill in the rest of the fields in the sentence.
   - Use <Lunch> and <LPayment> for the second set of (amount) and (name) in the sentence.
   - Use <Supper> and <SPayment> for the third set of (amount) and (name) in the sentence.
7) Final result: On <Date>, our breakfast cost <Breakfast> paid by <BPayment>, our lunch cost <Lunch> paid by <LPayment>, and our supper cost <Supper> paid by <SPayment>.
8) Add data to the fields of the sentence:
   - Click the gray box to the left of the row of data you want to add. That row should be highlighted like the second row of Figure 230.
   - Click the *Data to Fields* icon (circled). This should fill the fields with the data from the row you chose.
   - Click another row and then click this icon again. The data in the sentence changes to this selected row of data.
   - Save the document if you want to use it as an example later.

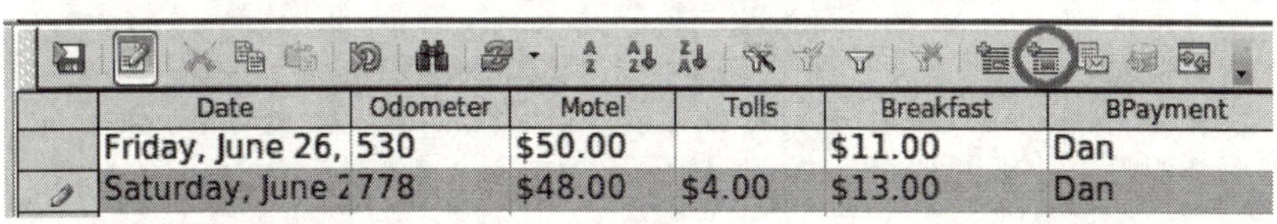

	Date	Odometer	Motel	Tolls	Breakfast	BPayment
	Friday, June 26,	530	$50.00		$11.00	Dan
	Saturday, June 2	778	$48.00	$4.00	$13.00	Dan

Figure 230: Selected row in data source window

Adding data in table format is a little easier and takes perhaps fewer steps. Some of the steps will be quite similar.

1) Navigate to the place you want to place the table and click the location.
2) *Control+Click* the gray box to the left of each row of the data source that you want to be a row in your table if the rows are not consecutive. To select consecutive rows, click the gray box to the left of the top desired row and *Shift+click* the bottom desired row.
3) Click the *Data to text* icon to open the Insert Database Columns dialog (Figure 231). (The *Data to text* icon is to the left of the Data to Fields icon in Figure 230.)
4) Move the fields you want in your table from the *Database Columns* list to the *Table column(s)* list.
   - To place the fields in the order you select, click the field and use the *single arrow* to move the fields in the order you desire. You can also limit the fields you use to less than all of the fields available.
   - If you want to use all of the fields, use the *double arrow* pointing to the right to move all of them at one time. The order of the fields in the table you create will be the same as in the data source table.
   - To remove a single field from the *Table Column(s)* list, click the field and use the *single arrow* pointing to the left.
5) To start over, click the *double arrow* pointing to the left.
6) Select the settings for your table. Use the default settings as in Figure 231.
7) Click **OK**. Save the document.

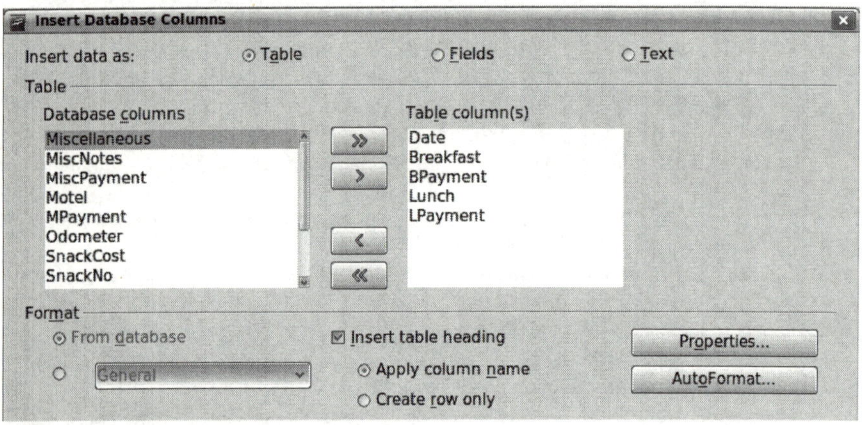

Figure 231: Insert Database Columns dialog

Calc spreadsheets

There are two ways to transfer data into a Calc spreadsheet. One enters the data into the spreadsheet cells. The other creates complete new records in the spreadsheet. While you can directly access the data inserted into the spreadsheet cells, new records created in the spreadsheet are read-only.

Entering data directly to the spreadsheet cells uses the *Data to Text* icon as when making a table in a Writer document. But there are certain differences.

The steps are straightforward.

1) Click the cell of the spreadsheet which you want to be the top left cell of your data, including the column names.

2) Use *F4* to open the database source window and select the table whose data you want to use.
3) Select the rows of data you want to add to the spreadsheet:
   - Click the gray box to the left of the row you want to select if only selecting one row. That row is highlighted.
   - To select multiple rows, hold down the *Control* key while clicking the gray box of the rows you need. Those rows are highlighted.
   - To select all the rows, click the gray box in the upper left corner. All rows are highlighted.
4) Click the *Data to text* icon to insert the data into the spreadsheet cells.
5) Save the spreadsheet.

Adding records to a spreadsheet is fairly easy. You need to have the Data Source window open, your spreadsheet open, and the table you want to use selected.

1) Click the gray box containing the field name for the table's ID field.
2) Drop and drag the gray box for the table's ID field to where you want the record to appear in the spreadsheet.
3) Repeat until you have moved all of the fields you need to where you want them.
4) Name and save the spreadsheet.
5) Click a row of the table in the Data Source window.
6) Drag the data in the ID field in the selected row onto the ID field in the spreadsheet. The Save icon should activate.
7) Click the *Edit File* button to make the spreadsheet read-only. Click **Save** when asked if you want to save the file.

The Data Sources window goes blank, the fields in the spreadsheet are populated with data from the row you selected, and the Form Navigation toolbar appears at the bottom of the spreadsheet.

Click the arrows on the Form Navigation toolbar to view the different records of the table. (The arrows are circled in red.) The number in the box changes when you change the record number by clicking an arrow. The data in the fields changes correspondingly to the data for that particular record number.

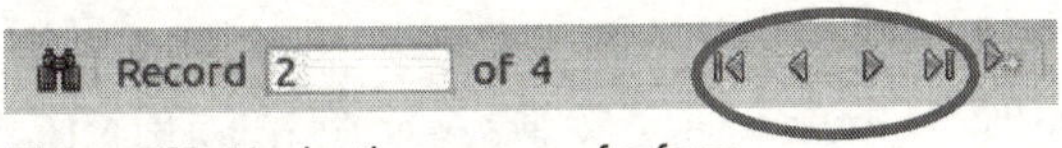

Figure 232: Navigation arrows of a form

Entering data in a form

Records are used to organize the data we enter into a form. They also organize the data we enter into a subform

Different types of field allow different methods of data entry. In many cases, more than one method can be used.

The first step to entering data in a form is to open it from the main database window (Figure 199).

1) Click the Forms icon in the *Database* list.
2) Find the form's name in the *Forms* list (Vacations).
3) Double-click the form's name.

The quickest way to enter a date in the Date field is to click the arrow that opens the drop down calendar (Figure 233). Then click the day the you want. Then press the *Tab* key to go to the Odometer field.

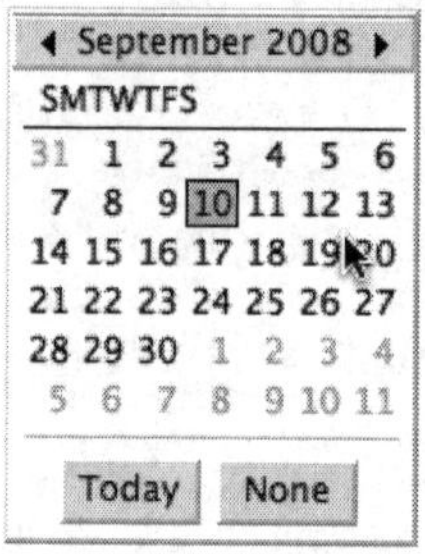

Figure 233: Calendar drop down

The Odometer, Tolls, and Motel fields are numeric fields. Enter values directly into them, or use the *up* and *down arrows*. When the value has been entered, use the *Tab* key to go to the next field.

- Clicking the *up arrow* increases the value, and the *down arrow* decreases the value by one unit.
- These two arrows only change the numerals to the left of the decimal place.
- Numerals to the right of the decimal place must be changed by deleting them and typing the desired ones.

The Motel's Payment field is a drop-down list. If, as in my case, all of the elements of the list start with different letters, typing the first letter selects the desired entry.

- If two or more elements of the list have the same first letter, repeated typing of the first letter will cycle through these elements.
- When the selection is correct, use the *Tab* key to go to the Misc. field.

The rest of the fields of the main form are either numeric fields or drop-down lists until we reach the Misc. Notes field. It is a text field. Type anything you desire in this field just as you would any simple text editor.

Note

Since the *Tab* key is used to move between fields, it can not be used in a text field. All spacing must be done by the *spacebar*. Furthermore in text fields, the *Enter* key acts only as a line break to move the cursor to the next line. While the *Enter* key will move between non-text fields, it will not do so from a text field. Use the *Tab* key instead.

If we did not have a subform for fuel data, pressing the *Tab* key in the last field would save all of the fields, clear them, and make the form ready to accept data on the second record.

Since we have a subform, using the *Tab* key places the cursor in the first Date field of the subform with the date automatically entered to match the Date field of the main form.

The FuelCost, FuelQuantity, and Odometer fields are numeric fields. The Payment field is a drop-down list. Enter the data just as you did in the main form, and use the *Tab* key to go to the next field.

When you use the *Tab* key to leave the Payment field, it goes to the Date field of the next line and automatically enters the date. Now you can enter your second set of fuel data for this day.

To move to another record when the form has a subform, click any of the fields of the main form. In this case, click the Date field of the main form. Then use the directional arrows at the bottom. There are four of them from left to right: *First Record, Previous Record, Next Record*, and *Last Record* (Figure 232). To the right of these arrows is the *New Record* icon.

To create a new record while in another record in the main form, click either the *Next Record* icon or the *New Record* icon.

Tip	The number in the Record box is the number of the record whose data is shown in the form. If you know the number of the record you want, you can enter it into the record box and then press *Enter* to take you to that record.

Figure 234 is a record with data inserted in its fields.

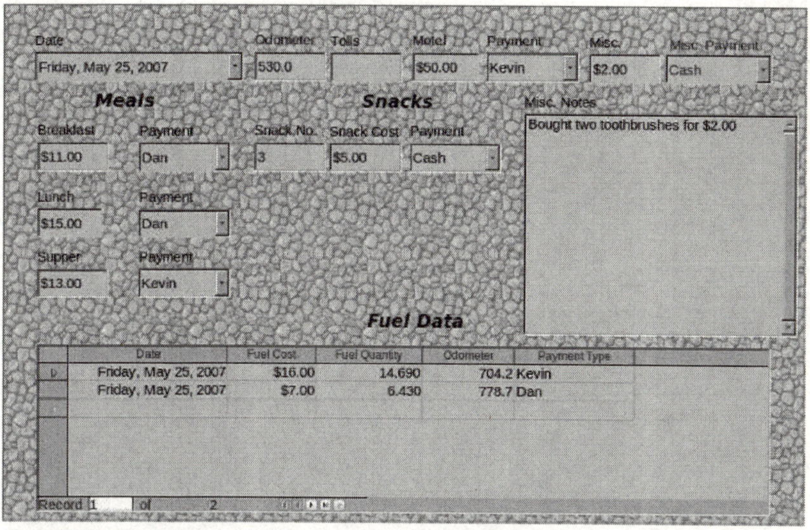

Figure 234: Sample record of the Vacation form and sub form

Creating queries

Queries are used to get specific information from a database. Query results are special tables within the database.

To demonstrate the use of queries, we will use two different methods:

- Using our CD-Collection table, we will create a list of albums by a particular artist. We will do this using the Wizard.
- The information we might want from the Fuel table includes what our fuel economy is. We will do this using the Design View. (Queries that require calculations are best created with the Design view.)

Using the Wizard to create a query

Queries created by the wizard provide a list or lists of information based upon what one wants to know. It is possible to obtain a single answer or multiple answers, depending upon the circumstances.

In the main database window (Figure 199), click the Queries icon in the Databases section, then in the Tasks section, click *Use Wizard to Create Query*. The Query Wizard window opens (Figure 235). The information we want is what albums are by a certain musical group or individual (the album's author). We can include when each album was bought.

Note	When working with a query, more than one table can be used. Since different tables may contain the same field names, the format for naming fields in a query is *Table name.field name*, with a period (.) between the table name and the field name. For example, the Lunch field of the Vacation table used in a query has the name *Vacation.Lunch*.

Step 1: Select the fields.

1) Select the CD-Collection table from the drop down list of tables.
2) Select fields from the CD-Collection table in the *Available fields* list.
   a) Click *Artist*, and use the **>** button to move it to the *Fields in the Query* list.
   b) Move the AlbumTitle and DatePurchased fields in the same manner.
   c) Click **Next**.

Tip	To change the order of the fields, select the field you want to move and click the up or down arrow.

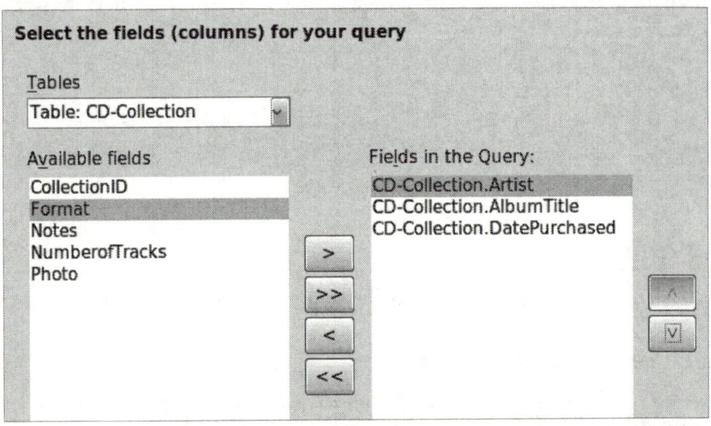

Figure 235: First page of the Query Wizard

Step 2: Select the sorting order.

Up to four fields can be used to sort the information of our query. A little simple logic helps at this point. Which field is most important?

In our query, the artist is most important. The album title is less important, and the date purchased is of least importance. Of course, if we were interested in what music we bought on a given day, the date purchased would be the most important.

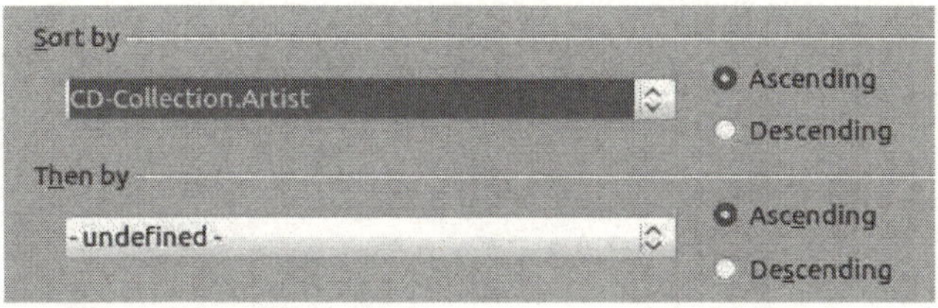

Figure 236: Sorting order page

1) Click the first *Sort by* drop down list.
   a) Click *CD-Collection.Artist* to select it.
   b) To list the artists in alphabetical order (a-z), select *Ascending* on the right.
2) Click the second *Sort by* drop down list.
   - Click *CD-Collection.ArtistTitle*. and select *Ascending*.
3) Repeat this process for *CD-Collection.DatePurchased.*
4) Click **Next**.

Step 3: Select the search conditions.

The search conditions allow us to compare the name we entered with the names of the artist in our database and decide whether to include a particular artist in our query or not.

- *is equal to*: the same as
- *is not equal to*: not the same as
- *is smaller than*: comes before
- *is greater than*: comes after
- *is equal or less than*: the same as or comes before
- *is equal or greater than*: the same as or comes after
- *like*: similar to in some way

Note	These conditions apply to numbers, letters (using alphabetical order), and dates.

1) Since we are only searching for one thing, we will use the default setting of *Match all of the following.*
2) We are looking for a particular artist, so select *CD-Collection. Artist* in the Fields list and *is equal to* as the Condition.
3) Type the name of the artist in the *Value* box. Click **Next**.

Step 4: Select type of query.

We want simple information, so the default setting: *Detailed query* is what we want. Click **Next** at the bottom of the window.

Note	Since we have a simple query, the *Grouping* and *Grouping conditions* are not needed. Steps 5 and 6 of the wizard are skipped in our query.

Step 5: Assign aliases if desired.

We want the default settings. Click **Next**.

Step 6: Overview.

Name the query (suggestion: *Query_Artists*). To the right of this are two choices. Select *Display Query*. Click **Finish**.

Using the Design View to create a query

Creating a query using Design View is not as difficult as it may first seem. It may take multiple steps, but each step is fairly simple.

What fuel economy is our vehicle getting (miles per gallon in the USA)? This question requires creating two queries, with the first query used as part of the second query.

Step 1: Open the first query in Design View.

- Click **Create Query in Design View.**

Step 2: Add tables.

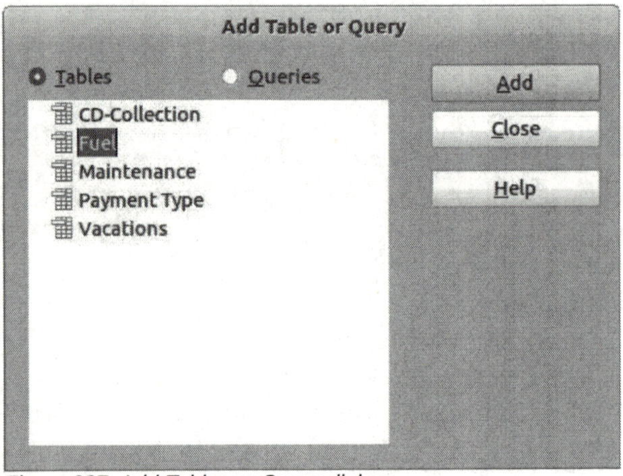

Figure 237: Add Tables or Query dialog

1) Click *Fuel* to highlight it.
2) Click **Add**. Click **Close.**

Tip	Move the cursor over the bottom edge of the fuel table (Figure 238) and drag the edge to make it longer and easier to see all of the fields in the table.

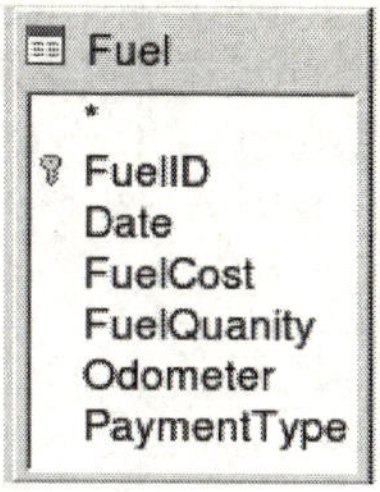

Figure 238: Fuel table in query

Step 3: Add fields to the table at the bottom.

1) Double-click the *FuelID* field in the Fuel table.
2) Double-click the Odometer field.
3) Double-click the FuelQuantity field.

The table at the bottom of the query window should now have three columns.

Field	FuelID	Odometer	FuelQuantity
Alias			
Table	Fuel	Fuel	Fuel
Sort			
Visible	☑	☑	☑
Function			
Criterion			

Figure 239: Query table

Step 4: Set the criterion for the query.

We want the query's FuelID to begin with the numeral 1.

1) Type *>0* in the Criterion cell under FuelID in the query table.
2) Click the *Run Query* icon in the Query Design toolbar.

Figure 240: Query Design toolbar

Figure 241 contains the Fuel table with my entries and the query results based upon the Fuel table: the query results are in Figure 242.

FuelID	Date	FuelCost	FuelQuantity	Odometer
0	Friday, May 25, 2007	$16.00	14.690	704.2
1	Friday, May 25, 2007	$7.00	6.430	778.7
2	Saturday, May 26, 2007	$20.00	19.570	1032.3
3	Saturday, May 26, 2007	$16.00	15.150	1239.4
5	Saturday, May 26, 2007	$16.00	15.144	1639.4
<AutoFielc				

Figure 241: Fuel table

FuelID	Odometer	FuelQuantity
1	778.7	6.430
2	1032.3	19.570
3	1239.4	15.150
4		
<AutoFie		

Figure 242: Query of Fuel table

Step 5: Save and close the query.

Since this query contains the final odometer reading for our calculations, name it *End-Reading* when saving it. Then close the query.

Step 6: Create the query to calculate the fuel economy.

1) Click **Create Query in Design View** to open a new query.
2) Add the Fuel table to the query just as you did in step 2: Add tables But, **do not** close the Add Tables window.
3) Add the End-Reading query to this query.
   a) Click *Queries* to get the list of queries in the database (Figure 243).
   b) Click End-Reading.
   c) Click **Add**, and then click **Close**.

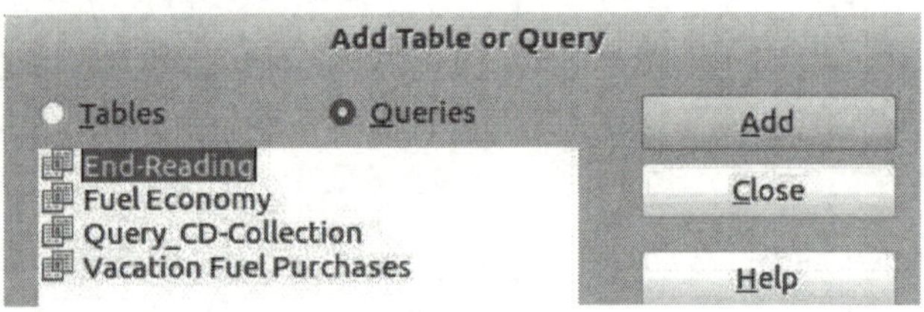

Figure 243: Selecting queries to add to another query

Step 7: Add fields to the table at the bottom of the query.

We are going to calculate the fuel economy. To do this we need the FuelQuantity and distance traveled. Since the FuelQuantity we want to use is the final odometer reading, we will use the End-Reading query to get it. We will also use the Odometer field from the Fuel table and End-Reading query.

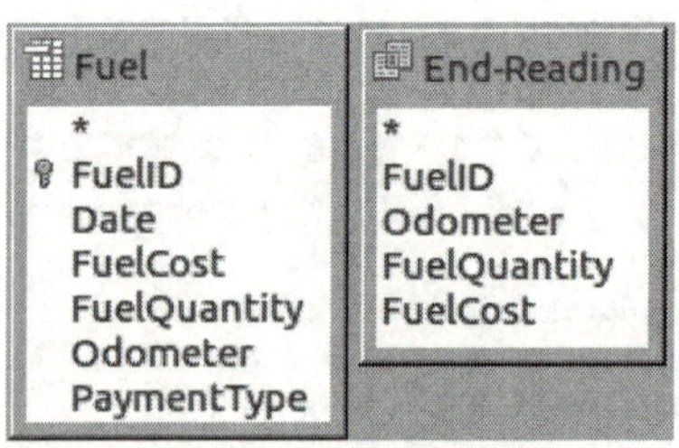

Figure 244: Tables in this query

1) Double-click *FuelQuantity* in the End-Reading query.

2) Double-click *Odometer* in the End-Reading query.
3) Double-click *Odometer* in the Fuel table.

Field	FuelQuantity	Odometer	Odometer
Alias			
Table	End-Reading	End-Reading	Fuel
Sort			
Visible	☑	☑	☑

Figure 245: Added fields to the query

Step 8: Enter the FuelID difference field.

We want the difference between the FuelID value of the Fuel table and FuelID value of the End-Reading query to equal one (1).

1) Type `"End-Reading"."FuelID" - "Fuel"."FuelID"` in the field to the right of the Odometer field of the Fuel Table.
2) Type the numeral 1 (one) in the Criterion cell of this column.
3) Calculate the distance traveled:
   - Type `"End-Reading"."Odometer" – "Fuel"."Odometer"` in the Field cell.
   - Type >0 in the Criterion cell.
4) Calculate fuel economy: Type `("End-Reading"."Odometer" – "Fuel"."Odometer")/"End-Reading"."FuelQuantity"` in the next column to the right of the word Field.

FuelQuantity	Odometer	Odometer	"End-Reading"."FuelID" - "Fuel"."FuelID"
Quantity	Begin	End	
End-Reading	Fuel	End-Reading	
☑	☑	☑	☐
			1

Figure 246: Typing in calculation of fields

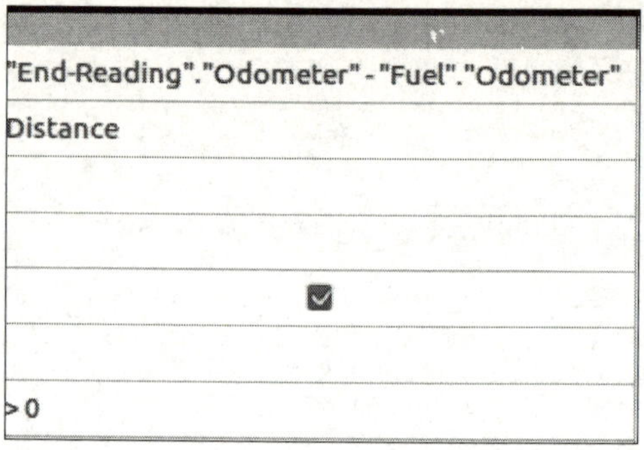

Figure 247: Field for distance traveled calculations

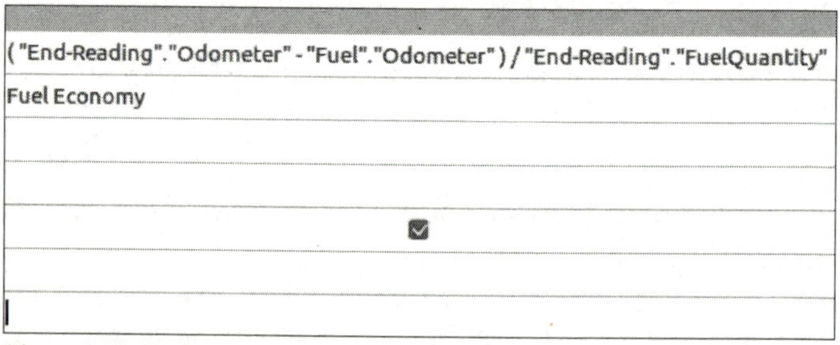

Figure 248: Fuel economy calculation field

Note	When entering fields for these calculations, you must follow this format: table or query name followed by a period follow by the field name. For hyphenated or multiple-word names (table or query), use double quotes around the table or query name. The query will then add the rest of the double quotes as in Figure 248. Use the arithmetical symbol between the two. More than one calculation can be done by using parentheses to group the arithmetical operations.

Step 9: Run the query and make some modification.

After we run the query to make sure it works correctly, we will hide all of the fields that we do not need.

FuelQuantity	Odometer	Odometer	("End-Reading"."Odometer" - "Fuel"."
6.430	704.2	778.7	11.59
19.570	778.7	1032.3	12.96
15.150	1032.3	1239.4	13.67

Figure 249: Result of running the fuel economy query

1) Click the Run Query icon in the Design Query toolbar (Figure 240). The results are in Figure 249.

   Notice that not all of the last column label is visible because some of the labels are long. We can fix this problem by using an alias for many of the fields. The labels are replaced by their aliases.
2) Add Aliases:

Type in the aliases as they are listed in Figure 250.

FuelQuantity	Odometer	Odometer	"End-Reading	("End-Reading"."
Quanity	Begin	End		Fuel Economy
End-Reading	End-Reading	Fuel		

Figure 250: Query table with aliases added

3) Run the query again. The results are in Figure 251.

Quantity	Begin	End	Distance	Fuel Economy	Fuel Cost	Cents per mile	"End-Reading"."FuelID" - "Fuel"."FuelID"
6.430	704.2	778.7	74.5	11.59	7	9.4	1
19.570	778.7	1032.3	253.6	12.96	20	7.9	1
15.150	1032.3	1239.4	207.1	13.67	16	7.7	1

Figure 251: Query run with aliases

We really do not need the column showing the difference between the FuelID fields from the table and query, so we will hide it. While it will not be visible, it will still be used in the calculations.

4) Hide a column that does not need to be seen.

Remove the check in the box of the Visible cell as in Figure 252.

Field	Date	FuelQuantity	Odometer	Odometer	"End-Reading"."FuelID" - "Fuel"."FuelID"
Alias		Quanity	Begin	End	
Table	Fuel	End-Reading	Fuel	End-Reading	
Sort					
Visible	☑	☑	☑	☑	☐

Figure 252: Making a field invisible in a query run

5) Rerun the query (Figure 253).

Date	Quantity	Begin	End	Distance	Fuel Economy	Fuel Cost	Cents per mile
Friday, May 25, 2007	6.430	704.2	778.7	74.5	11.59	7	9.4
Friday, May 25, 2007	19.570	778.7	1032.3	253.6	12.96	20	7.9
Saturday, May 26, 2007	15.150	1032.3	1239.4	207.1	13.67	16	7.7

Figure 253: Query run with a hidden column

Step 10: Close, save, and name the query.

My suggestion for a name is *Fuel Economy*.

1) Click the Save icon.
2) Name the query.
3) Close the query.
4) Save the database file.

There are obviously other calculations that can be made in this query such as cost per distance traveled and how much of the cost belongs to each of the payment types.

Note	To fully use queries requires a knowledge of set operations (*unions, intersections, and, or, complements,* and any combinations of these). Having a copy of the HSQLDB *User Guide*, available from http://hsqldb.org/, is also extremely useful.

Creating reports

Reports provide information found in the database arranged in a useful way. In this respect, they are similar to queries. Reports are generated from the database's tables, views, or queries.

All reports are based upon a single table, view, or query, so you need first to decide what fields you want to use in the report. If you want to use fields from different tables, you must first combine these fields in a single query or view. Then you can create a report from this.

For example, a report on vacation expenses includes both fuel costs and meal costs. These values are contained in fields of two different tables: Vacations and Fuel. So this report requires you to create a query or view.

Caution	Dynamic reports update only the *data* that is changed or added to a table or query. They do **not** show any modifications made to the table or query itself. For example, **after** creating the report below, open the fuel economy query created in the previous section. For the "End-Reading"."Odometer" – "Fuel."Odometer" column, change the number 1 to the number 3. The report will be identical before and after you make the change. But if you add more data to the query and run the report again, it will contain the new data.

Creating a report

We will create a report on vacation expenses. Certain questions need to be asked before creating the report.

- What information do we want in the report?
- How do we want the information arranged?
- What fields are required to provide this information?
- Will a query or view have to be created because these fields are in different tables?
- Are there any calculations required in the data before being added to the report?

The expenses for our vacation are motel, tolls, miscellaneous, breakfast, lunch, supper, snacks, and fuel. One possible report could list the totals of each of these expense groups. Another could list the expense totals for each day of the vacation. A third could list the totals for each expense group for each type of payment. (This would let us know where the money came from to pay the expenses.) Once you create a query to do any one of these, you can create a report based upon the query.

We will create two reports, one listing the expenses each day (other than fuel) and the second listing fuel statistics. The fields we need for the first report from the Vacations table are: Date, Motel, Toll, Breakfast, Lunch, Supper, SnackCost, and Miscellaneous. This report only requires the Vacation table. Had the report listed the total expenses for each of these fields, we would have to create a query to provide us with these totals.

The second report involves the Fuel table. Since this table includes fuel purchases at times other than during the vacation, we need to create a query that contains only the fuel purchased during the vacation.

Static vs dynamic reports

When creating a report using the Report Wizard, you have a choice of two types of reports in the last page of the wizard: static or dynamic. What you should select depends more upon whether you have a working Report Builder extension or not. If this extension works in your version of LibreOffice, you should select dynamic every time. Otherwise, your selection should depend upon whether you want to update the report later. In this case, select dynamic. If you choose static, the report will always contain the data for the original report date.

LibreOffice has always included the Report Builder extension. For some reason, it does not work in some versions. For these, creating a report is done the same way as is done using OpenOffice.org 3.3, and the Getting Started with Base chapter for OpenOffice.org 3.3 explains the basics for creating a report that can be used.

With the report builder extension working, selecting the type of report as static gives only a table layout of the report's data similar to Figure 258 on page 257. The area above the data can contain things like the author of the report, its date, and its name. A company logo can be placed there as well. The area below the data can also contain text and fields such as *page number* of *page count*.

Note	Editing a static report will be discussed in Chapter 4 of the Base Guide, Data Output.

When dynamic is selected as the report type and the report builder extension is working, the report can be edited. Its layout can be in one of two formats: a text document or a spreadsheet. Also, it can be saved in a variety of formats that are available for Writer and Calc documents.

My recommendation for those that have the report builder extension working in their version of LibreOffice is that they always select dynamic as the report type. You will have more control over the layout of the report than if you had selected static instead.

Vacations table report

To create a new report.

1) Click the *Reports* icon in the Database list in the Automobile – LibreOffice Base window (Figure 199).
2) In the Tasks list, click **Use Wizard to Create Report**. The Report Wizard opens.

Tip	When the Report Wizard opens, the Oracle Report Builder opens in the background. As you perform the steps of the wizard, it applies these steps to the Report Builder. You will not be directly using the Report Builder in these steps.

Step 1: Field selection

1) Select *Table: Vacations* in the Tables or Queries drop down list.
2) Use the **>** to move these fields from the *Available fields* list to the *Fields in report* list: Date, Motel, Tolls, Miscellaneous, Breakfast, Lunch, Supper, and SnackCost. Click **Next**.

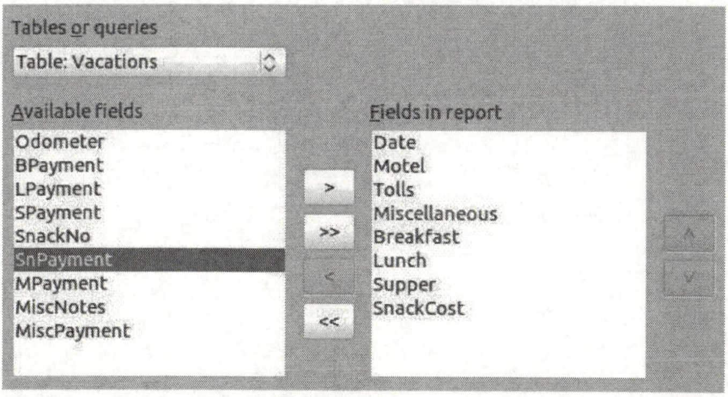

Figure 254: Adding fields to a report

Step 2: Labeling fields

Change any field labels you wish. We will shorten Miscellaneous to Misc. and make SnackCost into two words.

1) Shorten Miscellaneous to Misc.
2) Add a space to separate SnackCost into Snack Cost.
3) Click **Next**.

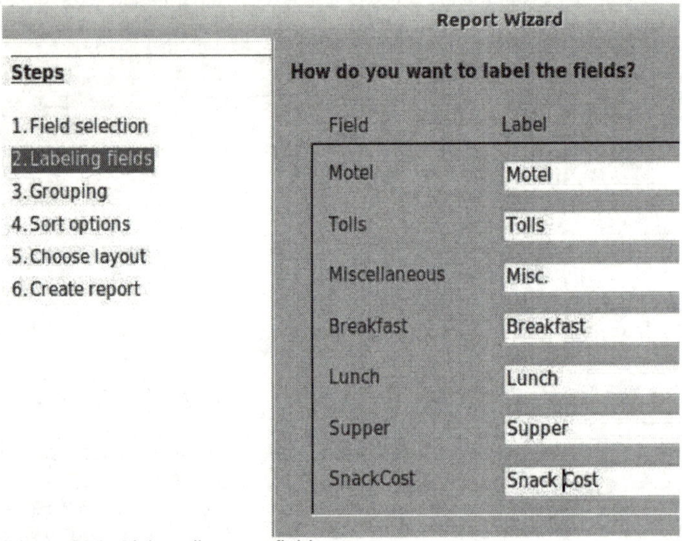

Figure 255: Giving aliases to fields

Step 3: Grouping

Since we are grouping by the date, use the **>** button to move the *Date* field to the Grouping list. Click **Next**.

Figure 256: Selecting fields for grouping data

Step 4: Sort options

We do not want to do any additional sorting.

- Click **Next**.

Step 5: Choose layout

Use *Columnar, three columns* for the layout.

1) Select *Columnar, three columns* for the Layout of data.
2) *Layout of headers and footers* has no possible selections.
3) Select Landscape as the Orientation for the page layout.
4) Click **Next**.

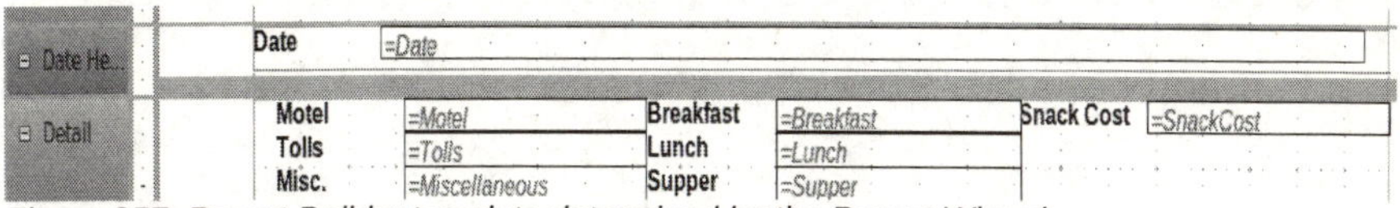

Figure 257: Report Builder template determined by the Report Wizard

Step 6: Create report

1) Label the report: Vacation Expenses.
2) Select *Dynamic report.*
3) Click **Finish**.

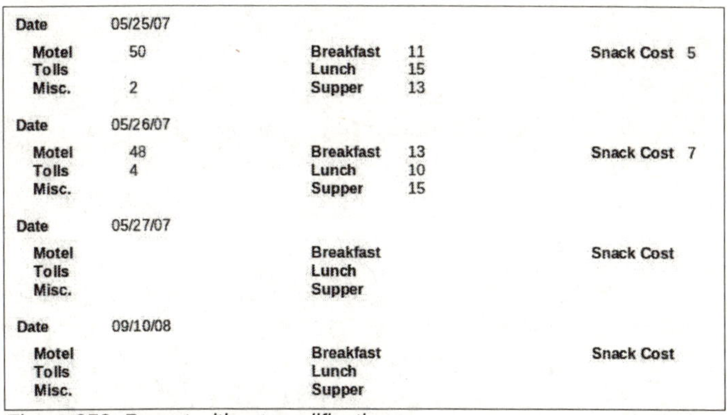

Date	05/25/07				
Motel	50	**Breakfast**	11	**Snack Cost**	5
Tolls		**Lunch**	15		
Misc.	2	**Supper**	13		
Date	05/26/07				
Motel	48	**Breakfast**	13	**Snack Cost**	7
Tolls	4	**Lunch**	10		
Misc.		**Supper**	15		
Date	05/27/07				
Motel		**Breakfast**		**Snack Cost**	
Tolls		**Lunch**			
Misc.		**Supper**			
Date	09/10/08				
Motel		**Breakfast**		**Snack Cost**	
Tolls		**Lunch**			
Misc.		**Supper**			

Figure 258: Report without modifications

The report has been created, but it needs some editing. The date could be formatted better, and all the numbers need to be formatted as currency. It could use a heading that includes its name, its author, and the date it was prepared. If the report had more than one page, the page numbers could be put in a footer of each page, perhaps including the total number of pages.

Report Builder: another way to create reports

When we used the Report Wizard, we created a template in Report Builder for our report. If we edit our report, we open Report Builder with this template. By modifying the template, we also modify the report. For example, we can change the Date field's format, and it will change the format of all the dates contained in that field in the above report. Similarly, we can change the field formatting of any of the other fields and change the format everywhere that field appears in the report.

Report Builder can also create reports by itself. To do this you click **Create Report in design View**. For instructions on how to use the Report Builder, see Chapter 4 of the Base Guide, Data Output. We will discuss it in detail there.

For detailed instructions on using Report Builder, see Dmitri Popov's *Sun Report Builder Guidebook*, available in PDF (search for "Sun Report Builder Guidebook") and printed versions from Lulu.com: http://www.lulu.com/spotlight/writertools

Note	Report Builder is a LibreOffice extension to assist in report creation. With Report Builder, you can create stylish, complex database reports. You can define group and page headers, group and page footers, and calculation fields. It is installed by default with LibreOffice.

Chapter 9
Getting Started with Math

LibreOffice's Equation Editor

What is Math?

Math is LibreOffice's component for writing mathematical and chemical equations. It is most commonly used as an equation editor for text documents, but it can also be used with other types of documents or stand-alone. When used inside Writer, the equation is treated as an object inside the text document.

Note	The equation editor is for writing equations in symbolic form, as in equation 1. If you want to evaluate a numeric value, see the *Calc Guide*.

$$\frac{df(x)}{dx} = \ln(x) + \tan^{-1}(x^2) \qquad (1)$$

or

$$NH_3 + H_2O \rightleftharpoons NH_4^+ + OH^-$$

Getting started

You can create an equation (formula) as a separate document or insert it into a document in Writer or another component of LibreOffice.

Creating an equation as a separate document

To create an equation as a separate document, open the Math component of LibreOffice using one of these methods:

- On the menu bar, choose **File > New > Formula**.
- On the Standard Toolbar, click the triangle to the right of the **New** icon and choose **Formula**.
- From the Start Center, click **Formula**.

An empty formula document opens (see Figure 259).

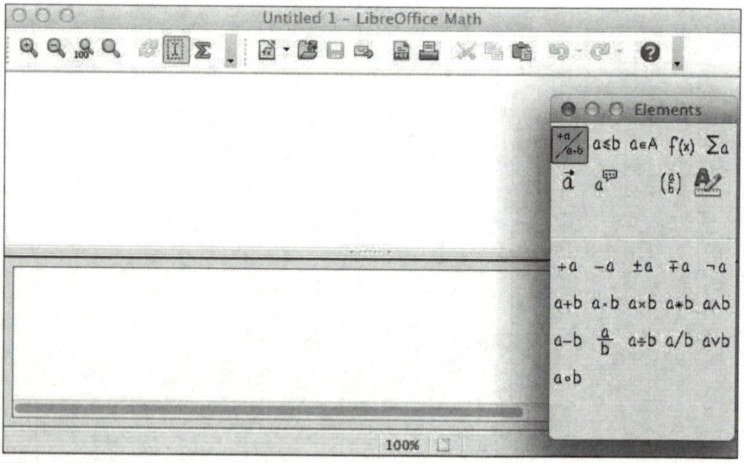

Figure 259: An empty formula document

The upper area is the preview window, where the equation will appear during and after input. The lower area is the equation editor, where the markup code for the equation is entered. The floating Elements window will also appear.

Inserting a formula into a Writer document

To insert a formula into a Writer document, open the document and then choose **Insert > Object > Formula** from the menu bar.

The formula editor opens at the bottom of the Writer window, and the floating Elements window appears. You will also see a small box with a gray border in your document, where the formula will be displayed, as shown in Figure 260.

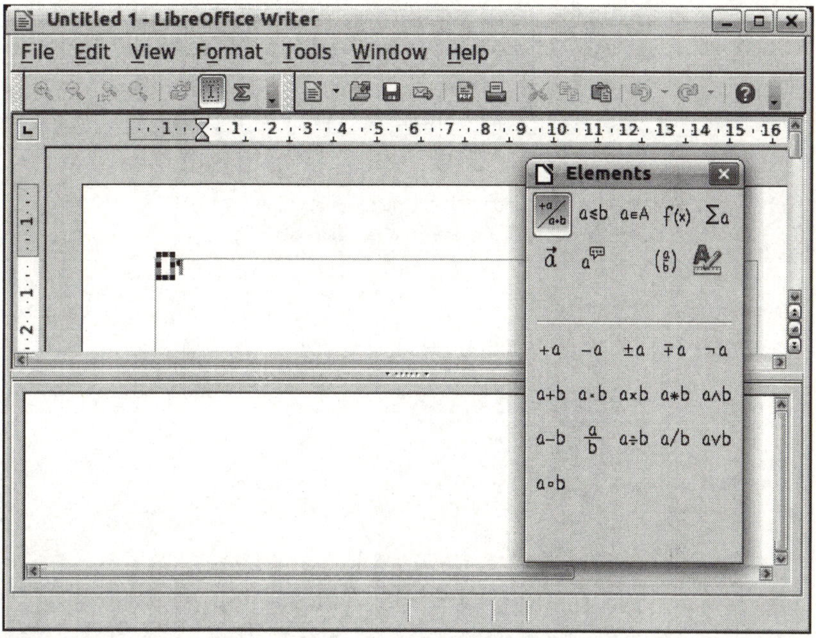

Figure 260: Equation Editor, Elements window, and location of resulting equation in Writer

Tip	If the Elements window is missing, show it with **View > Elements**.

When you are done entering the formula, you can close the editor by pressing the *Esc* key or by clicking an area outside the formula in the main document. A double-click on the box will open the editor again, so you can edit the formula.

Formulas are inserted as OLE objects. In a Writer document, the formula is anchored as a character, so it is embedded in the continuous text. You can, as with any other OLE object, change the anchor and make the formula floating. In Calc, Impress and Draw documents, formulas are embedded as floating OLE objects.

If you frequently need to insert formulas, it is advisable to add the Formula button to the Standard toolbar or create a keyboard shortcut. See Chapter 14, Customizing LibreOffice, for more information.

Entering a formula

The equation editor uses a markup language to represent formulas. For example, *%beta* creates the Greek character beta (β). This markup is designed to read similar to English whenever possible. For example, *a over b* produces a fraction: $\frac{a}{b}$.

You can enter a formula in three ways:

- Select a symbol from the Elements window.
- Right-click on the equation editor and select the symbol from the context menu.
- Type markup in the equation editor.

The context menu and the Elements window insert the markup corresponding to a symbol. This provides a convenient way to learn the LibreOffice Math markup.

Note	Click on the document body to exit the formula editor. Double-click on a formula to enter the formula editor again.

The Elements window

The simplest method for entering a formula is the Elements window.

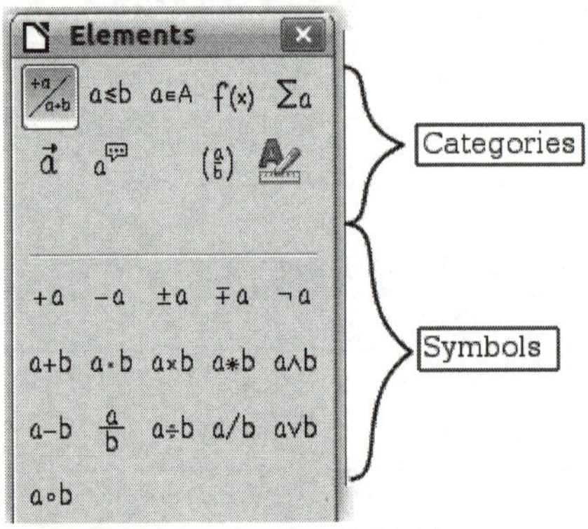

Figure 261: Symbols are divided into categories

The Elements window is divided into two main parts.

- The **top** shows the symbol categories. Click on these to change the list of symbols.
- The **bottom** shows the symbols available in the current category.

Tip	You can hide or show the Elements window with **View > Elements**.

Example 1: 5×4

For this example we will enter a simple formula: 5×4 . On the Elements window:

1) Select the top-left button of the categories (top) section.
2) Click on the multiplication symbol.

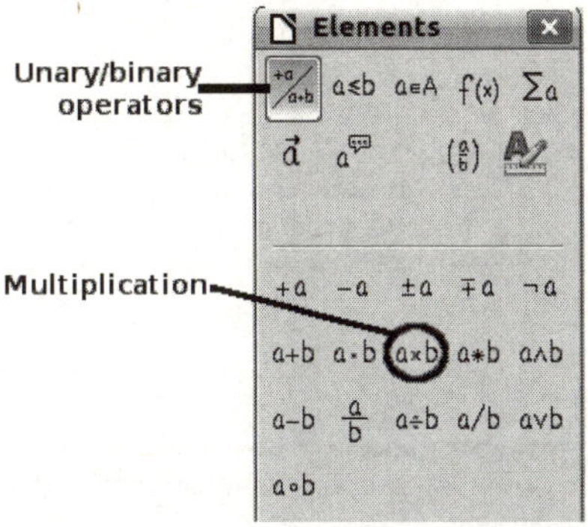

Figure 262: Selecting the multiplication symbol

When you select the multiplication symbol on the Elements window, two things happen:

- The equation editor shows the markup: <?> times <?>
- The body of the document shows a gray box like this: ❑×❑

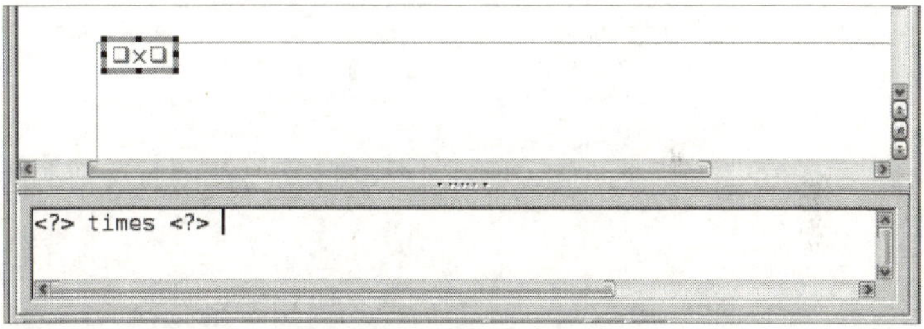

Figure 263: Result of selecting the multiplication symbol

The **<?>** symbols shown in Figure 263 are placeholders that you can replace by other text, for example **5** and **4**. The equation will update automatically, as shown in Figure 264.

Tip	When you add a formula, reserved placeholders are indicated by squares in the formula and **<?>** in the command window. You can navigate through these placeholders using *F4* and *Shift+F4*.

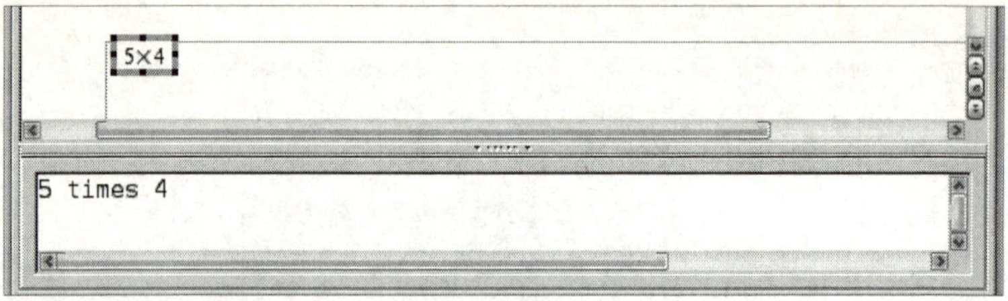

Figure 264: Result of entering 5 and 4 next to the times operator

Tip	To keep the equation from updating automatically, select **View > AutoUpdate display** to deselect it. To update a formula manually, press *F9* or select **View > Update**.

Right-click (context) menu

Another way to access mathematical symbols is to right-click on the equation editor. This pops up the menu shown in Figure 265. The items in this menu correspond to those in the Elements window, with some extra commands.

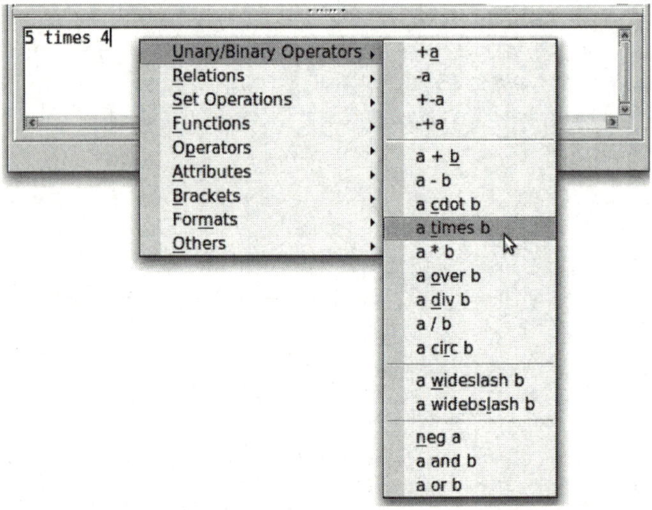

Figure 265: Right-click (context) menu

Note	Neither the window elements, nor the context menu contain a complete list of commands. For some seldom-used commands, you must always enter the markup. A complete list of commands can be found in Appendix of the Math Guide.

Markup

You can type the markup directly in the equation editor. For example, you can type **`5 times 4`** to obtain 5×4 . If you know the markup, this can be the fastest way to enter a formula.

Tip	The formula markup resembles the way the formula reads in English.

Below is a short list of common equations and their corresponding markup.

Display	*Command*	*Display*	*Command*
$a=b$	a = b	$\sqrt{a}$	sqrt {a}
a^2	a^2	a_n	a_n
$\int f(x)dx$	int f(x) dx	$\sum a_n$	sum a_n
$a \leq b$	a <= b	∞	infinity
$a \times b$	a times b	$x \cdot y$	x cdot y

Greek characters

Greek characters ($\alpha, \beta, \gamma, \theta$, etc) are common in mathematical formulas. *These characters are not available in the Elements window or the right-click menu*. Fortunately, the markup for Greek characters is simple: Type a **%** sign followed by the name of the character, in English.

- To write a *lowercase* character, type the name of the character in lowercase.
- To write an *uppercase* character, type the name of the character in uppercase.
- To write in italic, just add an `i` between **%** sign and the name of the character.

A complete table of Greek characters is provided in appendix of the Math Guide. See the table below for some examples.

Lowercase	*Uppercase*	*Italic lowercase*	*Italic uppercase*
`%alpha` → α	`%ALPHA` → A	`%ialpha` → α	`%iALPHA` → A
`%beta` → β	`%BETA` → B	`%ibeta` → β	`%iBETA` → B
`%gamma` → γ	`%GAMMA` → Γ	`%igamma` → γ	`%iGAMMA` → $\mathit{\Gamma}$
`%psi` → ψ	`%PSI` → Ψ	`%ipsi` → ψ	`%iPSI` → $\mathit{\Psi}$
`%phi` → φ	`%PHI` → Φ	`%iphi` → φ	`%iPHI` → $\mathit{\Phi}$
`%theta` → θ	`%THETA` → Θ	`%itheta` → θ	`%iTHETA` → $\mathit{\Theta}$

Another way to enter Greek characters is by using the Symbols catalog window. Choose **Tools > Catalog**. This window is shown in Figure 266. Under *Symbol set*, select **Greek** and double-click on a Greek letter from the list. The markup name of the character is shown below the list window.

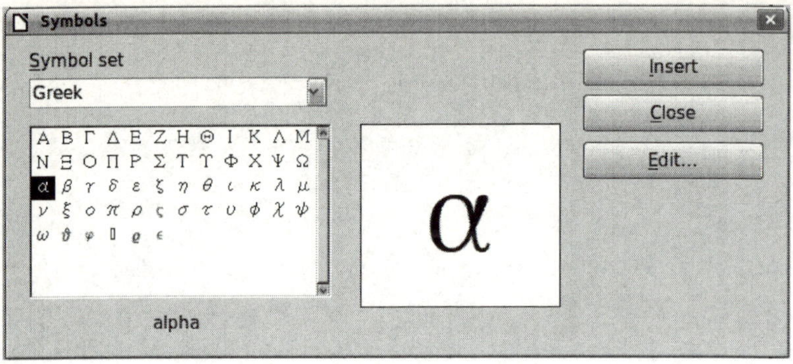

Figure 266: Symbols catalog, used for entering Greek characters and some special symbols

Example 2: $\pi \simeq 3.14159$

For this example we will suppose that:

- We want to enter the above formula (the value of pi rounded to 5 decimal places).
- We know the name of the Greek character (pi).
- But we do not know the markup associated with the $\simeq$ symbol.

Step 1: Type **%** followed by the text **`pi`**. This displays the Greek character π .

Step 2: Open the Elements window (**View > Elements**).

Step 3: The $\simeq$ symbol is a relation, so we click on the Relations button. If you hover the mouse over this button you see the tooltip *Relations* (Figure 267).

Figure 268 shows the Elements window after clicking the Relations button. The symbol we want is circled.

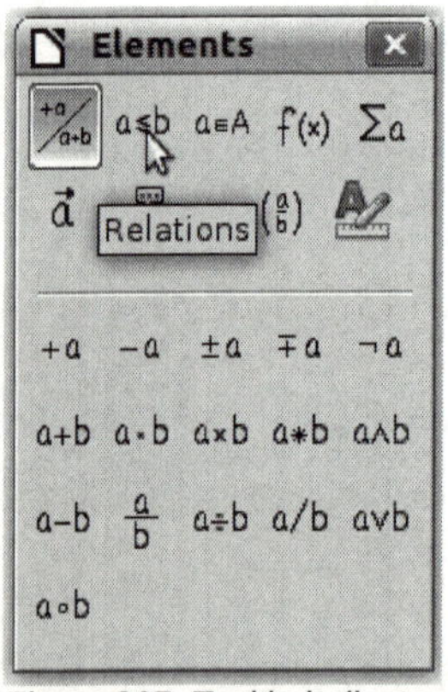

Figure 267: Tooltip indicates the Relations button

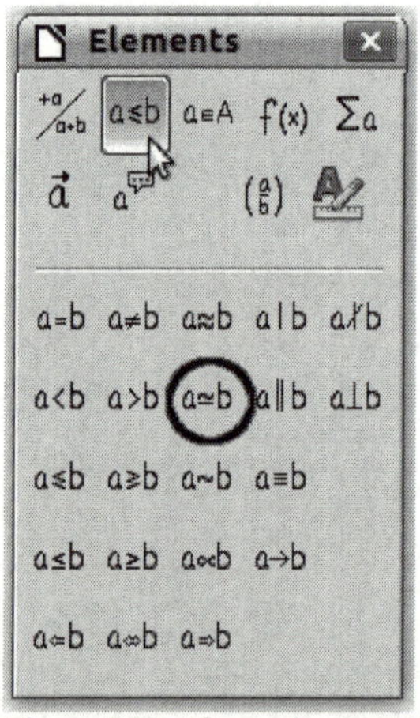

Figure 268: After selecting Relations

Step 4: Click on the a $\simeq$ b symbol. The equation editor now shows the markup **%pi<?> simeq <?>**.

Step 5: Delete the **<?>** text, press *F4* key and type **`3.14159`** at the end of the equation. We end up with the markup **%pi simeq 3.14159**. The result is shown in Figure 269.

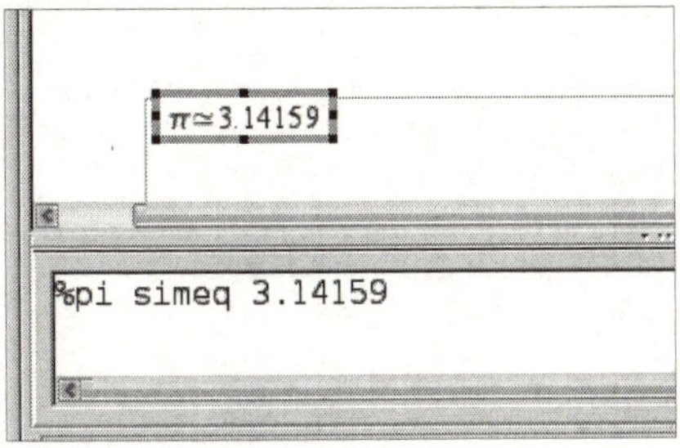

Figure 269. Final result

Changing a formula

You can change a formula at any time. To switch into edit mode, double-click on the formula.

To get to the appropriate section in the markup code, do any one of the following:

- In the equation editor, click on the location.
- Select an area of the markup code that you wish to change.
- Click on an element in the preview area; the cursor will automatically move to the corresponding point in the equation editor.
- Double-click on an element in the preview area; the corresponding section in the equation editor will be selected.

To be able to work in the upper (preview) area in the stand-alone Math window (Figure 259), the formula cursor must be activated. Use the **Formula Cursor** button on the *Tools* toolbar.

You can change an equation by overwriting selected text or by inserting new markup code at the cursor position.

Formula layout

The most difficult part of using LibreOffice Math comes when writing complicated formulas. This section provides some advice.

Brackets are your friends

Math knows nothing about order of operation. You must use brackets to state the order of operations explicitly. Consider the following examples.

Markup	*Result*	*Markup*	*Result*
`2 over x + 1`	$\frac{2}{x}+1$	`2 over {x + 1}`	$\frac{2}{x+1}$
`- 1 over 2`	$\frac{-1}{2}$	`- {1 over 2}`	$-\frac{1}{2}$

In the first example, Math has recognized that the **2** before and the **x** after the **over** belong to the fraction, and has represented them accordingly. If you want **x+1** rather than **x** to be the denominator, you must bracket them together so that both will be placed there.

In the second example, Math has recognized the minus sign as a prefix for the **1** and has therefore placed it in the numerator of the fraction. If you wish to show that the whole thing is negative, with the minus sign in front of the fraction, you must put the fraction in brackets in order to signify to Math that the characters belong together.

The braces belong solely to the layout of the markup code and are not printed. If you wish to use braces in the formula, use the commands **lbrace** and **rbrace.**

Compare the following examples:

Markup	***Result***	***Markup***	***Result***
`x over {-x + 1}`	$\frac{x}{-x+1}$	`x over lbrace -x + 1 rbrace`	$\frac{x}{\{-x+1\}}$

Brackets with matrices look ugly!

For background, we start with an overview of the matrix command.

Markup	***Result***
`matrix { a # b ## c # d }`	$\begin{matrix} a & b \\ c & d \end{matrix}$

Note	Rows are separated by two # symbols and entries within each row are separated by one #.

The first problem people have with matrices is that brackets do not scale with the matrix:

Markup	***Result***
`(  matrix { a # b ## c # d }  )`	$(\begin{matrix} a & b \\ c & d \end{matrix})$

Math provides scalable brackets. That is, the brackets grow in size to match the size of their contents. Use the commands *left(* and *right)* to make scalable brackets.

Markup	***Result***
`left(  matrix { a # b ## c # d }  right)`	$\left(\begin{matrix} a & b \\ c & d \end{matrix}\right)$

Tip	Use *left[* and *right]* to obtain square brackets. The list of all available brackets is available in the appendix of the *Math Guide*.

These scalable brackets may also be used with any element, such as a fraction, square root, etc.

Isolated and unpaired brackets

Math expects that for every opening bracket there will be a closing one. If you forget a bracket, Math places an inverted question mark by the corresponding bracket. This disappears when all brackets are matched. Sometimes forgetting a bracket causes the whole structure of the formula to fall apart.

However, an unpaired bracket is sometimes necessary. In such cases, you have two options:

- With non-scalable brackets, use a preceding backslash \ to indicate that the following character should not be regarded as a bracket but as a literal character. So the half-open interval **[a;b[** is represented by **\[a;b\[** — try comparing this with **[a;b[**
- Scalable brackets can also be unpaired. The same half-open interval is represented by

  ```
  left [ a; b right [
  ```

For scalable brackets, you can also use the command **none** to replace a non-existent paired bracket.

$$|x| = \left\lbrace \begin{array}{l} x \text{ for } x \geq 0 \\ -x \text{ for } x < 0 \end{array} \right.$$

can be represented by

```
abs x = left lbrace stack {x "for" x >= 0 # -x "for" x < 0} right none
```

Recognizing functions in Math

In the basic installation, Math outputs variables in italics. If you enter a function, Math usually recognizes it and outputs it normally (a list of recognized functions is available in the *Math Guide*). If Math fails to recognize a function, you can inform Math about it. Enter the markup code **func** before the function, and the following text will be recognized as a function.

Some functions recognized by Math need to be followed by numbers or variables. If these are missing, Math puts an inverted red question mark ¿ in their place, which you can only remove by correcting the formula: enter a variable or a number, or a pair of empty braces { } as a placeholder.

Tip	You can navigate through errors using *F3* and *Shift+F3*.

Equations over more than one line

Suppose you want to make an equation covering more than one line, for example: $\begin{array}{c} x=3 \\ y=1 \end{array}$

Your first reaction would be to simply press the *Enter* key. However, if you press the *Enter* key, although the markup goes to a new line, the resulting equation does not. You must type the newline command explicitly. This is illustrated in the table below.

Markup	*Result*
`x = 3` `y = 1`	$x=3\,y=1$
`x = 3 newline` `y = 1`	$x=3$ $y=1$

Continuing the calculation on a new line without writing a complete new equation is not directly possible, because Math expects a term on the left hand side of an equals sign. You can substitute:

- Empty quotes **""**. This will automatically cause the line to be left-justified.
- Empty braces **{ }**. The following line will then be centered.
- Spaces characters ` or ~. The line will be centered with the spaces.

The alignment of equals signs under each other is described on page 272.

As well, spacing between elements in formulas are not set by space characters in the code. You need to use special markup to add spaces: ` (grave) for a small space, ~ (tilde) for a large space. Another solution would be to add space characters between quotes, to be considered as text. Space markup at the end of a formula are ignored by default.

How do I add limits to my sum/integral?

The **sum** and **int** commands (see complete list in the appendix of the *Math Guide*) can (optionally) take the parameters *from* and *to*. These are used for lower and upper limits respectively. These parameters can be used singly or together.

Markup	***Result***
`sum from k = 1 to n a_k`	$\sum_{k=1}^{n} a_k$

`int from 0 to x f(t) dt`
or
`int_0^x f(t) dt`
	$\int\limits_{0}^{x} f(t)dt$ or $\int_0^x f(t)dt$

`int from Re f`	$\int\limits_{\Re} f$
`sum to infinity 2^{-n}`	$\sum^{\infty} 2^{-n}$

How do I write a derivative?

Writing derivatives essentially comes down to one trick: *Tell LibreOffice it's a fraction*.

In other words, you have to use the *over* command. Combine this with either the letter *d* (for a total derivative) or the *partial* command (for a partial derivative) to achieve the effect of a derivative.

Markup	***Result***
`{df} over {dx}`	$\frac{df}{dx}$
`{partial f} over {partial y}`	$\frac{\partial f}{\partial y}$
`{partial^2 f} over {partial t^2}`	$\frac{\partial^2 f}{\partial t^2}$

Note	Notice that we have to use braces (squiggly brackets) to make the derivative.

To write function names with primes, as is usual in school notation, you must first add the signs to the catalog. Using single and double quotes is typographically ugly. See “Customizing the catalog” on page 278.

Markup characters as regular characters

Characters that are used for controlling markup cannot be entered directly as normal characters. The characters concerned are: **%**, **{**, **}**, **&**, **|**, **_**, **^** and **"**. So, for example, you cannot write **2% = 0.02** or **1" = 2.56cm.** Two methods are available to overcome this limitation:

- Use double quotes to mark the character as text, for example **2"%"= 0.02.** This is not possible for the double-quote character itself.
- Add the character to the catalog. See the section “Customizing the catalog” on page 278.

In some cases you can use commands:

- **lbrace** and **rbrace** give you literal braces $\{\}$.
- **mline** gives you the vertical line, for example **2 mline 3** for $(2|3)$

Conversion into a character entity as in HTML or the use of an escape character is not possible in Math.

Text in a formula

To include text in a formula, enclose it in straight double-quotes:

```
abs x = left lbrace matrix {x # "for " x >= 0 ## -x # "for " x < 0} right none
```

$$|x| = \begin{cases} x & \text{for } x \geq 0 \\ -x & \text{for } x < 0 \end{cases}$$

All characters except double quotes are permissible in text. Unfortunately the Special characters dialog is not available. If necessary, you can write the text in a text document and copy it into the equation editor via the clipboard. In this way smart quotes can be inserted, as shown below.

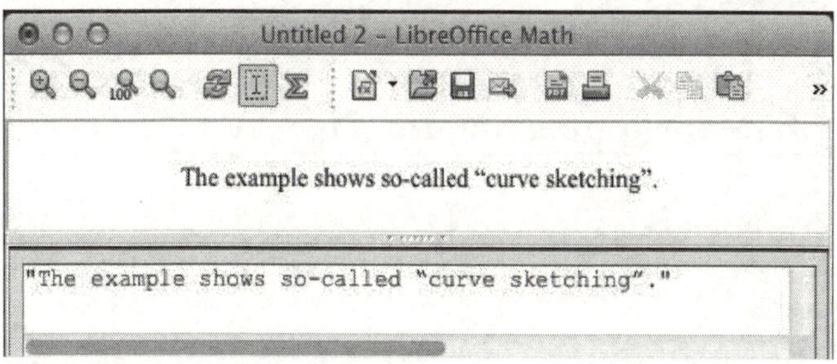

Figure 270: Smart quotes included by copy and paste from Writer.

Text is shown in the font that was selected from the **Text** list in the **Fonts** dialog (compare with the section Changing the font page 273). To use a font from the lower window of the equation editor, set the attribute **Serif**, **Sans** or **Fixed** before the text.

By default, text is left-justified. You can change the justification with **alignc** or **alignr**.

Commands are not interpreted within text. Use quotes to break up the text if you wish to use special formatting commands.

```
"In " color blue bold "isosceles" " triangles, the base angles are equal"
```

In **isosceles** triangles, the base angles are equal

How do I align my equations at the equals sign?

Math does not have a command for aligning equations on a particular character, but you can use a matrix to do this, as shown below.

Markup	*Result*

`matrix{`
`   alignr x+y # {}={} # alignl 2 ##`
`   alignr x   # {}={} # alignl 2-y`
`}`
	$x+y = 2$
	$x = 2-y$

The empty braces around = are necessary because = is a binary operator and thus needs an expression on each side.

You can reduce the spacing around = if you change the inter-column spacing of the matrix:

1) With the equation editor open, choose **Format > Spacing** from the menu bar.
2) In the Spacing dialog (Figure 271), click the **Category** button and select **Matrices** in the drop-down menu.
3) Enter **0%** for Column spacing and click **OK**.

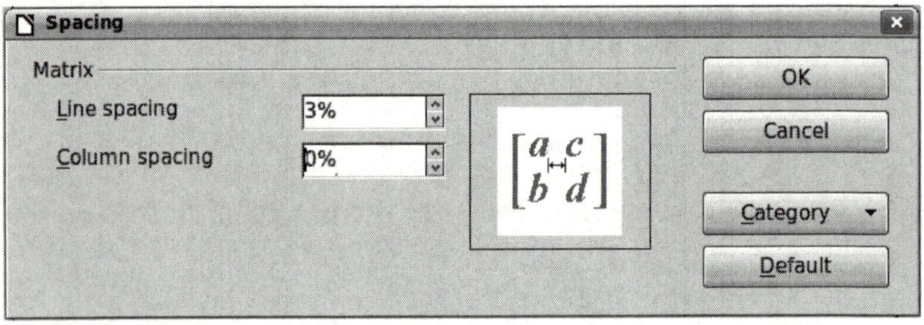

Figure 271: Changing spacing in a matrix formula

Changing the appearance of formulas

Changing the font size

This is one of the most common questions people ask about LibreOffice Math. The answer is simple, but not intuitive:

1) Start the formula editor and choose **Format > Font size**.
2) Select a larger font size under *Base size* (top-most entry).

The result of this change is illustrated in Figure 273.

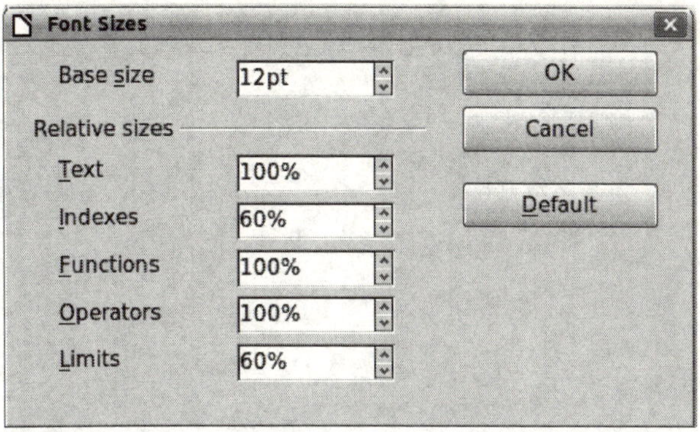

Figure 272. Edit Base size (top) to make a formula bigger

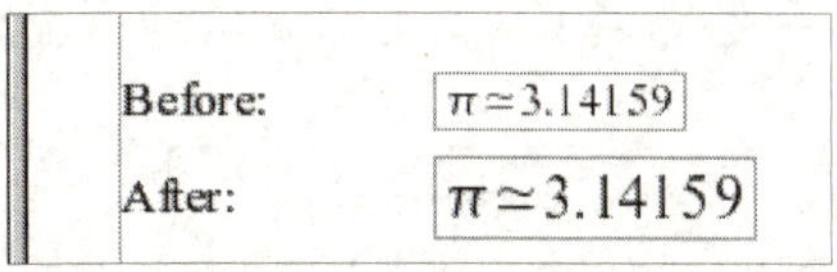

Figure 273. Result of changing the base font size

Note	
	The change in font size applies only to the current formula. To change the default font size, click on the **Default** button and then **OK**. A change in the default font size might, for example, make your work easier when you are preparing a big presentation and want all the formulas in it to have a base size of 28pt—but do not forget to set the font size back to its original value when the work is finished. Warning: this will modify only the current formula and future formulas you write. To modify existing formulas in the document, you need to use a macro (see section about macros in Math Guide).

The size of a subset of characters in a formula may be modified using the **`size`** command. For example: **`b size 5{a}`** gives the result *b* a. In the Elements window, the icon on the *Attributes* tab gives the **`size`** command. The value just after **`size`** may be absolute (numeric value) or relative to the context (base size by default): for example, **+6**, **-3**, **/2**, or ***2/**

Changing the font

The fonts used in formulas can be changed using **Format > Fonts.**

The **Formula fonts** section of the *Fonts* dialog (Figure 274) refers to the four specified formula elements. The font for operators, relationships and brackets is not affected, as these elements normally come from the OpenSymbol font. Similarly elements from the catalog (see “Customizing the catalog” on page 278) continue to be displayed in the font specified there.

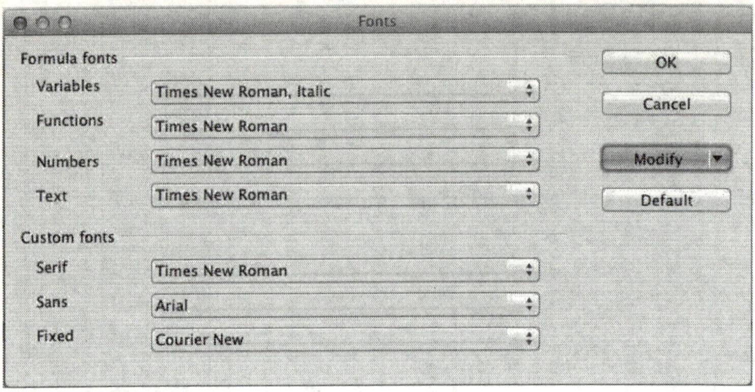

Figure 274: Fonts dialog

The *Custom fonts* section determines which font will be used when the attribute **font serif**, **font sans** or **font fixed** is specified.

To change a font, first click on **Modify** and choose the type of entry you wish to modify. The Fonts dialog opens, showing all the fonts available on your system.

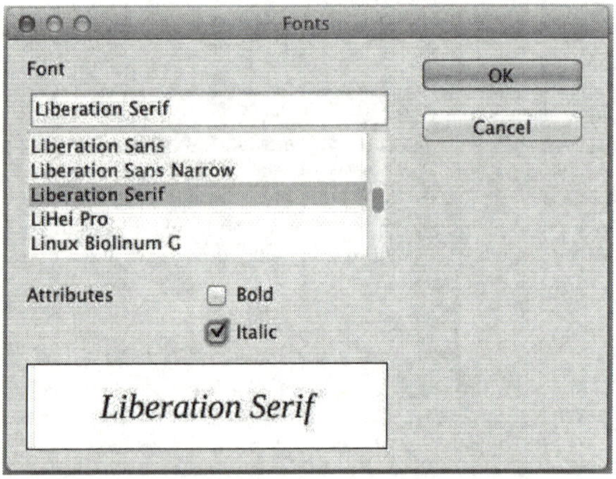

Figure 275: Font dialog

The Font text input box uses predictive text as you type to assist locating the wanted font. If you do not know its name, use the scrollbar to scroll through them. Click on any name and the preview box will show a sample.

Variables should be written in italics, so make sure that the **Italic** box is checked. For all other elements, use the basic (Roman) form. The style can be easily altered in the formula itself by using the commands **`italic`** or **`bold`** to set these characteristics and **`nitalic`** or **`nbold`** to unset them.

When you have chosen a new font for a formula, the old font remains in the list alongside the new one and can be selected again. This applies only to the current session; the old font is not stored permanently.

You can choose whatever fonts you like, but if you are exchanging documents with someone else, you should choose fonts that are present on your colleague's computer.

Changing the color

Use the command **`color`** to change the color of a subset of a formula: **`color red ABC`** gives *ABC* . Choose from 8 colors: **`white`**, **`black`**, **`cyan`**, **`magenta`**, **`red`**, **`blue`**, **`green`**, **`yellow`**.

You may set a color for a subset of a formula if it is enclosed between **`{ }`** or other parentheses. For instance: **`A B color green {C D} E`** gives *ABCDE* .

Color commands can be nested in subsets of formulas as shown in this example : **`color blue {A B color yellow C D}`** gives *AB D* . The space between C and D limits the color to the variable following the command.

It is not possible to select a background color: it is always transparent in Math. The background color of the whole formula is then the same as the background of the document or frame (in a text document for instance). In Writer, you can use object properties (right-click the formula **Object**) to choose a background color for the whole formula (see "Background, borders, and size" on page 277).

Formulas in Writer documents

Numbering equations

Equation numbering is one of Writer's best hidden features. The steps are simple, but obscure:

1) Start a new line.
2) Type **`fn`** and then press *F3*. Note this is **NOT** the keyboard *Fn* key.

The *fn* is replaced by a numbered formula:

$$E=mc^2 \qquad (2)$$

Now you can double-click on the formula to edit it.

You can insert a cross-reference to an equation (for example "as shown in Equation (2)") as follows:

1) Choose **Insert > Cross-reference** from the Menu bar.
2) On the *Cross-references* tab (Figure 276), under *Type*, select **Text**.
3) Under *Selection*, select the equation number.
4) Under *Insert reference to*, select **Reference**.
5) Click **Insert**.

If you later add more equations to the paper before the referenced equation, all the equations will automatically renumber and the cross-references will update.

Tip	To insert the equation number in the cross-reference without parentheses around it, choose **Numbering** instead of **Reference** under *Insert reference to.*

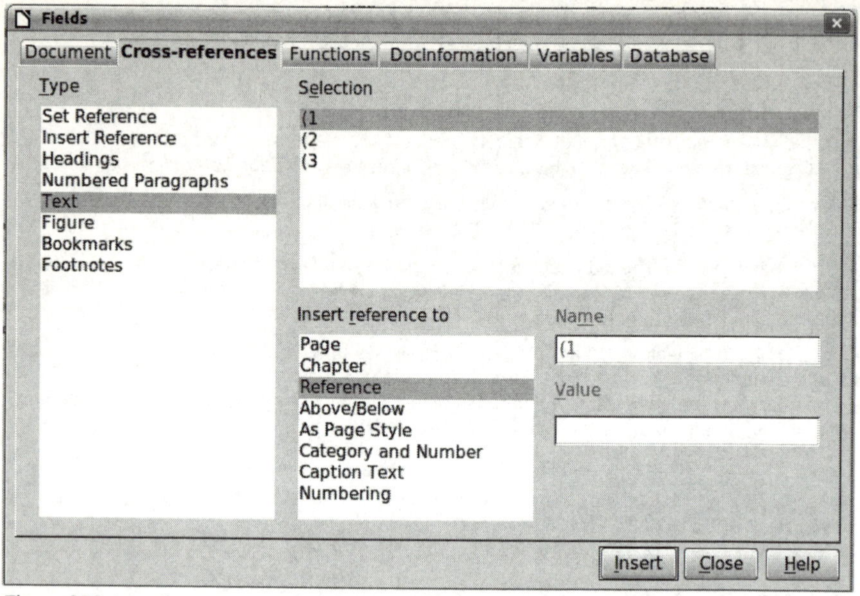

Figure 276. Inserting a cross-reference to an equation number

The AutoText inserted as a result of the above procedure consists of a 1x2 table. The left cell contains the formula and the right one the number. The number is an automatic counter named Text. You can edit the AutoText if, for example, you prefer square rather than round brackets, or if you want formula and number to be separated by tabs rather than formatted as a table. Read the section on "Using AutoText" in Chapter 3 (Working with Text) in the *Writer Guide*.

Position

Normally a formula is anchored *As character* in a Writer document. But as with any other OLE object, you can change the anchoring mode to position the formula where you want it. For more information, see Chapter 11 (Graphics, the Gallery, and Fontwork) of the *Getting Started* guide.

By default, formula objects anchored *As character* are automatically aligned vertically to the baseline of the surrounding text. To align the formula manually, go to **Tools > Options > LibreOffice Writer > Formatting Aids** and uncheck the option **Math baseline alignment**. This setting is stored with the document and applies to all formulas within it. New documents use the current setting from this dialog.

Margins

An inserted Math object has margins to left and right of it, separating it from surrounding text. If you do not want this, it is best to alter the frame style for formulas, as this will apply simultaneously to all existing formulas and those still to be inserted in the document. Proceed as follows:

1) Press *F11*. The Styles and Formatting dialog opens.
2) Click on the **Frame Styles** icon.
3) Find the **Formula** frame style and right-click on it.
4) Choose **Modify** from the context menu. The Frame Style dialog opens.

5) Switch to the **Wrap** tab of the dialog. Change the values for **Left** and **Right** in the Spacing section to 0.00.
6) Click **OK** to close the dialog.

This changes the spacing for all formulas that have not had their spacing adjusted manually. You can find more information on using styles in "Default layout with style" on page 280 and in Chapter 3 (Using Styles and Templates) of the *Getting Started* guide.

Text mode

Larger formulas should always be in a paragraph of their own, separated from the text. When you use formula elements in running text, they can often be higher than the letter height.

However, if it is necessary to place a formula within running text, switch into the equation editor and go to **Format > Text** mode. Math will try to shrink the formula to fit the letter height. The numerators and denominators of fractions are shrunk, and the limits of integrals and sums are placed beside the integral/sum sign.

Example:

A formula in a separate paragraph:

$$\sum_{i=2}^{5} i^2$$

and the same formula embedded in text mode: $\textstyle\sum_{i=2}^{5} i^2$

Background, borders, and size

With regard to formatting, formulas are treated as objects of the *Frame Style* type with the Formula frame style. Background color and borders can be set using this style or directly with **Format > Frame/Object**, or by right-clicking the formula and choosing **Object** from the context menu. In the default installation, formulas have a transparent background and no borders. The size of a formula cannot be adjusted; in a Writer document it depends directly on the way the formula is constructed (see "Changing the font size" on page 272).

Creating a formula library

When you use the Math component of LibreOffice directly with **File > New > Formula**, you create documents with the file suffix ODF, each containing a single formula. You can use these to build up a library of frequently-used formulas. Embedded formulas can also be stored as separate Math documents by right-clicking on the formula and choosing **Save copy as** from the context menu. To insert such a Math document into a Writer document, use **Insert > Object > OLE Object.** Select the option **Create from file** and enter the path name of the file or browse for it using your system's file manager by pressing the **Search** button.

Note	You cannot insert the document by dragging and dropping with the mouse, nor by using **Insert > File**.

Formulas cannot be stored in the gallery because they are not in graphical format. You can however store a formula as AutoText. Write the formula in a separate paragraph, select it and go to **Edit > AutoText**. For further information see "Using AutoText" in Chapter 3 (Working with Text) in the *Writer Guide*.

Fast insertion of formulas

If you already know the markup of your formula, here is a faster method to build your formula:

- Write the formula markup in Writer.
- Select the markup.
- Insert the formula using a toolbar button, a menu item, or a keyboard shortcut.

This method avoids the need to open and close the Math window and thus saves time.

Customizations

Customizing the catalog

If you need to use a symbol that is not available in Math, you can add it to the catalog yourself. The following example shows the procedure for symbols that are used in marking school work.

1) Go to **Tools > Catalog** or click on the catalog button Σ to open the Symbols catalog (Figure 266).
2) Click the **Edit** button. The Edit symbols dialog (Figure 277) opens.
3) The symbols are arranged in symbol sets. In the lower part of the window, choose an available set for your new symbol from the Symbol set list, for example the *Special* set. Or you can type the name of a new symbol set directly into the box.
4) From the Font list, choose a font that contains the desired symbol.

   When you have selected a font, its characters appear in the font summary window. You can scroll through it using the scrollbar at the side, or use the Subset list to go straight to the place you need.

   To follow this example, choose the font *DejaVu Sans* and the subset *General punctuation*.
5) Click on the desired symbol (here Ux2032). It appears enlarged in the right-hand preview box (see Figure 278). Make sure that the symbol set is set to **Special**.
6) In the Symbol field, enter a name for the symbol, for example *prime*.
7) If the name is not already in use, the **Add** button becomes active. Click on it.
8) You can immediately add more symbols. In the example, the "U+2033" symbol, named dblprime, and the "U+2034" symbol, named triprime, are added (see Figure 279).
9) Click **OK** to close the dialog.

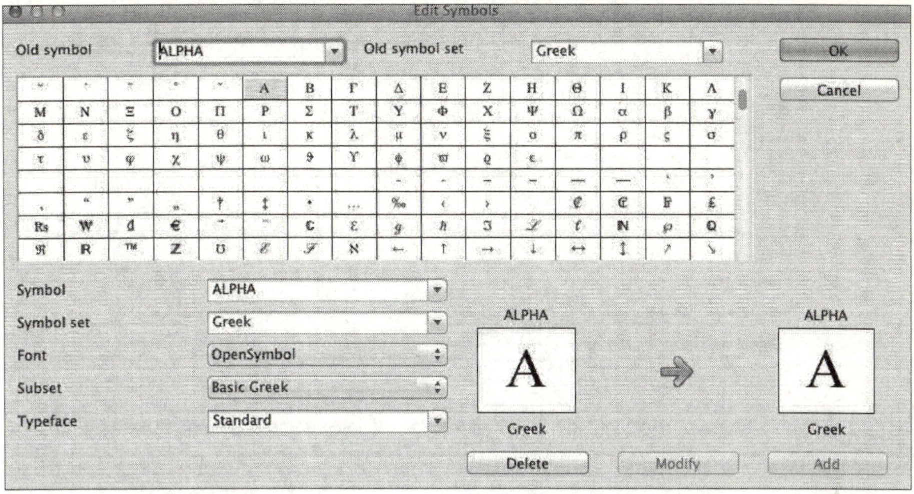

Figure 277: Edit Symbols dialog

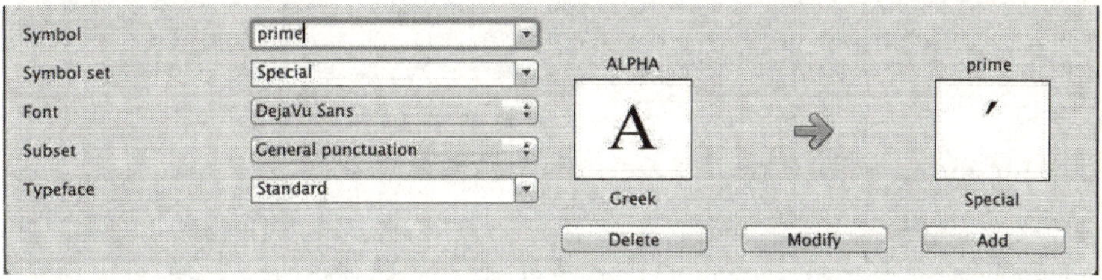

Figure 278: Edit Symbols dialog: characters selected

Now the Symbol set view area shows the new symbol. It can be selected just like the other symbols, either from here, or by writing them directly into the equation editor in the form %prime.

Caution

Symbols (Greek or Special), in contrast to commands, are case sensitive (lowercase/uppercase).

Numerous free fonts contain a great number of mathematical symbols. The "STIX[1]" font is worthy of special mention here. It was developed specially for writing mathematical/technical texts. The DejaVu[2] and Lucida[3] fonts also have a wide range of symbols.

1 Font files for STIX are available from http://www.stixfonts.org
2 Font files for DejaVu Sans are available from http://www.dejavu-fonts.org
3 Lucida Sans belongs to the JRE package, which is probably already on your computer.

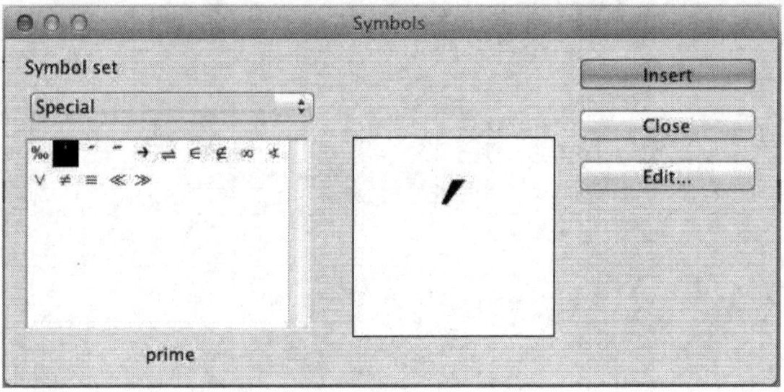

Figure 279: Catalog with new symbol

Note	Many symbols occur in more than one font. If you want to exchange documents with others, take care to use a font that is installed on their machine.

In the default LibreOffice installation, only those user-defined symbols that actually occur in the document are stored with it. Sometimes it is useful to embed all the user-defined symbols, for example when the document is going to be further edited by another person. Go to **Tools > Options > LibreOffice Math** and on the **Settings** page, uncheck the option **Embed only used symbols (smaller file size)**.This setting is only available when you are working on a Math document.

Default layout with style

In Writer, formulas are formatted according to the Formula frame style. In the Style and Formatting window (displayed with *F11*), click on the third icon at the top: **Frame Styles**. Right-click on **Formula** and select **Modify**. By this means, you can directly modify all formulas in your document, regarding spacing (page 276) or background (page 277), unless you manually modify formula formatting.

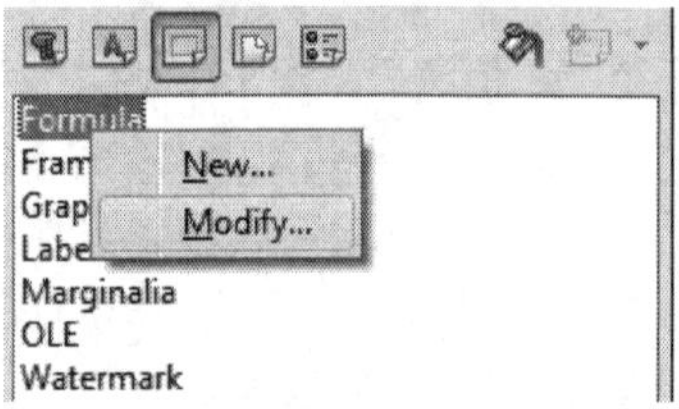

Figure 280 : Modify Frame Style Formula

To apply this style in all your new Writer documents, you must include the Formula style in your default template. To do so, create a new Writer document and modify the Formula frame style as you wish. Save the document using **File > Save as Template** and save it into **My Templates** with a name of your choice. To define this template as your default template, select the template you just created and choose **Set as default**. If you wish to return to the default template given at installation, open the Template Manager, click on the **Action Menu** and point to **Reset Default Template**, on the drop-down menu, and click **Text Document**. This menu choice does not appear unless a custom template has been set as the default.

The next time that you create a document by choosing **File > New**, the document will be created from the new default template.

For more information on the Template Manager, see Chapter 9, Styles and Templates.

Application to chemical formulas

Math was designed to build mathematical formulas, but it can also be used to write chemical formulas. In chemistry, formulas look like H_2O: names are usually non-italic uppercase. To write chemical formulas with Math, deselect the **Italic** attribute in the Fonts dialog (see "Changing the font" on page 273).

Here some examples of chemical formulas:

Construction	*Example*	*Entry*
Molecules	H_2SO_4	**`H_2 SO_4`** (please note the space!)
Isotopes	${}^{238}_{92}U$	**`U lsub 92 lsup 238`**
Ions	SO_4^{2-}	**`SO_4^{2-{}}`** or **`SO_4^{2"-"}`**

Notes: **`lsub`** or **`lsup`** are abreviations for *left subscript* and *left superscript*. Empty braces after **`2-`** are necessary to avoid errors as there is no right member after the minus sign.

For reversible reactions, there is no satisfactory double arrow in *Math*. If you have a font with a suitable symbol, you may use the method described in "Customizing the catalog" on page 278. For instance, DejaVu fonts have these double arrows ⇄ ⇆ ⇋ ⇌.

Alternatively, if you find a special character in a document you can copy it, for example here in this formula: C+O⇌ CO "⇌". Other double arrows can be found here: http://dev.w3.org/html5/html-author/charref from character x021C4, or here: http://www.unicode.org/charts/PDF/U2190.pdf, which is a subset of this location: http://www.unicode.org/charts/#symbols

Math commands – Reference

The complete list of commands and reserved words used by Math is available in the *Math Guide*:

- Unary / binary operators
- Relations
- Set operations
- Functions
- Operators
- Attributes
- Brackets
- Formats
- Others
- Characters – Greek
- Characters – Special
- Reserved words in alphabetic order

LibreOffice
The Document Foundation

Chapter 10
Printing, Exporting, and E-mailing

Introduction

This chapter provides general information about printing, exporting, and e-mailing documents from LibreOffice.

Quick printing

Click the **Print File Directly** icon to send the entire document to the default printer defined for your computer.

Note	You can change the action of the **Print File Directly** icon to send the document to the printer defined for the document instead of the default printer for the computer. Go to **Tools > Options > Load/Save > General** and select the **Load printer settings with the document** option.

Controlling printing

Note for Mac users	If you prefer to use the standard Mac Print dialogs, deselect the **Print dialogs – Use LibreOffice dialogs** option in **LibreOffice > Preferences > General**. This book uses the LibreOffice Print dialogs in illustrations.

For more control over printing, use the Print dialog (**File > Print** or *Ctrl+P*).

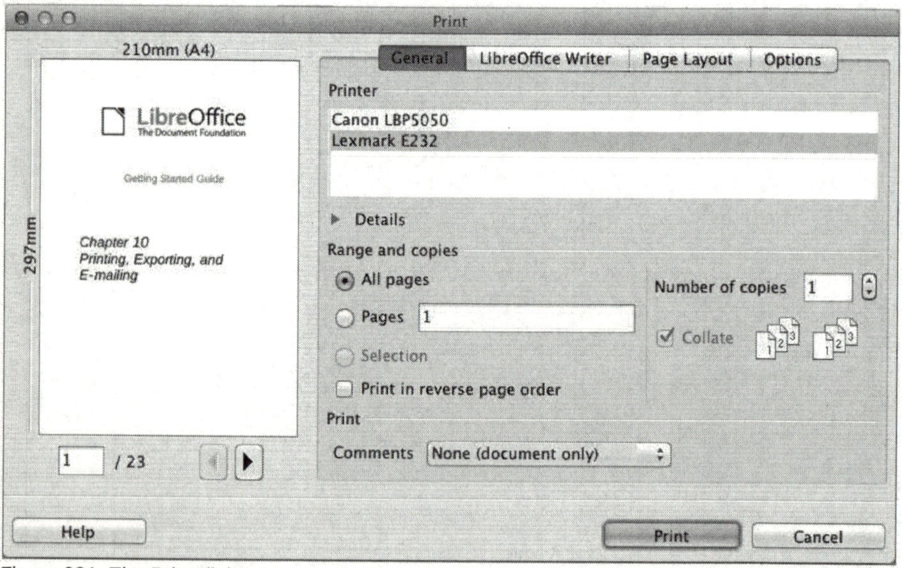

Figure 281. The Print dialog

The Print dialog has four pages, from which you can choose a range of options, as described in the following sections.

Note	The options selected on the Print dialog apply to this printing of this document only. To specify default printing settings for LibreOffice, go to **Tools > Options > LibreOffice – Print** and **Tools > Options > LibreOffice Writer – Print**. See Chapter 2, Setting Up LibreOffice, for more details.

The different components of LibreOffice have different available print settings, as summarized in Table 5.

Table 5: Print options in LibreOffice components

Feature	*Writer*	*Calc*	*Impress*	*Draw*
Select pages/sheets/slides to print	Yes	Yes	Yes	Yes
Print multiple pages/sheets/slides on one page	Yes	Yes	Yes	Yes
Print a brochure	Yes	No	Yes	Yes
Print envelopes	Yes	No	No	No
Print labels or business cards	Yes	No	No	No
Preview pages/sheets before printing	Yes	Yes	No	No

Selecting general printing options

On the *General* tab of the Print dialog, you can choose:

- The **printer** (from the printers available)
- Which **pages** to print, the number of copies to print, and whether to collate multiple copies (*Range and copies* section)
- Whether to print any **comments** that are in the document, and where to print the comments.

Some selections may not be available all the time. For example, if the document contains no comments, the Print – Comments drop-down list does not work.

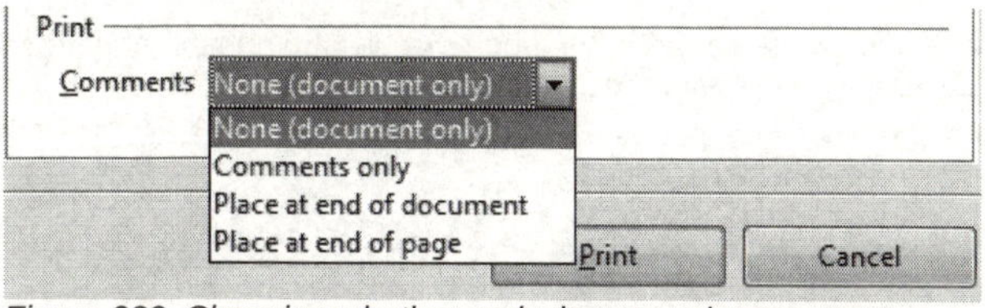

Figure 282: Choosing whether and where to print comments

Select the **Properties** button to display the selected printer's properties dialog where you can choose portrait or landscape orientation, which paper tray to use, and the paper size to print on.

On the Options tab of the Print dialog (Figure 283), the last item, *Use only paper tray from printer preference*, is not available in Calc.

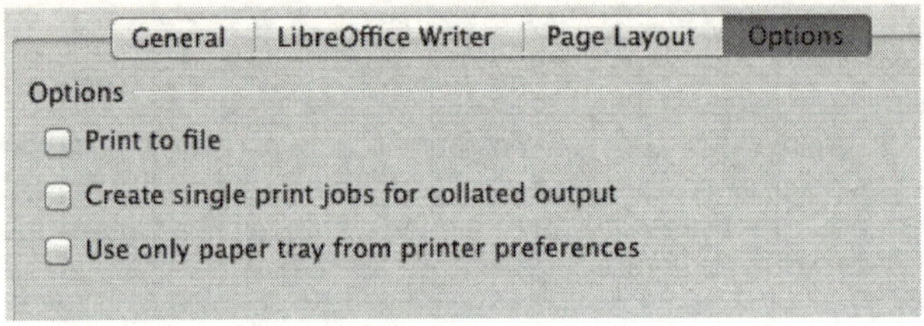

Figure 283: General print options

Printing multiple pages on a single sheet of paper

You can print multiple pages of a document on one sheet of paper. To do this:

1) In the Print dialog, select the *Page Layout* tab (Figure 284).

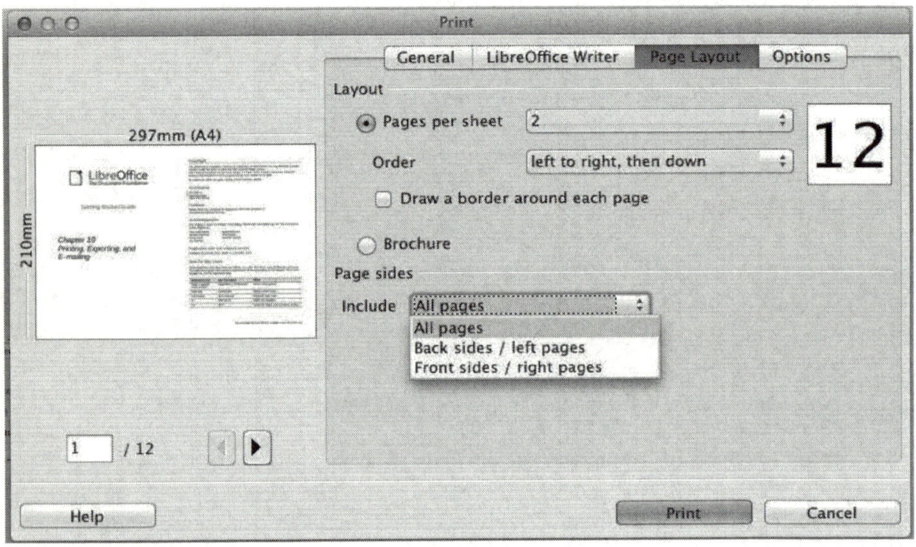

Figure 284: Printing multiple page per sheet of paper

2) In the *Layout* section, select from the drop-down list the number of pages to print per sheet. The preview panel on the left of the Print dialog shows how the printed document will look.

   When printing more than 2 pages per sheet, you can choose the order in which they are printing across and down the paper.

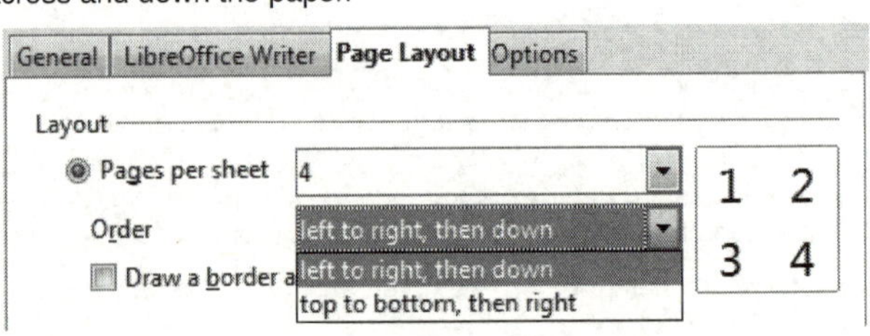

3) In the *Page sides* section, select whether to print all pages or only some pages. Click the **Print** button.

Tip	In Writer, to print two pages per sheet in "facing pages" (book layout) style, print from Print Preview instead. See page 292.

Selecting pages/sheets/slides to print

In addition to printing a full document, you can choose to print individual pages/sheets/slides, ranges of pages/sheets/slides, or a selection of a document. The details vary slightly in Writer, Calc, Draw and Impress, as described in this section.

Writer

Printing an individual page:

1) Choose **File > Print** from the menu bar, or press *Ctrl+P*.
2) On the Print dialog, select the page to print.
   a) In the *Ranges and copies* section of the General page, select the *Pages* option. The text input box displays the current page number.
   b) Enter the page number of the page you want to print. The preview box changes to show the selected page.
3) Click the **Print** button.

Printing a range of pages:

1) Choose **File > Print** from the menu bar, or press *Ctrl+P*.
2) On the Print dialog, select the range of pages to print.
   a) In the *Ranges and copies* section of the General page, select the *Pages* option.
   b) Enter the sequence numbers of the pages to print (for example, 1–4 or 1,3,7,11).
3) Click the **Print** button.

Printing a selection of text:

1) In the document, select the material (text and graphics) to print.
2) Choose **File > Print** from the menu bar, or press *Ctrl+P*.
3) The *Ranges and copies* section of the Print dialog now includes a *Selection* option and the preview box shows the selected material. See Figure 285.
4) Click the **Print** button.

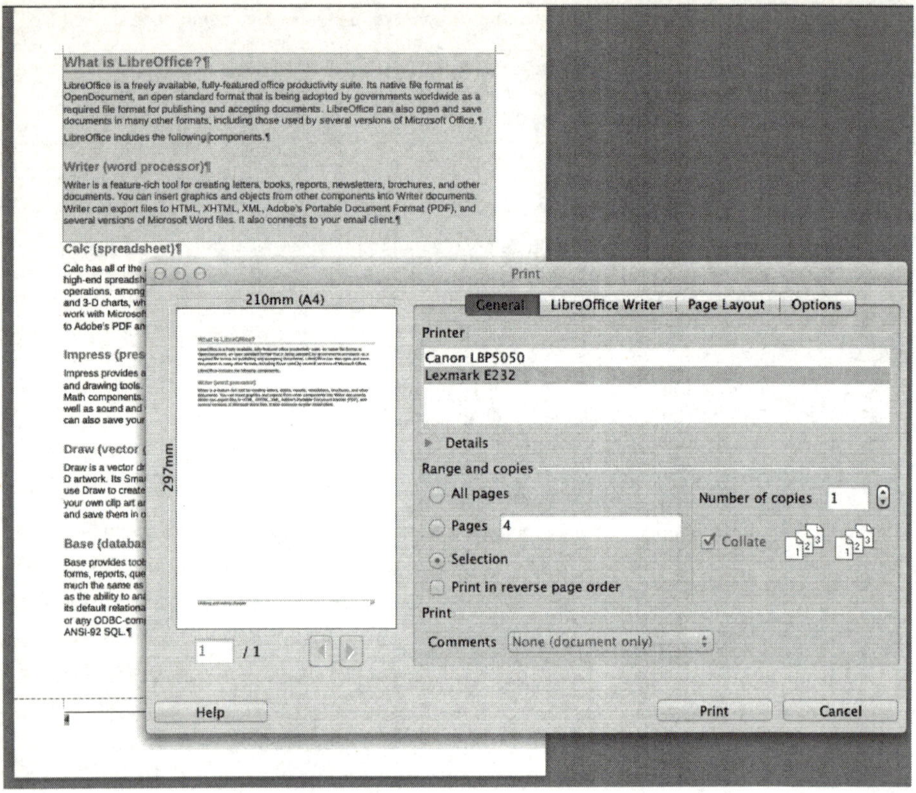

Figure 285: Printing a selection of text

Calc

You can choose single sheets, multiple sheets, and selections of cells for printing.

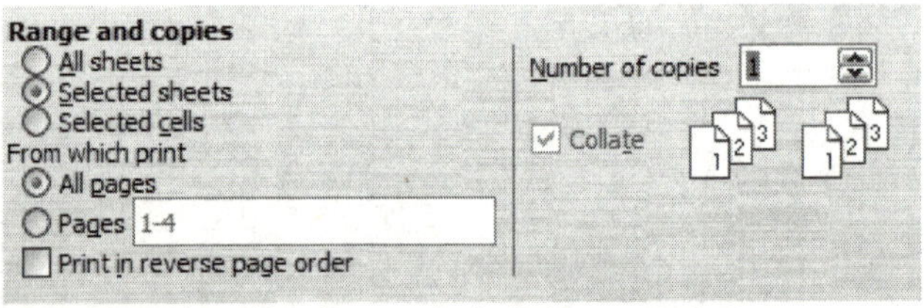

Figure 286: Choosing what to print in Calc

Printing an individual sheet:

1) In the spreadsheet, click on the sheet tab to select the sheet you want to print.
2) Choose **File > Print** from the menu bar, or press *Ctrl+P*.
3) In the *Ranges and copies* section of the Print dialog, choose the *Selected sheets* option.
4) Click the **Print** button.

Printing a range of sheets:

1) In the spreadsheet, select the sheets to print.
   a) Select the first sheet.
   b) Hold down the *Control* key.
   c) Click on the additional sheet tabs.
   d) Release the *Control* key when all required sheets are selected.
2) Choose **File > Print** from the menu bar, or press *Ctrl+P*.
3) In the *Ranges and copies* section of the Print dialog, choose the *Selected sheets* option.
4) Click the **Print** button.

Printing a selection of cells:

1) In the document, select the section of cells to print.
2) Choose **File > Print** from the menu, or press *Ctrl+P*.
3) In the *Ranges and copies* section of the Print dialog, select the *Selected cells* option.
4) Click the **Print** button.

Caution	After printing, be sure to deselect the extra sheets. If you keep them selected, the next time you enter data on one sheet, you enter data on all the selected sheets. This might not be what you want.

Impress and Draw

You can choose individual slides, ranges of slides, or selections of slides for printing.

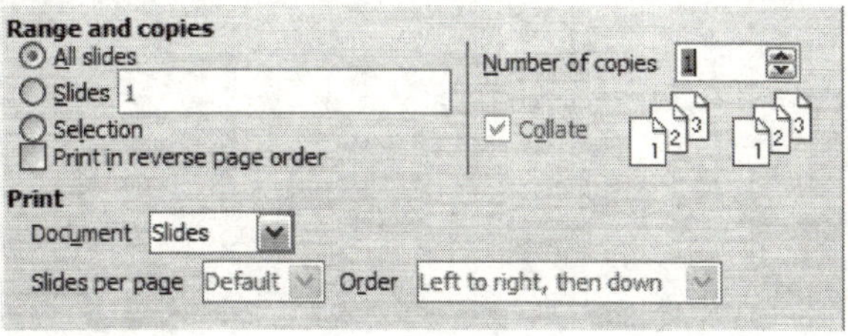

Printing an individual slide:

1) Choose **File > Print** from the menu bar, or press *Ctrl+P*.
2) Select the slide to print.
   a) In the *Ranges and copies* section of the Print dialog, select the *Slides* option.
   b) Enter the number of the slide to print.
3) Click the **Print** button.

Printing a range of slides:

1) Choose **File > Print** from the menu bar, or press *Ctrl+P*.
2) Select the slides to print.
   a) In the *Ranges and copies* section of the Print dialog, select the *Slides* option.
   b) Enter the number of the slides to print (for example 1-4 or 1,3,7,11).
3) Click the **Print** button.

Printing a selection from a slide, or a selection from multiple slides:

1) In the document, select the section of the slide to print.
2) Choose **File > Print** from the menu bar, or press *Ctrl+P*.
3) Select the *Selection* option in the *Ranges and copies* section of the Print dialog.
4) Click the **Print** button.

Printing handouts, notes, or outlines in Impress

Handouts prints the slides in reduced size on the page, from one to nine slides per page. The slides can be printed horizontally (landscape orientation) or vertically (portrait orientation) on the page.

Notes prints a single slide per page with any notes entered for that slide in Notes View.

Outline prints the title and headings of each slide in outline format.

To print handouts, notes, or outlines:

1) Choose **File > Print** from the menu bar, or press *Ctrl+P*.
2) In the *Print* section of the Print dialog, select the required option.
3) For Handouts, you can then choose how many slides to print per page, and the order in which they are printed.
4) Click the **Print** button.

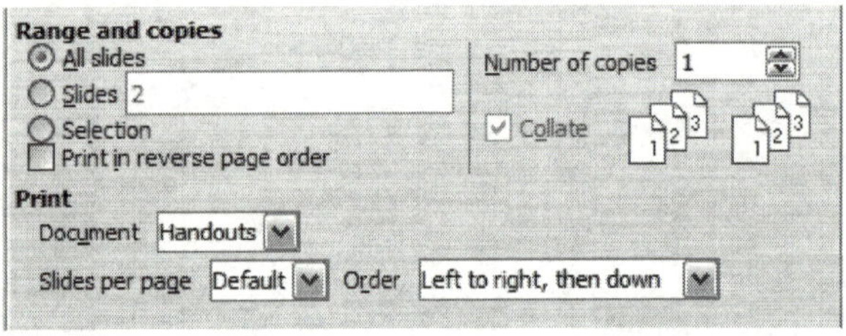

Printing a brochure

In Writer, Impress, and Draw, you can print a document with two pages on each side of a sheet of paper, arranged so that when the printed pages are folded in half, the pages are in the correct order to form a booklet or brochure.

Tip	Plan your document so it will look good when printed half size; choose appropriate margins, font sizes, and so on. You may need to experiment.

To print a brochure on a single-sided printer:

1) Choose **File > Print**, or press *Ctrl+P*.
2) In the Print dialog, click **Properties**.
3) Check the printer is set to the same orientation (portrait or landscape) as specified in the page setup for your document. Usually the orientation does not matter, but it does for brochures. Click **OK** to return to the Print dialog.
4) Select the *Page layout* tab in the Print dialog.
5) Select the **Brochure** option.
6) In the *Page sides* section, select *Back sides / left pages* option from the Include drop-down list.

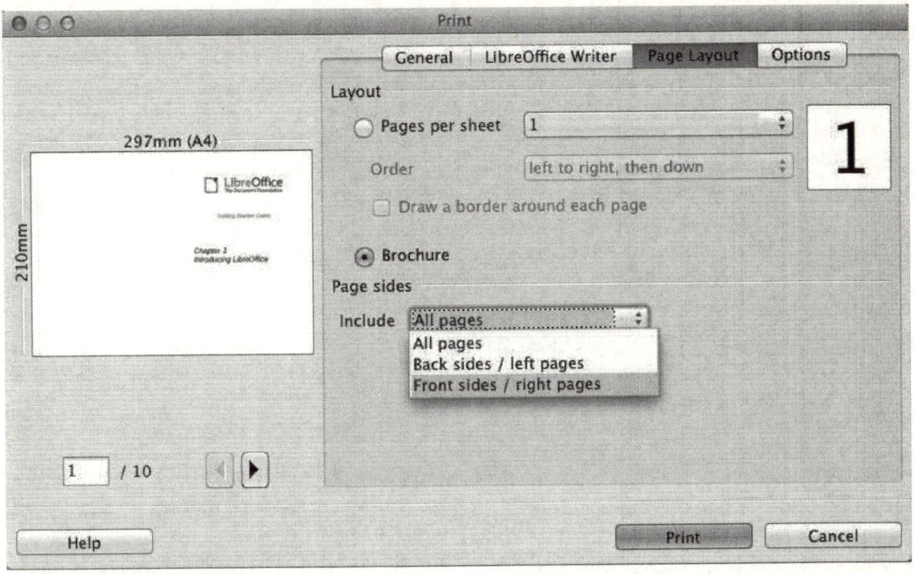

7) Click the **Print** button.
8) Take the printed pages out of the printer, turn the pages over, and put them back into the printer in the correct orientation to print on the blank side. You may need to experiment a bit to find out what the correct arrangement is for your printer.
9) On the Print dialog, in the *Page sides* section, select *Front sides / right pages* option from the Include drop down box.
10) Click the **Print** button.

Tip	If your printer can print double-sided automatically, choose **All pages**.

Printing envelopes, labels, business cards

Printing envelopes, labels, or business cards using Writer involves two steps: setup and printing.

For details of how to set these up, see Chapter 11, Using Mail Merge, in the *Writer Guide*. To print:

1) Choose **File > Print** from the menu bar, or press *Ctrl+P*.
2) On the Print dialog, under *Ranges and copies*, choose **Pages** and type **1** in the box. Click the **Print** button.

Printing in black and white (on a color printer)

You may wish to print documents in black and white on a color printer. Several choices are available. Please note that some color printers may print in color regardless of the settings you choose.

Change the printer settings to print in black and white or grayscale:

1) Choose **File > Print**, or press *Ctrl+P*, to open the Print dialog.

2) Click **Properties** to open the Properties dialog for the printer. The available choices vary from one printer to another, but you should find options for the Color settings. See your printer's help or user manual for more information.
3) The choices for color might include *black and white* or *grayscale*. Choose the required setting.
4) Click **OK** to confirm your choice and return to the Print dialog,
5) Click the **Print** button to print the document.

Tip	Grayscale is best if you have any graphics in the document.

Change the LibreOffice settings to print all color text and graphics as grayscale:

1) Choose **Tools > Options > LibreOffice > Print**.
2) Select the **Convert colors to grayscale** option. Click **OK** to save the change.
3) Open the Print dialog (**File > Print**), or press *Ctrl+P.*
4) Click the **Print** button to print the document.

Change the LibreOffice Writer (or Calc, Impress, Draw) settings to print all color text as black, and all graphics as grayscale:

1) Choose **Tools > Options > LibreOffice Writer > Print**.
2) Under *Contents*, select the **Print text in black** option. Click **OK** to save the change.
3) Open the Print dialog (**File > Print**), or press *Ctrl+P*.
4) Click the **Print** button to print the document.

Previewing pages/sheets before printing

You can use the previewing options in Writer and Calc to view the document as it will be printed. Different viewing options are available.

Writer

The normal page view in Writer shows you what each page will look like when printed and you can edit the pages in that view. If you are designing a document to be printed double-sided, you may want to see what facing pages look like. Writer provides two ways to do this:

- View Layout (editable view): use the Facing Pages (Book Preview) button on the status bar.

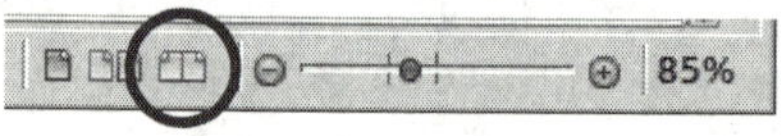

- Page Preview (read-only view).

To use Page Preview:

1) Choose **File > Page Preview**, click the **Page Preview** button on the Standard toolbar or press *Ctrl+Shift+O*.

   Writer now displays the **Page Preview** toolbar instead of the Formatting toolbar.

Figure 287. Page Preview toolbar (Writer)

2) Select the required preview icon: **Two Pages** ( ), **Multiple Pages** ( ) or **Book Preview** ( ).

3) To print the document from this view, click the **Print document** icon( ) to open the Print dialog. Choose the print options and click the **Print** button.

Calc

To preview the sheets in Calc before printing:

1) Choose **File > Page Preview**.

   The Calc window now displays the **Page Preview** toolbar instead of the Formatting toolbar.

Figure 288. Page Preview toolbar (Calc)

2) To print the document from this view, click the **Print document** icon to open the Print dialog.
3) Choose the print options and click the **Print** button.

Exporting to PDF

LibreOffice can export documents to PDF (Portable Document Format). This industry-standard file format is ideal for sending the file to someone else to view using Adobe Reader or other PDF viewers.

The process and dialogs are the same for Writer, Calc, Impress, and Draw, with a few minor differences mentioned in this section.

Quick export to PDF

Click the **Export Directly as PDF** icon to export the entire document using the PDF settings you most recently selected on the PDF Options dialog (see below). You are asked to enter the file name and location for the PDF file, but you do not get a chance to choose a page range, the image compression, or other options.

Controlling PDF content and quality

For more control over the content and quality of the resulting PDF, use **File > Export as PDF**. The PDF Options dialog opens. This dialog has five pages (General, Initial View, User Interface, Links, and Security). Select the appropriate settings, and then click **Export**. Then you are asked to enter the location and file name of the PDF to be created, and click **Save** to export the file.

General page of PDF Options dialog

On the *General* page, you can choose which pages to include in the PDF, the type of compression to use for images (which affects the quality of images in the PDF), and other options.

Range section

- **All**: Exports the entire document to PDF.
- **Pages**: To export a range of pages, use the format **3-6** (pages 3 to 6). To export single pages, use the format **7;9;11** (pages 7, 9 and 11). You can also export a combination of page ranges and single pages, by using a format like **3-6;8;10;12**.
- **Selection**: Exports all the selected material.

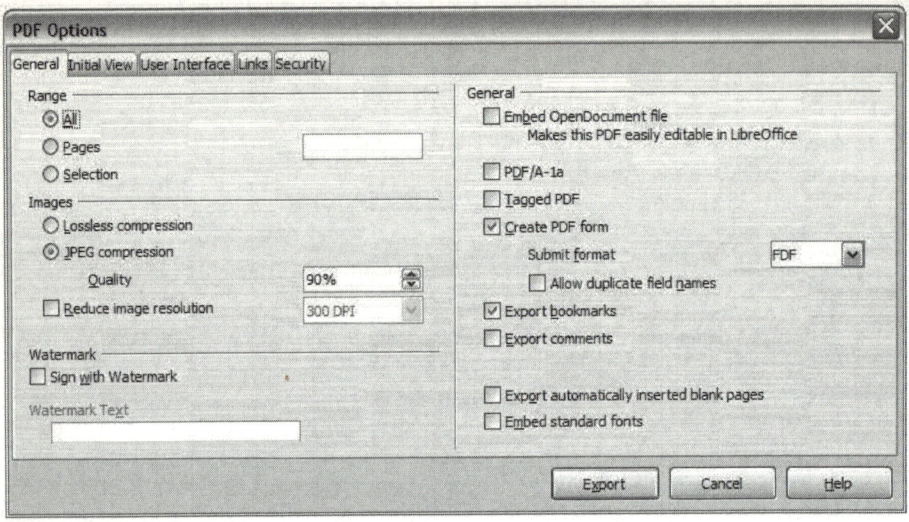

Figure 289: General page of PDF Options dialog

Images section

- **Lossless compression**: Images are stored without any loss of quality. Tends to make large files when used with photographs. Recommended for other kinds of images or graphics.
- **JPEG compression**: Allows for varying degrees of quality. A setting of 90% works well with photographs (small file size, little perceptible loss of quality).
- **Reduce image resolution**: Lower DPI (dots per inch) images have lower quality. For viewing on a computer screen, generally a resolution of 72dpi (for Windows) or 96dpi (GNU/Linux) is sufficient, while for printing it is generally preferable to use at least 300 or 600dpi, depending on the capability of the printer. Higher DPI settings greatly increase the size of the exported file.

Note	EPS (Encapsulated PostScript) images with embedded previews are exported only as previews. EPS images without embedded previews are exported as empty placeholders.

Watermark section

- **Sign with Watermark:** When this option is selected, a transparent overlay of the text you enter into the **Watermark Text** box will appear on each page of the PDF.

General section

- **Embed OpenDocument file**: Makes this PDF easily editable in LibreOffice or similar programs.
- **PDF/A-1a**: PDF/A is an ISO standard for long-term preservation of documents, by embedding all the information necessary for faithful reproduction (such as fonts) while forbidding other elements (including forms, security, and encryption). PDF tags are written. If you select PDF/A-1a, the forbidden elements are grayed-out (not available).
- **Tagged PDF**: Tagged PDF contains information about the structure of the document's contents. This can help to display the document on devices with different screens, and

when using screen reader software. Some tags that are exported are table of contents, hyperlinks, and controls. This option can increase file sizes significantly.

- **Create PDF form - Submit format:** Choose the format of submitting forms from within the PDF file. This setting overrides the control's URL property that you set in the document. There is only one common setting valid for the whole PDF document: PDF (sends the whole document), FDF (sends the control contents), HTML, and XML. Most often you will choose the PDF format.
- **Export bookmarks:** Exports headings in Writer documents, and page or slide names in Impress and Draw documents, as "bookmarks" (a table of contents list displayed by most PDF viewers, including Adobe Reader).
- **Export comments**: Exports comments as PDF notes. You may not want this!
- **Export automatically inserted blank pages**: If selected, automatically inserted blank pages are exported to the PDF. This is best if you are printing the PDF double-sided. For example, books usually have chapters set to always start on an odd-numbered (right-hand) page. When the previous chapter ends on an odd page, LibreOffice inserts a blank page between the two odd pages. This option controls whether to export that blank page.
- **Embed standard fonts:** Normally the 14 standard PostScript fonts are not embedded in a PDF file, because PDF reader software already contains these fonts. However, you can choose to embed these fonts in all PDF documents created by LibreOffice to enhance display accuracy in PDF viewers. Font embedding may also be required by some printers.

Initial View page of PDF Options dialog

On the *Initial View* page (Figure 290), you can choose how the PDF opens by default in a PDF viewer. The selections should be self-explanatory.

If you have Complex Text Layout enabled (in **Tools > Options > Language settings > Languages**), an additional selection is available under *Continuous facing*: **First page is left** (normally, the first page is on the right when using the *Continuous facing* option).

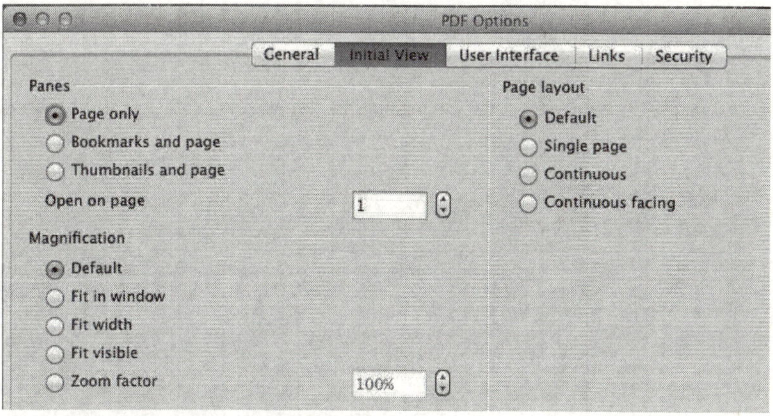

Figure 290: Initial View page of PDF Options dialog

User Interface page of PDF Options dialog

On the *User Interface* page (Figure 291), you can choose more settings to control how a PDF viewer displays the file. Some of these choices are particularly useful when you are creating a PDF to be used as a presentation or a kiosk-type display.

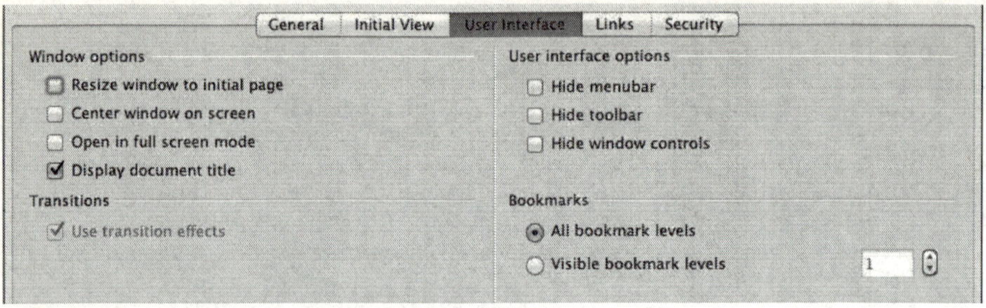

Figure 291: User Interface page of PDF Options dialog

Window options section

- **Resize window to initial page.** Causes the PDF viewer window to resize to fit the first page of the PDF.
- **Center window on screen.** Causes the PDF viewer window to be centered on the computer screen.
- **Open in full screen mode.** Causes the PDF viewer to open full-screen instead of in a smaller window.
- **Display document title.** Causes the PDF viewer to display the document's title in the title bar.

User interface options section

- **Hide menu bar.** Causes the PDF viewer to hide the menu bar.
- **Hide toolbar.** Causes the PDF viewer to hide the toolbar.
- **Hide window controls.** Causes the PDF viewer to hide other window controls.

Transitions

In Impress, displays slide transition effects as their respective PDF effects.

Bookmarks

Select how many heading levels are displayed as bookmarks, if *Export bookmarks* is selected on the General page.

Links page of PDF Options dialog

On the *Links* page, you can choose how links are exported to PDF.

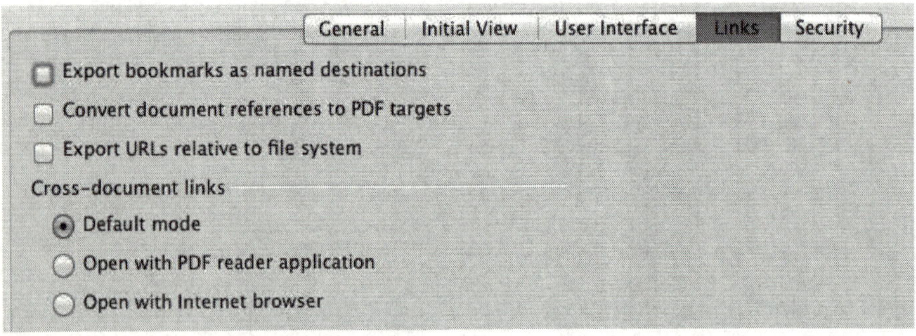

Figure 292: Links page of PDF Options dialog

Export bookmarks as named destinations

If you have defined Writer bookmarks, Impress or Draw slide names, or Calc sheet names, this option exports them as "named destinations" to which Web pages and PDF documents can link.

Convert document references to PDF targets

If you have defined links to other documents with OpenDocument extensions (such as .odt, .ods, and .odp), this option converts the files' extensions to .pdf in the exported PDF document.

Export URLs relative to file system

If you have defined relative links in a document, this option exports those links to the PDF.

Cross-document links

Defines the behavior of links clicked in PDF files.

Security page of PDF Options dialog

PDF export includes options to encrypt the PDF (so it cannot be opened without a password) and apply some digital rights management (DRM) features.

- With an *open password* set, the PDF can only be opened with the password. Once opened, there are no restrictions on what the user can do with the document (for example, print, copy, or change it).
- With a *permissions password set*, the PDF can be opened by anyone, but its permissions can be restricted. See Figure 293. After you set a password for permissions, the other choices on the Security page become available.
- With *both* the *open password* and *permission password* set, the PDF can only be opened with the correct password, and its permissions can be restricted.

Note	Permissions settings are effective only if the user's PDF viewer respects the settings.

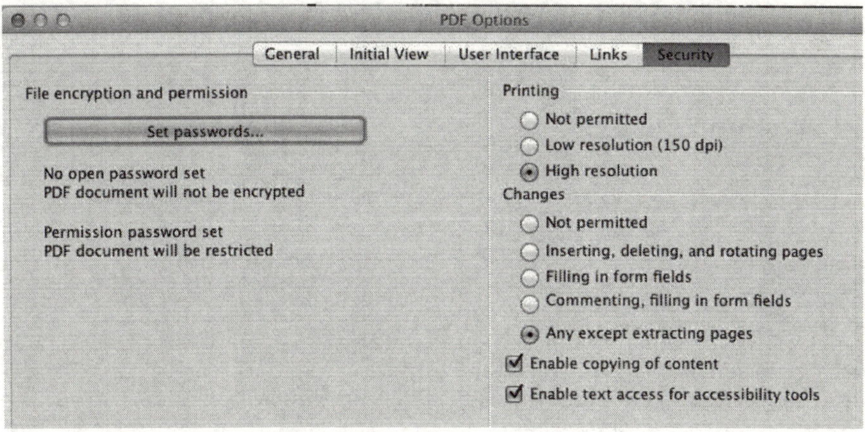

Figure 293: Security page of PDF Options dialog

Figure 294 shows the pop-up dialog displayed when you click the **Set open password** button on the Security page of the PDF Options dialog.

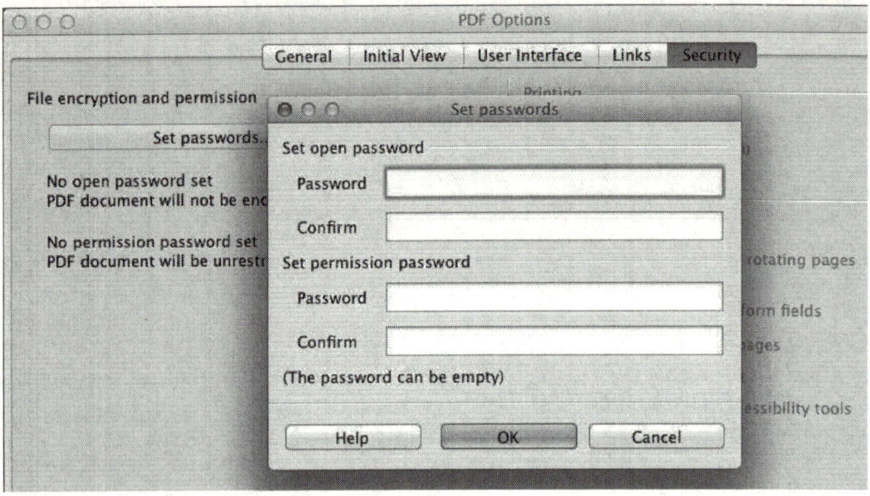

Figure 294: Setting a password to encrypt a PDF

Exporting to other formats

LibreOffice uses the term "export" for some file operations involving a change of file type. If you cannot find what you want under **File > Save As**, look under **File > Export** as well.

LibreOffice can export files to XHTML. In addition, Draw and Impress can export to Adobe Flash (SWF) and a range of image formats.

To export to one of these formats, choose **File > Export**. On the Export dialog, specify a file name for the exported document, then select the required format in the *File format* list and click the **Export** button.

E-mailing documents

LibreOffice provides several ways to send documents quickly and easily as e-mail attachments in one of three formats: OpenDocument (LibreOffice's default format), Microsoft Office formats, or PDF.

Note	Documents can only be sent from the LibreOffice menu if a mail profile has been set up in **Tools > Options > LibreOffice Writer > Mail Merge E-mail**.

To send the current document in OpenDocument format:

1) Choose **File > Send > Document as E-mail**. LibreOffice opens your default e-mail program. The document is attached.
2) In your e-mail program, enter the recipient, subject, and any text you want to add, then send the e-mail.

File > Send > E-mail as OpenDocument (Text, **Spreadsheet**, or **Presentation**) has the same effect.

If you choose **E-mail as Microsoft [Word**, **Excel**, or **Powerpoint]**, LibreOffice first creates a file in one of those formats and then opens your e-mail program with the file attached.

Similarly, if you choose **E-mail as PDF**, LibreOffice first creates a PDF using your default PDF settings (as when using the **Export Directly as PDF** toolbar button) and then opens your email program with the PDF file attached.

E-mailing a document to several recipients

To e-mail a document to several recipients, you can use the features in your e-mail program or you can use LibreOffice's mail merge facilities to extract email addresses from an address book.

You can use LibreOffice's mail merge to send e-mail in two ways:

- Use the Mail Merge Wizard to create the document and send it. See Chapter 11, Using Mail Merge, in the *Writer Guide* for details.
- Create the document in Writer without using the Wizard, then use the Wizard to send it. This method is described here.

To use the Mail Merge Wizard to send a previously-created Writer document:

1) Click **Tools > Mail Merge Wizard**. On the first page of the wizard, select **Use the current document** and click **Next**.

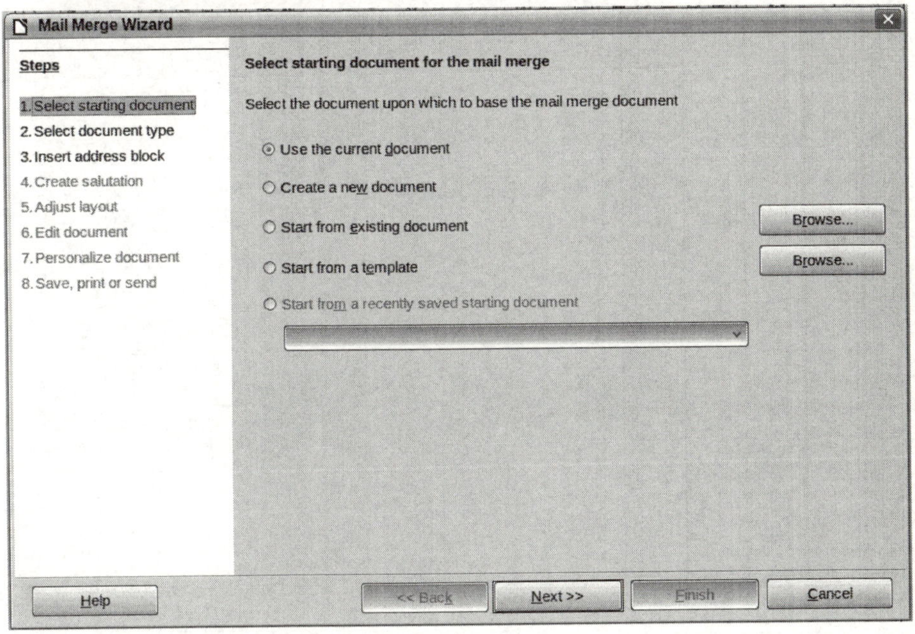

Figure 295: Select starting document

2) On the second page, select **E-mail message** and click **Next**.

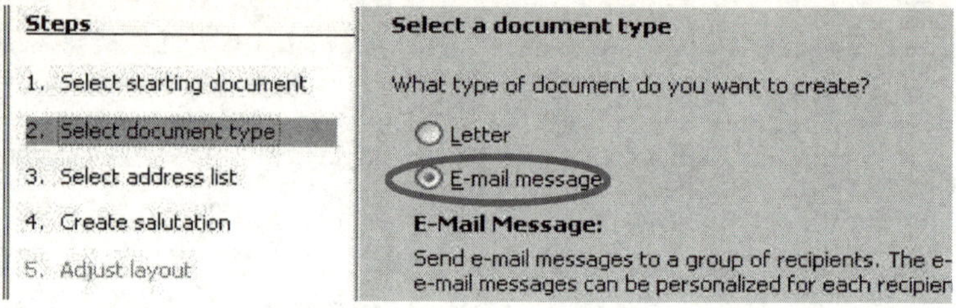

Figure 296: Select document type

3) On the third page, click the **Select Address List** button. Select the required address list (even if only one is shown) and then click **OK**. (If the address list you need is not shown here, you can click **Add** to find it and add it to the list.)

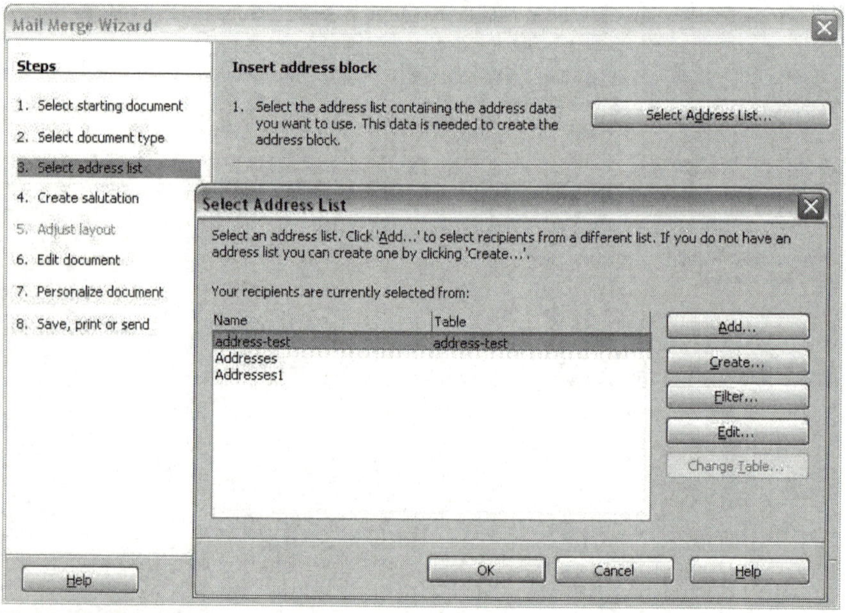

Figure 297: Selecting an address list

4) Back on the Select address list page, click **Next**. On the Create salutation page, deselect **This document should contain a salutation**.

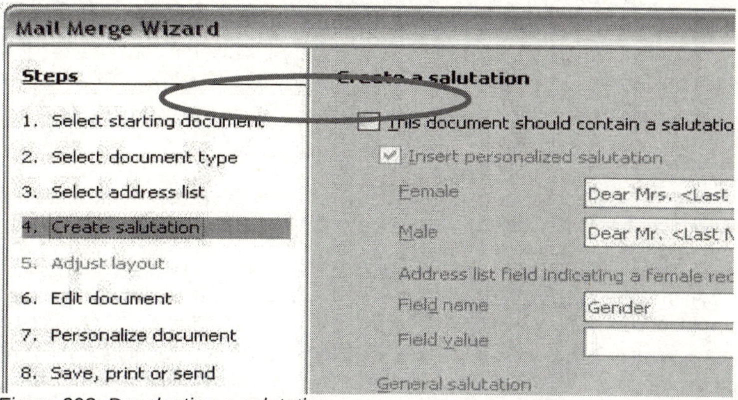

Figure 298: Deselecting a salutation

5) In the left-hand list, click **8. Save, print or send**. LibreOffice displays a "Creating documents" message and then displays the *Save, print or send* page of the Wizard.

6) Select **Send merged document as E-Mail**. The lower part of the page changes to show e-mail settings choices.

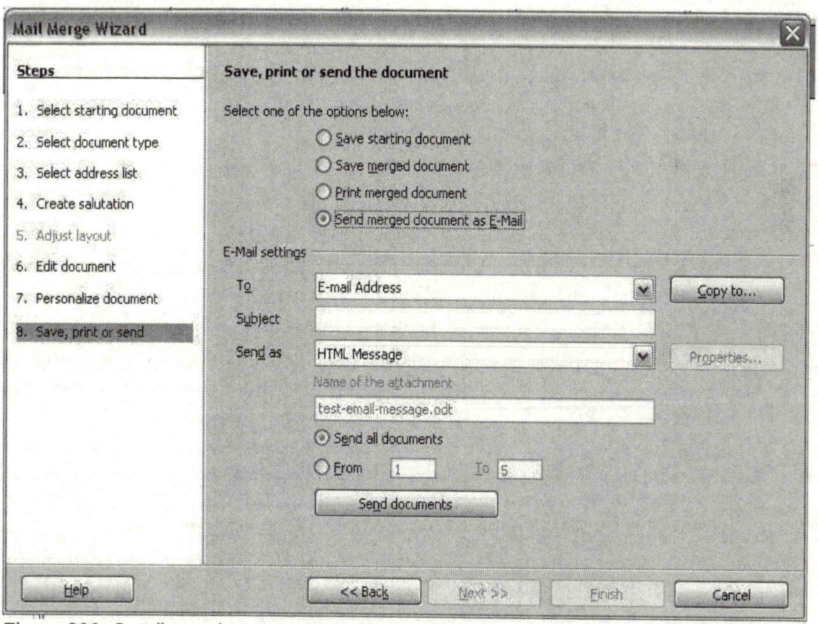

Figure 299: Sending a document as an email message

7) Type a subject for your email and click **Send documents**. LibreOffice sends the e-mails.

Digital signing of documents

To sign a document digitally, you need a personal key, also known as a *certificate*. A personal key is stored on your computer as a combination of a private key, which must be kept secret, and a public key, which you add to your documents when you sign them. You can get a certificate from a certification authority, which may be a private company or a governmental institution.

When you apply a digital signature to a document, a kind of checksum is computed from the document's content plus your personal key. The checksum and your public key are stored together with the document.

When someone later opens the document on any computer with a recent version of LibreOffice, the program will compute the checksum again and compare it with the stored checksum. If both are the same, the program will signal that you see the original, unchanged document. In addition, the program can show you the public key information from the certificate. You can compare the public key with the public key that is published on the web site of the certificate authority. Whenever someone changes something in the document, this change breaks the digital signature.

On Windows operating systems, the Windows features of validating a signature are used. On Solaris and Linux systems, files that are supplied by Thunderbird, Mozilla or Firefox are used. For a more detailed description of how to get and manage a certificate, and signature validation, see "About Digital Signatures" in the LibreOffice Help.

To sign a document:

1) Choose **File > Digital Signatures**.
2) If you have not saved the document since the last change, a message box appears. Click **Yes** to save the file.
3) After saving, you see the Digital Signatures dialog. Click **Add** to add a public key to the document.
4) In the Select Certificate dialog, select your certificate and click **OK**.
5) You see again the Digital Signatures dialog, where you can add more certificates if you want. Click **OK** to add the public key to the saved file.

A signed document shows an icon in the status bar. You can double-click the icon to view the certificate.

Removing personal data

You may wish to ensure that personal data, versions, notes, hidden information, or recorded changes are removed from files before you send them to other people or create PDFs from them.

In **Tools > Options > LibreOffice > Security > Options**, you can set LibreOffice to remind (warn) you when files contain certain information and remove personal information automatically on saving.

To remove personal and some other data from a file, go to **File > Properties**. On the *General* tab, uncheck **Apply user data** and then click the **Reset** button. This removes any names in the created and modified fields, deletes the modification and printing dates, and resets the editing time to zero, the creation date to the current date and time, and the version number to 1.

To remove version information, either (a) go to **File > Versions**, select the versions from the list and click **Delete;** or (b) use **File > Save As** and save the file with a different name.

LibreOffice
The Document Foundation

Chapter 11
Graphics, the Gallery, and Fontwork

Introduction

You can add graphic and image files, including photos, drawings, scanned images, and others, to LibreOffice documents. LibreOffice can import various vector (line drawing) and raster (bitmap) file formats. The most commonly used graphic formats are GIF, JPG, PNG, and BMP. See Appendix B for a full list of the graphic formats LibreOffice can import.

Graphics in LibreOffice are of three basic types:

- Image files, such as photos, drawings, and scanned images
- Diagrams created using LibreOffice's drawing tools
- Charts created using LibreOffice's Chart component

This chapter covers images and diagrams.

More detailed descriptions on working with drawing tools can be found in the *Draw Guide* and *Impress Guide*. Instructions on how to create charts are given in the *Calc Guide*.

Adding images to a document

Images can be added to a document in several ways: by inserting an image file, directly from a graphics program or a scanner, or by copying and pasting from a source being viewed on your computer.

Inserting an image file

When the image is in a file stored on the computer, you can insert it into a LibreOffice document using either of the following methods.

Drag and drop

1) Open a file browser window and locate the image you want to insert.
2) Drag the image into the LibreOffice document and drop it where you want it to appear. A faint vertical line marks where the image will be dropped.

This method embeds (saves a copy of) the image file in the document. To link the file instead of embedding it, hold down the *Ctrl+Shift* keys while dragging the image.

Insert Picture dialog

1) Click in the LibreOffice document where you want the image to appear.
2) Choose **Insert > Picture > From File** from the menu bar.
3) On the Insert Picture dialog, navigate to the file to be inserted, and select it.

   At the bottom of the dialog (Figure 300) are two options, **Preview** and **Link**. Select **Preview** to view a thumbnail of the selected image in the preview pane on the right, so that you can verify that you have the correct file. See page 305 for the use of **Link**.
4) Click **Open**.

Note	If you choose the **Link** option, a message box appears when you click **Open**. The message states that the picture will not be stored with the document, but only referenced as a link, and asks if you want to embed the graphic instead. Choose **Keep Link** if you want the link, or **Embed Graphic** if you do not. To prevent this message from appearing again, deselect the box by **Ask when linking a graphic** at the bottom of the message.

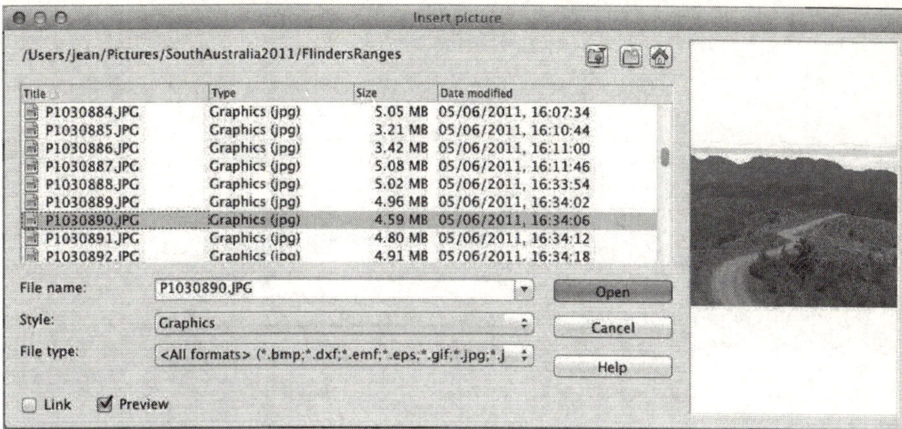

Figure 300. Insert picture dialog

Linking an image file

If the **Link** option in the Insert picture dialog is selected, LibreOffice creates a link to the file containing the image instead of saving a copy of the image in the document. The result is that the image is displayed in the document, but when the document is saved, it contains only a reference to the image file—not the image itself. The document and the image remain as two separate files, and they are merged together only when you open the document again.

Linking an image has two advantages and one disadvantage:

- Advantage – Linking can reduce the size of the document when it is saved, because the image file itself is not included. File size is usually not a problem on a modern computer with a reasonable amount of memory, unless the document includes many large graphics files; LibreOffice can handle quite large files.
- Advantage – You can modify the image file separately without changing the document because the link to the file remains valid, and the modified image will appear when you next open the document. This can be a big advantage if you (or someone else, perhaps a graphic artist) is updating images.
- Disadvantage – If you send the document to someone else, or move it to a different computer, you must also send the image files, or the receiver will not be able to see the linked images. You need to keep track of the location of the images and make sure the recipient knows where to put them on another machine, so that the document can find them. For example, you might keep images in a subfolder named Images (under the folder containing the document); the recipient of the file needs to put the images in a subfolder with the same name and in the same place relative to the document.

Note	When inserting the same image several times in the document, it would appear beneficial to link rather than embed; however, this is not necessary as LibreOffice embeds only one copy of the image file in the document.

Embedding linked images

If you originally linked the images, you can easily embed one or more of them later if you wish. To do so:

1) Open the document in LibreOffice and choose **Edit > Links**.

2) The Edit Links dialog (Figure 301) shows all the linked files. In the *Source file* list, select the files you want to change from linked to embedded.
3) Click the **Break Link** button.
4) Save the document.

Note	Going the other way, from embedded to linked, is not so easy—you must delete and reinsert the images, one at a time, selecting the **Link** option when you do so.

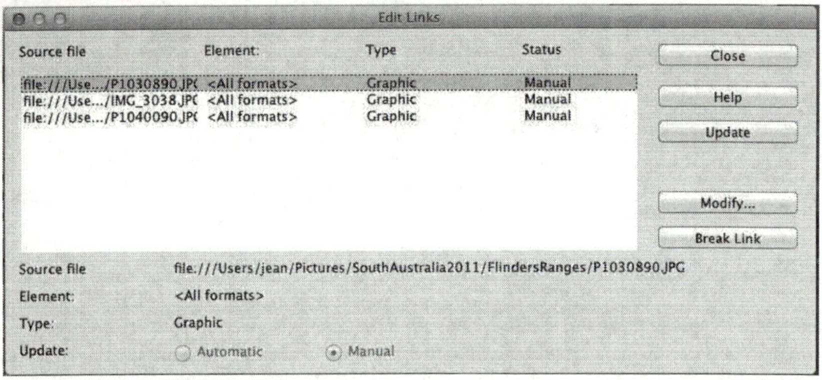

Figure 301: The Edit Links dialog

Inserting an image from the clipboard

Using the clipboard, you can copy images into a LibreOffice document from another LibreOffice document and from other programs. To do this:

1) Open both the source document and the target document.
2) In the source document, select the image to be copied.
3) Move the mouse pointer over the selected image and press *Ctrl+C* to copy the image to the clipboard.
4) Switch to the target document.
5) Click to place the cursor where the graphic is to be inserted.
6) Press *Ctrl+V* to insert the image.

Caution	If the application from which the graphic was copied is closed before the graphic is pasted into the target, the image stored on the clipboard could be lost.

Inserting an image using a scanner

If a scanner is connected to your computer, LibreOffice can call the scanning application and insert the scanned item into the LibreOffice document as an image. To start this procedure, place the cursor where you want the graphic to be inserted and choose **Insert > Picture > Scan > Select Source**.

Although this practice is quick and easy, it is unlikely to result in a high-quality image of the correct size. You may get better results by scanned material into a graphics program and cleaning it up there before inserting the resulting image into LibreOffice.

Inserting an image from the Gallery

The Gallery provides a convenient way to group reusable objects such as graphics and sounds that you can insert into your documents. The Gallery is available in all components of LibreOffice. See "Managing the LibreOffice Gallery" on page 308. You can copy or link an object from the Gallery into a document.

To insert an object:

1) Choose **Tools > Gallery** or click the Gallery icon on the Standard toolbar (in Writer and Calc) or the Drawing toolbar (in Impress, Writer, and Draw).
2) Select a theme.
3) Select an object with a single click.
4) Drag and drop the image into the document. (See Figure 302.)
   You can also right-click on the object and choose **Insert > Copy**.

This then causes the Graphics toolbar to replace the Formatting toolbar and opens the Pictures toolbar, docked to the Status bar.

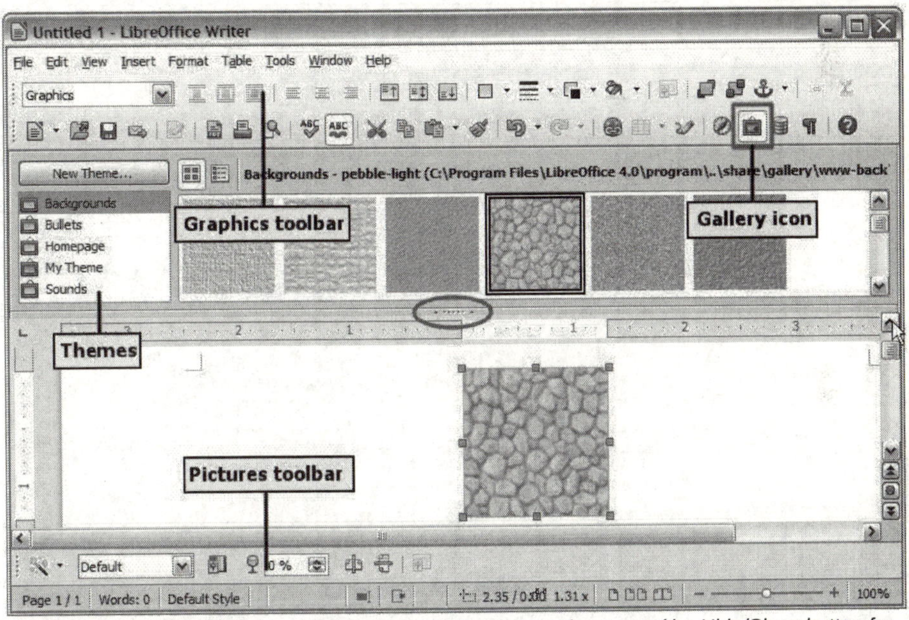

Figure 302. Copying a graphic object from the Gallery into a document (the Hide/Show button for the Gallery is indicated by the ellipse)

To insert an object as a link:

1) Choose **Tools > Gallery** and select a theme.
2) Select an object with a single click, then while pressing the *Shift* and *Ctrl* keys, drag and drop the object into the document.

Inserting an image as a background

To insert an image as the background to a page or paragraph:

1) Choose **Tools > Gallery** and select a theme.
2) Select an object with a single click, right-click on the object, and choose **Insert > Background > Page** or **> Paragraph**.

Modifying and positioning graphics

LibreOffice provides many tools for resizing, modifying, filtering, and positioning graphics; wrapping text around graphics; and using graphics as backgrounds and watermarks. These tools are described in relevant chapters of the other guides. Some sophisticated adjustments of the graphics are best done in an image manipulation program and the results brought into LibreOffice, rather than using LibreOffice's inbuilt tools.

Managing the LibreOffice Gallery

Graphics in the Gallery are grouped by themes, such as Bullets, Rulers, and Backgrounds. You can create other groups or themes and add your own pictures or find extensions containing more graphics.

The box on the left of the gallery window lists the available themes. Click on a theme to see its contents displayed in the Gallery window.

You can display the Gallery in *Icon View* (Figure 303) or *Detailed View*, and you can hide or show the Gallery by clicking on the *Hide* button (similar to the Hide button for the Navigator and the Styles and Formatting windows when they are docked).

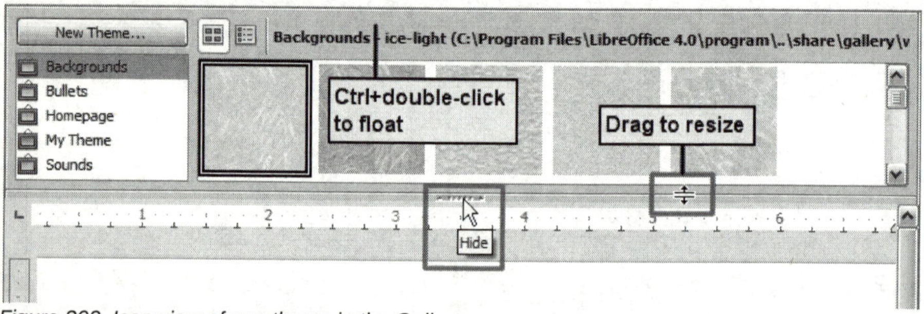

Figure 303. Icon view of one theme in the Gallery

By default, the Gallery is docked above the workspace. To expand the Gallery, position the pointer over the line that divides it from the top of the workspace. When the pointer changes to parallel lines with arrows, click and drag downward. The workspace resizes in response.

As with other docked windows, you can "float" the Gallery by moving the mouse pointer over an edge of the Gallery window, holding down the *Ctrl* key, and double-clicking. Repeat this procedure to dock the Gallery again.

The default themes are locked; no items can be added to or deleted from these themes. The locked themes are easily recognizable by right-clicking on them; the only available option in the pop-up menu is **Properties**.

In a default installation, only the *My themes* theme is customizable, although new themes can be added as explained in "Adding a new theme to the Gallery" on page 310.

Adding objects to the Gallery

You may wish to add to the Gallery any images that you use frequently, for example, a company logo. You can then very easily insert these graphics into a document later.

You can add images only to "My Theme" or to any other theme that you have created; these are indicated by a differently colored icon from the defaults, in the list of themes. You cannot add images to the built-in themes.

Method 1 (selecting a file)

1) Right-click on the desired theme and select Properties from the context menu.
2) In the theme's Properties dialog, go to the *Files* page and click the **Find Files** button.
3) The Select path dialog (not shown) opens. You can enter the path for the file's directory in the *Path* text box, or you can navigate to locate the file's directory.
4) Click the **Select** button to start the search. A list of graphic files is then displayed in the Properties dialog. You can use the *File type* drop-down list to limit the files displayed.
5) To add all of the files shown in the list, click **Add All.** Otherwise, select the files to add and then click **Add**. (Hold down either the Shift key or the *Ctrl* key while you click on the files.)

Figure 304. Gallery Properties dialog

Method 2 (drag and drop)

You can drag and drop an image into the Gallery from a document.

1) Open the document containing an image you want to add to the Gallery, and display the Gallery theme to which you want to add it.
2) Position the mouse pointer above the image, without clicking.
3) If the mouse pointer changes to a hand symbol, the image refers to a hyperlink. In this case, press the *Alt* key while you click the image, to select it without activating the link. If the mouse pointer does not change to a hand symbol, you can simply click the image to select it.
4) Once the image is selected, evident from the colored selection handles around it, release the mouse button. Click again on the image, keeping the mouse button pressed for more than two seconds. Without releasing the mouse button, drag the image into the Gallery.
5) Release the mouse button.

Deleting images from the Gallery

To delete an image from a theme that you created:

1) Right-click on the name of the image file or its thumbnail in the Gallery.
2) Click **Delete** in the context menu. A message appears, asking if you want to delete this object. Click **Yes.**

Note	Deleting the name of a file from the list in the Gallery does not delete the file from the hard disk or other location. This includes the drag-drop folder in the Gallery.

Adding a new theme to the Gallery

To add a new theme to the Gallery:

1) Click the **New Theme** button above the list of themes (Figure 303).
2) In the Properties of New Theme dialog, click the *General* tab and type a name for the new theme.
3) Click the *Files* tab and add images to the theme, as described earlier.

Deleting a theme from the Gallery

You can delete only themes that you have added to the Gallery; you cannot delete any of the built-in themes. To delete a theme from the Gallery:

1) Go to **Tools > Gallery.**
2) In the left part of the Gallery, select in the list the theme you wish to delete.
3) Right-click on the theme, then click **Delete** on the pop-up menu.

Location of the Gallery and the objects in it

Graphics and other objects shown in the Gallery can be located anywhere on your computer's hard disk, on a network drive, or on a CD-ROM. Listings in the Gallery show the location of each object. When you add graphics to the Gallery using method 1, the files are not moved or copied; only the location of each new object is added as a reference. When files are added using drag and drop, they are copied into a folder (dragdrop) in the Gallery, and allocated a file name.

Figure 305 shows in *Detailed View*, two files in the *My Theme* in the Gallery, one is contained in the dragdrop folder, and the other is a reference path to its actual location.

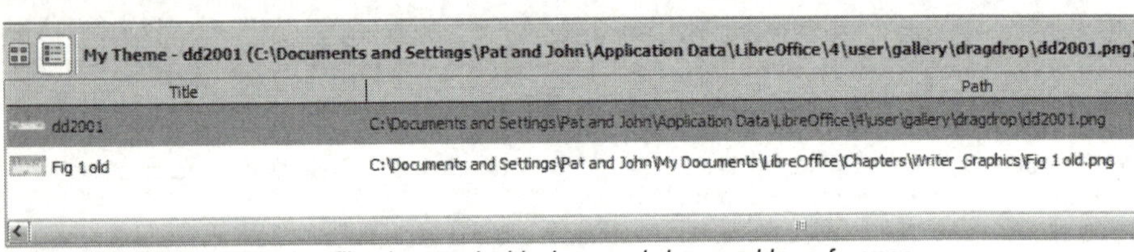

Figure 305: Theme showing files inserted with drag-and-drop and by reference

In a workgroup, you may have access to a shared Gallery (where you cannot change the contents unless authorized to do so) and a user Gallery, where you can add, change, or delete objects.

The location of the user Gallery is specified in **Tools > Options > LibreOffice > Paths**. You can change this location, and you can copy your gallery files (SDV) to other computers.

Gallery contents provided with LibreOffice are stored in a different location. You cannot change this location.

Creating an image map

An image map defines areas of an image (called *hotspots*) with hyperlinks to web addresses, other files on the computer, or parts of the same document. Hotspots are the graphic equivalent of text hyperlinks (described in Chapter 12). Clicking on a hotspot causes LibreOffice to open the linked page in the appropriate program (for example, the default browser for an HTML page; LibreOffice Calc for an ODS file; a PDF viewer for a PDF file). You can create hotspots of various shapes and include several hotspots in the same image.

To use the image map editor:

1) In your LibreOffice document, select the picture where you want to define the hotspots.
2) Choose **Edit > ImageMap** from the menu bar. The ImageMap Editor (Figure 306) opens.
3) Use the tools and fields in the dialog (described below) to define the hotspots and links necessary.
4) Click the **Apply** icon  to apply the settings.
5) When done, click the **Save** icon  to save the image map to a file, then click the **X** in the upper right corner to close the dialog.

Figure 306: The dialog to create or edit an image map

The main part of the dialog shows the image on which the hotspots are defined. A hotspot is identified by a line indicating its shape.

The toolbar at the top of the dialog contains the following tools:

- **Apply** button: click this button to apply the changes.
- **Load, Save,** and **Select** icons.
- Tools for drawing a hotspot shape: these tools work in exactly the same way as the corresponding tools in the Drawing toolbar.
- **Edit**, **Move**, **Insert**, **Delete Points**: advanced editing tools to manipulate the shape of a polygon hotspot. Choose the Edit Points tool to activate the other tools.
- **Active** icon: toggles the status of a selected hotspot between active and inactive.
- **Macro**: associates a macro with the hotspot instead of just associating a hyperlink.
- **Properties**: sets the hyperlink properties and adds the Name attribute to the hyperlink.

Below the toolbar, specify for the selected hotspot:

- **Address:** the address pointed to by the hyperlink. You can also point to an anchor in a document; to do this, write the address in this format: file:///<path>/document_name#anchor_name
- **Text**: type the text that you want to be displayed when the mouse pointer is moved over the hotspot.
- **Frame:** where the target of the hyperlink will open: pick among _blank (opens in a new browser window), _self (opens in the active browser window), _top or _parent.

Tip	The value _self for the target frame will usually work just fine. It is therefore not recommended to use the other choices unless absolutely necessary.

Using LibreOffice's drawing tools

You can use LibreOffice's drawing tools to create graphics such as simple diagrams using rectangles, circles, lines, text, and other predefined shapes. You can also group several drawing objects to make sure they maintain their relative position and proportion.

You can place the drawing objects directly on a page in your document, or you can insert them into a frame.

You can also use the drawing tools to annotate photographs, screen captures, or other illustrations produced by other programs, but this is not recommended because:

- You cannot include images in a group with drawing objects, so they may get out of alignment in your document.
- If you convert a document to another format, such as HTML, the drawing objects and the graphics will not remain associated; they are saved separately.

In general, if you need to create complex drawings, it is recommended to use LibreOffice Draw, which includes many more features such as layers, styles, and so on.

Creating drawing objects

To begin using the drawing tools, display the Drawing toolbar (Figure 307) by clicking **View > Toolbars > Drawing**.

If you are planning to use the drawing tools repeatedly, you can tear off this toolbar and move it to a convenient place on the window.

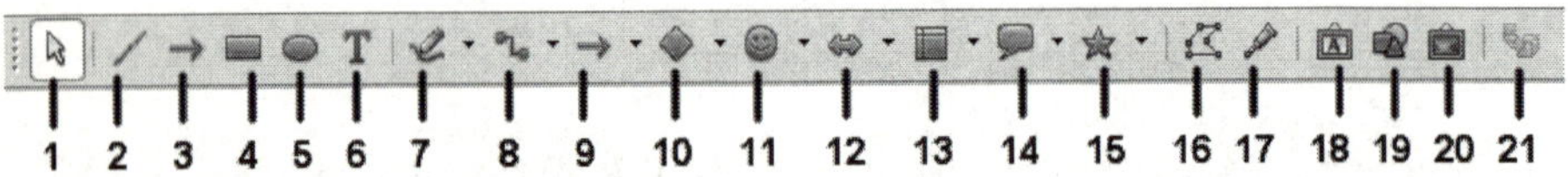

1 Select
2 Line
3 Line Ends with Arrow
4 Rectangle
5 Ellipse
6 Text
7 Curve
8 Connector
9 Lines and Arrows
10 Basic Shapes
11 Symbol Shapes
12 Block arrows
13 Flowcharts
14 Callouts
15 Stars
16 Points
17 Glue Points
18 Fontwork Gallery
19 From File
20 Gallery
21 Extrusion On/Off

Figure 307. The Drawing toolbar

To use a drawing tool:

1) Click in the document where you want the drawing to be anchored. You can change the anchor later, if necessary.
2) Choose the tool from the Drawing toolbar (Figure 307). The mouse pointer changes to a drawing-functions pointer .
3) Move the cross-hair pointer to the place in the document where you want the graphic to appear and then click and drag to create the drawing object. Release the mouse button. The selected drawing function remains active, so that you can draw another object of the same type.
4) To cancel the selected drawing function, press the *Esc* key or click on the **Select** icon (the arrow) on the Drawing toolbar.
5) You can now change the properties (fill color, line type and weight, anchoring, and others) of the drawing object using either the Drawing Object Properties toolbar (Figure 308) or the choices and dialogs reached by right-clicking on the drawing object.

Set or change properties for drawing objects

To set the properties for a drawing object before you draw it:

1) On the Drawing toolbar (Figure 307), click the **Select** tool.
2) On the Drawing Object Properties toolbar (Figure 308), click on the icon for each property and select the value you want for that property.
3) For more control, or to define new attributes, you can click on the **Area** or **Line** icons on the toolbar to display detailed dialogs.

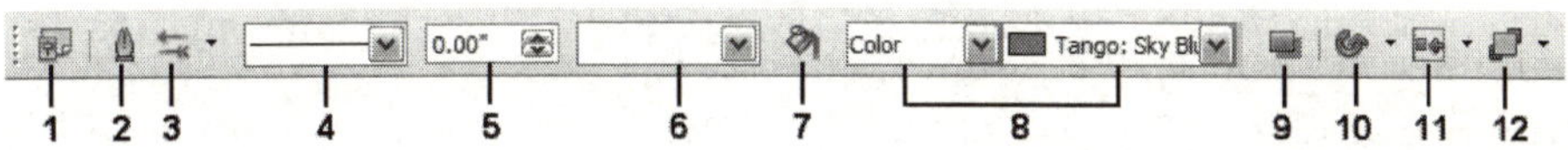

1 Styles and Formatting	**4** Line Style	**7** Area	**10** Effects
2 Line	**5** Line Width	**8** Area Style / Filling	**11** Alignment
3 Arrow Style	**6** Line Color	**9** Shadow	**12** Arrange

Figure 308. Drawing Object Properties toolbar

The default you set applies to the current document and session. It is not retained when you close the document or close Writer, and it does not apply to any other document you open. The defaults apply to all the drawing objects except text objects.

To change the properties for an existing drawing object:

1) Select the object.
2) Continue as described above.

You can also specify the position and size, rotation, and slant and corner radius properties of the drawing object:

1) Right-click on the drawing object and then choose **Position and Size** from the context menu. The Position and Size dialog is displayed.
2) Choose any properties, as required.

Resizing a drawing object

An object is resized in a similar way to an image. Select the object, click on one of the eight handles around it and drag it to its new position. For a scaled resizing, select one of the corner handles and keep the *Shift* key pressed while dragging the handle to its new position.

For more sophisticated control of the size of the object, choose **Format > Object > Position and Size** from the menu bar. Use the Position and Size dialog to set the width and height independently. If the **Keep ratio** option is selected, then the two dimensions change so that the proportion is maintained, allowing for a scaled resizing.

Grouping drawing objects

To group drawing objects:

1) Select one object, then hold down the *Shift* key and select the others you want to include in the group. The bounding box expands to include all the selected objects.
2) With the objects selected, hover the mouse pointer over one of the objects and choose **Format > Group > Group** from the menu bar or right-click and choose **Group > Group** from the pop-up menu.

Note	You cannot include an embedded or linked graphic in a group with drawing objects.

Using Fontwork

With Fontwork you can create graphical text art objects to make your work more attractive. There are many different settings for text art objects (line, area, position, size, and more), so you have a large choice. You will surely find one that fits your document.

Fontwork is available with each component of LibreOffice, but you will notice small differences in the way that each component displays it.

The Fontwork toolbars

You can use two different toolbars for creating and editing a Fontwork object.

Choose either **View > Toolbars > Fontwork** or **View > Toolbars > Drawing**.

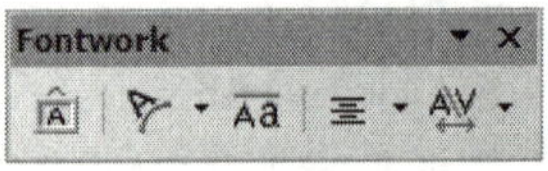

Figure 309. The floating Fontwork toolbar

If you click on an existing Fontwork object, the Formatting toolbar changes to display the Fontwork options as shown in Figure 314. The contents of this toolbar vary depending on the LibreOffice component with which it is being used.

Creating a Fontwork object

1) On the chosen toolbar, click the Fontwork Gallery icon .
2) In the Fontwork Gallery (Figure 310), select a Fontwork style, then click **OK**. The Fontwork object will appear in your document. Notice the colored squares around the edge (indicating that the object is selected) and the yellow dot; these are discussed in "Moving and resizing Fontwork objects" on page 319.

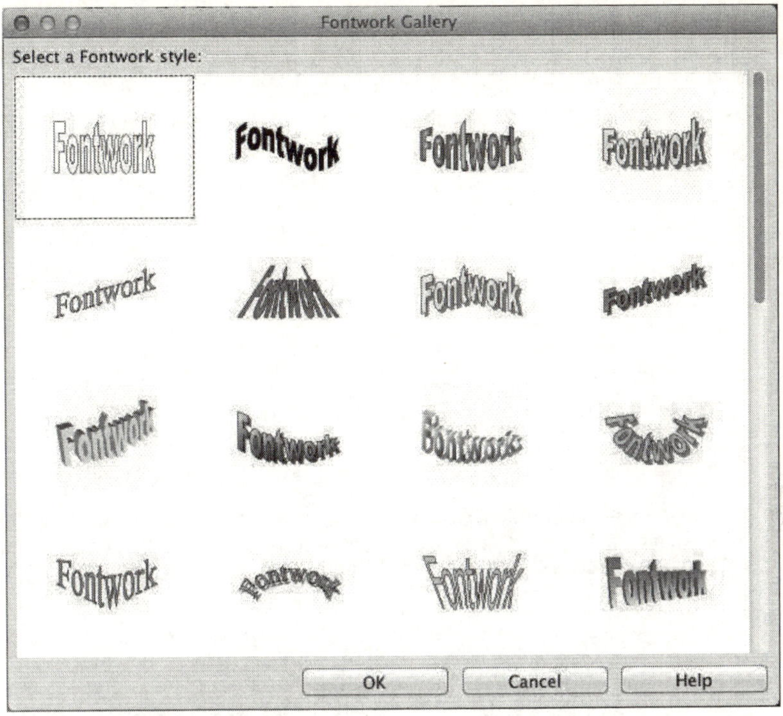

Figure 310. The Fontwork Gallery

3) Double-click the object to edit the Fontwork text (see Figure 311). Select the text and type your own text in place of the black *Fontwork* text that appears over the object.
4) Click anywhere in a free space or press *Esc* to apply your changes.

Figure 311. Editing Fontwork text

Editing a Fontwork object

Now that the Fontwork object is created, you can edit some of its attributes. To do this, you can use the Fontwork toolbar, the Formatting toolbar, or menu options as described in this section. If the selected Fontwork object is a 3-D object, you can also use the 3D-Settings toolbar.

Using the Fontwork toolbar

Make sure that the Fontwork toolbar, shown in Figure 309, is visible. If you do not see it, go to **View > Toolbars > Fontwork**. Click on the different icons to edit Fontwork objects.

Fontwork Shape: Edits the shape of the selected object. You can choose from a palette of shapes.

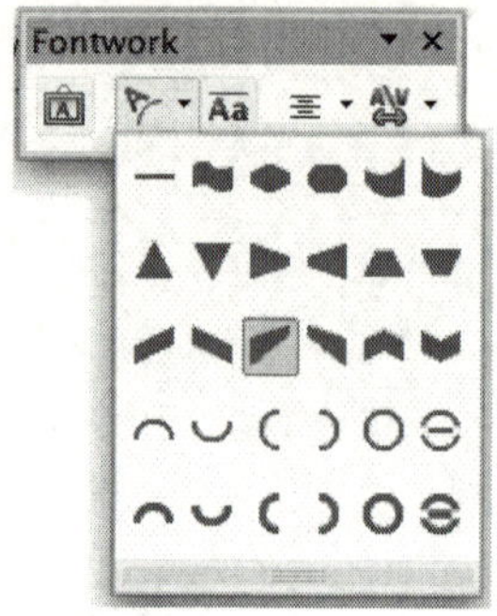

Figure 312. Fontwork toolbar showing palette of shapes

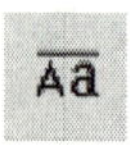

Fontwork Same Letter Heights: Changes the height of characters in the object. Toggles between normal height (some characters taller than others, for example capital letters, d, h, l and others) and all letters the same height.

Figure 313. Left: normal letters; right: same letter heights

Fontwork Alignment: Changes the alignment of characters. Choices are left align, center, right align, word justify, and stretch justify. The effects of the text alignment can only be seen if the text spans over two or more lines. In the stretch justify mode, all the lines are filled completely.

Fontwork Character Spacing: Changes the character spacing and kerning in the object. Select from the choices in the drop-down list.

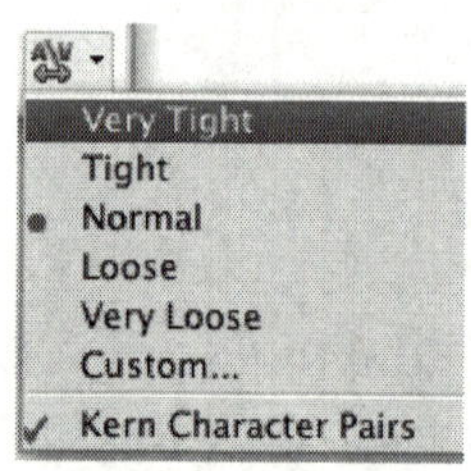

Using the Formatting toolbar

Now let us go further and customize the Fontwork object with several more attributes.

Click on the Fontwork object. The Formatting toolbar changes to show the options for editing the object. (The toolbar shown in Figure 314 appears when you use Fontwork in Writer.)

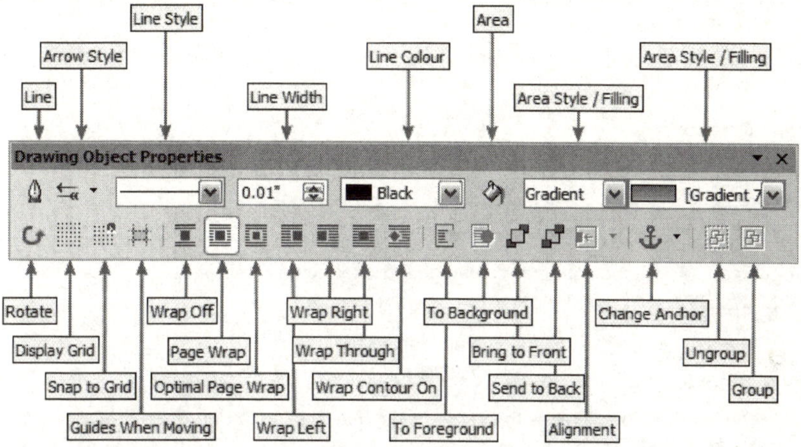

Figure 314. Formatting toolbar for a Fontwork object in Writer

This figure shows the toolbar floating. In its default, docked position it is one of the toolbars located below the menu bar. The example toolbar has also been customized to show all of the available options; by default only a subset of these options is shown.

On the Formatting toolbar you have a large choice of options for customizing your object. These choices are the same as the ones for other drawing objects. For more information, see the *Draw Guide*.

Line options

Line icon: Opens a dialog with three tabs: **Line**, **Line Styles**, **Arrow Styles**. Use the **Line** tab to edit the most common properties of the line around the selected Fontwork object, by choosing from previously-defined attributes including line style, line color, and arrow styles. Use the **Line Styles** and **Arrow Styles** tabs to edit the properties of line and arrow styles, and define new styles.

Arrow Style icon: Choose from the different arrow styles.

Line Style box: Choose from the available line styles.

Line Width box: Set the width of the line.

Line Color box: Select the color of the line.

Area options

Area icon: Opens a dialog with seven tabs: **Area**, **Shadow**, **Transparency**, **Colors**, **Gradients**, **Hatching**, **Bitmaps**.

- **Area** tab: Choose from the predefined list a color, bitmap, gradient or hatching pattern to fill the selected object.
- **Shadow** tab: Set the shadow properties of the selected object.
- **Transparency** tab: Set the transparency properties of the selected object.

- **Colors** tab: Modify the available colors or add new ones to appear on the Area tab.
- **Gradients** tab: Modify the available gradients or add new ones to appear on the Area tab.
- **Hatching** tab: Modify the available hatching patterns or add new ones to appear on the Area tab.
- **Bitmaps** tab: Create simple bitmap patterns and import bitmaps, to make them available on the Area tab.

Area Style / Filling boxes: Select the type of the fill of the selected object. For more detailed settings, use the Area icon.

Positioning options

Rotate icon: Rotate the selected object manually using the mouse to drag the object.

To Foreground icon: Move the selected object in front of the text.

To Background icon: Move the selected object behind the text.

Alignment icon: Modify the alignment of the selected objects.

Bring to front icon: Move the selected object in front of the others.

Send to back icon: Move the selected object behind the others.

Change Anchor icon: Choose between anchoring options:

- To Page—The object keeps the same position in relation to the page margins. It does not move as you add or delete text.
- To Paragraph—The object is associated with a paragraph and moves with the paragraph. It may be placed in the margin or another location.
- To Character—The object is associated with a character but is not in the text sequence. It moves with the paragraph but may be placed in the margin or another location. This method resembles anchoring to a paragraph.
- As Character—The object is placed in the document like any character and moves with the paragraph as you add or delete text before the object.

Ungroup icon: Ungroup the selected objects, so you can manage them individually.

Group icon: Group the selected objects, so you can manage them as a single object.

Using menu options

You can use some the choices on the **Format** menu to anchor, align, arrange and group selected Fontwork objects, wrap text around them, and flip them horizontally and vertically.

You can also right-click on a Fontwork object and choose many of the same options from the pop-up menu. The pop-up menu also provides quick access to the Line, Area, Text, and Position and Size dialogs. The Text dialog offers only a few options for Fontwork objects and is not discussed here. On the Position and Size dialog, you can enter precise values concerning size and position. For more information on all of these menu options, see the *Draw Guide*.

Using the 3D-Settings toolbar

If the selected Fontwork object is a 3-D object, you can also use the options on the 3D-Settings toolbar. You can also change a 2-D Fontwork object into a 3-D object (or change a 3-D object into a 2-D object) by clicking the Extrusion On/Off icon on the 3D-Settings toolbar. For more information, see the *Draw Guide*.

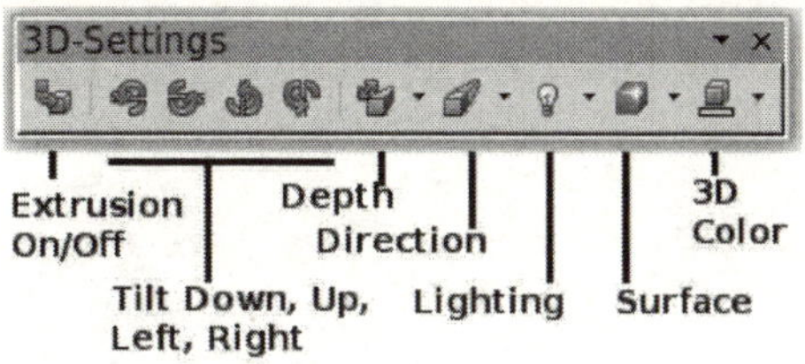

Figure 315: 3D-Settings toolbar

Moving and resizing Fontwork objects

When you select a Fontwork object, eight colored squares (known as *handles*) appear around the edge of the object, as shown below. You can drag these handles to resize the object.

A yellow dot also appears on the object. This dot may be along an edge of the object, or it may be somewhere else; see figure to right for an example. If you hover the pointer over this yellow dot, the pointer turns into a hand symbol. You can drag the dot in different directions to distort the object.

Hovering the pointer over other parts of the object turns the pointer into the usual symbol for dragging the object to another part of the page.

For precise control of the location and size of the object, use the Position and Size dialog.

LibreOffice
The Document Foundation

Chapter 12
Creating Web Pages

Saving Documents as HTML Files

Introduction

This chapter describes how to do the following in Writer, Calc, Impress and Draw:

- Create hyperlinks within a document and to other documents such as web pages, PDFs, and other files.
- Save documents as web pages (HTML documents).

When creating a document that you plan to deliver as a web page, you need to consider the following:

- In an HTML document, hyperlinks are active (clickable), but other cross-references inserted by LibreOffice are not active links.
- An object such as a image is saved as a separate file. However, if that object has been placed in a frame (for example, with an associated caption), it is not saved and does not appear in the HTML document; instead, the name of the frame appears.

Relative and absolute hyperlinks

Hyperlinks stored within a file can be either relative or absolute.

A relative hyperlink says, *Here is how to get there starting from where you are now* (meaning from the folder in which your current document is saved) while an absolute hyperlink says, *Here is how to get there no matter where you start from.*

An absolute link will stop working if the target is moved. A relative link will stop working if the start and target locations change relative to each other. For instance, if you have two spreadsheets in the same folder linked to each other and you move the entire folder to a new location, an absolute hyperlink will break but a relative one will not.

To change the way that LibreOffice stores the hyperlinks in your file, select **Tools > Options > Load/Save > General** and choose if you want URLs saved relatively when referencing the *File System*, or the *Internet*, or both.

Calc will always display an absolute hyperlink. Do not be alarmed when it does this even when you have saved a relative hyperlink. This 'absolute' target address will be updated if you move the file.

Note	Make sure that the folder structure on your computer is the same as the file structure on your web server if you save your links as relative to the file system and you are going to upload pages to the Internet.

Tip	When you rest the mouse pointer on a hyperlink, a help tip displays the absolute reference, because LibreOffice uses absolute path names internally. The complete path and address can only be seen when you view the result of the HTML export (saving the spreadsheet as an HTML file), by loading the HTML file as text, or by opening it with a text editor.

Creating hyperlinks

When you type text (such as a website addresses or URL) that can be used as a hyperlink, and then press the spacebar or the *Enter* key, LibreOffice automatically creates the hyperlink and applies formatting to the text (usually a color and underlining). If this does not happen, you can enable this feature by going to **Tools > AutoCorrect Options > Options** on the main menu bar and selecting the **URL Recognition** option.

If you do not want LibreOffice to convert a specific URL to a hyperlink, go to **Edit > Undo Insert** on the main menu bar, or press *Ctrl+Z* immediately after the formatting has been applied, or place the cursor in the hyperlink, right-click, and select **Remove Hyperlink** from the context menu.

Tip	To change the color of hyperlinks, go to **Tools > Options > LibreOffice > Appearance**, scroll to *Unvisited links* and/or *Visited links*, pick the new colors and click **OK**. Caution: this will change the color for all hyperlinks in all components of LibreOffice; this may not be what you want. In Writer and Calc (but not Draw or Impress), you can also change the *Internet link* character style or define and apply new styles to selected links.

Using the Navigator

You can insert hyperlinks using the Navigator and this is an easy way to insert a hyperlink to another part of the same document.

1) Open the documents containing the items you want to cross-reference.
2) Click on theNavigator icon , or go to **View > Navigator** on the main menu bar, or press the *F5* key to open the Navigator dialog.
3) Click the triangle to right of the **Drag Mode** icon and select **Insert as Hyperlink** (Figure 316). Note that the Drag Mode icon changes shape depending on the type of insert that was previously selected. The default icon for Drag Mode is to show the Hyperlink icon .
4) Select the document from the drop down list at the bottom of the Navigator that contains the item that you want to cross-reference.
5) In the Navigator list, select the item that you want to insert as a hyperlink.
6) Drag the item to where you want to insert the hyperlink in the document. The name of the item is inserted in the document as an active hyperlink.

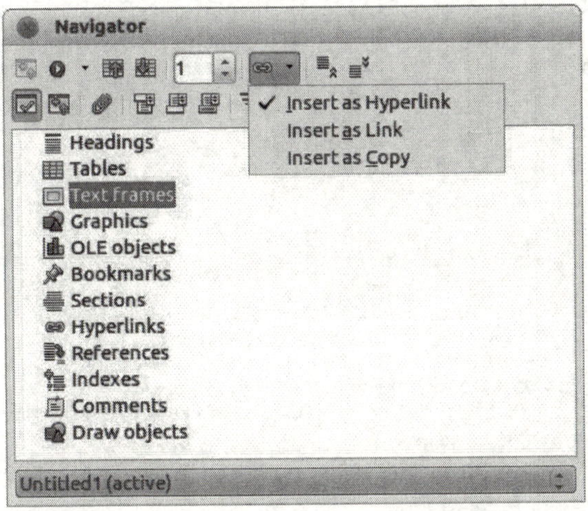

Figure 316: Inserting hyperlink using the Navigator

When using the Navigator to insert a hyperlink to an object such as a graphic, it is recommended to have the hyperlink show a useful name, for example *2009 Sales Graph*. You need to give such objects useful names instead of leaving them as the default names, for example Graphics6, or you will have to edit the name of the resulting link using the Hyperlink dialog, as described below.

You can also use the Navigator to insert a hyperlink from one document (the source) to a specific place in another document (the target). Open the Navigator in the target document and drag the item to the position in the source document where you want the hyperlink to appear.

Using the Hyperlink dialog

You can the Hyperlink dialog to insert a hyperlink and modify all hyperlinks.

1) Highlight the existing text you want to use as a link.
2) Click the **Hyperlink** icon on the Standard toolbar or go to **Insert > Hyperlink** on the main menu bar to open the Hyperlink dialog (Figure 317).
3) On the left side, select one of the four categories of hyperlink:
   - **Internet**: the hyperlink points to a web address, normally starting with http://.
   - **Mail & News**: the hyperlink opens an email message that is pre-addressed to a particular recipient.
   - **Document**: the hyperlink points to another document or to another place in the current document
   - **New document**: the hyperlink creates a new document.
4) The Hyperlink dialog changes depending on the type of hyperlink selected. Enter all necessary details to create the hyperlink.
5) Click **Apply** to create the hyperlink and the Hyperlink dialog remains open allowing you to create another hyperlink.
6) Click **Close** to close the Hyperlink dialog.

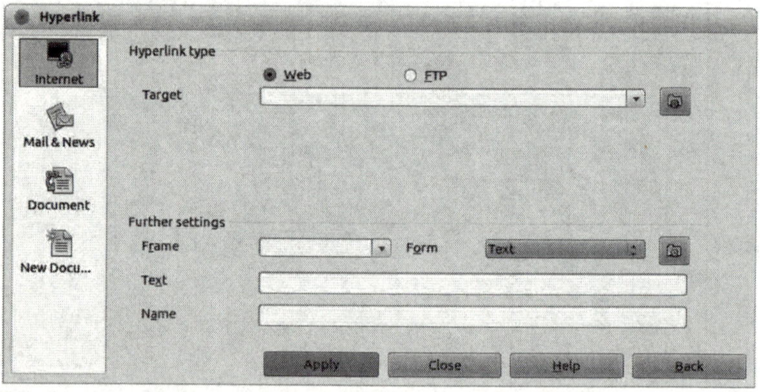

Figure 317. Hyperlink dialog showing details for Internet links

The dialog changes according to the choice made for the hyperlink category in the left panel. A full description of all the choices and their interactions is beyond the scope of this chapter. Here is a summary of the most common choices.

- For an *Internet* hyperlink, choose the type of hyperlink (Web, FTP, or Telnet), and enter the required web address (URL).
- For a *Mail and News* hyperlink, specify whether it is a mail or news link, the address of the receiver and, for email, the subject.
- For a *Document* hyperlink, specify the document path (clicking **Open File** opens a file browser) or leave this blank if you want to link to a target in the same document. Optionally

specify the target in the document (for example a specific slide). Click the **Target in Document** icon to open the Target in Document dialog where you can select the type of target; or, if you know the name of the target, you can type it into the box.

- For a *New Document* hyperlink, specify whether to edit the newly created document immediately (**Edit now**) or just create it (**Edit later**). Enter the file name and select the type of document to create (text, spreadsheet, and so on). Click the **Select Path** icon to open a file browser and choose where to store the file.

The *Further settings* section in the bottom right part of the dialog is common to all the hyperlink categories, although some choices are more relevant to some types of links.

- **Frame** value determines how the hyperlink will open. This applies to documents that open in a Web browser.
- **Form** specifies if the link is to be presented as text or as a button.See the *Writer Guide Chapter 15 Using Forms in Writer* for more information.
- **Text** specifies the text that will be visible to the user. If you do not enter anything here, LibreOffice uses the full URL or path as the link text. Note that if the link is relative and you move the file, this text will not change, though the target will.
- **Name** is applicable to HTML documents. It specifies text that will be added as a NAME attribute in the HTML code behind the hyperlink.
- **Events** : click this icon to open the Assign Macro dialog and select a macro to run when the link is clicked. See *Chapter 13 Getting Started with Macros* for more information.

Editing hyperlinks

To edit an existing link:

1) Click anywhere in the hyperlink text.
2) Click the **Hyperlink** icon on the Standard toolbar or go to **Edit > Hyperlink** on the main menu bar or right-click and select **Edit Hyperlink** from the context menu. The Hyperlink dialog opens.
3) Make your changes and click **Apply** to save your changes. The Hyperlink dialog remains open allowing you to continue editing hyperlinks. Click **Apply** after editing each hyperlink.
4) When you are finished editing hyperlinks, click **Close**.

The standard (default) behavior for activating hyperlinks within LibreOffice is to use *Ctrl+click*. This behavior can be changed in **Tools > Options > LibreOffice > Security > Options** and deselecting the option **Ctrl-click required to follow hyperlinks**. If clicking in your links activates them, check that page to see if the option has been deselected.

Removing hyperlinks

You can remove the link from hyperlink text and leave just the text by right-clicking on the link and selecting **Remove Hyperlink** from the context menu. You may then need to re-apply some formatting to match the text with the rest of your document.

To erase the link text or button from the document completely, select it and press the *Backspace* or *Delete* key.

Creating web pages using the Web Wizard

The Web Wizard in LibreOffice allows you to create several types of standard web pages and is available all LibreOffice modules. However, each time you open the Web Wizard in a LibreOffice module, Writer will automatically start before the Web Wizard dialog opens. The Web Wizard is linked to Writer and is normally used in Writer for creating web pages.

1) Go to **File > Wizards > Web Page** on the main menu bar to open the Web Wizard dialog (Figure 318).

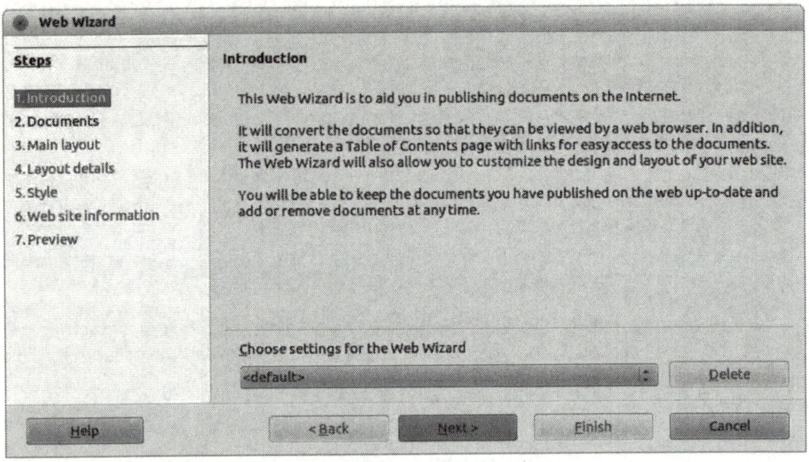

Figure 318: Introduction page of Web Wizard dialog

2) On the first page of the Wizard, choose settings and click **Next >**. If this is your first web page, the only choice is <default>.
3) Select or browse to the document you would like to format. The information for *Title*, *Summary* and *Author* is taken from the document properties. If necessary, edit this information (Figure 319).

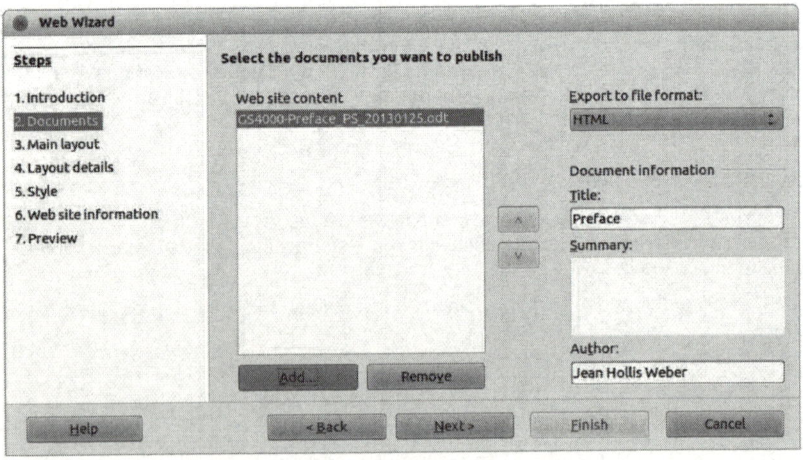

Figure 319: Documents page of Web Wizard dialog

4) Click **Next >** and select a layout for the web site by clicking on the layout boxes (Figure 320).

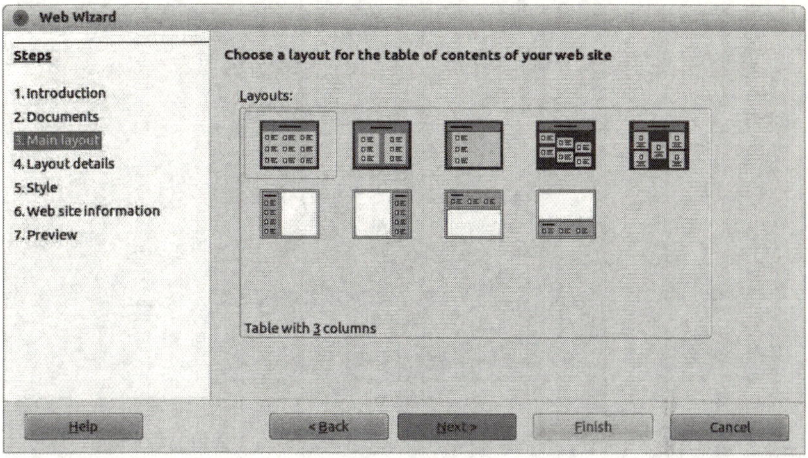

Figure 320: Main layout page of Web Wizard dialog

5) Click **Next >** to customize the layout and select the information to be listed and screen resolution (Figure 321).
6) Click **Next >** and select a style for the page. Use the drop-down list to choose different styles and color combinations. Browse to select a background image and icon set from the Gallery (Figure 322).

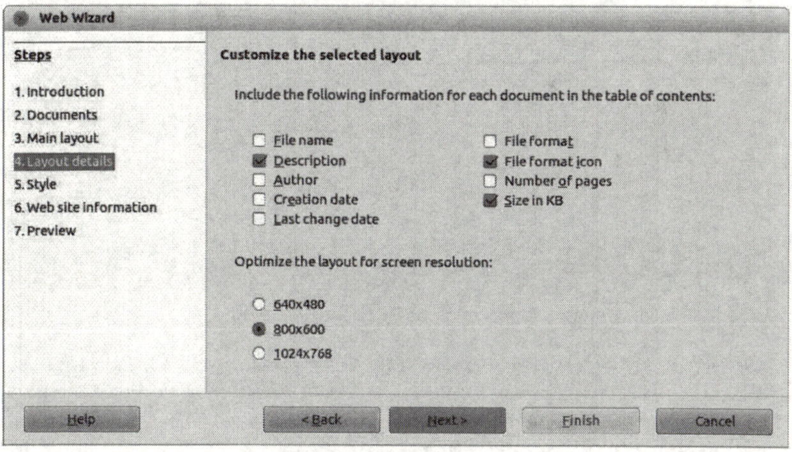

Figure 321: Layout details page of Web Wizard dialog

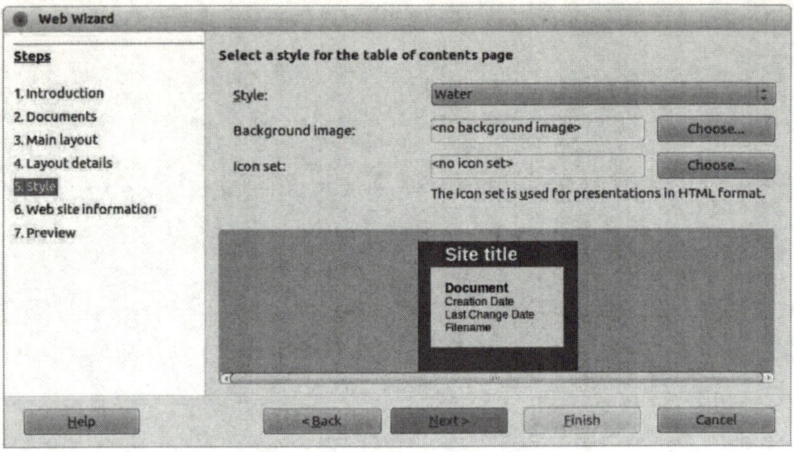

Figure 322: Style page of Web Wizard dialog

7) Click **Next >** and enter general information for the web site such as Title and HTML Metadata information (Figure 323).

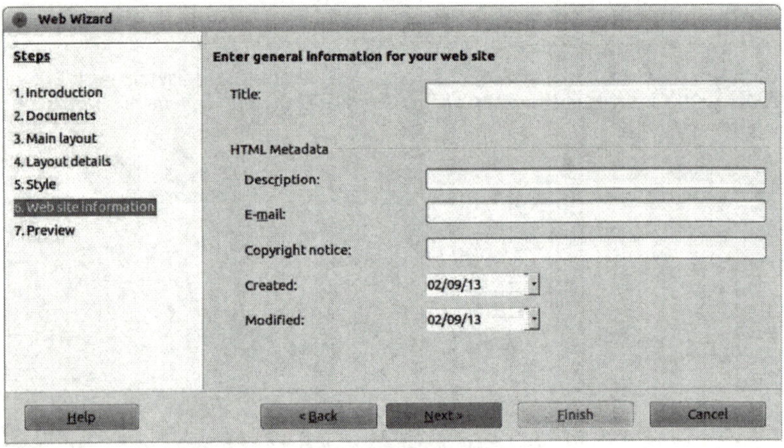

Figure 323: Web site information page of Web Wizard dialog

8) Click **Next >** and select where to save the file and preview the page if you wish (Figure 324).
9) Enter the information of where to publish your new web site.
10) Click **Finish** to save the file and close the Web Wizard.

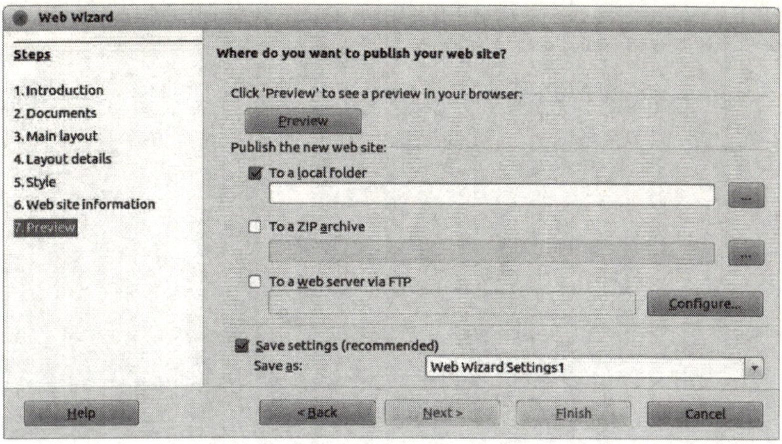

Figure 324: Preview page of Web Wizard dialog

Saving documents as web pages

HTML capabilities in LibreOffice include saving and exporting existing documents in HTML format. You can also create several different types of web pages using the Web Wizard included with LibreOffice, see "Creating web pages using the Web Wizard" on page 326 for more information.

The easiest way to create HTML documents is to start with an existing document. You can get a good idea of how it will appear as a web page by using **View > Web Layout**. However, web layout view does not show you which features will or will not be saved correctly in HTML format. Refer to "Error: Reference source not found" on page Error: Reference source not found on what to consider before creating a web page from a document.

Writer documents

Single web page

To save a document as a single web page (HTML format) by going to **File > Save As** on the main menu bar and specify **HTML Document (Writer)** as the file type or **File > Export** and specifying **XHTML** format as the file type.

Note	Writer does not replace multiple spaces in the original document with the HTML code for non-breaking spaces. If you want to have extra spaces in your HTML file or web page, you need to insert non-breaking spaces in LibreOffice. To do this, press *Ctrl+Spacebar* instead of just *Spacebar*.

Series of web pages

Writer can save a large document as a series of web pages (HTML files) with a table of contents page.

1) Decide which headings in the document should start on a new page and make sure all those headings have the same paragraph style (for example, Heading 1).

2) Go to **File > Send > Create HTML Document** on the main menu bar to open the Name and Path of the HTML Document dialog (Figure 325).

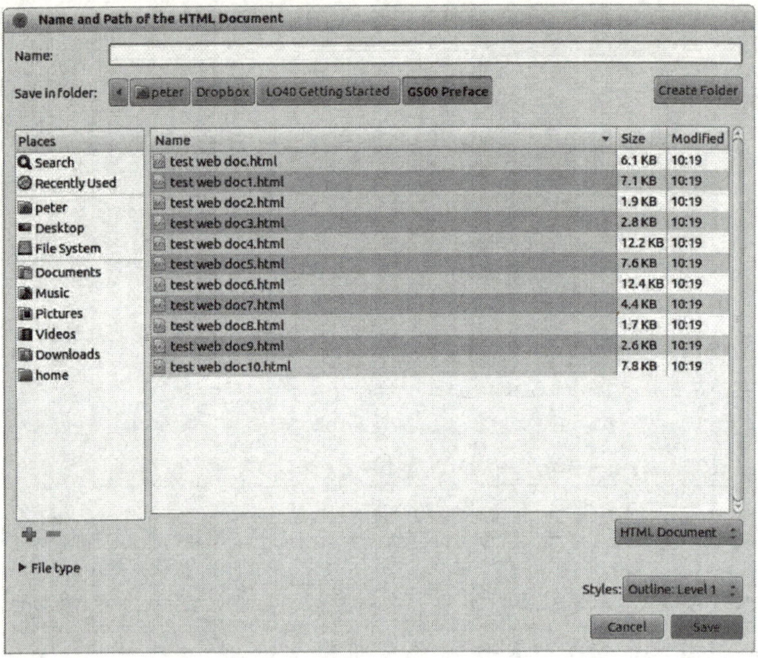

Figure 325. Creating a series of web pages from one document

3) Type the file name to save the pages under.

4) Specify which style indicates a new page using the Styles drop list at the bottom of the dialog (for example Heading 1).

5) Click **Save** to create the multi-page HTML document. The resulting HTML files conforms to the HTML 4 Transitional.

Calc spreadsheets

Calc can save files as HTML documents by going to **File > Save As** on the main menu bar and select **HTML Document (Calc)** format as the file type. This is similar to "Single web page" on page 329.

If the file contains more than one sheet and the web pages are created using the Web Wizard (see "Creating web pages using the Web Wizard" on page 326), the additional sheets will follow one another in the HTML file. Links to each sheet will be placed at the top of the document.

Calc also allows the insertion of links directly into the spreadsheet using the Hyperlink dialog. See "Creating hyperlinks" on page 322 for more information on hyperlinks.

Impress presentations

Note	Saving as web pages in HTML format does not retain animation and slide transitions.

Impress presentations cannot be saved in HTML format, but have to be be exported as HTML documents. Note that you can click **Create** at any step in the following procedure. The web pages created will then use the default settings that you have not changed in any way.

1) Go to **File > Export** on the main menu bar and specify the file name and location of where to save the web page version of your presentation.
2) Select **HTML document (Impress)** as the file type and click **Save** to open the HTML Export dialog (Figure 326).
3) On the *Assign design* page you can choose to create a new design and select or delete an existing design. Specify a *New design* or an *Existing design* and click **Next>>**. If you have not previously saved a web page design, the *Existing Design* choice is not available.
   - *New design* – creates a new design in the next pages of the Wizard.
   - *Existing design* – loads an existing design from the design list to use as a starting point for the steps that follow. The list box displays all existing designs.

   Delete Selected Design deletes the selected design from the design list. If you delete a design, you will only delete the design information. An export file will not be deleted by this action.

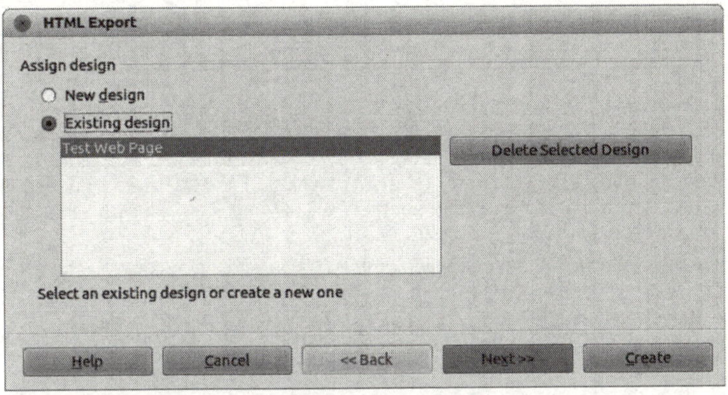

Figure 326: HTML Export dialog - Assign design page

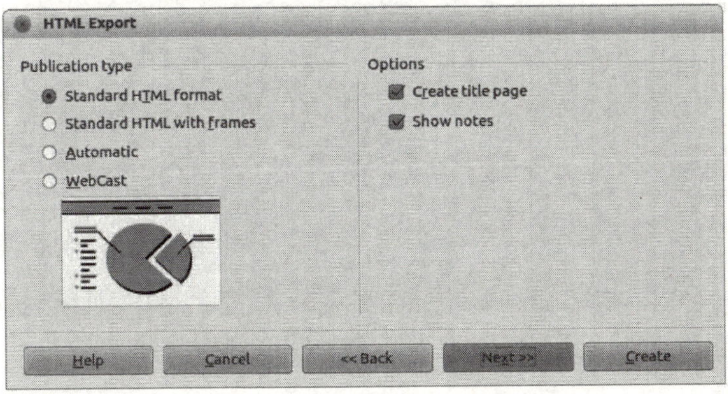

Figure 327: HTML Export dialog – Publication type page

4) Specify the *Publication type* for the web pages (Figure 327), then click **Next>>**. The publication type defines the basic settings for the intended export. The choices are:
   - *Standard HTML format* – creates standard HTML pages from export pages.
   - *Standard HTML with frames* – creates standard HTML pages with frames. The exported page will be placed in the main frame and the frame to the left will display a table of contents in the form of hyperlinks.
   - *Automatic* – creates a default HTML presentation as a kiosk export in which the slides are automatically advanced after a specified amount of time.
   - *WebCast* – in a WebCast export, automatic scripts will be generated with Perl or ASP support. This enables the speaker (for example, a speaker in a telephone conference using a slide show on the Internet) to change the slides in the web browsers used by the audience.

   For more information on the options available for this page of the HTML Export dialog, click **Help** to open the help pages.

5) Specify the options for *Save graphics as*, *Monitor resolution* and *Effects* used for the web pages (Figure 328), then click **Next>>**. The options for this page of the HTML Export dialog are as follows:
   - *Save graphics as* – determines the image format. You can also define the compression value for the export.
   - *Monitor resolution* – defines the resolution for the target screen. Depending on the selected resolution, the image will be displayed in a reduced size. You can specify a reduction of up to 80% from the original size. When selecting a resolution, consider what the majority of your viewers might be using. If you specify a high resolution, then a viewer with a medium-resolution monitor will have to scroll sideways to see the entire slide, which is probably not desirable.
   - *Effects* – specifies that sound files defined as an effect for slide transitions and whether any hidden slides are exported.

   For more information on the options available for this page of the HTML Export dialog, click **Help** to open the help pages.

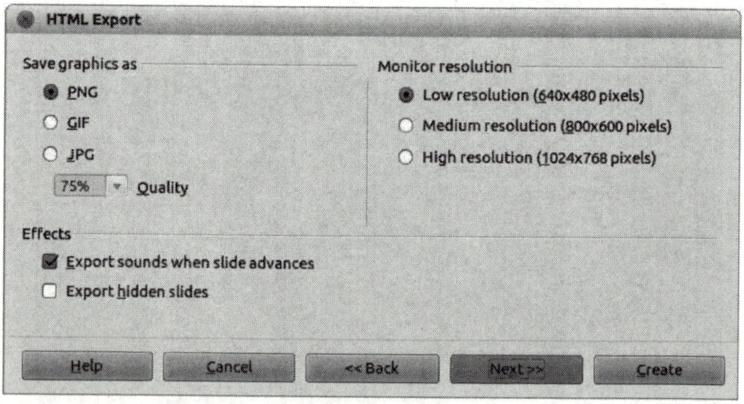

Figure 328: HTML Export dialog – graphics and monitor resolution

6) Specify the *Information for the title page* to be used with the web version of your presentation (Figure 329). The title page normally contains the author's name, an e-mail address and home page, along with any additional information you may want to include. This page is not available if you have selected not to create a title page and either Automatic or WebCast publication type.

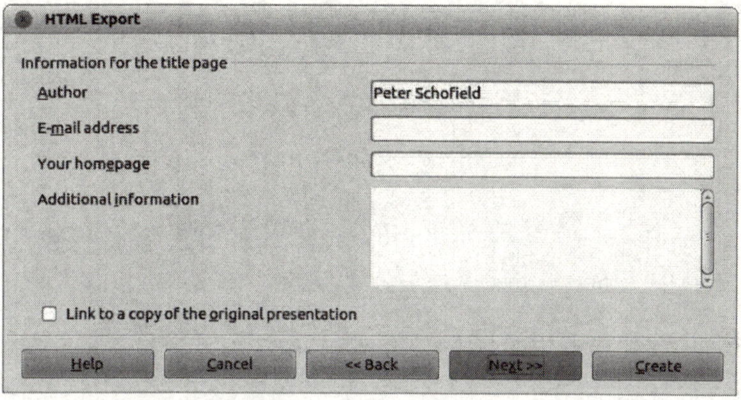

Figure 329: HTML Export dialog – title page information

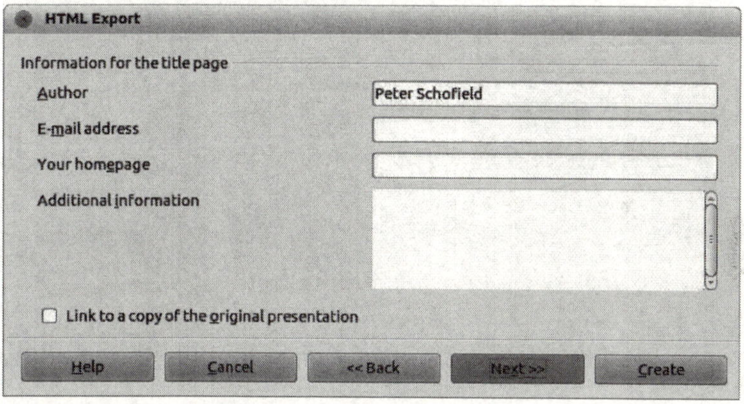

Figure 330: HTML Export dialog – title page information

7) Select *Link to a copy of the original presentation* if you want to create a hyperlink to download a copy of the presentation file and then click **Next>>**.
8) *Select button style* to be used for the web pages from the designs available (Figure 331) and then click **Next>>**.

   If you do not select a button style, LibreOffice will create a text navigator.
   This page is not available if you have selected either Automatic or WebCast publication type.
9) *Select color scheme* to be used for the web pages (Figure 332) such as the color scheme and colors for text and background. This page is not available if you have selected either Automatic or WebCast publication type.

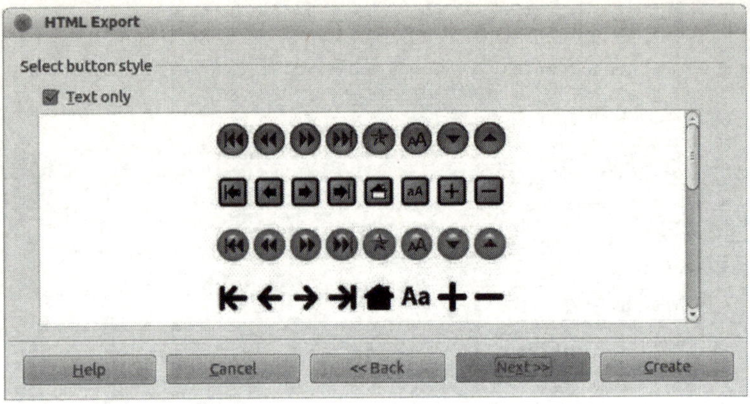

Figure 331: HTML Export dialog – button style page

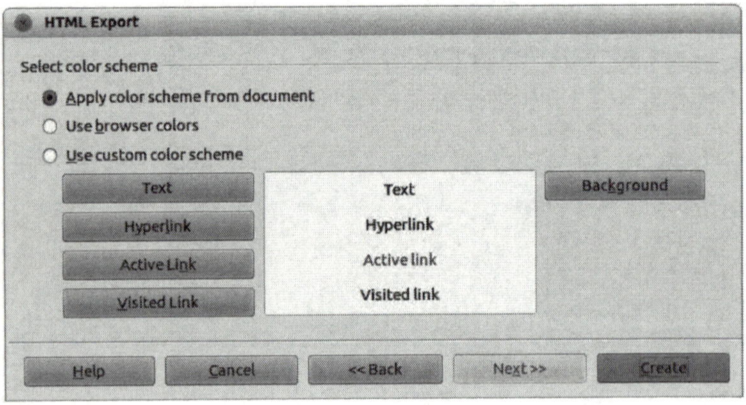

Figure 332: HTML Export dialog – color scheme page

10) Click **Create**.
11) If you have created a new design for your web pages, type in a name for your design and click **Save**.

Note	Depending on the size of your presentation and the number of graphics it contains, the HTML export function creates several HTML, JPG, and GIF files. For example, if you simply save to your desktop and not in a specific folder, these separate HTML and graphics files will be placed all over your desktop. It is recommended to create a folder to hold all the files created for the web version of your presentation.

Draw documents

Draw documents cannot be saved in HTML format, but have to be be exported as HTML documents. Exporting drawings as web pages from Draw is similar to exporting a presentation from Impress. Go to **File > Export** and select **HTML Document (Draw)** as the file type, then follow the procedure above for exporting Impress presentations.

Chapter 13
Getting Started with Macros

Using the Macro Recorder … and Beyond

Introduction

A macro is a saved sequence of commands or keystrokes that are stored for later use. An example of a simple macro is one that "types" your address. The LibreOffice macro language is very flexible, allowing automation of both simple and complex tasks. Macros are very useful when you have to repeat the same task in the same way over and over again.

LibreOffice macros are usually written in a language called LibreOffice Basic, sometimes abbreviated to Basic. Although you can learn Basic and write macros, there is a steep learning curve to writing macros from scratch. The usual methods for a beginner are to use macros that someone else has written or use the built-in macro recorder, which records keystrokes and saves them for use.

Most tasks in LibreOffice are accomplished by "dispatching a command" (sending a command), which is intercepted and used. The macro recorder works by recording the commands that are dispatched (see "Dispatch framework" on page 345).

Your first macros

Adding a macro

The first step in learning macro programming is to find and use existing macros. This section assumes that you have a macro that you want to use, which may be in an email, on a web page, or even in a book. For this example, the macro in Listing 1 is used. You must create a library and module to contain your macro; see "Macro organization" on page 346 for more information.

Listing 1: Simple macro that says hello

```
Sub HelloMacro
  Print "Hello"
End Sub
```

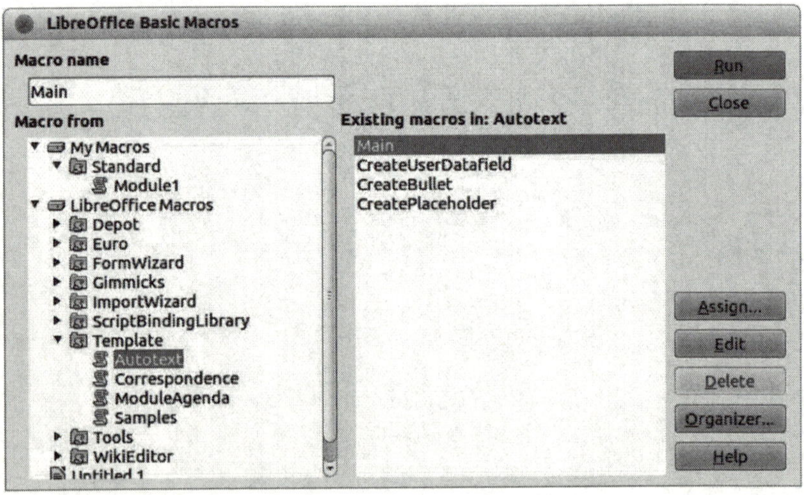

Figure 333: LibreOffice Basic Macros dialog

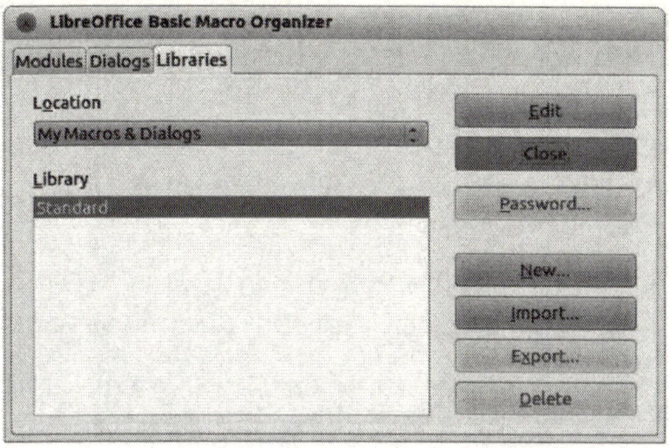

Figure 334: LibreOffice Basic Macro Organizer dialog

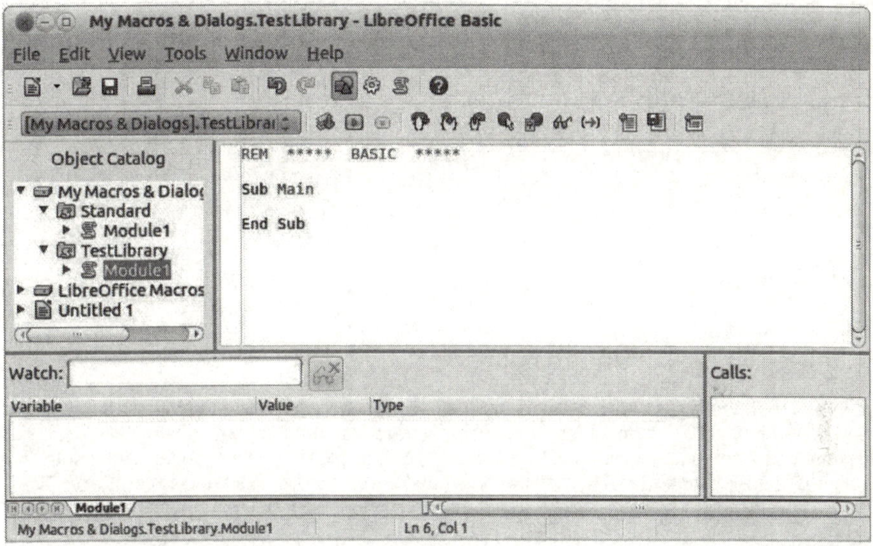

Figure 335: Integrated Debugging Environment dialog

Use the following steps to create a library to contain your macro:

1) Use **Tools > Macros > Organize Macros > LibreOffice Basic** to open the LibreOffice Basic Macro dialog (Figure 333).
2) Click **Organizer** to open the Basic Macro Organizer dialog (Figure 334) and select the *Libraries* tab.
3) Set the *Location* to *My Macros & Dialogs*, which is the default location.
4) Click **New** to open the New Library dialog.
5) Enter a library name, for example TestLibrary, and click **OK**.
6) Select the *Modules* tab.
7) In the *Module* list, expand *My Macros* and select, for example TestLibrary. A module named Module1 already exists and can contain your macro. If you wish, you can click **New** to create another module in the library.

8) Select Module1, or the new module that you created, and click **Edit** to open the Integrated Debugging Environment (IDE) (Figure 335). The IDE is a text editor included with LibreOffice that allows you to create and edit macros.
9) When a new module is created, it contains a comment and an empty macro named Main, which does nothing.
10) Add the new macro either before Sub Main or after End Sub. Listing 2 shows the new macro has been added before Sub Main.
11) Click the **Compile** icon on the Macro toolbar to compile the macro.
12) Place the cursor in the HelloMacro subroutine and click the **Run BASIC** icon on the Macro toolbar, or press the *F5* key, to run the HelloMacro in the module. A small dialog will open with the word "Hello" displayed. If the cursor is not in a subroutine or function, a dialog will open; select the macro to run.
13) Click **OK** to close this small dialog.
14) To select and run any macro in the module, click the **Select Macro** icon on the Standard toolbar or go to **Tools > Macros > Organize Macros > LibreOffice Basic.**
15) Select a macro and then click **Run**.

Listing 2: Module1 after adding the new macro.

```
REM  *****  BASIC  *****

Sub HelloMacro
  Print "Hello"
End Sub

Sub Main

End Sub
```

Recording a macro

If you have to repeatedly enter the same information, you can copy this information after it has been entered into your document for the first time, then paste the information into your document each time you want to use it. However, if something else is copied to the clipboard, the contents on the clipboard are changed. This means that you have to re-copy your repeated information. To overcome this problem, you can create a macro that enters your repeated information.

Note	For some types of information that you want to repeatedly enter into a document, it may be more convenient to create an AutoText file. See the *Writer Guide Chapter 3 Working with Text* for more information.

1) Make sure macro recording is enabled by going to **Tools > Options > LibreOffice > Advanced** on the main menu bar and selecting the option **Enable macro recording**. By default, this feature is turned off when LibreOffice was installed on your computer.
2) Go to **Tools > Macros > Record Macro** on the main menu bar to start recording a macro. A small dialog is displayed indicating that LibreOffice is recording a macro.
3) Type the desired information or perform an appropriate series of operations. As an example, type your name.
4) Click **Stop Recording** on the small Recording dialog to stop recording and the LibreOffice Basic Macros dialog opens (Figure 333 on page 336).
5) Open the library container *My Macros*.
6) Find the library named *Standard* in My Macros. Note that every library container has a

library named Standard.

7) Select the Standard library and click **New Module** to create a new module to contain the macro. This opens the New Module dialog (Figure 336).

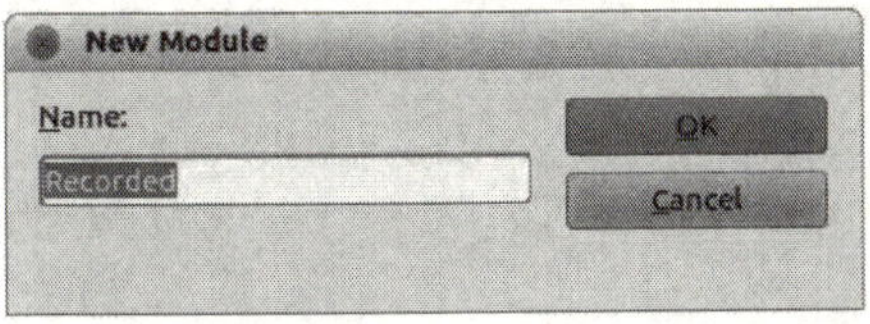

Figure 336: New Module dialog

8) Type a descriptive name for the new module, for example *Recorded* and click **OK** to create the module. The LibreOffice Basic Macros dialog now displays the name of the new module in the Standard library.
9) In the **Macro name** text box, type a name for the macro you have just recorded, for example *EnterMyName*.
10) Click **Save** to save the macro and close the LibreOffice Basic Macros dialog.
11) If you followed all of the above steps, the Standard library now contains a module named Recorded and this module contains the EnterMyName macro.

Note	When LibreOffice creates a new module, it automatically adds the macro named Main.

Running a macro

1) Go to **Tools > Macros > Run Macro** on the main menu bar to open the Macro Selector dialog (Figure 337).
2) For example, select your newly created macro EnterMyName and click **Run**.
3) Alternatively, go to **Tools > Macros > Organize Macros > LibreOffice Basic** on the main menu bar to open the LibreOffice Basic Macros dialog, select your macro and click **Run**.

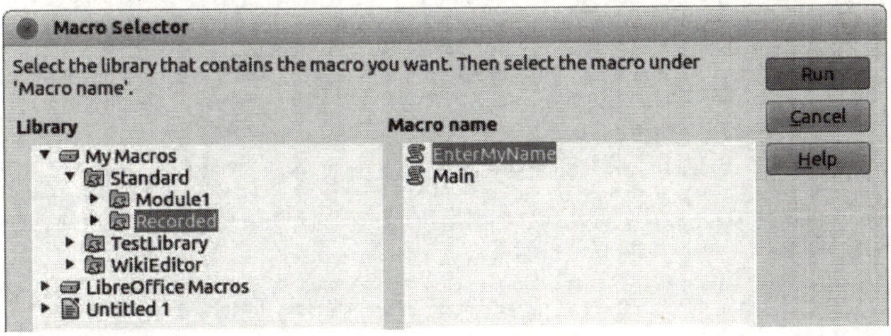

Figure 337: Macro Selector dialog

Viewing and editing macros

To view and/or edit the macro that you created:

1) Go to **Tools > Macros > Organize Macros > LibreOffice Basic** to open the LibreOffice Basic Macros dialog.

2) Select your new macro EnterMyName and click **Edit** to open the macro in the Basic IDE. The macro EnterMyName is shown in Listing 3.

The EnterMyName macro is not as complicated as it first appears. Learning a few things helps significantly in understanding macros. The discussion starts with features near the top of the macro listing and describes them.

Listing 3: Generated "EnterMyname" macro

```
REM  *****  BASIC  *****
Sub Main

End Sub

sub EnterMyName
rem -------------------------------------------------------------
rem define variables
dim document   as object
dim dispatcher as object
rem -------------------------------------------------------------
rem get access to the document
document   = ThisComponent.CurrentController.Frame
dispatcher = createUnoService("com.sun.star.frame.DispatchHelper")

rem -------------------------------------------------------------
dim args1(0) as new com.sun.star.beans.PropertyValue
args1(0).Name = "Text"
args1(0).Value = "Your name"

dispatcher.executeDispatch(document, ".uno:InsertText", "", 0, args1())
end sub
```

REM comments

All comments in macro coding begin with REM, which stands for remark. All text after REM and on the same line is ignored. As a short cut, the single quote character (') can also be used to start a comment.

LibreOffice Basic is not case-sensitive for keywords, so REM, Rem, and rem can all start a comment. If you use symbolic constants defined by the Application Programming Interface (API), it is safer to assume that the names are case-sensitive. Symbolic constants are an advanced topic not covered by this user guide and are not required when using the macro recorder in LibreOffice.

Defining subroutines with SUB

Individual macros are stored in subroutines and these subroutines begin with the keyword SUB. The end of a subroutine is indicated by the words END SUB. The code starts by defining the subroutine named Main, which is empty and does nothing. The next subroutine, EnterMyName, contains the generated code for your macro.

Note	LibreOffice always creates an empty subroutine named Main when it creates a module.

There are advanced topics that are beyond the scope of this user guide, but knowing about them might be of interest:

- You can write a macro so that values can be passed to the subroutine. The values are called arguments. However, recorded macros in LibreOffice do not accept arguments.

- Another kind of subroutine is called a function, which is a subroutine that returns a value. Functions are defined by the keyword FUNCTION at the beginning. However, recorded macros in LibreOffice always create subroutines, not functions.

Defining variables using Dim

You can write information on a piece of paper so that you can look at it later. A variable, like a piece of paper, contains information that can be changed and read. The Dim keyword originally stood for Dimension and was used to define the dimensions of an array. The dim statement used in the EnterMyName macro is similar to setting aside a piece of paper to be used to store a message or note.

In the EnterMyName macro, the variables `document` and `dispatcher` are defined as the type *object*. Other common variable types include *string*, *integer*, and *date*. A third variable, named *args1,* is an array of property values. A variable of type *array* allows a single variable to contain multiple values, similar to storing multiple pages in a single book. Values in an array are usually numbered starting from zero. The number in the parentheses indicates the highest usable number to access a storage location. In this example, there is only one value, and it is numbered zero.

Explaining macro code

The following is an explanation of the code used in the EnterMyName macro. You may not understand all the details, but the explanation of each line of code may give you some idea of how a macro works.

```
sub EnterMyName
```

Defines the start of the macro

```
dim document   as object
```

Defined as a variable

```
dim dispatcher as object
```

Defined as a variable

```
document = ThisComponent.CurrentController.Frame
```

ThisComponent refers to the current document.

CurrentController is a property referring to a service that controls the document. For example, when you type, it is the current controller that takes note of what you type. CurrentController then dispatches the changes to the document frame.

Frame is a controller property that returns the main frame for a document. Therefore, the variable named document refers to a document's frame, which receives dispatched commands.

```
dispatcher = createUnoService("com.sun.star.frame.DispatchHelper")
```

Most tasks in LibreOffice are accomplished by dispatching a command. LibreOffice includes a dispatch helper service, which does most of the work when using dispatches in macros. The method CreateUnoService accepts the name of a service and it tries to create an instance of that service. On completion, the dispatcher variable contains a reference to a DispatchHelper.

```
dim args1(0) as new com.sun.star.beans.PropertyValue
```

Declares an array of properties. Each property has a name and a value. In other words, it is a name/value pair. The created array has one property at index zero.

```
args1(0).Name = "Text"
args1(0).Value = "Your name"
```

Gives the property the name "Text" and the value "Your name", which is the text that is inserted when the macro is run.

```
dispatcher.executeDispatch(document, ".uno:InsertText", "", 0, args1())
```

This is where the magic happens. The dispatch helper sends a dispatch to the document frame (stored in the variable named document) with the command .uno:InsertText. The next two arguments, frame name and search flags, are beyond the scope of this document. The last argument is the array of property values to be used while executing the command InsertText.

```
end sub
```

The last line of the code ends the subroutine.

Creating a macro

When creating a macro, it is important to ask two questions before recording:

1) Can the task be written as a simple set of commands?
2) Can the steps be arranged so that the last command leaves the cursor ready for the next command or entering text or data into the document?

A more complicated example of a macro

A common task is to copy rows and columns of data from a web site and format them as a table in a text document as follows:

1) Copy the data from the web site to the clipboard.
2) To avoid strange formatting and fonts, paste the text into a Writer document as unformatted text.
3) Reformat the text with tabs between columns so that it can be converted into a table using **Table > Convert > Text to Table** on the main menu bar.

DONTKNOW	The font weight is not specified/known.
THIN	specifies a 50% font weight.
ULTRALIGHT	specifies a 60% font weight.
LIGHT	specifies a 75% font weight.
SEMILIGHT	specifies a 90% font weight.
NORMAL	specifies a normal font weight.
SEMIBOLD	specifies a 110% font weight.
BOLD	specifies a 150% font weight.
ULTRABOLD	specifies a 175% font weight.
BLACK	specifies a 200% font weight.

Figure 338: Example of copied data

With the two questions given above in mind, inspect the text to see if a macro can be recorded to format the text. An example of copied data showing the FontWeight constants group from the API web site (Figure 338). The first column in this example indicates a constant name and each name is followed by a space and a tab, and each line has two trailing spaces.

The first column in the table should contain a numeric value, the second column the name, and the third column the description. This conversion is easily accomplished for every row except for DONTKNOW and NORMAL, which do not contain a numeric value, but the values are between 0 and 100 and can be entered manually.

The data can be cleaned up in several ways, all of them easy to accomplish. The example given below uses keystrokes that assume the cursor is at the start of the line with the text THIN.

1) Make sure macro recording is enabled by going to **Tools > Options > LibreOffice > Advanced** on the main menu bar and selecting the option **Enable macro recording**. By default, this feature is turned off when LibreOffice was installed on your computer.
2) Go to **Tools > Macros > Record Macro** on the main menu bar to start recording.
3) Press *Ctrl+Right Arrow* to move the cursor to the start of "specifies".
4) Press *Backspace* twice to remove the tab and the space.
5) Press *Tab* to add the tab without the space after the constant name.
6) Press *Delete* to delete the lower case s and then press *Shift+S* to add an upper case S.
7) Press *Ctrl+Right Arrow* twice to move the cursor to the start of the number.
8) Press *Ctrl+Shift+Right Arrow* to select and move the cursor before the % sign.
9) Press *Ctrl+C* to copy the selected text to the clipboard.
10) Press *End* to move the cursor to the end of the line.
11) Press *Backspace* twice to remove the two trailing spaces.
12) Press *Home* to move the cursor to the start of the line.
13) Press *Ctrl+V* to paste the selected number to the start of the line.
14) Pasting the value also pasted an extra space, so press *Backspace* to remove the extra space.
15) Press *Tab* to insert a tab between the number and the name.
16) Press *Home* to move to the start of the line.
17) Press *down arrow* to move to the next line.
18) Stop recording the macro and save the macro, see "Recording a macro" on page 338.

It takes much longer to read and write the steps than to record the macro. Work slowly and think about the steps as you do them. With practice this becomes second nature.

The generated macro code in Listing 4 has been modified to contain the step number in the comments to match the code to the step above.

Listing 4: Copying numeric value to start of the column.

```
sub CopyNumToCol1
rem -------------------------------------------------------------
rem define variables
dim document   as object
dim dispatcher as object
rem -------------------------------------------------------------
rem get access to the document
document   = ThisComponent.CurrentController.Frame
dispatcher = createUnoService("com.sun.star.frame.DispatchHelper")

rem (3) Press Ctrl+Right Arrow to move the cursor to the start of "specifies".
dispatcher.executeDispatch(document, ".uno:GoToNextWord", "", 0, Array())

rem (4) Press Backspace twice to remove the tab and the space.
dispatcher.executeDispatch(document, ".uno:SwBackspace", "", 0, Array())

rem -------------------------------------------------------------
dispatcher.executeDispatch(document, ".uno:SwBackspace", "", 0, Array())

rem (5) Press Tab to add the tab without the space after the constant name.
dim args4(0) as new com.sun.star.beans.PropertyValue
args4(0).Name = "Text"
```

```
args4(0).Value = CHR$(9)

dispatcher.executeDispatch(document, ".uno:InsertText", "", 0, args4())

rem (6) Press Delete to delete the lower case s ....
dispatcher.executeDispatch(document, ".uno:Delete", "", 0, Array())

rem (6) ... and then press Shift+S to add an upper case S.
dim args6(0) as new com.sun.star.beans.PropertyValue
args6(0).Name = "Text"
args6(0).Value = "S"

dispatcher.executeDispatch(document, ".uno:InsertText", "", 0, args6())

rem (7) Press Ctrl+Right Arrow twice to move the cursor to the number.
dispatcher.executeDispatch(document, ".uno:GoToNextWord", "", 0, Array())

rem -------------------------------------------------------------
dispatcher.executeDispatch(document, ".uno:GoToNextWord", "", 0, Array())

rem (8) Press Ctrl+Shift+Right Arrow to select the number.
dispatcher.executeDispatch(document, ".uno:WordRightSel", "", 0, Array())

rem (9) Press Ctrl+C to copy the selected text to the clipboard.
dispatcher.executeDispatch(document, ".uno:Copy", "", 0, Array())

rem (10) Press End to move the cursor to the end of the line.
dispatcher.executeDispatch(document, ".uno:GoToEndOfLine", "", 0, Array())

rem (11) Press Backspace twice to remove the two trailing spaces.
dispatcher.executeDispatch(document, ".uno:SwBackspace", "", 0, Array())

rem -------------------------------------------------------------
dispatcher.executeDispatch(document, ".uno:SwBackspace", "", 0, Array())

rem (12) Press Home to move the cursor to the start of the line.
dispatcher.executeDispatch(document, ".uno:GoToStartOfLine", "", 0, Array())

rem (13) Press Ctrl+V to paste the selected number to the start of the line.
dispatcher.executeDispatch(document, ".uno:Paste", "", 0, Array())

rem (14) Press Backspace to remove the extra space.
dispatcher.executeDispatch(document, ".uno:SwBackspace", "", 0, Array())

rem (15) Press Tab to insert a tab between the number and the name.
dim args17(0) as new com.sun.star.beans.PropertyValue
args17(0).Name = "Text"
args17(0).Value = CHR$(9)

dispatcher.executeDispatch(document, ".uno:InsertText", "", 0, args17())
rem (16) Press Home to move to the start of the line.
dispatcher.executeDispatch(document, ".uno:GoToStartOfLine", "", 0, Array())

rem (17) Press Down Arrow to move to the next line.
dim args19(1) as new com.sun.star.beans.PropertyValue
args19(0).Name = "Count"
args19(0).Value = 1
args19(1).Name = "Select"
args19(1).Value = false

dispatcher.executeDispatch(document, ".uno:GoDown", "", 0, args19())
```

```
end sub
```

Cursor movements are used for all operations (as opposed to searching). If run on the DONTKNOW line, the word *weight* is moved to the front of the line, and the first "The" is changed to "She". This is not perfect, but you should not run the macro on the lines that did not have the proper format. You need to do these manually.

Running a macro quickly

It is tedious to repeatedly run the macro using **Tools > Macros > Run Macro** on the main menu bar when the macro can be run from the IDE (Figure 335 on page 337).

1) Go to **Tools > Macros > Organize Macros > LibreOffice Basic** on the main menu bar to open the Basic Macro dialog (Figure 333 on page 336).
2) Select your macro and click **Edit** to open the macro in the IDE.
3) Click the **Run BASIC** icon  on the Macro toolbar, or press the *F5* key, to run the macro.
4) Unless you change the first macro, it is the empty macro named Main. Modify Main so that it reads as shown in Listing 5.
5) Now, you can run CopyNumToCol1 by repeatedly clicking the **Run Basic** icon in the toolbar of the IDE. This is very fast and easy, especially for temporary macros that will be used a few times and then discarded.

Listing 5: Modify Main to call CopyNumToCol1.

```
Sub Main
  CopyNumToCol1
End Sub
```

Macro recorder failures

Sometimes the macro recorder has a failure and understanding LibreOffice internal workings helps to understand how and why the macro recorder sometimes fails. The primary offender is related to the dispatch framework and its relationship to the macro recorder.

Dispatch framework

The purpose of the dispatch framework is to provide uniform access to components (documents) for commands that usually correspond to menu items. Using **File > Save** from the main menu bar, the shortcut keys *Ctrl+S*, or clicking the **Save** icon are all of commands that are translated into the same "dispatch command".

The dispatch framework can also be used to send "commands" back to the User Interface (UI). For example, after saving the document, the File Save command is disabled. As soon as the document has been changed, the File Save command is enabled.

A dispatch command is text, for example .uno:InsertObject or .uno:GoToStartOfLine. The command is sent to the document frame and this passes on the command until an object is found that can handle the command.

How the macro recorder uses the dispatch framework

The macro recorder records the generated dispatches. The recorder is a relatively simple tool to use and the same commands that are issued are recorded for later use. The problem is that not all dispatched commands are complete. For example, inserting an object generates the following code:

```
dispatcher.executeDispatch(document, ".uno:InsertObject", "", 0, Array())
```

It is not possible to specify what kind of object to create or insert. If an object is inserted from a file, you cannot specify which file to insert.

When recording a macro and using **Tools > Options** on the main menu bar to open and modify configuration items, the generated macro does not record any configuration changes. In fact, the generated code is commented so it will not even be run.

```
rem dispatcher.executeDispatch(document,
    ".uno:OptionsTreeDialog", "", 0, Array())
```

If a dialog is opened, a command to open the dialog is likely to be generated. Any work done inside the dialog is not usually recorded. Examples of this include macro organization dialogs, inserting special characters, and similar types of dialogs. Other possible problems using the macro recorder include things such as inserting a formula, setting user data, setting filters in Calc, actions in database forms, and exporting a document to an encrypted PDF file. You never know for certain what will work unless you try it. For example, the actions from the search dialog are properly captured.

Other options

When the macro recorder is not able to solve a specific problem, the usual solution is to write code using the LibreOffice objects. Unfortunately, there is a steep learning curve for these LibreOffice objects. It is usually best to start with simple examples and then increase the scope of macros as you learn more. Learning to read generated macros is a good place to start.

If you record Calc macros, and the recorder can correctly generate a macro, there is an add-in available which converts Calc macros when they are recorded. The final code manipulates LibreOffice objects rather than generating dispatches. This can be very useful for learning the object model and can be downloaded directly from the web site:

http://www.paolo-mantovani.org/downloads/DispatchToApiRecorder/

Macro organization

In LibreOffice, macros are grouped in modules, modules are grouped in libraries, and libraries are grouped in library containers. A library is usually used as a major grouping for either an entire category of macros, or for an entire application. Modules usually split functionality, such as user interaction and calculations. Individual macros are subroutines and functions. Figure 339 shows an example of the hierarchical structure of macro libraries in LibreOffice.

Go to **Tools > Macros > Organize Macros > LibreOffice Basic** on the main menu bar to open the LibreOffice Basic Macros dialog (Figure 333 on page 336). All available library containers are shown in the *Macro from* list. Every document is a library container, capable of containing multiple libraries. The application itself acts as two library containers, one container for macros distributed with LibreOffice called LibreOffice Macros, and one container for personal macros called My Macros.

The LibreOffice Macros are stored with the application runtime code, which may not be editable to you unless you are an administrator. This helps protect these macros because they should not be changed and you should not store your own macros in the LibreOffice container.

Unless your macros are applicable to a single document, and only to a single document, your macros will probably be stored in the My Macros container. The My Macros container is stored in your user area or home directory.

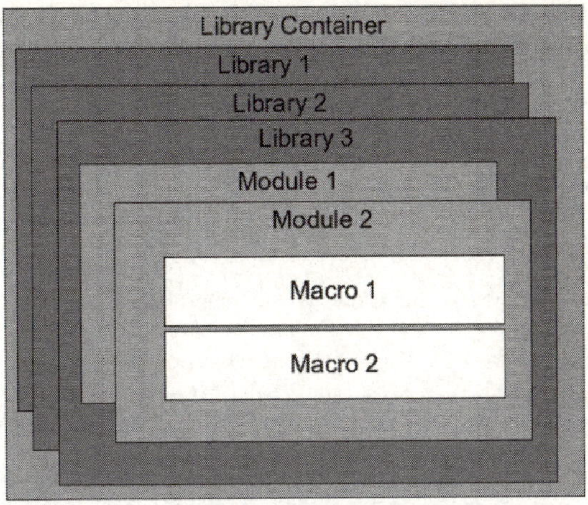

Figure 339: Macro Library hierarchy

If a macro is contained in a document, then a recorded macro will attempt to work on that document; because it primarily uses "ThisComponent" for its actions.

Every library container contains a library named *Standard*. It is better to create your own libraries with meaningful names than to use the Standard library. Not only are meaningful names easier to manage, but they can also be imported into other library containers whereas the Standard library cannot.

Caution	LibreOffice allows you to import libraries into a library container, but it will not allow you to overwrite the library named Standard. Therefore, if you store your macros in the Standard library, you cannot import them into another library container.

Just as it makes good sense to give your libraries meaningful names, it is prudent to use meaningful names for your modules. By default, LibreOffice uses names such as Module1, Module2 and so on.

As you create your macros, you must decide where to store them. Storing a macro in a document is useful if the document will be shared and you want the macro to be included with the document. Macros stored in the application library container named My Macros, however, are globally available to all documents.

Macros are not available until the library that contains them is loaded. The Standard library and Template library, however, are automatically loaded. A loaded library is displayed differently from a library that is not loaded. To load the library and the modules it contains, double-click on the library.

Where are macros stored?

LibreOffice stores user-specific data in a directory in the home directory for each user. The location is operating system specific. Go to **Tools > Options > LibreOffice > Paths** on the main menu bar to view where other configuration data are stored. For example, on computer running Windows XP, this is `C:\Documents and Settings\<user name>\Application Data`. User macros are stored in `LibreOffice\4\user\basic`. Each library is stored in its own directory off the basic directory.

It is not important to understand where macros are stored for casual use. If you know where they are stored, however, you can create a backup, share your macros, or inspect them if there is an error.

Go to **Tools > Macros > Organize Dialogs** on the main menu bar to open the LibreOffice Macro Organizer dialog (Figure 334 on page 337). Alternatively, go to **Tools > Macros > Organize Macros > LibreOffice Basic** on the main menu bar to open the LibreOffice Macros dialog (Figure 333 on page 336) and then click the **Organizer** button.

Importing macros

The LibreOffice Macro Organizer dialog allows you to import macro libraries into your document as well as creating, deleting, and renaming libraries, modules, and dialogs.

1) Select the library container to use and then click **Import** to import macro libraries (Figure 334 on page 337).
2) Navigate to the directory containing the library to import (Figure 340). There are usually two files from which to choose, dialog.xlb and script.xlb. It does not matter which of these two files you select; both will be imported. Macros can be stored in libraries inside LibreOffice documents. Select a document rather than a directory on disk to import libraries contained in a document.

Note	You cannot import the library named Standard.

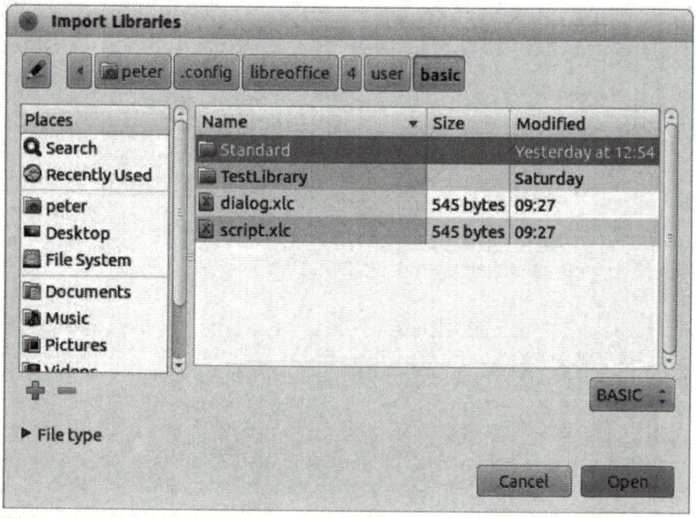

Figure 340: Navigating to a macro library

Tip	On a computer operating Linux, the LibreOffice specific files are stored in the home directory of a user in a directory whose name begins with a period. Directories and files with names beginning with a period may be hidden and not shown in a normal selection dialog. If using LibreOffice dialogs, rather than the operating system specific dialogs, type the name of the desired directory in the Name field.

3) Select a file and click **Open** to continue and open the Import Libraries dialog (Figure 341).

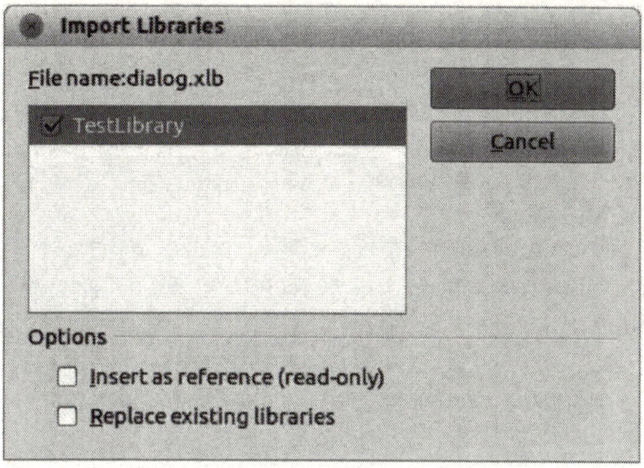

Figure 341: Choose library import options

4) Select the following options for importing libraries:
   a) If no options are selected, the library is copied to your user macro directory. However, if the library you are importing has the same name and you are importing into the same location, it will not be copied.
   b) Select **Replace existing libraries** if the library you want to import has the same name and you want to replace the existing library.
   c) Select **Insert as reference** if you want to use the library as reference, but not import the library into your document. When a library is used as a reference, it remains in its current location and is read only.
5) Click **OK** to import the macro library you selected.

Downloading macros to import

Macros are available for download. Some macros are contained in documents, some as regular files that you must select and import, and some as macro text that should be copied and pasted into the Basic IDE. See “Adding a macro” on page 336 on how to add macros to your macro library and “Viewing and editing macros” on page 339 on how to edit macros using the Basic IDE..

Some macros are available as free downloads on the Internet (see Table 6).

Table 6. Macro examples

Location	***Description***
http://www.pitonyak.org/oo.php	Reference materials regarding macros.
http://www.pitonyak.org/database/	Reference materials regarding database macros.
http://development.openoffice.org/	Lots of links to everything.
http://forum.openoffice.org/	A forum, with many examples and help.

How to run a macro

Although you can use **Tools > Macros > Run Macro** to run all macros, this is not efficient for frequently run macros. See "Running a macro" on page 339 for more information.

A more common technique for frequently used macros is to assign the macro a toolbar icon, menu item, keyboard shortcut, or a button embedded in a document. While choosing a method, it is also good to ask questions such as:

- Should the macro be available for only one document, or globally for all documents?
- Is the macro for a specific document type, such as a Calc document?
- How frequently will the macro be used?

The answers will determine where to store the macro and how to make it available. For example, you will probably not add a rarely used macro to a toolbar. To help determine your choices, see Table 7.

Table 7. Methods for starting a macro

Type	LibreOffice	Document Type	Document
Toolbar	No	Yes	Yes
Menu	No	Yes	Yes
Shortcut	Yes	Yes	No
Event	Yes	No	Yes

Toolbars, menu items and keyboard shortcuts

To add a menu item, keyboard shortcut, or toolbar icon that calls a macro, use the Customize dialog (Figure 342). The Customize dialog contains pages to configure menus, keyboard shortcuts, toolbars, and events. To open this dialog, go to **Tools > Customize** on the main menu bar or right-click in an empty space on a toolbar and select **Customize Toolbar** from the context menu.

Complete coverage of the Customize dialog is beyond the scope of this chapter. Click the **Help** button to access the help pages included with LibreOffice or see *Chapter 14 Customizing LibreOffice*.

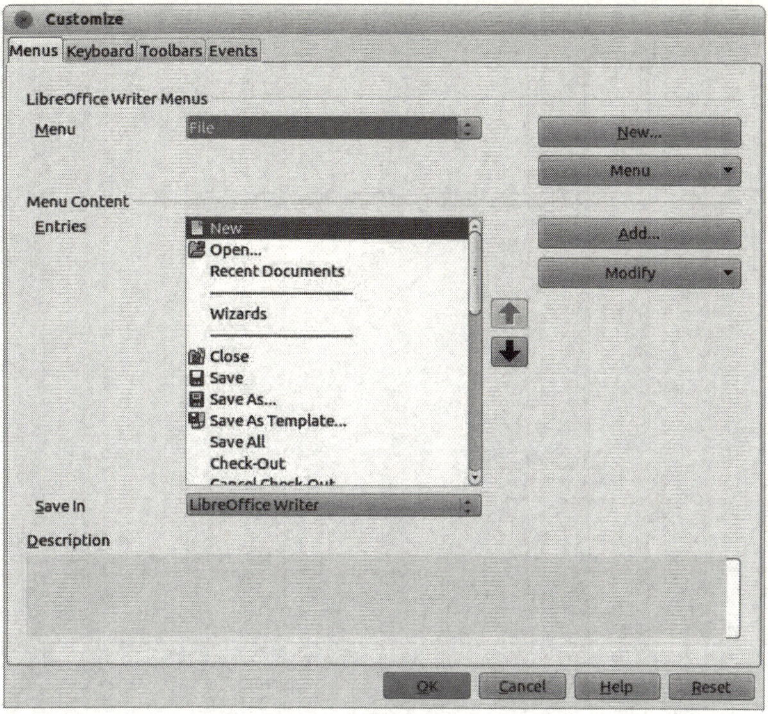

Figure 342: Menus page in Customize dialog

Events

In LibreOffice, when something happens it means that an event occurred. For example, opening a document, pressing a key, or moving the mouse cursor. LibreOffice allows events to cause a macro to be called; the macro is then called an event handler. Full coverage of event handlers is well beyond the scope of this document, but a little knowledge can accomplish much.

Caution ⚠	Be careful when you configure an event handler. For example, assume that you write an event handler that is called every time that a key is pressed, but you make a mistake so the event is not properly handled. One possible result is that your event handler will consume all key presses, forcing you to forcibly terminate LibreOffice.

1) Go to **Tools > Customize** on the main menu bar to open the Customize dialog and select the Events tab (Figure 343). The events in the Customize dialog are related to the entire application and specific documents.
2) In **Save In**, select LibreOffice, or a specific document from the drop down menu to save your event.
3) A common use is to assign the Open Document event to call a specific macro. The macro then performs certain setup tasks for the document. Select the desired event and click **Macro** to open the Macro Selector dialog (Figure 337 on page 339).
4) Select the desired macro and click **OK** to assign the macro to the event. The Events page shows that the event has been assigned to a macro.

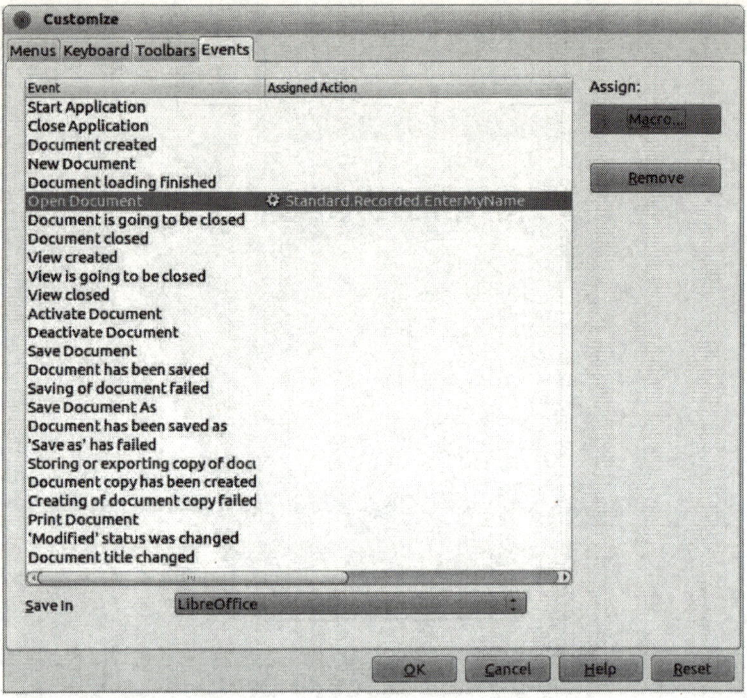

Figure 343: Events page in Customize dialog

Many objects in a document can be set to call macros when events occur. The most common use is to add a control, such as a button, into a document. Even double-clicking on a graphic opens a dialog with a Macros tab that allows you to assign a macro to an event.

Extensions

An extension is a package that can be installed into LibreOffice to add new functionality. Extensions can be written in almost any programming language and may be simple or sophisticated. Extensions can be grouped into types:

- Calc Add-Ins, which provide new functionality for Calc, including new functions that act like normal built-in functions
- New components and functionality, which normally include some level of User Interface (UI) integration such as new menus or toolbars
- Pivot Tables that are used directly in Calc
- Chart Add-Ins with new chart types
- Linguistic components such as spell checkers
- Document templates and images

Although individual extensions can be found in several places, there is currently an extension repository at: http://extensions.libreoffice.org/ and some documentation at http://libreplanet.org/wiki/Group:OpenOfficeExtensions/List

For more about obtaining and installing extensions, see *Chapter 14 Customizing LibreOffice*.

Writing macros without the recorder

The examples covered in this chapter are created using the macro recorder and the dispatcher. You can also write macros that directly access the objects that comprise LibreOffice if you are confident in writing computer code. In other words, you can create a macro that directly manipulates a document.

Directly manipulating LibreOffice internal objects is an advanced topic that is beyond the scope of this chapter. A simple example, however, demonstrates how this works.

Listing 6: Append the text "Hello" to the current document.

```
Sub AppendHello
  Dim oDoc
  Dim sTextService$
  Dim oCurs

  REM ThisComponent refers to the currently active document.
  oDoc = ThisComponent

  REM Verify that this is a text document
  sTextService = "com.sun.star.text.TextDocument"
  If NOT oDoc.supportsService(sTextService) Then
    MsgBox "This macro only works with a text document"
    Exit Sub
  End If

  REM Get the view cursor from the current controller.
  oCurs = oDoc.currentController.getViewCursor()

  REM Move the cursor to the end of the document
  oCurs.gotoEnd(False)

  REM Insert text "Hello" at the end of the document
  oCurs.Text.insertString(oCurs, "Hello", False)
End Sub
```

Finding more information

Numerous resources are available that provide help with writing macros. Use **Help > LibreOffice Help** to open the LibreOffice help pages. The upper left corner of the LibreOffice help system contains a drop-down list that determines which help set is displayed. To view the help for Basic, choose *LibreOffice Basic* from this list.

Included material

Many excellent macros are included with LibreOffice. Use **Tools > Macros > Organize Macros > LibreOffice Basic** to open the Macro dialog. Expand the Tools library in the LibreOffice library container. Inspect the Debug module—some good examples include WritedbgInfo(document) and printdbgInfo(sheet).

Online resources

The following links and references contain information regarding macro programming:

http://ask.libreoffice.org/ (a Q & A site where volunteers answer questions related to LibreOffice) http://forum.openoffice.org/en/forum/ (Apache OpenOffice community forum; volunteers answer questions about LibreOffice as well)

http://api.*openoffice.org*/docs/common/ref/com/sun/star/module-ix.html (official IDL reference; here you will find almost every command with a description)

https://wiki.documentfoundation.org/Documentation/Other_Documentation_and_Resources (look in Programmers section for *BASIC Programmers' Guide* and *Developers' Guide*; the latter contains a detailed explanation)

http://www.pitonyak.org/oo.php (macro page for Andrew Pitonyak)

http://www.pitonyak.org/AndrewMacro.odt (numerous examples of working macros)

http://www.pitonyak.org/OOME_3_0.odt (Andrew Pitonyak's book on macros)

http://www.pitonyak.org/database/ (numerous macro examples using Base)

Printed and eBook materials

There are currently no books specific to LibreOffice macros that are available for download.

Information in the following books is mostly applicable to LibreOffice; the books are available for purchase in both printed and eBook form from their publishers:

Dr. Mark Alexander Bain's *Learn OpenOffice.org Spreadsheet Macro Programming*.
See http://www.packtpub.com/openoffice-ooobasic-calc-automation/book.

Roberto Benitez's *Database Programming with OpenOffice.org Base & Basic*.
See http://www.lulu.com/product/paperback/database-programming-with-openofficeorg-base-basic/3568728

LibreOffice
The Document Foundation

Chapter 14
Customizing LibreOffice

Introduction

This chapter describes some common customizations that you may wish to do.

You can customize menus, toolbars, and keyboard shortcuts in LibreOffice, add new menus and toolbars, and assign macros to events. However, you cannot customize context (right-click) menus.

Other customizations are made easy by extensions that you can install from the LibreOffice website or from other providers.

Note	Customizations to menus and toolbars can be saved in a template. To do so, first save them in a document and then save the document as a template as described in Chapter 3, Using Styles and Templates.

Customizing menu content

In addition to changing the menu font (described in Chapter 2, Setting up LibreOffice), you can add and rearrange categories on the menu bar, add commands to menus, and make other changes.

To customize menus:

1) Choose **Tools** > **Customize.**
2) On the **Customize** dialog, choose the **Menus** page.

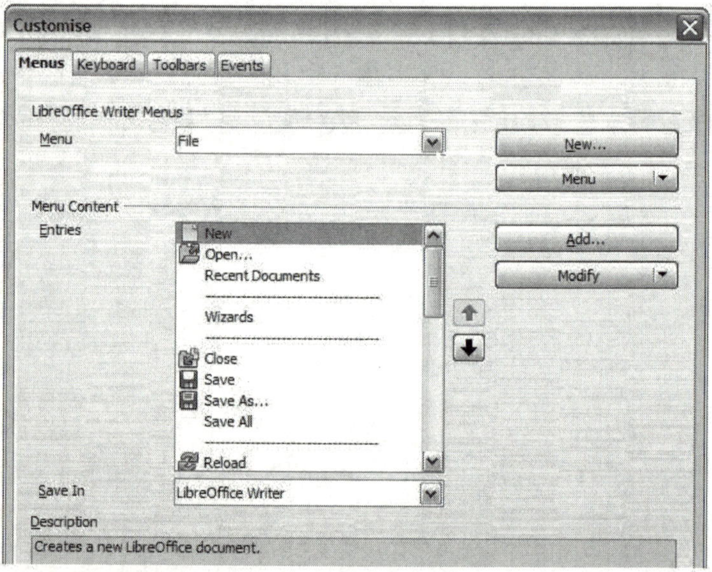

Figure 344. The Menus page of the Customize dialog

3) In the *Save In* drop-down list, choose whether to save this changed menu for the application (for example, LibreOffice Writer) or for a selected document (for example, SampleDocument.odt).
4) In the section **LibreOffice [name of the program (example: Writer)] Menus**, select from the *Menu* drop-down list the menu that you want to customize. The list includes all the main menus as well as submenus (menus that are contained under another menu). For

example, in addition to *File*, *Edit*, *View*, and so on, there is *File* | *Send* and *Edit* | *Changes*. The commands available for the selected menu are shown in the central part of the dialog.

5) To customize the selected menu, click on the **Modify** button. You can also add commands to a menu by clicking on the **Add** button. These actions are described in the following sections. Use the up and down arrows next to the Entries list to move the selected menu item to a different position.
6) When you have finished making all your changes, click **OK** (not shown in illustration) to save them.

Creating a new menu

In the *Menus* page of the Customize dialog, click **New** to display the New Menu dialog, shown in Figure 345.

1) Type a name for your new menu in the **Menu name** box.
2) Use the up and down arrow buttons to move the new menu into the required position on the menu bar.
3) Click **OK** to save.

The new menu now appears on the list of menus in the Customize dialog. (It will appear on the menu bar itself after you save your customizations.)

After creating a new menu, you need to add some commands to it, as described in "Adding a command to a menu" on page 358.

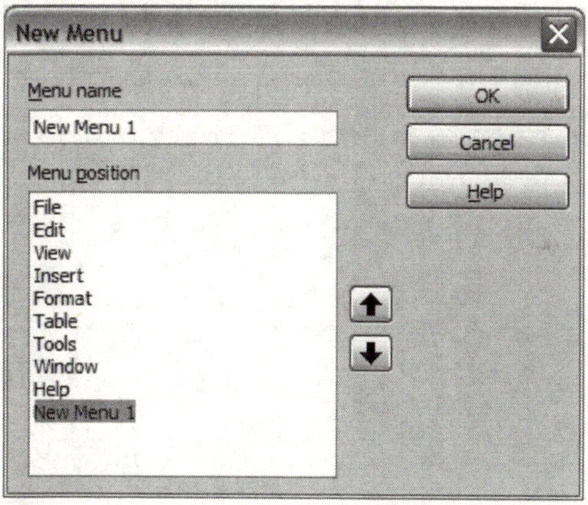

Figure 345: Adding a new menu

Modifying existing menus

To modify an existing menu, either user-made or inbuilt, select it in the *Menu* list and click the **Menu** button to drop down a list of modifications: **Move**, **Rename**, **Delete**. Not all of these modifications can be applied to all the entries in the *Menu* list. For example, **Rename** and **Delete** are not available for the supplied menus, and **Move** is not available for submenus.

To move a menu (such as *File*), choose **Menu > Move**. A dialog similar to the one shown in Figure 345 (but without the **Menu name** box) opens. Use the up and down arrow buttons to move the menu into the required position.

To move submenus (such as *File* | *Send*), select the main menu (**File**) in the Menu list and then, in the *Menu Content* section of the dialog, select the submenu (**Send**) in the *Entries* list and use the arrow keys to move it up or down in the sequence. Submenus are easily identified in the *Entries* list by a small black triangle on the right hand side of the name.

In addition to renaming, you can allocate a letter in a custom menu's name, which will become underlined, to be used as a keyboard shortcut, that allows you to select that menu when you press *Alt*+ that letter. Existing submenus can be edited to change the letter which is used to select them from the keyboard once the menu is open.

1) Select a custom menu or a submenu in the *Menu* drop-down list.
2) Click the **Menu** button and select **Rename**.
3) Add a tilde (~) in front of the letter that you want to use as an accelerator. For example, to select the **Send** submenu command by pressing *S* (after opening the File menu using *Alt+F*), enter **~Send**. This changes it from the default *d*.

Note	It is possible to use a letter already in use in the menu list (for example, in the Insert menu, the letter *v* is used in *Envelope* and in *Movie and sound* as an accelerator). However, you should use an unused letter if possible, to make it simpler for the user to navigate.

Adding a command to a menu

You can add commands to the supplied menus and to menus you have created. On the Customize dialog, select the menu in the *Menu* list and click the **Add** button in the *Menu Content* section of the dialog.

On the Add Commands dialog (Figure 346), select a category and then the command, and click **Add**. The dialog remains open, so you can select several commands. When you have finished adding commands, click **Close**. Back on the Customize dialog, you can use the up and down arrow buttons to arrange the commands in your preferred sequence.

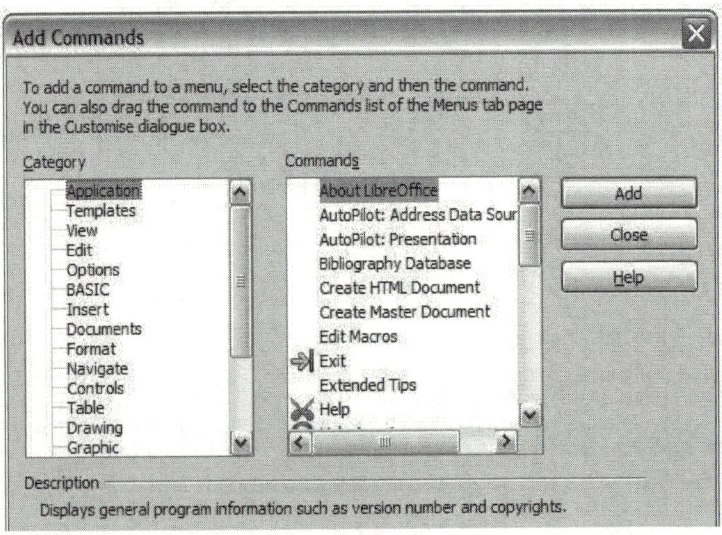

Figure 346: Adding a command to a menu

Modifying menu entries

In addition to changing the sequence of entries on a menu or submenu, you can add submenus, rename or delete the entries, and add group separators.

To begin, select the menu or submenu to be modified, from the *Menu* list near the top of the Customize page, then select the entry in the *Entries* list under *Menu Content*. Click the **Modify** button and choose the required action from the drop-down list of actions.

Most of the actions should be self-explanatory. **Begin a group** adds a separator line after the highlighted entry.

Customizing toolbars

You can customize toolbars in several ways, including choosing which icons are visible and locking the position of a docked toolbar (as described in Chapter 1, Introducing LibreOffice), and adding or deleting icons (commands) in the list of those available on a toolbar. You can also create new toolbars. This section describes how to create new toolbars and add or delete icons on existing ones.

To get to the toolbar customization dialog, do any of the following:

- On the toolbar, right-click in the toolbar and choose **Customize Toolbar**.
- Choose **View > Toolbars > Customize** from the menu bar.
- Choose **Tools > Customize** from the menu bar and go to the *Toolbars* page.

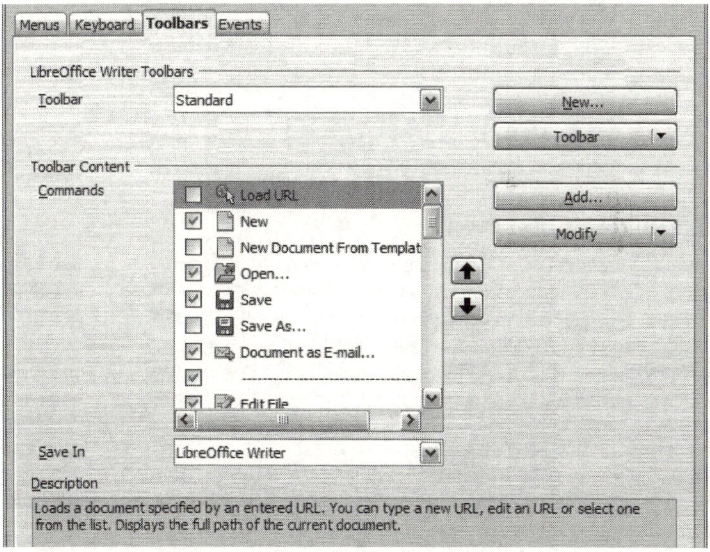

Figure 347. The Toolbars page of the Customize dialog

Modifying existing toolbars

To modify an existing toolbar:

1) In the *Save In* drop-down list, choose whether to save this changed toolbar for the application (for example, Writer) or for a selected document.
2) In the section **LibreOffice [name of the program (example: Writer)] > Toolbars**, select from the *Toolbar* drop-down list the toolbar that you want to customize.
3) Click on the **Toolbar** or **Modify** buttons, and add commands to a toolbar by clicking on the **Add** button. You can also create a new toolbar by clicking on the **New** button. These actions are described in the following sections.
4) When you have finished making all your changes, click **OK** to save them.

Creating a new toolbar

To create a new toolbar:

1) Choose **Tools > Customize > Toolbars** from the menu bar.
2) Click **New**. On the Name dialog, type the new toolbar's name and choose from the Save In drop-down list where to save this changed menu: for the application (for example, Writer) or for a selected document. Click **OK**.

The new toolbar now appears on the list of toolbars in the Customize dialog. After creating a new toolbar, you need to add some commands to it, as described below.

Adding a command to a toolbar

If the list of available buttons for a toolbar does not include all the commands you want on that toolbar, you can add commands. When you create a new toolbar, you need to add commands to it.

1) On the *Toolbars* page of the Customize dialog, select the toolbar in the Toolbar list and click the **Add** button in the Toolbar Content section of the dialog.
2) The Add Commands dialog is the same as for adding commands to menus (Figure 346). Select a category and then the command, and click **Add**. The dialog remains open, so you can select several commands. When you have finished adding commands, click **Close**. If you insert an item which does not have an associated icon, the toolbar will display the full name of the item: the next section describes how to choose an icon for a toolbar command.
3) Back on the Customize dialog, you can use the up and down arrow buttons to arrange the commands in your preferred sequence.
4) When you are done making changes, click **OK** to save.

Choosing icons for toolbar commands

Toolbar buttons usually have icons, not words, on them, but not all of the commands have associated icons.

To choose an icon for a command, select the command and click **Modify > Change icon**. On the Change Icon dialog, you can scroll through the available icons, select one, and click **OK** to assign it to the command.

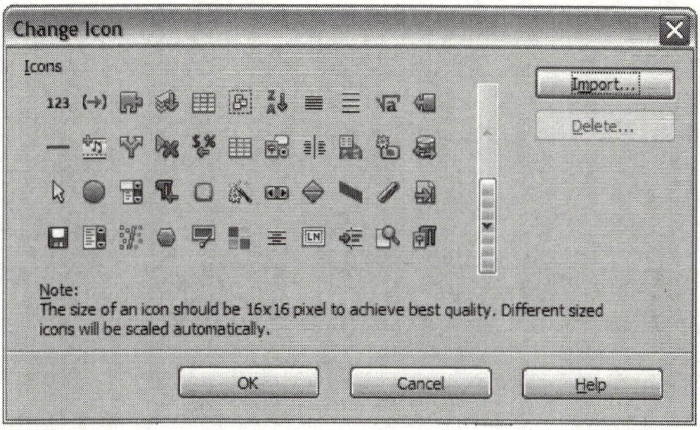

Figure 348: Change Icon dialog

To use a custom icon, create it in a graphics program and import it into LibreOffice by clicking the **Import** button on the Change Icon dialog. Custom icons should be 16 x 16 pixels in size to achive the best quality and should not contain more than 256 colors.

Example: Adding a Fax icon to a toolbar

You can customize LibreOffice so that a single click on an icon automatically sends the current document as a fax.

1) Be sure the fax driver is installed. Consult the documentation for your fax modem for more information.
2) Choose **Tools > Options > LibreOffice Writer > Print**. The dialog shown in Figure 349 opens.
3) Select the fax driver from the **Fax** list and click **OK**.
4) Right-click in the Standard toolbar. In the drop-down menu, choose **Customize Toolbar**. The *Toolbars* page of the Customize dialog appears (Figure 347). Click **Add**.
5) On the Add Commands dialog (Figure 350), select **Documents** in the *Category* list, then select **Send Default Fax** in the *Commands* list. Click **Add**. Now you can see the new icon in the Commands list.
6) In the *Commands* list, click the up or down arrow button to position the new icon where you want it. Click **OK** and then click **Close**.

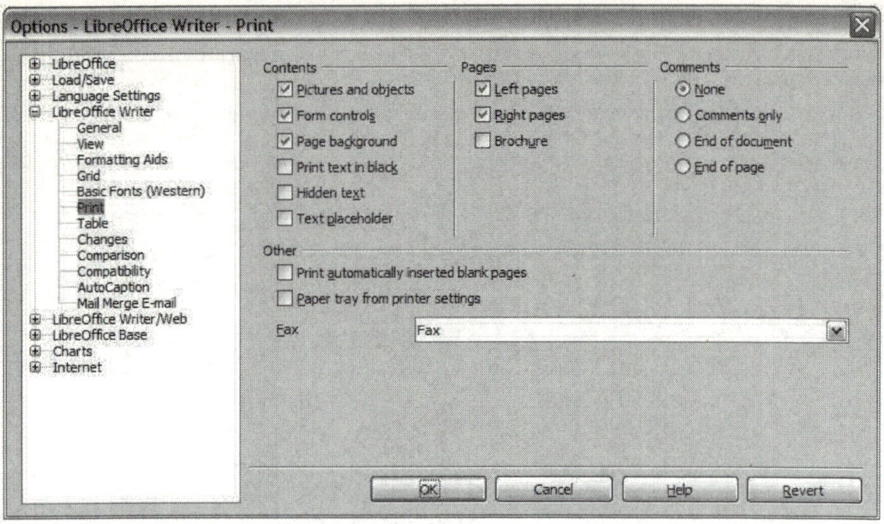

Figure 349: Setting up LibreOffice for sending faxes

Your toolbar now has a new icon to send the current document as a fax.

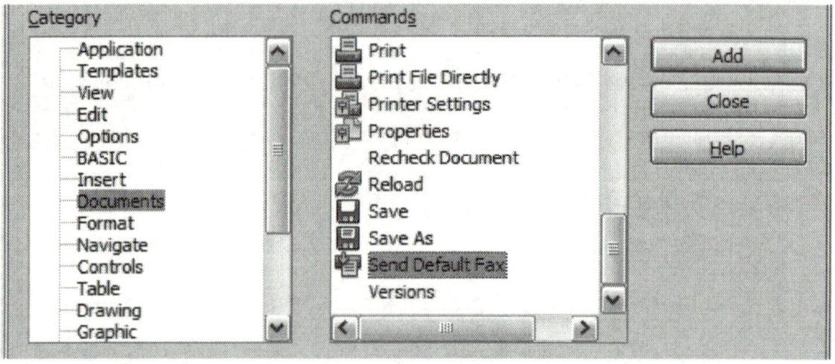

Figure 350: Adding a Send Fax command to a toolbar

Assigning shortcut keys

In addition to using the built-in keyboard shortcuts (listed in Appendix A), you can define your own. You can assign shortcuts to standard LibreOffice functions or your own macros and save them for use with the entire LibreOffice suite.

Caution	Be careful when reassigning your operating system's or LibreOffice's predefined shortcut keys. Many key assignments are universally understood shortcuts, such as *F1* for Help, and are always expected to provide certain results. Although you can easily reset the shortcut key assignments to the LibreOffice defaults, changing some common shortcut keys can cause confusion, especially if other users share your computer.

To adapt shortcut keys to your needs, use the Customize dialog, as described below.

1) Select **Tools > Customize > Keyboard**. The Customize dialog opens.
2) To have the shortcut key assignment available in all components of LibreOffice select the **LibreOffice** button.
3) Next select the required function from the *Category* and *Function* lists.
4) Now select the desired shortcut keys in the *Shortcut keys* list and click the **Modify** button at the upper right.
5) Click **OK** to accept the change. Now the chosen shortcut keys will execute the function chosen in step 3 above whenever they are pressed.

Note	All existing shortcut keys for the currently selected *Function* are listed in the *Keys* selection box. If the *Keys* list is empty, it indicates that the chosen key combination is free for use. If it were not, and you wanted to reassign a shortcut key combination that is already in use, you must first delete the existing key. Shortcut keys that are greyed-out in the listing on the Customize dialog, such as *F1* and *F10,* are not available for reassignment.

Example: Assigning styles to shortcut keys

You can configure shortcut keys to quickly assign styles in your document. Some shortcuts are predefined, such as *Ctrl+0* for the *Text body* paragraph style, *Ctrl+1* for the *Heading 1* style, and *Ctrl+2* for *Heading 2*. You can modify these shortcuts and create your own.

1) Click **Tools > Customize > Keyboard**. The Keyboard page of the Customize dialog (Figure 351) opens.
2) To have the shortcut key assignment available only with one component (for example, Writer), select that component's name in the upper right corner of the page; otherwise select **LibreOffice** to make it available to every component.
3) Choose the shortcut keys you want to assign a style to. In this example, we have chosen *Ctrl+9*. This enables the **Modify** button.
4) In the *Functions* section at the bottom of the dialog, scroll down in the *Category* list to *Styles*. Click the expansion symbol (usually a + sign or triangle) to expand the list of styles.
5) Choose the category of style. (This example uses a paragraph style, but you can also choose character styles and others.) The *Function* list will display the names of the available styles for the selected category. The example shows some of LibreOffice's predefined styles.
6) To assign *Ctrl+9* to be the shortcut key combination for the List 1 style, select *List 1* in the *Function* list, and then click **Modify**. *Ctrl+9* now appears in the *Keys* list on the right, and *List 1* appears next to *Ctrl+9* in the Shortcut keys box at the top.
7) Make any other required changes, and then click **OK** to save these settings and close the dialog.

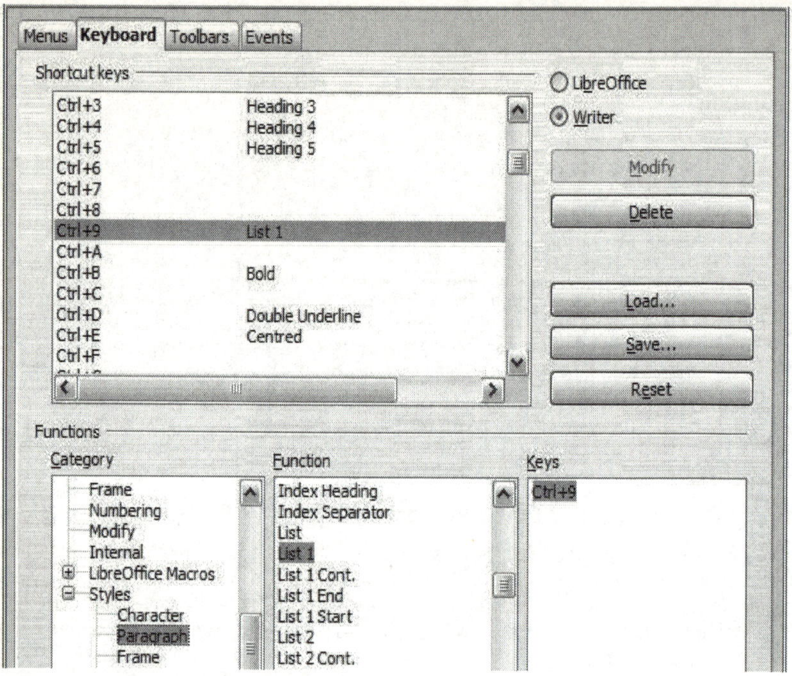

Figure 351. Defining keyboard shortcuts for applying styles

Saving changes to a file

Changes to the shortcut key assignments can be saved in a keyboard configuration file for use at a later time, thus permitting you to create and apply different configurations as the need arises. To save keyboard shortcuts to a file:

1) After making your keyboard shortcut assignments, click the **Save** button at the right of the Customize dialog (Figure 351).
2) In the Save Keyboard Configuration dialog, select *All files* from the **Save as Type** list.
3) Next enter a name for the keyboard configuration file in the **File name** box, or select an existing file from the list. If you need to, browse to find a file from another location.
4) Click **Save**. A confirmation dialog appears if you are about to overwrite an existing file, otherwise there will be no feedback and the file will be saved.

Loading a saved keyboard configuration

To load a saved keyboard configuration file and replace your existing configuration, click the **Load** button at the right of the Customize dialog, and then select the configuration file from the Load Keyboard Configuration dialog.

Resetting the shortcut keys

To reset all of the keyboard shortcuts to their default values, click the **Reset** button near the bottom right of the Customize dialog. Use this feature with care as no confirmation dialog will be displayed; the defaults will be set without any further notice or user input.

Assigning macros to events

In LibreOffice, when something happens, we say that an event occurred. For example, a document was opened, a key was pressed, or the mouse moved. You can associate a macro with an event, so the macro is run when the event occurs. A common use is to assign the "open document" event to run a macro that performs certain setup tasks for the document.

To associate a macro with an event, use the Events page of the Customize dialog. For more information, see Chapter 13, Getting Started with Macros.

Adding functionality with extensions

An extension is a package that can be installed into LibreOffice to add new functionality.

Several extensions are shipped bundled with LibreOffice and are installed with the program. Others can be downloaded from various websites. The official extension repository is located at http://extensions.libreoffice.org/. These extensions are free of charge.

Some extensions from other sources are free of charge; others are available for a fee. Check the descriptions to see what licenses and fees apply to the ones that interest you.

Installing extensions

Extensions can be installed in any of three ways.

1) Directly from the *.oxt file in your system's file browser.
2) From your web browser if it can be configured to open this file type from a web page hyperlink.
3) Directly from **Tools > Extension Manager** by clicking **Add**.

To install directly from a saved *.oxt file on your system, double-click the file.

To install from a suitably enabled web browser, select the hyperlink, and then select to Open the file.

In both cases, after the Extension Manager opens, a warning dialog opens for you to verify the installation and then continue. The file is installed as a "user only" file in a multi user system.

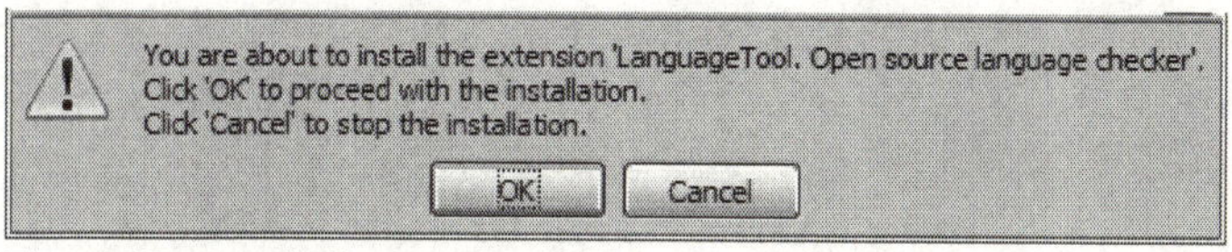

Figure 352: Installation warning dialog

To install directly from Extension Manager:

1) In LibreOffice, select **Tools > Extension Manager** from the menu bar. The option to view the extensions bundled with LibreOffice can be deselected to easier view those installations which have been added by a user.
2) In the Extension Manager dialog (Figure 354), click **Add**.
3) A file browser window opens. Find and select the extension you want to install and click **Open**.
4) Users with administrator or root privileges will see a dialog where they can choose to install extensions "for all users" (**shared**) or "only for me" (**user**). Normal users without those privileges can install, remove, or modify extensions only for their own use (**user**).

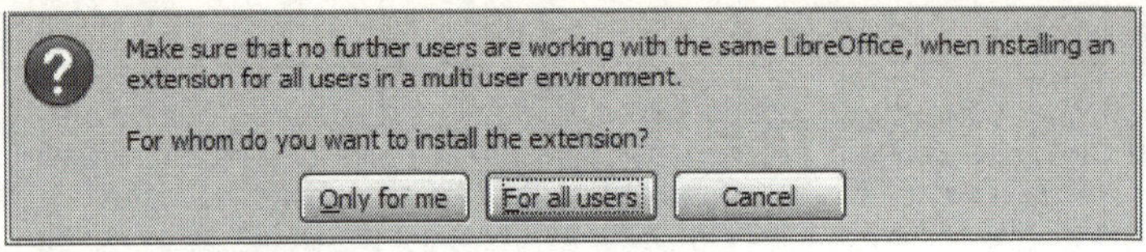

Figure 353: Dialog showing the installation choices

5) The extension begins installing.
6) In all three cases, during the process you may be asked to accept a license agreement. When the installation is complete, the extension is listed in the Extension Manager dialog.

Tip	To get extensions that are listed in the repository, you can open the Extension Manager and click the **Get more extensions online** link. You do not need to download them separately.

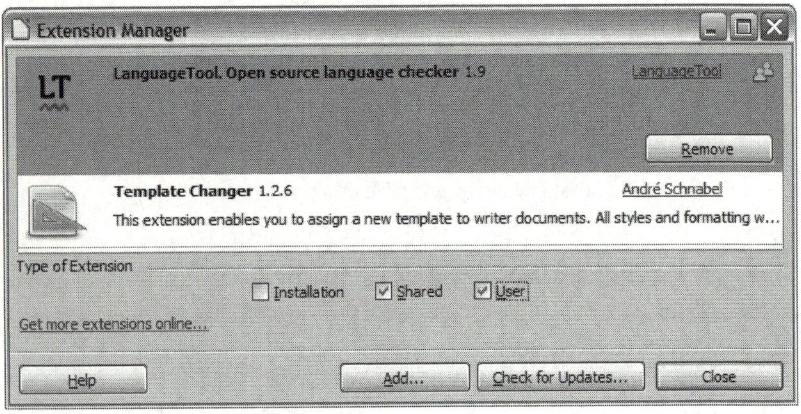

Figure 354: Using the Extension Manager

LibreOffice
The Document Foundation

Appendix A
Keyboard Shortcuts

Introduction

You can use LibreOffice without requiring a pointing device, such as a mouse or touchpad, by using its built-in keyboard shortcuts.

This appendix lists some of the most common built-in keyboard shortcuts that apply to all components of LibreOffice. For shortcuts specific to Writer, Calc, Impress, Draw, or Base, read the relevant component guide or search the application Help.

Note	Some of the shortcuts listed here may not work if your operating system uses the same shortcuts for other tasks. To resolve any conflicts, assign different keys to these shortcuts by reconfiguring either LibreOffice (see Chapter 14) or your operating system (see system documentation).

Tip for Macintosh users

Some keystrokes are different on a Mac from those used in Windows and Linux. The following table gives some common substitutions for the instructions in this chapter. For a more detailed list, see the application Help.

Windows or Linux	***Mac equivalent***	***Effect***
Right-click	*Control+click*	Opens a context menu
Ctrl (Control)	*⌘ (Command)*	Used with other keys
F5	*Shift+⌘+F5*	Opens the Navigator
F11	*⌘+T*	Opens the Styles and Formatting window

General keyboard shortcuts

Opening menus and menu items

Shortcut Keys	*Result*
Alt+<?>	Opens a menu where <?> is the underlined character of the menu you want to open. For example, *Alt+F* opens the menu **File** With the menu open, you will again find underlined characters. You can access these menu items directly by simply pressing the underlined character key. Where two menu items have the same underlined character, press the character key again to move to the next item. *Example*: to access the **Printer Settings** item of the **File** menu after opening it, press *R* twice to move from the initial **Digital Signatures** selection to **Printer Settings**. There may be instances where an item in a menu has no underlined character. This will have to be clicked directly.
Esc	Closes an open menu.
F6	Repeatedly pressing *F6* switches the focus and circles through the following objects: • Menu bar • Every toolbar from top to bottom and from left to right • Every free window from left to right • Document
Shift+F6	Switches through objects in the opposite direction.
Ctrl+F6	Switches the focus to the document.
F10 or *Alt*	Switches to the Menu bar and back.

Accessing a menu command

Press *Alt* or *F6* or *F10* to select the first item on the menu bar (the **File** menu). With the *right-arrow*, the next menu to the right is selected; with the *left-arrow*, the previous menu. The *Home* and *End* keys select the first and the last item on the Menu bar.

The *down-arrow* opens a selected menu. An additional *down-arrow* and *up-arrow* moves the selection through the menu commands. The *right-arrow* opens any existing submenus.

Press *Enter* to execute the selected menu command.

Executing a toolbar command

Press *F6* repeatedly until the first icon on the toolbar is selected. Use the right and left arrows to select an icon on a horizontal toolbar. Similarly, use the up and down arrows to select an icon on a vertical toolbar. The *Home* key selects the first icon on a toolbar and the *End* key, the last.

Press *Enter* to execute the selected icon. If the selected icon normally demands a consecutive mouse action, such as inserting a rectangle, then pressing the *Enter* key is not sufficient: in these cases press *Ctrl+Enter*.

- Press *Ctrl+Enter* on an icon for creating a draw object. A draw object will be placed into the middle of the view, with a predefined size.

- Press *Ctrl+Enter* on the Selection tool to select the first draw object in the document. If you want to edit, size, or move the selected draw object, first use *Ctrl+F6* to move the focus into the document.

Navigating and selecting with the keyboard

You can navigate through a document and make selections with the keyboard.

- To move the cursor, press the key or key combination given in the following table.
- To select the characters under the moving cursor, additionally hold down the *Shift* key when you move the cursor.

Key	***Function***	***Plus Ctrl key***
Right, left arrow keys	Moves the cursor one character to the left or to the right.	Moves the cursor one word to the left or to the right.
Up, down arrow keys	Moves the cursor up or down one line.	(*Ctrl+Alt*) Moves the current paragraph up or down.
Home	Moves the cursor to the beginning of the current line.	Moves the cursor to the beginning of the document.
End	Moves the cursor to the end of the current line.	Moves the cursor to the end of the document.
PgUp	Scrolls up one page.	Moves the cursor to the header.
PgDn	Scroll down one page.	Moves the cursor to the footer.

Controlling dialogs

When you open any dialog, one element (such as a button, an option field, an entry in a list box, or a checkbox) is highlighted or indicated by a dotted box around the field or button name. This element is said to have the focus on it.

Shortcut Keys	***Result***
Enter	Activates selected button. In most cases where no button is selected, *Enter* is equivalent to clicking **OK**.
Esc	Closes dialog without saving any changes made while it was open. In most cases, *Esc* is equivalent to clicking Cancel. When an open drop-down list is selected, *Esc* closes the list.
Spacebar	Checks an empty checkbox. Clears a checked checkbox.
Up, down arrow keys	Moves focus up and down a list. Increases or decreases value of a variable. Moves focus vertically within a section of dialog.
Left, right arrow keys	Moves focus horizontally within a section of a dialog.
Tab	Advances focus to the next section or element of a dialog.
Shift+Tab	Returns focus to the previous section or element in a dialog.
Alt+Down Arrow	Shows items in a drop-down list.

Macros

Shortcut Keys	*Result*
*Ctrl+** (multiplication sign: on number pad only)	Runs a macro field.
Shift+Ctrl+Q	Stops a running macro.

Getting help

Shortcut Keys	*Result*
F1	Opens the LibreOffice Help dialog. In LibreOffice Help: jumps to the first help page of the selected tab.
Shift+F1	Turns the cursor into the *What's This?* question mark. Shows the tip for an item underneath the cursor.
Shift+F2	Shows tip for a selected item.
Esc	In LibreOffice Help: goes up one level.

Managing documents

Shortcut Keys	*Result*
Ctrl+F4 or Alt+F4	Closes the current document. Closes LibreOffice when the last open document is closed.
Ctrl+O	Launches the Open dialog to open a document.
Ctrl+S	Saves the current document. If you are working on a previously unsaved file, the shortcut launches the Save As dialog.
Ctrl+N	Creates a new document.
Shift+Ctrl+N	Opens the Templates and Documents dialog.
Ctrl+P	Opens the Print dialog to print the document.
Ctrl+Q	Closes the application.
Del	In the Save and Open dialogs, deletes the selected files or folders. Items can be retrieved from the Recycle Bin (Trash).
Shift+Del	In the Save and Open dialogs, deletes the selected files or folders. Items are permanently deleted: they can not be retrieved from the Recycle Bin.
Backspace	In the Save and Open dialogs, shows contents of the current directory's parent folder.

Editing

Shortcut Keys	*Result*
Ctrl+X	Cuts selected items.
Ctrl+C	Copies selected items.
Ctrl+V	Pastes copied or cut items from the clipboard.
Ctrl+Shift+V	Opens the Paste Special dialog.
Ctrl+A	Selects all.
Ctrl+Z	Undoes last action.
Ctrl+Y	Redoes last action.
Ctrl+Shift+Y	Repeats last command.
Ctrl+F	Opens the Find dialog
Ctrl+H	Opens the Find & Replace dialog.
Ctrl+Shift+F	Searches for the last entered search term.
Ctrl+Shift+R	Refreshes (redraws) the document view.
Ctrl+Shift+I	Shows or hides the cursor in read-only text.

Selecting rows and columns in a database table opened by F4

Shortcut keys	*Result*
Spacebar	Toggles row selection, except when the row is in edit mode.
Ctrl+Spacebar	Toggles row selection.
Shift+Spacebar	Selects the current column.
Ctrl+Page Up	Moves pointer to the first row.
Ctrl+Page Down	Moves pointer to the last row.

Shortcut keys for drawing objects

Shortcut keys	*Result*
Select the toolbar with *F6*. Use the *Down Arrow* and *Right Arrow* to select the desired toolbar icon and press *Ctrl+Enter*.	Inserts a Drawing Object.
Select the document with *Ctrl+F6* and press *Tab*.	Selects a Drawing Object.

Shortcut keys	Result
Tab	Selects the next Drawing Object.
Shift+Tab	Selects the previous Drawing Object.
Ctrl+Home	Selects the first Drawing Object.
Ctrl+End	Selects the last Drawing Object.
Esc	Ends Drawing Object selection.
Esc (in Handle Selection Mode)	Exit Handle Selection Mode and return to Object Selection Mode.
Up/Down/Left/Right Arrow	Move the selected point (the snap-to-grid functions are temporarily disabled, but end points still snap to each other).
Alt+Up/Down/Left/Right Arrow	Moves the selected Drawing Object one pixel (in Selection Mode). Re-sizes a Drawing Object (in Handle Selection Mode). Rotates a Drawing Object (in Rotation Mode). Opens the properties dialog for a Drawing Object. Activates the Point Selection mode for the selected drawing object.
Spacebar	Select a point of a drawing object (in Point Selection mode) / Cancel selection. The selected point blinks once per second.
Shift+Spacebar	Select an additional point in Point Selection mode.
Ctrl+Tab	Select the next point of the drawing object (Point Selection mode). In Rotation mode, the center of rotation can also be selected.
Ctrl+Shift+Tab	Select the previous point of the drawing object (Point Selection mode).
Ctrl+Enter	A new drawing object with default size is placed in the center of the current view.
Ctrl+Enter at the Selection icon	Activates the first drawing object in the document.
Esc	Leave the Point Selection mode. The drawing object is selected afterwards. Edit a point of a drawing object (Point Edit mode).
Any text or numerical key	If a drawing object is selected, switches to edit mode and places the cursor at the end of the text in the drawing object. A printable character is inserted.
Alt key while creating or scaling a graphic object	The position of the object's center is fixed.

Shortcut keys	*Result*
Shift key while creating or scaling a graphic object	The ratio of the object's width to height is fixed.

Defining keyboard shortcuts

In addition to using the built-in keyboard shortcuts listed in this Appendix, you can define your own. See Chapter 14, Customizing LibreOffice, for instructions.

Further reading

For help with LibreOffice's keyboard shortcuts, or using LibreOffice with a keyboard only, search the application Help using the "shortcut keys" or "accessibility" keywords.

LibreOffice
The Document Foundation

Appendix B
Open Source, Open Standards, OpenDocument

Introduction

LibreOffice is a productivity suite that is compatible with other major office suites and available on a variety of platforms. It is open source software and therefore free to download, use, and distribute. If you are new to LibreOffice, this appendix will provide some information regarding its history, its community and some of its technical specifications.

A short history of LibreOffice

The OpenOffice.org project began when Sun Microsystems released the source code ("blueprints") for its StarOffice® software to the open source community on October 13, 2000. OpenOffice.org 1.0, the product, was released on April 30, 2002. Major updates to OpenOffice.org included version 2.0 in October 2005 and version 3.0 in October 2008. On January 26, 2010, Oracle Corporation acquired Sun Microsystems.

On September 28, 2010, the community of volunteers who develop and promote OpenOffice.org announced a major change in project structure. After ten years' successful growth with Sun Microsystems as founding and principle sponsor, the project launched an independent foundation called The Document Foundation, to fulfill the promise of independence written in the original charter. This foundation is the cornerstone of a new ecosystem where individuals and organizations can contribute to and benefit from the availability of a truly free office suite.

Unable to acquire the trademarked OpenOffice.org name from Oracle Corporation, The Document Foundation named its product LibreOffice. Continuing the version numbers from OpenOffice.org, LibreOffice 3.3 was released in January 2011.

In February 2012, The Document Foundation was incorporated in Berlin as a German Stiftung. You can read more about The Document Foundation at: http://www.documentfoundation.org/

The LibreOffice community

The Document Foundation's mission is:

> "...to facilitate the evolution of the OpenOffice.org Community into a new open, independent, and meritocratic organizational structure within the next few months. An independent Foundation is a better match to the values of our contributors, users, and supporters, and will enable a more effective, efficient, transparent, and inclusive Community. We will protect past investments by building on the solid achievements of our first decade, encourage wide participation in the Community, and co-ordinate activity across the Community."

Some of our corporate supporters include Canonical, The GNOME Foundation, Google, Novell and Red Hat. Additionally, over 450,000 people from nearly every part of the globe have joined this project with the idea of creating the best possible office suite that all can use. This is the essence of an "open source" community!

With its open source software license, LibreOffice is key in the drive to provide an office suite that is available to anyone, anywhere, for commercial or personal use. The software has been translated into many languages and runs on all major operating systems. New functionality can be added in the form of extensions.

The LibreOffice community invites contributors in all areas, including translators, software developers, graphic artists, technical writers, editors, donors and end-user support. Whatever you do best, you can make a difference in LibreOffice. The Community operates internationally in all time zones and in many languages, linked through the internet at www.libreoffice.org and www.documentfoundation.org.

How is LibreOffice licensed?

LibreOffice is distributed under the Open Source Initiative (OSI) approved Lesser General Public License (LGPL).

The LGPL license is available from the LibreOffice website:
http://www.libreoffice.org/download/license/

What is "open source"?

The four essential rights of open-source software are embodied within the Free Software Foundation's *General Public License* (GPL):

- The right to use the software for any purpose.
- Freedom to redistribute the software for free or for a fee.
- Access to the complete source code of the program (that is, the "blueprints").
- The right to modify any part of the source, or use portions of it in other programs.

The basic idea behind open source is very simple: When programmers can read, redistribute, and modify the source code for a piece of software, the software evolves. People improve it, people adapt it, people fix bugs.

For more information on Free and Open Source software, visit these websites:

Open Source Initiative (OSI): http://www.opensource.org

Free Software Foundation (FSF): http://www.gnu.org

What are "open standards"?

An open standard provides a means of doing something that is independent of manufacturer or vendor, thus enabling competing software programs to freely use the same file formats. HTML, XML, and ODF are examples of open standards for documents.

An open standard meets the following requirements:

- It is well documented with the complete specification publicly available, either free or at a nominal charge.
- It can be freely copied, distributed and used. The intellectual property of the standard is made irrevocably available on a royalty-free basis.
- It is standardized and maintained in an independent, open forum (also called "standards organization") using an open process.

What is OpenDocument?

OpenDocument (ODF) is an XML-based file format for office documents (text documents, spreadsheets, drawings, presentations and more), developed at OASIS (http://www.oasis-open.org/who/), an independent, international standards group.

Unlike other file formats, ODF is an open standard. It is publicly available, royalty-free, and without legal or other restrictions; therefore ODF files are not tied to a specific office suite and anybody can build a program that interprets these files. For this reason ODF is quickly becoming the preferred file format for government agencies, schools and other companies who prefer not to be too dependent on any one software supplier.

Since version 2.0, OpenOffice.org has supported the open standard OASIS OpenDocument as its default file format. LibreOffice saves documents in OpenDocument Format by default. LibreOffice 3 adopted version 1.2 of the OpenDocument standard and this version of LibreOffice continues to use this standard. LibreOffice can also open and save many other file formats; see "File formats LibreOffice can open" on this page, "File formats LibreOffice can save to" on page 380, and "Exporting to other formats" on page 382.

OpenDocument filename extensions

The most common filename extensions used for OpenDocument documents are:

*.odt for word processing (text) documents

*.ods for spreadsheets

*.odp for presentations

*.odb for databases

*.odg for graphics (vector drawings)

*.odf for formulas (mathematical equations)

File formats LibreOffice can open

LibreOffice can open a wide variety of file formats in addition to the OpenDocument formats, including Portable Document Format (PDF), if an ODF file is embedded in the PDF (see *Chapter 10 Printing, Exporting, and Emailing* for more information).

Opening text documents

In addition to OpenDocument formats (.odt, .ott, .oth, .odm, and .fodt), Writer can open the formats used by OpenOffice.org 1.x (.sxw, .stw, and .sxg) and the following text document formats:

Microsoft Word 6.0/95/97/2000/XP) (.doc and .dot)
Microsoft Word 2003 XML (.xml)
Microsoft Word 2007/2010 XML (.docx, .docm, .dotx, .dotm)
Microsoft WinWord 5 (.doc)
WordPerfect Document (.wpd)
Microsoft Works (.wps)
Lotus WordPro (.lwp)
Rich Text Format (.rtf)
Text CSV (.csv and .txt)
StarWriter formats (.sdw, .sgl, .vor)
DocBook (.xml)
Unified Office Format text (.uot, .uof)
Ichitaro 8/9/10/11 (.jtd and .jtt)
Hangul WP 97 (.hwp)
T602 Document (.602, .txt)
AportisDoc (Palm) (.pdb)
Pocket Word (.psw)
HTML Document (.htm, .html)

Most of these file types are automatically detected by LibreOffice, so they can be opened without explicitly selecting the document type in the file picker.

When opening .htm or .html files (used for web pages), LibreOffice customizes Writer for working with these files.

Opening spreadsheets

In addition to OpenDocument formats (.ods, .ots, and .fods), Calc can open the formats used by OpenOffice.org 1.x (.sxc and .stc) and the following spreadsheet formats:

Microsoft Excel 97/2000/XP (.xls, .xlw, and .xlt)
Microsoft Excel 4.x–5.0/95 (.xls, .xlw, and .xlt)
Microsoft Excel 2003 XML (.xml)
Microsoft Excel 2007/2010 XML (.xlsx, .xlsm, .xlts, .xltm)
Microsoft Excel 2007/2010 binary (.xlsb)
Lotus 1-2-3 (.wk1, .wks, and .123)
Data Interchange Format (.dif)
Rich Text Format (.rtf)
Text CSV (.csv and .txt)
StarCalc formats (.sdc and .vor)
dBASE (.dbf)
SYLK (.slk)
Unified Office Format spreadsheet (.uos, .uof)
HTML Document (.htm and .html files, including Web page queries)
Pocket Excel (pxl)
Quattro Pro 6.0 (.wb2)

Opening presentations

In addition to OpenDocument formats (.odp, .odg, .otp, and .fodp), Impress can open the formats used by OpenOffice.org 1.x (.sxi and .sti) and the following presentation formats:

Microsoft PowerPoint 97/2000/XP (.ppt and .pot)
Microsoft PowerPoint 2007/2010 (.pptx, .pptm, .potx, .potm)
StarDraw and StarImpress (.sda, .sdd, .sdp, and .vor)
Unified Office Format presentation (.uop, .uof)
CGM – Computer Graphics Metafile (.cgm)
Portable Document Format (.pdf)

Opening graphic files

In addition to OpenDocument formats (.odg and .otg), Draw can open the formats used by OpenOffice.org 1.x (.sxd and .std) and the following graphic formats:

Adobe Photoshop (*.psd)
AutoCAD Interchange Format (*.dxf)
Corel Draw (*.cdr)
Corel Presentation Exchange (*.cmx)
Microsoft Publisher 98-2010 (*.pub)
Microsoft Visio 2000-2013 (*.vdx; *.vsd; *.vsdm; *.vsdx)
WordPerfect Graphics (*.wpg)

BMP	JPEG, JPG	PCX	PSD	SGV	WMF
DXF	MET	PGM	RAS	SVM	XBM
EMF	PBM	PLT	SDA	TGA	XPM
EPS	PCD	PNG	SDD	TIF, TIFF	
GIF	PCT	PPM	SGF	VOR	

Opening formula files

In addition to OpenDocument Formula (.odf) files, Math can open the format used by OpenOffice.org 1.x (.sxm), StarMath, (.smf), and MathML (.mml) files.

When opening a Word document that contains an embedded equation editor object, if the option for it (MathType to LibreOffice Math or reverse) is checked in **Tools > Options > Load/Save > Microsoft Office**, the object will be automatically converted to a LibreOffice Math object.

File formats LibreOffice can save to

Saving in an OpenDocument format guarantees the correct rendering of the file when it is transferred to another person or when the file is re-opened with a later version of LibreOffice or with another program. It is strongly recommended that you use OpenDocument as the default file formats. However, you can save files in other formats, if you wish.

Tip	When sharing a document that you do not expect or want the recipient to modify, the safest option is to convert the document to PDF. LibreOffice provides a very straightforward way to convert documents to PDF. See *Chapter 10 Printing, Exporting, and E-Mailing* in this guide.

Saving text documents

In addition to OpenDocument formats (.odt, .ott, and .fodt), Writer can save in these formats:

OpenOffice.org 1.x Text Document (.sxw)
OpenOffice.org 1.x Text Document Template (.stw)
Microsoft Word 6.0, 95, and 97/2000/XP (.doc)
Microsoft Word 2003 XML (.xml)
Microsoft Word 2007/2010 XML (.docx)
Office Open XML Text (.docx)
Rich Text Format (.rtf)
StarWriter 3.0, 4.0, and 5.0 (.sdw)
StarWriter 3.0, 4.0, and 5.0 Template (.vor)
Text (.txt)
Text Encoded (.txt)
Unified Office Format text (.uot, .uof)
HTML Document (OpenOffice.org Writer) (.html and .htm)
DocBook (.xml)
AportisDoc (Palm) (.pdb)
Pocket Word (.psw)

Encryption support within the Microsoft Word 97/2000/XP filter allows password protected Microsoft Word documents to be saved.

Note	The .rtf format is a common format for transferring text files between applications, but you are likely to experience loss of formatting and images. For this reason, other formats should be used.

Saving spreadsheet files

In addition to OpenDocument formats (.ods and .ots), Calc can save in these formats:

OpenOffice.org 1.x Spreadsheet (.sxc)
OpenOffice.org 1.x Spreadsheet Template (.stc)
Microsoft Excel 97/2000/XP (.xls and .xlw)
Microsoft Excel 97/2000/XP Template (.xlt)
Microsoft Excel 5.0 and 95 (.xls and .xlw)
Microsoft Excel 2003 XML (.xml)
Microsoft Excel 2007/2010 XML (.xlsx)
Office Open XML Spreadsheet (.xlsx)
Data Interchange Format (.dif)
dBase (.dbf)
SYLK (.slk)
Text CSV (.csv and .txt)
StarCalc 3.0, 4.0, and 5.0 formats (.sdc and .vor)
Unified Office Format spreadsheet (.uos)
HTML Document (OpenOffice.org Calc) (.html and .htm)
Pocket Excel (.pxl)

Note	The Java Runtime Environment is required to use the mobile device filters for AportisDoc (Palm), Pocket Word, and Pocket Excel.

Saving presentations

In addition to OpenDocument formats (.odp, .otp, .fodp, and .odg), Impress can save in these formats:

OpenOffice.org 1.x Presentation (.sxi)
OpenOffice.org 1.x Presentation Template (.sti)
Microsoft PowerPoint 97/2000/XP (.ppt)
Microsoft PowerPoint 97/2000/XP Template (.pot)
Microsoft PowerPoint 2007/2010 XML (.pptx, .potm)
Office Open XML Presentation (.pptx, .potm, .ppsx)
StarDraw, StarImpress (.sda, .sdd, and .vor)
Unified Office Format presentation (.uop)

Impress can also export to MacroMedia Flash (.swf) and any of the graphics formats listed for Draw.

Saving drawings

Draw can only save in the OpenDocument Drawing formats (.odg, .otg, and .fodg), the OpenOffice.org 1.x formats (.sxd and .std) and StarDraw format (.sda, .sdd, and .vor).

However, Draw can also export to BMP, EMF, EPS, GIF, JPEG, MET, PBM, PCT, PGM, PNG, PPM, RAS, SVG, SVM, TIFF, WMF, and XPM.

Writer/Web can save in these formats

HTML document (.html and .htm), as HTML 4.0 Transitional
OpenOffice.org 1.0 HTML Template (.stw)
OpenOffice.org 2.x HTML Template (.oth)
StarWriter/Web 4.0 and 5.0 (.vor)
Text and Text Encoded (LibreOffice Writer/Web) (.txt)

Exporting to other formats

LibreOffice uses the term "export" for some file operations involving a change of file type. If you cannot find the file type you are looking for under **Save As**, look under **Export** for additional types.

LibreOffice can export files to HTML and XHTML. In addition, Draw and Impress can export to Adobe Flash (.swf) and a range of image formats.

To export to one of these formats, choose **File > Export**. On the Export dialog, specify a file name for the exported document, then select the desired format in the *File format* list and click the **Export** button.

Index

E